CISTERCIAN FATHERS SERIES: NUMBER EIGHTY-THREE

Aelred of Rievaulx

Homilies on the Prophetic Burdens of Isaiah

Translated by
Lewis White

Introduction by
Marsha L. Dutton

D1452585

CISTERCIAN FATHERS SERIES: NUMBER EIGHTY-THREE

Aelred of Rievaulx

Homilies on the Prophetic Burdens of Isaiah

Translated by
Lewis White

Introduced by
Marsha L. Dutton

Cistercian Publications
www.cistercianpublications.org

LITURGICAL PRESS
Collegeville, Minnesota
www.litpress.org

A Cistercian Publications title published by Liturgical Press

BS
1515.54
.A3513
2018

Cistercian Publications
Editorial Offices
161 Grosvenor Street
Athens, Ohio 45701
www.cistercianpublications.org

English translation of Gaetano Raciti's critical edition, *Sermones in oneribus propheticis Isaiae*, translated by Lewis White. Corpus Christianorum Continuatio Mediaevalis, 2D (Turnhout: Brepols, 2005). Permissions in process.

Library of Congress Control Number: 2017963026

ISBN 978-0-87907-183-7   ISBN 978-0-87907-638-2 (e-book)

Contents

Abbreviations

Ant	Antiphon
CCCM	Corpus Christianorum, Continuatio Mediaevalis
CCSL	Corpus Christianorum Series Latina
CF	Cistercian Fathers series
CS	Cistercian Studies series
CSQ	*Cistercian Studies Quarterly*
Ep	Epistola, letter
H, HH	Homilia, homily, homilies
Hesbert	René-Jean Hesbert. *Antiphonale Missarum Sextuplex*. Brussels and Paris: Vromant et Cie, 1935.
LXX	The Greek Septuagint version
PL	Patrologia Latina, ed. J.-P. Migne
Pref	Preface
Pref Mass	Preface to the Mass
Prol	Prologue
RB	*Regula sancti Benedicti; Regula Monachorum*
Resp	Responsory

S, SS	Sermo, Sermones
Symb apost	*Symbolum apostolorum*
Tract	Tractatus, tract
Var	Old Latin version
Vita A	*Vita Aelredi*; Walter Daniel, *The Life of Aelred of Rievaulx and the Letter to Maurice*. Trans. Maurice Powicke. CF 57. 1950; Kalamazoo, MI: Cistercian Publications, 1994.
Vulg	Vulgate

Works of Aelred

Adv	Sermo in adventu Domini
Anima	*De anima*
Ep	Epistle to Gilbert Foliot
Iesu	*De Iesu puero duodenni*
Inst incl	*De institutione inclusarum*
Mira	*De quodam miraculum mirabili*
Oner	Homilia de oneribus
Orat past	*Oratio pastoralis*
Spec car	*Speculum caritatis*
Spir amic	*De spiritali amicitia*

Works of Other Writers

Alexander III

Ep Aet	Epistola *Aeterna et incommutabilis*

Antiphons (ed. Hesbert)

In ass	In assumptione Sanctae Mariae
In comm Confess	In communi Confessorum
In comm Dedic Eccl	In communi Dedicationis Ecclesiae
In comm Martyr et Confess	In communi Martyrum et Confessorum
In comm Virg	In communi Virginum
In nat Dom	In nativitate Domini
Pro defunct	Pro defunctis
5 HM	Feria V in cena Domini

Augustine

C acad	*Contra academicos*
C Adim	*Contra Adimantum Manichaeum*
C Faust Manich	*Contra Faustum Manichaeum*
Civ Dei	*De civitate Dei*
C Max Arrian	*Contra Maximinium Arrianum*
Conf	*Confessiones*
Div quaest	*De diversis quaestionibus*
Doct chr	*De doctrina Christiana*
Enchir	*Enchiridion*
Gen ad litt	*De Genesi ad litteram*

In ev Ioann	*In Evangelium Ioannis tractatus*
In Ps	*Enarrationes in Psalmos*
Trin	*De Trinitate*

Bede

In Cant	*In Cantica Canticorum*
In Gen	*In principium Genesis*

Benedict

RB	*Regula sancti Benedicti; Regula Monachorum*

Bernard

OS	Sermo in festivitate omnium sanctorum
SC	*Sermones super Cantica Canticorum*

Cassian

Conl	*Conlationes*

Cicero

De fini bon et mal	*De finibus bonorum et malorum*
Off	*De officiis*
Tusc	*Tusculanae disputationes*

Pseudo-Dionysius

Cael Hier	*De caelesti hierarchia*

Gregory the Great

Mo	*Moralia in Iob*
Eu	*Homeliae in Euangelia*
Hiez	*Homiliae in Ezechielem*
Reg past	*Regula pastoralis*

Hugh of St. Victor

Didasc	*Didascalicon*

Isidore

Etym	*Etymologiae*

Jerome

Ep	*Epistulae*
In Ez	*Homeliae in Ezechielem*
In Isa	*In Isaiam*
In Matt	*In Matthaeum*
In Naum	*In Naum prophetam*
In Zach	*In Zachariam prophetam*
Nom	*Interpretatio Hebraicorum nominum*

Leo the Great

Tract	*Tractatus*

Lucretius

Rer nat	*De rerum natura*

Origen

In Cant	*In Canticum Canticorum*
In Ex	*Homeliae in Exodum*
In Gen	*Homeliae in Genesin*

Responsories (ed. Hesbert)

In comm Apost	In communi Apostolorum
In comm Confess	In communi Confessorum
In comm Dedic Eccl	In communi Dedicationis Ecclesiae
In comm Martyr et Confess	In communi Martyrum et Confessorum
In Dom Quinq	Dominica in Quinquagesima
In nat Dom	In nativitate Domini

Virgil

Aen	*Aeneis*

Introduction to *Prophetic Burdens of Isaiah*[1]

Marsha L. Dutton

> In the beginning was the Word, and the Word was with God and
> the Word was God. . . . What has come into being in him was
> life, and the life was the light of all people. The light shines in the
> darkness, and the darkness did not overcome it. (John 1:1-5, 14)

The thirty-one homilies on *The Prophetic Burdens of Isaiah,* an
extended commentary on Isaiah chapters 13 through 16, are far
and away the least read of the works of Aelred, a twelfth-century
abbot of the Yorkshire Cistercian abbey of Rievaulx. To some extent
their neglect reflects the fact that until recently they were only
widely available in J.-P. Migne's Patrologia Latina, as *Sermones de
oneribus.*[2] But in 2005 Gaetano Raciti's critical edition appeared in
Corpus Christianorum, Continuatio Mediaevalis,[3] and Pierre-Yves
Emery's French translation was published in 2006.[4] The homilies
now appear here in English for the first time in Lewis White's
translation.

---

[1] I am grateful to Christopher Coski, Fr. Brendan Freeman, ocso, Br. Brian
Kerns, ocso, Fr. Stephen Muller, ocso, Lewis White, and the monks of Our Lady
of Guadalupe Abbey for their contributions to my understanding of this work.

[2] Aelredi Rievallis Abbatis, *Sermones de Oneribus,* ed. J.-P. Migne, PL 195 (Paris,
1855), 361–500.

[3] *Homiliae de oneribus propheticis Isaiae,* ed. Gaetano Raciti, CCCM 2D (Turnhout:
Brepols, 2005).

[4] *Homélies sur les fardeaux selon le prophète Isaïe,* trans. Pierre-Yves Emery, Pain
de Cîteaux 25, 3rd series (Oka, Québec: Abbaye Notre-Dame-du-Lac, 2006).

The title of this translation, like Emery's, retains Raciti's use of *homilies,* but, unlike the French, it replaces Migne's title with the English version of Raciti's title: *Homilies on the Prophetic Burdens of Isaiah.* Aelred refers to the work in this way in his cover letter to Gilbert Foliot, bishop of London from 1163–1187 (Ep 6). His distinction between sermon and homily also comes from that letter, though unexplained: "to the sermon that was written previously . . . we have attached nineteen homilies on the burden of Babylon, three on the burden of the Philistines, and nine on the burden of Moab" (Ep 9).

These homilies are the most ambitious and challenging of Aelred's works. They are also puzzling, raising numerous questions, such as, Why is this work a series of homilies rather than a unified treatise? Is its date significant? Who is its intended audience? Why did Aelred ask Gilbert Foliot, bishop of London, to evaluate his work?

The complexity of the homilies raises problems of its own with its constant shifting of the signification of words and images. White argues that such ambivalence is essential to their meaning, that as human life and experience are inherently equivocal, these homilies directly confront that equivocality: "Far from being a symptom of confusion, Aelred's ambivalence provides a glimpse into his worldview. His bold reinterpretations . . . illustrate a world in which everything is confused and everyone is weighed down. *De Oneribus* is ambivalent because the world is ambivalent: any phenomenon can lead either to redemption or perdition."[5]

Because of the multiple meanings that Aelred assigns to words and images over the course of his commentary, reading the homilies requires particular effort. In explaining *Babylon,* for example, the subject of well over half of the thirty-one homilies, he ranges from the relatively straightforward "confusion" (H 1.17) to "the world as Christ found it" (H 3.9) to much greater complexity with "that world that is always impure, the world that *dwells in wickedness,* the world for which the one who overcame the world does not pray, the world from which those who conquer the world are chosen to greater obscurity" (H 13.2). Not surprisingly, then, the dark confusion represented by

---

[5] Lewis White, "*Bifarie itaque potest legi:* Ambivalent Exegesis in Aelred of Rievaulx's *De Oneribus,*" CSQ 42, no. 3 (2007): 299–327; rept. CSQ 52, no. 3 (2017): 395–423, here 395–96.

Babylon seems tacitly to govern the work. White warns of the burden the constant shifting meanings place on its readers: "Any attempt to understand *De oneribus* in its integrity . . . must confront its brash ambivalence by investing Scriptural images with contradictory referents."[6]

At the same time, Aelred is clear about the spiritual obligation to emerge from confusion. Early on he points to the value of instruction in aiding humans to return to their "original form . . . when he who formed us reforms us" and defines that form as wisdom (H 1.3). He also makes it clear that he is undertaking the responsibility of providing that instruction. Any reader of these homilies must thus remain alert to the way their equivocalities extend outward from terminology to subject matter to textual interpretation to questions of audience and purpose, because Aelred intends his work to lead the audience not just to acquaintance with Isaiah but to wisdom. He insists on the importance of his work's explication of Isaiah when he writes, "This holy prophet is so deep in meaning, so lofty in mysteries, so clear sighted in foretelling future events, so delightful in moral instruction . . . that at times it seems as though he were carried to heaven itself to lay bare the secrets of divine wisdom" (H 1.8).

Aelred's Life

Aelred was born in 1110 to a family embedded in the church of England's north country. Nothing is known of his female ancestors except that they were the wives and mothers of priests at a time when such families were usual and valued. The names and occupations of several of his paternal predecessors, however, are well documented. His father, Eilaf, and paternal grandfather—also Eilaf—were both priests of the church of St. Andrew in Hexham. His grandfather had previously been sacristan of the cathedral of Durham until in 1083 William of Saint-Calais, the new Norman bishop of Durham, expelled the married priests of the cathedral chapter; only the one widowed priest stayed behind. The elder Eilaf's father, Alfred son of Westou,

---

[6] White, "*Bifarie itaque potest legi*," 395.

had also been a priest at Durham, with responsibility for the shrine of Saint Cuthbert, and he is credited with having brought the bones of Bede there.[7] Earlier yet, a member of the family had reportedly been among the Lindisfarne priests who carried Cuthbert's body in flight from the Viking invaders who ravaged England's coast.[8]

This genealogy explains a great deal about Aelred's life. Above all, faith in God and service to God were an old family tradition. But Aelred must also have grown up on stories showing that even the most protected and apparently secure of lives are vulnerable to sudden overturning, with either terroristic raids or new ecclesiastical policies coming to the same thing in the end: expulsion from home, exile, and search for refuge, followed by new beginnings. Safety, Aelred learned early, is always fragile; here there is no true city.

Before Aelred was born, Gregorian reform had struck down another of the family's certainties: that priests' sons could become priests as well. After the church had repeatedly and unsuccessfully endeavored to end clerical marriage, in 1093 the policies of Pope Gregory VII won out when the synod of Melfi ruled that sons of priests could only be admitted to holy orders if they first took vows of celibacy as monks or canons.[9] For Aelred and his brothers Samuel and Æthelwold, like other sons of priests around the Christian world, this decision required

---

[7] See *De Sanctis Ecclesie Haugustaldensis et Eorum Miraculis*, in *Aelredi Rievallensis: Opera Historica et Hagiographica*, ed. Domenico Pezzini, CCCM 3 (Turnhout: Brepols, 2017), 75–110; Aelred of Rievaulx, "The Saints of the Church of Hexham and their Miracles," in *Lives of the Northern Saints*, trans. Jane Patricia Freeland, ed. Marsha L. Dutton, CF 71 (Kalamazoo, MI: Cistercian Publications, 2006), 65–107.

[8] James Raine, ed., *The Priory of Hexham*, 2 vols., Surtees Society 44 (Durham, UK: Andrews, 1864), 1:l–li. Raine includes a genealogical chart tracing Alfred, son of Westou, back to one of the Lindisfarne priests. See also Squire, *Aelred of Rievaulx*, 5.

[9] Johannes Dominicus Mansi, *Sacrorum conciliorum . . . collectio* (Florence, 1775), 20:724; Melfi, canon 14: "Presbyterorum filios a sacris altaris ministeriis removendos decernimus, nisi aut in coenobiis aut in canonicis religiose probati fuerint conversari." See Christopher Brooke, "Gregorian Reform in Action: Clerical Marriage in England: 1050–1200," *Cambridge Historical Journal* 12, no. 1 (1956): 1–21; Jennifer D. Thibodeaux, *The Manly Priest: Clerical Celibacy, Masculinity, and Reform in England and Normandy, 1066–1300* (Philadelphia: University of Pennsylvania Press, 2015).

new vocational choices.[10] Aelred's brothers pursued secular lives, and it appears that Aelred considered doing the same, in his case as a member of the court of King David I of Scotland, where he apparently spent the years 1124 to 1134. But after this decade of discernment, he returned to the path of his male ancestors as a monk in the Cistercian monastery of Rievaulx, founded in 1132.

After entering Rievaulx, perhaps with help from King David and Archbishop Thurstan of York,[11] Aelred seems to have taken on significant responsibility in the young abbey. In 1142 his abbot, William, sent him to Rome along with three other prelates to protest the political appointment of the new archbishop of York, a relative of King Stephen. On their return—perhaps after a stop at the abbey of Clairvaux, where Bernard was abbot—Aelred became Rievaulx's novice master; soon afterward he was appointed the first abbot of Rievaulx's second daughter house, St. Laurence of Revesby. There he stayed for five years, until in 1147 being elected third abbot of Rievaulx itself.[12] Until his death in January 1167, he continued as abbot while Rievaulx grew in size and prominence; he himself, like many Cistercian abbots of the time, traveled widely, preached regularly, and wrote prolifically. When he died, Walter Daniel says, he was buried in the chapter house at Rievaulx, next to Abbot William.[13]

Aelred delivered most of his known sermons—182 in Gaetano Raciti's critical edition—as chapter talks for the year's liturgical feasts, the dates on which Cistercian abbots were required to preach to their communities.[14] He also wrote the thirty-one Isaian homilies

---

[10] Richard of Hexham, "History of the Church of Hexham," in Raine, ed., *The Priory of Hexham*, 2:1–62, here 55.

[11] See Marsha L. Dutton, "The Conversion and Vocation of Aelred of Rievaulx: A Historical Hypothesis," in *England in the Twelfth Century*, ed. Daniel Williams (London: Boydell, 1990), 31–49, here 42–47.

[12] See Walter Daniel, *The Life of Aelred of Rievaulx and the Letter to Maurice,* [chap.] 26, trans. Maurice Powicke, CF 57 (1950; Kalamazoo, MI: Cistercian Publications, 1994), 115 (hereafter Vita A).

[13] Vita A 60; CF 57:140.

[14] *Sermones I–XLVI, LXVII–LXXXIV, LXXXV–CLXXXII,* ed. Gaetano Raciti, CCCM 2A, B, C (Turnhout: Brepols, 1989, 2001, 2012). Peter Jackson has identified a sermon as the one preached by Aelred at the translation of the relics of King Edward the Confessor in 1163: "*In translacione sancti Edwardi confessoris*: The Lost

and thirteen treatises, six devoted to monastic and spiritual subjects, three about the lives and miracles of English saints, and four concerning historical and political topics, three of which he addressed to King Henry II (r. 1154–1189).[15] By the end of 2017 all of Aelred's treatises and sermons had been published in critical editions through Brepols Publishers' Corpus Christianorum, Continuatio Mediaevalis series; all have also appeared or are forthcoming in French and English translations, and many have been translated into Dutch, Italian, and Spanish.[16]

It is easy to assume that English clergy in these centuries were sheltered from the rough and tumble of the world that surrounded them, but Aelred's family history dispels that image. It also, of course, helps to explain the activity that characterized Aelred's life and writing and perhaps led, toward the end of his life, to his authorship of these homilies, filled with scenes of threatened apocalypse but permeated with promises of God's forgiveness, protection, and blessing to those who repent of their sin, seek God in faith, hope, and love, and look toward God's light.

The Prophetic Homilies

Manuscript and Editorial History

The original manuscript of Aelred's homilies apparently no longer exists, but according to Walter Daniel, Aelred wrote it "with his own hand" (*manu sua scribendo consummauit*).[17] Aelred seems to confirm that claim when he says toward the end of the introductory Epistle to Foliot, "I have written thirty-one homilies [*cum XXXI homelias stilo*

Sermon by Aelred of Rievaulx Found?" ed. Peter Jackson, trans. Tom License, CSQ 40, no. 1 (2005): 46–83. On the sermons, see n. 51 below.

[15] Two of these were written in 1153–1154, before Henry of Anjou became king; a third dates to 1161–1163.

[16] See Pierre-André Burton, "Bibliotheca aelrediana secunda supplementa," in *A Companion to Aelred of Rievaulx (1110–1167)*, ed. Marsha L. Dutton (Leuven: Brill, 2017), 295–324. For an overview of Aelred's works, see my chapter in the same book, "Aelred of Rievaulx: Abbot, Teacher, and Author," 17–47, here 35–43.

[17] Vita A 32; CF 57:121.

tradidissem]," and at the end of the final homily, "I now lay down my pen [*stilum suspendo*]" (H 31.26). Raciti cautiously argues on the basis of the surviving manuscripts that the homilies were written in under a year and a half, perhaps between spring 1163 and before mid-1164. He bases the *terminus a quo* on the assumption that the first meeting between Aelred and Foliot took place after Foliot ascended the episcopal throne in March 1163, and the *terminus ad quem* depends on the April 1164 death of the antipope Victor IV, as Aelred seems to indicate in the twenty-third homily that as he wrote the papal contest between Victor and Alexander III was still underway.[18]

The epistle that begins the work indicates that Aelred sent the autograph manuscript to Foliot, but he probably first arranged for two copies to be made, as Raciti speculates that the two best surviving twelfth-century manuscripts, one from Clairvaux, derive from it.[19] Nineteen essentially complete manuscripts of the work survive, all but one from the twelfth or thirteenth centuries. Another eleven manuscripts containing partial versions or fragments of the work also survive from the thirteenth through the sixteenth centuries.[20]

The *editio princeps* of the work, published by Richard Gibbon in 1616, depends on the somewhat abbreviated version of the homilies found in one twelfth-century manuscript, though supplemented with readings from another early manuscript. In 1662 Bertrand Tissier produced a new edition, using the two manuscripts known to Gibbon but for the most part accepting the abbreviated text, judging it the more authentic. As Raciti points out, though, Tissier "tacitly readjusted" that text by incorporating various readings from the more complete version, "borrowed in an eclectic fashion." Tissier's version appeared in 1855 in the Patrologia Latina.

---

[18] Gaetano Raciti, Introduction to Ælred of Rievaulx, *Homeliae de oneribus propheticis Isaiae*, CCCM 2D (Turnhout: Brepols, 2005), V. Aelred could have begun writing before Foliot's consecration, and even if he wrote homily 23 before learning of Victor's death, the fact that another eight homilies follow it means that the total time of writing may well have taken longer than Raciti calculates.

[19] Raciti, Introduction, VIII.

[20] This survey of the manuscript and editorial history comes from Raciti, Introduction, VII–XV.

The shorter text was regarded as Aelred's original version until in 1957 Charles Dumont, at work on a critical edition of the homilies that never appeared, reported that he had examined sixteen manuscripts of the work. Of these only two, from the thirteenth century, contained the shorter version, while the longer text was present in six twelfth-century manuscripts, four of English provenance and one probably from Rievaulx's daughter house of Wardon. Three thirteenth-century manuscripts with Cistercian provenance also contained the longer version. From this evidence Dumont concluded that the longer version must have been Aelred's original: "the conformity of the manuscripts from the Order is thus frankly in favor of the longer reading. . . . As for the short reading, it seems that we are in the presence of an abbreviation of the text . . . . That conviction rests not only on the majority of manuscripts (14 against 2), but also on their age and their origin."[21]

Aelred's Sources

(1) The principal source for Aelred's homilies is Isaiah 13 through 24, immediately following the familiar passages on the Peaceable Kingdom and the prophecy of celebration and divine praise in chapters 11 and 12. In sharp contrast to these promises of peace, Isaiah devotes the next nine chapters to proclaiming the devastation to come upon Babylon, Philistia, Moab, Assyria, Damascus, Ethiopia, Egypt, Edom, Arabia, and Tyre, as well as the destruction of Jerusalem herself, and finally judgment upon the entire earth:

> Listen, a tumult on the mountains as of a great multitude!
> Listen, an uproar of kingdoms, of nations gathering together!
> The Lord of hosts is mustering an army for battle.
> They come from a distant land, from the end of the heavens,
> The Lord and the weapons of his indignation, to destroy the whole
>   earth.

---

[21] Charles Dumont, "Autour des Sermons 'De Oneribus' d'Ælred de Rievaulx," *Collectanea Cisterciensia* 19 (1957): 114–21, here 116–17 [my translation]; White, "*Bifarie itaque potest legi*," 398.

Wail, for the day of the Lord is near; it will come like destruction
from the Almighty! . . .
See, the day of the Lord comes, cruel, with wrath and fierce anger,
To make the earth a desolation, and to destroy its sinners from
it. . . .
I will punish the world for its evil, and the wicked for their
iniquity;
I will put an end to the pride of the arrogant and lay low the
insolence of tyrants. (Isa 13:4-6, 9, 11)

Isaiah's visions offer little hope of rescue for the people of the nations that have wreaked violence upon Israel and Judah. Of Babylon he declares, "I will blot out all remembrance of Babylon and destroy all her people, including the offspring she produces" (Isa 14:22), and of the Moabites he promises only that "Moab's splendor will disappear, along with all her many people; there will be just a few insignificant survivors left" (Isa 16:14).

Aelred is explicit from the beginning about his focus on these prophecies, and his reference to Isaiah's work in the epistle to Foliot anticipates the emphasis he puts on it as prophetic. In the first homily he explains his general pedagogical purpose: "I will now take up the book of Isaiah to examine a small portion of it with you. Although you may be quite familiar with it from the commentaries of the saints, I think it is highly useful for us to repeat what they said, if not differently, at least in another fashion" (H 1.7). Later, addressing Jesus, he again links himself and his project to Isaiah: "You who inspired holy Isaiah to write, inspire me too, I beg you, to understand what he wrote" (H 1.25). He devotes the second homily to the nature of prophecy, determining that Isaiah's visions were prophetic because received through intellectual vision, "by which the mind, transcending all matter and all physical images and likenesses, rests in the very light of Truth" (H 2.14). He concludes, "only the intellectual vision makes someone a prophet . . . that which is perceived in the Truth, in whom whatever will be is made, is both bright and certain" (H 2.24).

Isaiah's abrupt movement away from the beauty of peace promised through the prophet by God and to the damnation that awaits the sinful—the insolent, the arrogant—is of particular interest to

Aelred, who in historical works such as *Genealogy of the Kings of the English* repeatedly called attention to God's promise of peace and prosperity to England when her monarchs walk in God's way but in other works juxtaposed promises of blessing with the terrors that await the damned, as in the last section of *Formation of Recluses* and in Sermon 48.[22]

Aelred's Isaian homilies, however, offer much more hope to those who listen than do Isaiah's prophecies. Although Aelred too writes extensively of the misery that will come upon those who have turned away from God in their arrogance and love of the world, he also regularly interposes promises of blessing. In the tenth homily, for example, commenting on Isaiah's prophecy of destruction to Babylon (Isa 13:14), he moves rapidly back and forth from hope to destruction: "Beginning from *The voice of the crowd in the mountains,* [the prophecy] announced the peace that the conversion of the kings and nations bestowed upon the church. It went on to speak of the ruin or conversion of those who fell away by yielding to persecutions, or who disgraced themselves with vices during times of peace" (H 10.2). Later, after explaining Moab as "the wisdom of the world" (H 23.7) and "the wise people of the world who oppose the Gospel's teaching" (H 25.1), he says that the church by appropriating worldly wisdom, which he identifies with "dialectical argument," has accepted and transformed it: "Such argument, which had opposed the church, has begun to serve it in the wise who have converted" (H 25.4). And he ends the work as a whole with a vision of harmony.

Such changes reflect the three ways in which Aelred primarily departs from Isaiah. The first, of course, is that he presents the Isaian burdens from the perspective of explicitly Christian teaching, with God's love made known through Christ's coming and cross. He signals that shift in the manuscript by preceding his homilies with the sermon for Advent, which redefines the prophets' Day of the Lord from a day of darkness and damnation to the day of light in which mercy precedes and so redefines Judgment. As White points

---

[22] Aelred, *De institutione inclusarum* 33 (hereafter Inst incl); CCCM 1:678–79; CF 2:99; S 48; CCCM 2B:17–21; CF 80.

out, "thematically, Aelred interprets Isaiah in light of the Lord's coming, which means that implicit in any text describing destruction is the possibility of redemption."[23]

A second departure from Isaiah, directly related to the first, is Aelred's three-part exegesis of Isaiah's prophecies of devastation. Aelred repeatedly explains to his audience how to respond morally to Isaiah's warnings by replacing pride with humility or vice with virtue, often going on to provide the allegorical meaning of a passage and interpreting Isaiah's threats to the nations as relating to the soul of the Christian. He does not, however, apply each of these meanings to each verse, and indeed different homilies present different exegetical levels, with the moral interpretation most often divided from the literal in different homilies and signaled explicitly in the work's Table of Contents present in the manuscripts. Additionally, as White notes, the literal and the allegorical readings tend to coalesce in the homilies, because Aelred understands Isaiah to be consciously writing of the incarnation and the early church, with his visions expressed in figurative language but pointing to literal fulfillment in the future, as Aelred demonstrates: "There, this same Isaiah, gazing upon the incarnation of the Word, spoke of what had not happened yet as if it had, saying, *A little one was born to us, a son was given to us* [Isa 46:10]. There too, looking on his passion, he said, *We saw him, and there was no beauty* [Is 53:2]" (H 17.11).[24]

Aelred is often explicit about his movement from one level to another and about his allegorical rephrasing of Isaiah's language even while insisting on its literal truth. In the fifteenth homily he writes, "Let us break open the heavenly storehouses that holy Isaiah hid under the husk of parables, since the Holy Spirit has poured forth the light of truth . . . . But because we gave an allegorical interpretation in our last sermon to you concerning these matters, let us continue with the moral reading of this same part" (H 15.3). In his commentary on the burden of the Philistines, he explains Isaiah's reference to the death of Ahaz (Isa 14:28) as allegorically referring to the devil and to the life of Ahaz as the devil's kingdom (H 20.4); he moves back and forth from historical to allegorical

[23] White, "*Bifarie itaque potest legi*," 398.
[24] Personal communication.

meaning throughout that homily. At the beginning of the next homily he again calls attention to a change in exegetical level: "So, brothers, descending from the allegorical mountains to the moral plains [*allegoricis montibus ad plana tropologica*], let us return to the beginning of the burden itself. . . . Take a look at what happens, dear brothers, when the virtues naturally take the place of uprooted vices. The more progress one makes, the more pride, now closer to the virtues than to the vices, grows bitterly strong" (H 21.1–2).[25]

A third Aelredian departure that is inseparable from the others is the interpretive mode most characteristic of these homilies, an almost infinite multiplication of meanings. Burton has referred to this pattern as a "lecture aux éclats" or "splintered reading," recalling the fragmentation that results from an explosion, visible in the cloud of debris that arises from the detonation of a building.[26] The splintering is partially accomplished by Aelred's fluctuating redefinitions of words with consequent application to new situations. This approach represents the equivocal and ever-shifting nature of reality, which both causes and results from the human inability since the Fall to see truth, something that Aelred emphasizes toward the end of the homilies (H 22.10).[27]

The pattern of verbal and hence substantive differentiation begins immediately in the first homily and expands with the incrementally growing meaning of the work's two core terms, *burden* (*onus*) and *Babylon*. Of *burden* Aelred writes, "There is a burden that weighs down, and a burden that crushes. Sickness weighs down; iniquity crushes. Temptation weighs down; damnation crushes" (H 1.12). After defining *Babylon* as "confusion," Aelred explains that it "represents the world. The world is surely the place where all things are

---

[25] Aelred uses the same three-part exegetical pattern in *Iesu puero duodenni*, again following Gregory in placing the allegorical level before the moral, unlike, e.g., Cassian.

[26] Burton, *Aelred de Rievaulx*, 554–55. See also Pierre-André Burton, "Une lecture 'aux éclats' du Cantique des cantiques. Les enjeux de l'herméneutique biblique selon saint Bernard. Un commentaire du *Sermon 23 sur le Cantique*," *Cîteaux* 57 (2006): 165–241.

[27] See, e.g., *Speculum caritatis* (hereafter Spec car) 1.3.9; CCCM 1:16; CF 17:91–92; *De Anima* (hereafter Anima) 1.32, 36; CCCM 1:694, 695; CF 22:50, 52–53; S 49.5; CCCM 2B:23; CF 80.

confused. Here the good live with the wicked, the chosen with the condemned" (H 1.17). He then divides the condemned into three groups—those still alive and participating in the Christian community, those alive but already separated from the community, and the third already dead and "handed over to eternal punishment" (H 1.18, 19). He similarly groups the chosen into three groups: those not yet called (Jews or pagans), those called but not yet justified (Christian sinners), and saints, those already justified but not yet glorified (H 1.18, 19). So the splintering progresses.

Both White and Elias Dietz have used the word *ambivalence* to reflect the postlapsarian reality that characterizes Aelred's homilies. White explains this pattern of multiplying possibilities as not merely a rhetorical device but in many ways the substantive core of the homilies, mirroring both the confusion of the world and the multiple ways in which God acts in the world to warn, to test, to punish, and to reward. And Dietz has shown the complexity of meaning that it reveals to be key to all of Aelred's works, noting that "Aelred is always keenly aware of the multiplicity of possible meanings and of the numerous consequences that flow from any choice or act."[28]

While Aelred's thirty-one homilies closely follow Isaiah 13–16 in articulating the destruction that will come upon those who turn away from God in arrogance and disbelief, they are also profoundly informed by a Christian understanding of the world as complex rather than simple, infused with moral and spiritual meaning and informed by an ever-increasing multiplicity of possibilities demonstrating God's power and purpose. By juxtaposing these possibilities, he allows them to illuminate one another: "Holy Isaiah . . . also includes a word concerning the happiness of those whom this sinking burdens not for ruin, but for salvation. And everywhere it is clear that the power is God's, and yours, Lord, mercy; *because you render to all according to their works,* dividing *day from night, light from darkness.* Thus the darkness appears even thicker when compared to the light, and the light shines more abundantly by the gathering darkness" (H 1.13).

---

[28] White, "*Bifarie itaque potest legi,*" 395; Elias Dietz, "Ambivalence Well Considered," CSQ 47, no. 1 (2012): 71–85, here 72; Burton, *Aelred de Rievaulx,* 566–67.

(2) A second principal source for Aelred's work is three books of Jerome's eighteen-book *Commentary on Isaiah,* one of his seventeen commentaries on the Hebrew prophets written between 392 and 416.[29] In 397, reportedly at the request of Bishop Amabilis in Gaul,[30] Jerome commented on Isaiah's eleven visions of doom to the foreign nations, at the literal or historical level in the first book, then in the second and third books moving into the moral and anagogical levels. When in 408–410 he expanded his work into a three-part exegesis of all of Isaiah, he inserted the earlier portion, on Isaiah 13 through 23, unchanged, as books five, six, and seven.

At the beginning of the fifth book Jerome explains his interpretive plan: "I will attach the beginning of the sixth book in accordance with tropology, and . . . I will pursue the summit of the spiritual understanding [*spiritalis intelligentiae*]."[31] A little later he develops this image: "I will briefly annotate what I have learned, laying down the foundations of the Scriptures. For the rest . . . we must build the spiritual edifice upon these foundations, in order to point to the perfect adornment of the church by setting in place a roof."[32] He expands his plan in book 6: "Thus, by the same effort by which the fifth book summarized history, the sixth and seventh will touch upon anagogy."[33]

Early in his fifth book Jerome articulates his understanding of Isaiah's prophecies in characteristically lexical terms, focusing on

---

[29] *Commentaire de Jérôme sur le prophète Isaïe,* I–IV, V–VII, ed. R. Gyson et al., Vetus Latina: Aus der Geschichte der lateinischen Bibel 23, 27 (Freiburg: Verlag Herder, 1993–1994), 24 (cited as In Isa); Jerome, *Commentariorum in Isaiam Prophetam Libri Duodeviginti,* PL 24. For the dates of Jerome's biblical commentaries see *St. Jerome: Commentary on Isaiah,* trans. Thomas P. Scheck, Ancient Christian Writers no. 68 (New York and Mahwah, NJ: The Newman Press, 2015), 20. Scheck's Introduction is my source for what follows.

[30] William Henry Fremantle reports of Hereclius, "a deacon of Pannonia at the end of the 4th century," that "his bishop, Amabilis, after urging Jerome many times by letters to interpret for him the visions of Isaiah, and receiving no reply, enforced his request by the personal agency of Heraclius" ("Hereclius [23]," in *A Dictionary of Christian Biography, Literature, Sects and Doctrines,* ed. William Smith and Henry Wace, vol. 2 [London: John Murray, 1880], 904).

[31] Jerome, In Isa 5.1; Scheck, *St. Jerome,* 226.

[32] Jerome, In Isa 5.2; Scheck, *St. Jerome,* 227.

[33] Jerome, In Isa 6.1; Scheck, *St. Jerome,* 292.

the Hebrew word *messa* (משא) from Isaiah 13:1 and objecting to the Septuagint's translation: "The Hebrew word *messa* [משא] can be understood either as a 'burden' or a 'weight' (*onus*). And everywhere the word is used, what follows is full of threats. I marvel, then, that the translators of the LXX wanted to render 'vision' [ὅρασις] for such a wretched condition."[34] He continues with Isaiah's prophecies of God's punishment to the nations, to be followed by eternal damnation.

Like Isaiah, Jerome occasionally writes of God's rescuing his people, but whereas Isaiah promised that to Israel, Jerome considers it either in purely allegorical terms or with specific reference to Christians. So he allegorizes Isaiah 14:1-4, itself a promise of redemption to Israel: "Now here is the progression: after Babylon has been deserted forever . . . *the Lord will have mercy upon Jacob,* namely upon the one who throws down his vices, *and he will choose Israel,* the one who sees God with his mind."[35] When commenting on Isaiah 14:24-25, in which God promises to crush the Assyrian and remove his yoke from his people, he interprets the beneficiaries of the promise as Christians: "when all the enemies will have been placed under Christ's feet, so that the last death is destroyed, then the very heavy yoke of the *Assyrian* will be *taken away from* the saints. . . . Thus, with the yoke of the Assyrians removed, they see the resting place, that it is good, and the land, that it is very abundant, and they place their necks under Christ's yoke to labor, and they become farmers of men."[36]

Jerome's commentary is useful to Aelred in presenting a Christian perspective on Isaiah rather than a Jewish one, though Jerome more commonly writes of Christ in terms of virtue or as Lord or Judge rather than as an agent of mercy. When he writes of God's sparing

---

[34] *Verbum Hebraicum messa uel onus uel pondus intellegi potest. Et ubicumque praepositum fuerit, minarum plena sunt quae dicuntur. Vnde miror LXX translatores in re tristi uoluisse ponere uisionem* (Jerome, In Isa, 160). Jerome translates *messa* as "burden" in his Vulgate translation of Isaiah, retained by some English Bibles (e.g., the King James and the Douay Rheims), but many other English Bibles (e.g., the New Revised Standard Version and the New American Bible) use either *prophecy* or *oracle.*

[35] Jerome, In Isa 6.21; Scheck, *St. Jerome,* 305.

[36] Jerome, In Isa 6.22; Scheck, *St. Jerome,* 318.

Zion, he explains, "*Because the Lord founded* it, and he is its foundation, but he founded it upon the foundation of prudence, justice, strength, and moderation, by which names Christ is understood."[37]

But Aelred differs from Jerome in offering much more opportunity for individual repentance and salvation. As White notes, "For Jerome, Babylon is simply the land of wickedness. The prophecies against Babylon unambiguously foretell universal doom . . . Without exception, Babylon's inhabitants will be burdened with torment on the Day of the Lord."[38] Thus while Jerome explains that the Moabites will suffer for only three years, Aelred allegorizes the three years as both the three ages of the church ("the times of calling, of trial, and of consolation") and the three stages of spiritual progress, conversion, purgation, and contemplation (H 31.16, 19), both of which systems end in blessing. Further, toward the end of the homilies Aelred depicts the daughters of Moab as ready for spiritual progress, able to emerge from the darkness of sin, to climb toward the spiritual marriage, and to seek the light of God. In his final homily he offers their reconciliation, relying now on the passage from Isaiah 16:11 but enlarged to refer to God and the church. Jerome takes Isaiah's passage "Therefore my heart will sound like a harp for Moab" as referring to the time "when the false joy has been changed into mourning and tears. . . . Moab . . . will try to enter into the sanctuaries of the church to make them his own, and to pray and implore, but he will not prevail."[39] But Aelred uses the passage precisely to speak to the various voices of the church singing in harmony through the cross (H 31). As White comments, however, Aelred is not consistently more encouraging than Jerome, in some places countering Jerome's positive outlook with cautious ambivalence.[40]

Although Aelred never names Jerome's commentary, so deviating from his usual practice of frequently citing his sources, he relies heavily on it. About ten times he uses passages from Jerome's fifth book, through the end of his discussion of Moab (In Isa 5.75), and around

---

[37] Jerome, In Isa 6.35; Scheck, *St. Jerome*, 322.

[38] White, "*Bifarie itaque potest legi*," 400.

[39] Jerome, In Isa 6.43; Scheck, *St. Jerome*, 332.

[40] White, "*Bifarie itaque potest legi*," 405.

175 times from the sixth book, which covers only the first three burdens and which is thus coterminous with Aelred's own homilies.

(3) Aelred incorporates numerous readings from other patristic sources; Raciti lists fifteen in his edition, ranging from Origen through Ps-Dionysius through the Venerable Bede, as well as medieval authors such as Bernard of Clairvaux. He also catalogues liturgical citations and reminiscences of Aelred's other works.[41] Prominent among the patristic sources, not surprisingly, are Augustine (sixteen works), Gregory the Great (four), and Jerome (seven besides the *Commentary on Isaiah*). Of Augustine's works Aelred most frequently cites *On Genesis according to the Letter*, predominantly in the second homily, where he cites but expands Augustine's taxonomy of visions.[42]

Although Raciti has noted only seven passages in the homilies from Augustine's *City of God*, its thematic influence is obvious in the numerous homilies concerned with the historical development of the church, which Burton and Philippe Molac have explained as fundamentally concerned with the theology of history. Most obviously, Isaiah's juxtaposition of the peace promised to Israel with the damnation due the nations recalls Augustine's distinction between the City of God and the City of Man by distinguishing the joint presence in this world of the blessed and the damned. Aelred makes much the same point in his eleventh homily: "O brothers, there are two peoples, two nations, and two kingdoms: the good and the wicked, the wise and the foolish, the chosen and the condemned. But at the time in which all things are mingled together and confused, one cannot detect to which nation or people any given person belongs. This is because many people are good insofar as outward appearance goes but are wicked in the depths of their conscience" (H 11.10). Similarly Aelred seems to echo Augustine in identifying Nero as a type of both the Antichrist and of the devil, both of whom

---

[41] Raciti, *Homeliae de oneribus*, 362–86.

[42] Guglielmo Scannerini explains both Aelred's treatment of Augustine's visionary types and his inclusion of the visionary experience of the Gilbertine nun in H 2 as indicating "a pastoral sensibility" in its effort to make the subject of the homily accessible ("Mystica o misticismo? Un approcio patristico ad Aelredo di Rievaulx, *De oneribus* S. 2 [3]," *Analecta cisterciensia* 54, no. 1–2 [2002]: 134–85, here 165).

appear throughout: "The Romans' emperor at that time, the wicked Nero, is fittingly compared to a poisonous basilisk" (H 20.17).[43]

Of Gregory's works, Aelred most often relies on the lengthy *Moralia in Iob*, whose thematic and methodological echoes are particularly pervasive in these homilies. Time and again Gregory returns to the explanation of human suffering as sent by God both to punish the wicked and to give them a chance to reform, and to warn good people of the suffering that will ensue if they abandon God, or to give them pain now so that it will not await them in the life to come: "[Almighty God] liberally anticipates many of those who perpetrate unlawful and perverse actions and converts them to the performance of holy deeds, and other people who are dedicated to upright behavior he corrects by means of a trial that intervenes. By this means he afflicts those who please him as though he were not pleased."[44]

Gregory's three-part exegetical method in the *Moralia*—interpreting passages in Job at literal, allegorical, and moral levels—also influenced Aelred's work. Using Jerome's imagery, Gregory explains his use of the method in a letter to Bishop Leander of Seville:

> We must make it clear that some passages are subjected only to a brief literal commentary and others to a thorough allegorical interpretation in order to bring out the typical sense; others are discussed using only the tools of allegory to make clear the moral sense, and others again are interpreted using all these means together, the three senses that we diligently search out. First and foremost we base ourselves on the sacred history, then we elevate the mind's construction into an edifice of faith through the typical meaning, and finally we adorn the building with exterior color through the charm of moral action.[45]

---

[43] See further Philippe Molac, "Théologie de l'histoire chez Aelred d'après les sermons *De oneribus*," in Intentio Cordis: *Temps, histoire, mémoire chez Aelred de Rievaulx. Collectanea Cisterciensia* 73 (2011): 86–98, here 91.

[44] Gregory the Great, *Moralia in Iob* 24.XVIII.14 (hereafter Mo); ed. Marcus Adriaen, CCCM 43, 43A, 43B (Turnhout: Brepols, 1979); *Moral Reflections on the Book of Job,* trans. Brian Kerns, 6 vols., CS 249, 257, 258, 259 (Collegeville, MN: Cistercian Publications, 2014–2017) (vols. 5–6 forthcoming 2019–2020).

[45] Gregory, Letter to Leander 3, in Mo 1:4; *Moral Reflections on Job,* 1:51. A little earlier in the letter Gregory explains the allegorical sense as "the higher sense leading to contemplation."

Like Aelred, Gregory offers differing meanings for most images and scriptural passages. For example, at the historical level he explains Job as a good man suffering unearned pain, but at the allegorical level he presents him as Christ, or the church, as in *Moralia* 6.I.1. Aelred's use of this method allows him to complicate his commentary on Isaiah's prophetic message, showing each threat as able to lead either to repentance or to recalcitrance, and so to salvation as well as damnation.

(4) Finally, Aelred's deep familiarity with Scripture and the liturgy of the church and monastery informs these homilies in both language and argument. Repeatedly he silently incorporates liturgical antiphons and responses into the text. The prophetic books and the Psalms are particularly full of passages in which God condemns his ungrateful people, promising for example that the day of the Lord will be a day of darkness not light (Amos 5:18) and declaring his ability to turn plowshares into swords and rivers into deserts (Joel 3:10; Ps 106:33). In the New Testament as well God declares that he will cast sinners into outer darkness (e.g., Matt 8:12). Both the Old and New Testaments also tell of God's promise to rescue and save his people, as he remembers that his creatures are his people and the sheep of his pasture: "For he remembered that they were but flesh; a wind that passes away and does not come again" (Ps 77:39).[46]

Aelred's Audience

Most scholars have assumed with good reason that the intended audience of this work is the monks of Rievaulx. Aelred says in the letter to Foliot that he wrote the homilies as a response to his monks' request; in the first homily he explains his rhetorical choices as a preacher and teacher to his community, he regularly ends homilies by acknowledging his listeners' need for rest, and he concludes his final homily by saying that while waiting for a response from Foliot, "we will attempt something else that seems either useful or pleasing for your instruction or for the instruction of others" (H 31.26). He

---

[46] Marginal notes in the translation below indicate Aelred's incorporation of scriptural passages and their liturgical use.

often says that both he and his community need a break or promises to return to the same topic on the next day. Even the homiletic form of the work indicates his desire that it be understood as personal, addressed to those whom he hopes to inspire and guide. Of particular interest in that regard in terms of both audience and rhetorical intention is a passage in the first homily:

> Because many of you grow bored with the same sermon and the same reading repeated again and again, we need to renew what seems old and familiar, either by adding certain ideas or at least by changing the words. In this way we can rouse the attentiveness that we seek and call the heart back from its useless and vain digressions to what is useful. So the mind that in its boredom had fled the familiar can, after being renewed by the sweetness of a reading or sermon, beneficially return to that from which it had been unconsciously distracted. (H 1.6)

Later Aelred speaks more personally to his community: "I confess, dear brothers, that things have not worked out as I had thought. For it seemed to me that we could deal with the mysteries of our discourse's burdens in a few sermons. But this first burden, which we still have in our hands, has already detained us for many days" (H 11.1). One of the most expansive of such explanations comes at the end of a homily, apparently as he prepares to depart on a journey, perhaps to attend the annual Cistercian general chapter at Cîteaux:

> We have explained these things briefly, because the mind has already hastened to other things that must be said. For it is time to take a journey that the Order's law demands of us, to which desire rouses us and affection invites us. But how will I be separated for such a long time from my heart's desire [*a uisceribus meis*]? I will be separated, I say, *in the body*, but not *in the spirit*. And I know that I will be as present in affection and spirit as I am absent in body. . . .
> But think, beloved, of what was written of the Lord Jesus just when his physical presence was about to be taken from his disciples: *Eating with them, he ordered them not to leave Jerusalem.* We have already gotten up from the table after our sweet banquet, and in a little while we will depart. Following his example, we command you, we beseech you, we remind you not to leave Jerusalem.

> For Jerusalem means peace. We commend peace to you, we command peace among you. May Christ *himself*, who *is our peace*, making *both into one*, keep you in the unity of *spirit* and *in the bond of peace*. I commit you to his protection and consolation under the wings of the Holy Spirit. May he restore you to me and me to you in peace and safety. (H 14.17–19)

The following homily, implicitly preached after Aelred's return from his journey overseas, begins with his joy at finding the community living in that peace.

So it is not surprising that most scholars consider the work to be monastic teaching. Thomas Renna writes that its goal is to inculcate monastic culture: "Aelred gave his monks a lesson in how to read the scriptures . . . . actually a concealed lecture in the school of the cloister."[47] Molac similarly defines it as intended for monks: "Aelred thus in the first place aims to catechize his monks in the sense of the birth of Christ in the soul."[48] And Burton seems to take it for granted that Aelred's primary audience is his community, e.g., "Aelred applies to the spiritual exegesis of the Scriptures that same sharp pastoral sense he demonstrated throughout his two abbacies and that . . . led him to push to great extremes his efforts to adapt to and satisfy the personal needs of each one of his brothers."[49]

But several aspects of the homilies resist this view. They are in the first place too long for such use, even if so defined only rhetorically. And as Raciti points out, they "are not the fruit of actual preaching, recorded on the fly by secretaries. . . . This biblical commentary in the form of homilies is thus essentially a written creation."[50] Moreover, they are not clearly sited within the liturgical year. Whereas Cistercian abbots were required to preach at the beginning of Advent, no expectation existed for a long series of

---

[47] Thomas Renna, "Aelred of Rievaulx and Isaiah," in *The Joy of Learning and the Love of God: Studies in Honor of Jean Leclercq*, ed. E. Rozanne Elder, CS 160 (Kalamazoo, MI: Cistercian Publications, 1995), 253–68, here 261.

[48] Molac, "Théologie de l'histoire," 91.

[49] Burton, *Aelred de Rievaulx*, 555.

[50] Raciti, Introduction, V.

sermons explicating Isaiah.[51] Finally, the concerns and tone of the homilies that address themes of pride, hypocrisy, love of the world, carnal sin, vice, apostasy, the fall of Satan, and even the tripartite history of the church seem peripheral to the needs of monks; however thematically integrated into the work as a whole, as individual units they seem unlikely to resonate meaningfully within the monastery. While it is true that manuscripts of Aelred's liturgical sermons contain some sermons, such as SS 47, 48, and 76, that resemble some of these homilies, they are there grouped with many that are explicitly pastoral.

The rhetorical method and voice of many of these Isaian homilies castigating the powerful in church and kingdom seem to point instead to a message that is not primarily monastic or pastoral but one closer to Isaiah's, proclaiming a theological and ethical message to an audience that needs to be shaken, challenged, confronted, driven either to stay on the right path or to return to it, with damnation the sure result of failure. As White has noted, Aelred's letter to Foliot "reads like a document intended for public consumption."[52] His words thus suggest an overlap between two possible audiences, the monks of Rievaulx and the public figures represented by Foliot, to whom Aelred sends the homilies. Aelred's constant writing since at least the 1150s to and for those men whose decisions governed Scotland and England had surely not diminished by the mid-1160s, especially given the public conflict not just between church and crown but within the church itself.[53]

In offering the Isaian homilies to Foliot, Aelred seems to imply that they, like his better-known historical treatises, are intended for a public audience. Some of them in fact make that reading almost irresistible, as when in one of his fiercest attacks on prelates, he attacks the powerful and the hypocritical:

---

[51] Danièle Choisselet and Placide Vernet, eds., *Les* Ecclesiastica Officia *Cisterciens du XIIème siècle*, La Documentation Cistercienne 22 (Reiningue: Abbaye d'Œlenberg, 1989), 190. See Domenico Pezzini, "The Sermons of Aelred of Rievaulx," in *A Companion to Aelred of Rievaulx (1110–1167)*, ed. Marsha L. Dutton (Leuven: Brill, 2017), 73–97, here 74.

[52] White, "*Bifarie itaque potest legi*," 420.

[53] See Vita A 32; CF 57:121.

This is also the case for those in Christ's church whom pleasures and wantonness deform, whom ambition crushes, to whom poverty is a burden and the Gospel an object of ridicule. . . . Because the church now reigns in faith, many of them publicly preach it, although they secretly disparage it. They argue in the schools as though they were in favor of faith, but they mock the same faith in the bedroom and in hidden nooks. They use their profession of faith to obtain a full pantry, a stuffed pocketbook, and privileged *greetings and the highest seats*. But when it comes to the perfuming room and chalices, to the bedrooms and *hidden disgraceful things*, they casually dismiss the catholic faith, they explain away the resurrection of the body as impossible, they mock the Last Judgment, and they excuse lust as a natural need. (H 10.5)

Some of these passages echo another theme found in Aelred's historical works, about the necessity of close cooperation between public power and the church, echoing the tenth-century Benedictine Reform's emphasis on cooperation between church and crown[54] and, in Aelred's *Genealogy of the Kings of the English* (1153–1154), the lengthy address of King Edgar (r. 959–975) to "the fathers of the churches and monasteries":

I refrain from pointing out that their corona is not evident or their tonsure not appropriate, that the indecency of their clothing, the insolence of their bearing, and the filthiness of their speech express the madness of their inner being. What is more, the extent of their indifference at the divine offices is apparent when they scarcely deign to be present at the sacred Vigils, when they seem to gather at the holy solemnity of the Mass to fool around rather than to chant. . . . they wallow in reveling and drunkenness, in debauchery and licentiousness, so that the houses of clerics are reckoned brothels for prostitutes and gathering places for actors. There is gambling, dancing, and singing, and vigils drawn out to the middle of the night with frightful clamor.[55]

---

[54] See for a recent survey of this movement Jacob Riyeff, Introduction, in Saint Aethelwold of Winchester, *The Old English Rule of Saint Benedict with Related Old English Texts,* ed. Jacob Riyeff, CS 264 (Collegeville, MN: Cistercian Publications, 2017), 1–26, here 4–11.

[55] *Genealogia Regum Anglorum* IX; CCCM 3:41; CF 56:98–99.

Even scholars who assume Aelred's primary audience here to be monks recognize the homilies' suitability for those in the world outside as well. Pezzini, for example, assumes a more extensive audience: "The addressee of the work is Aelred's monastic community. . . . But considering his great personal effort in composing it and his public dedication of the work to Gilbert Foliot, the potential audience must be far larger, as is well expressed by the word *Babylon*. . . . It is necessary to keep this large horizon in mind while reading Aelred's large frescoes of past and contemporary history. Although the main perspective is certainly monastic, the perspective goes well beyond that world."[56] Burton too interprets them as intended for audiences outside the cloister, to invite emulation of monastic life: "Like Bede Aelred urged secular and ecclesiastical leaders to adopt something of the spirituality of the cloister."[57] And Renna, in fact, sees such passages on the church as sufficiently disruptive to his explication of the work as designing a monastic moral journey that he calls attention to that disruption: "This historical scheme, appearing as it does at the conclusion of the final sermon (as if this were a major theme in the entire set of sermons), comes as something of a jolt."[58]

Scholars' indecision on this question reflects the fact that Aelred seems intentionally to leave his audience as well as his argument imprecisely defined. So in his homily bewailing the current decline in collaboration between kings and bishops, he cries out, "Woe to us who have fallen on these unhappy times in which the sun seems to have turned to darkness!" He then poses the question that he expects his audience to ask—and he refuses to answer it: "What darkness, you ask? I do not want to say, brothers, I do not want to say, lest I should seem to place *my mouth in heaven*" (H 10.9).[59]

It is not unusual for Aelred to employ the rhetorical strategy of raising questions that he either thinks his listeners want to ask or that he thinks they should ask, especially in his dialogical treatises. In such cases he tends to evade the question he himself has raised, either promising to come back to it later or responding with another

---

[56] Pezzini, "The Sermons," 95.

[57] Burton, *Aelred de Rievaulx*, 262.

[58] Renna, "Aelred of Rievaulx and Isaiah," 259.

[59] Raciti notes Aelred's allusion here to Ps 72:3-9: "For I envied the arrogant. . . . Their mouths lay claim to heaven."

question.[60] Here he employs the same evasive strategy, placing a question on the lips of those to whom he apparently speaks but then explicitly deflecting the question, explaining his refusal as intended to avoid arrogance but in fact calling extra attention to the question by his refusal. It seems likely that he avoids the question about the target of his attack not—or not solely—out of desire to avoid personal arrogance but out of self-protectiveness, as the tenth homily and some others come close to castigating powerful living figures.

But if Aelred intends the homilies that contain such passages not for the monks of Rievaulx but for public figures, then for whom? As the named recipient of the work Foliot is the first obvious candidate. Despite Aelred's warm words of greeting in the epistle, he might well have viewed Foliot's public animosity from at least as early as 1162 toward the archbishop of Canterbury, Thomas Becket, as a matter of arrogance and resistance to lawful authority—as Becket certainly did. But scholars have not indicated that Foliot was corrupt, tyrannical, or heretical in his life or work, and even when criticizing his behavior with regard to Becket, they suggest no improbity in his life or episcopal role, the characteristics that Aelred most insistently attacks. The forcefulness of his condemnations in these passages seems out of proportion to what is known today about Foliot.

A more obvious Aelredian target in these homilies is Becket himself, on whom judgments are more widely mixed. After being Henry's close companion and then his chancellor between 1155 and 1162, when he became archbishop of Canterbury, Henry presumably anticipated a continuing close collaboration between them. But rather quickly Becket began to develop an understanding of his new office that drew him apart from Henry's political expectations, not only taking on habits of personal piety such as wearing a hair shirt underneath his vestments but also insisting on greater autonomy for the church in England and its authority over the lives of clerics. Soon a deep division had developed between crown and church and between Henry and Becket, and in 1164 Becket fled to France, taking refuge for two years in the Cistercian abbey of Pontigny.[61]

---

[60] See, e.g., *De spiritali amicitia* 1.69; CCCM 1:301; CF 5:69.

[61] Jean Truax examines the Becket affair and Becket's relationship with Cistercians in England and France, with particular attention to Aelred (*Aelred the Peacemaker,* CF 251 [Collegeville, MN: Cistercian Publications, 2017], 194–222).

While discussing the political context within which Aelred wrote these homilies, Burton implies a similar reading of the passages dealing with the church:

> if, in April 1164, the storm had not yet broken, the sky was nevertheless darkening, and lightning was violently scorching the horizon. In January 1164, Thomas had gathered all his strength to resist the king's desire to force the English episcopate to sign the Constitutions of Clarendon, severely limiting the judicial power that ecclesiastical authorities had until then exercised. He had even, as a supreme insult, presented himself before the court flaunting his archiepiscopal crosier before him. Gilbert Foliot would reproach him for this: "If the king were to brandish his sword . . . as you now brandish yours, what hope can there be at making peace between you?"[62]

It is hard to believe that Aelred would not have had Becket in mind during at least some of the period while he was writing these homilies. His relationship, however tenuous, with both Foliot and Henry II during that critical period—at just the time of Becket's flight to France—may have led him to want to state his own position on the conflict, either as another spokesman for the English church or as a supporter of Henry and Foliot. Aelred's close attention to public affairs in England and his praise and decades-long support for King Henry were already clear from his historical works. These homilies may indicate a desire to speak his own piece on current affairs, now as a preacher and prophet rather than a historian.

The Three Parts of the Work

Raciti's edition of Aelred's homilies and White's translation both follow the three-part manuscript composition. After the commendatory letter to Bishop Gilbert Foliot comes an Advent sermon devoted to Isaiah 13–16, titled "Sermon on the Coming of the Lord: On the Eleven Burdens" (*Sermo in Adventu Domini: de undecim oneribus*),

---

[62] Burton, *Aelred de Rievaulx*, 538.

which Aelred says he delivered to his community and which led the community to ask him to speak at more length on the topic.[63] The thirty-one homilies follow.

Bishop Gilbert Foliot and the Epistle from Aelred

Foliot (ca. 1110–1187), to whom Aelred apparently sent the homilies, is best remembered today as the bishop of London who stood by Henry II during his conflict with Becket. That familiar identification of Foliot has two consequences: his name is much better known than that of other medieval bishops of London, and he is reduced in popular memory to a simple antagonist, with his own great gifts both personal and public forgotten. Most of those today who recognize his name are simply unaware of him as a man of religion, scholarship, and integrity, all of which may have led Aelred to select him as recipient and arbiter of his homilies.[64]

Scholars have generally praised Foliot's character and accomplishments. David Knowles, for example, called him, "the man of probity whom even a pope reverenced for his austerity of life, the mirror of religion and glory of the age, the luminary who shed a lustre even on the great name of Cluny."[65] A little later he expanded on this description:

> [his character] is that of an able, efficient, prudent, tactful, eminently
> respectable churchman, a man in high position in a graded, orderly

[63] Migne numbered this sermon 1 of 32 in his 1855 printing, creating an enduring problem for scholars wishing either to locate or cite a particular passage. In Raciti and the translation below, this Advent sermon is designated as Adv, with the *De oneribus* homilies numbered 1 through 31.

[64] This brief biographical sketch of Gilbert Foliot depends for the most part on David Knowles, *The Episcopal Colleagues of Archbishop Thomas Becket: Being the Ford Lectures Delivered in the University of Oxford in Hilary Term 1949* (Cambridge: University Press, 1951), 37–49; and "Foliot, Gilbert (c. 1110–1187)," *The Dictionary of National Biography*, http://www.oxforddnb.com.proxy.library.ohio.edu/view /article/9792?docPos=1. The DNB entry focuses largely on Foliot's support of King Henry in his conflict with Becket.

[65] Knowles, *Episcopal Colleagues*, 37–38.

> society, obeying and enforcing its laws with an equitable recognition
> of the tribes without the law—barons, it might be, and kings. He
> would seem to have taken particular pains to be on good terms
> with his colleagues; letters of recommendation and support are
> numerous . . . . Foliot had the reputation of a man of letters and
> of an ascetic; he was a monk, and therefore had learned to obey
> and be obeyed . . . . He had been for many years a religious su-
> perior, and in outward behaviour and mental characteristics he
> bore the stamp of a dignified and cultured life.[66]

Foliot came from an English family with notable ecclesiastical ties.
His maternal uncle, Robert de Chesney, was the bishop of Lincoln
(1148–1166), and another uncle was a monk of Gloucester Abbey
before becoming abbot of Evesham Abbey. Although Foliot's paternal
line is uncertain, his father is thought to have been Robert Foliot I,
who served as steward to David of Scotland before David became
king, the same role that Aelred himself later filled in David's reign.[67]
After becoming a monk of Cluny, the younger Foliot became one of
its priors before in 1139 England's King Stephen, presumably because
of Foliot's already distinguished reputation, named him abbot of
Gloucester. In 1148 Theobald, archbishop of Canterbury, proposed
him to Pope Eugenius III as bishop of Hereford; Eugenius immediately appointed him to the see. Upon Theobald's death in 1161, it
was widely assumed that Henry would appoint Foliot, clearly a
rising man in the church, as archbishop of Canterbury, but those
expectations were dashed when in 1162 Henry instead named Becket.

Foliot was outspoken in his opposition to that appointment.
Indeed he was, as Knowles approvingly reports, the only bishop
to oppose the king's choice: "This of itself is creditable rather than
the reverse. . . . for a worldly chancellor to be forced upon a re-
calcitrant electing body was a thing deplorable in itself . . . . Indeed, we may feel that with such principles and in such a cause
Foliot should have refused consent come what might."[68] Over the

---

[66] Knowles, *Episcopal Colleagues*, 41–42.

[67] Although the origins of the family are unknown, it is usual to pronounce the
name in an English rather than Norman fashion, i.e., to rhyme with *got* rather
than *go*.

[68] Knowles, *Episcopal Colleagues*, 45.

following years, then, even as Becket increasingly militated for the rights of the church against the crown, Foliot supported Henry in his opposition. But here Knowles does not admire Foliot's course: "Disappointed ambition, perhaps all the more painful because unacknowledged, . . . the strong personal bias; the unfortunate series of accidents which made him an almost *ex officio* leader of the opposition and advocate of the king—all these contributed to make of Gilbert Foliot the adversary of his archbishop and, once adversary, his talents and reputation made him inevitably the one to whom all who opposed the archbishop looked for leadership and counsel."[69]

In the letter preceding the homilies, Aelred refers with unalloyed praise to Foliot's accomplishments and reputation as a man of faith and scholarship. And despite the public furor surrounding the conflict between Henry and Becket, he makes no reference to the conflict itself or to Foliot's role therein: "among the countless tasks that either the royal majesty's authority or the needs of pastoral care impose on you, you are a cultivator of wisdom, a friend of peace, eager for spiritual knowledge, attentive to reading, and, . . . among the sweet delights of prayer, you lighten the trouble of encroaching cares by frequent meditation on the Holy Scriptures" (Ep 2).

Like Knowles, David N. Bell combines praise for Foliot's strengths with criticism for Foliot's continuing animosity toward Becket:

> [Foliot] was the mirror of holiness, the exemplar of truth and justice, adorned with virtues, pre-eminent in learning, and pure in religion.
>
> What, then, can we say of his conduct between the years 1162 and 1170? How can we explain those major blemishes which mar the cold perfection of this model of pious integrity: perjury, personal ambition (though Gilbert himself denied it), and a fierce hatred . . . . Even John of Salisbury, whose cautious and balanced mind was one of the best of his age, could only see him as the *archisynagogus*, clamouring for innocent blood."[70]

---

[69] Knowles, *Episcopal Colleagues*, 49.

[70] David N. Bell, "The Commentary on the Lord's Prayer of Gilbert Foliot," *Recherches de théologie ancienne et médiévale* 56 (1999): 80–101, here 81–82.

Foliot's resistance led Becket to excommunicate Foliot twice. After the first instance, when in 1169 Becket excommunicated Foliot for insubordination, Foliot obtained papal absolution. But in 1170, after Foliot attended the illicit coronation of Henry's oldest son, known as the Young King,[71] Becket issued a second excommunication, which Knowles regards as "an essential link in the circumstances that led to the murder [of Becket]."[72]

Foliot's obvious preeminence in Henry's reign both before and during Becket's exile placed considerable distance of renown, rank, and power between him and Aelred. The common scholarly opinion is that the two men knew each other only slightly, having on some occasion been introduced in London,[73] as Aelred seems to imply in his epistle to Foliot: "the memory of your humility together with your kindness encourages me, you who came before me in the blessings of sweetness when I was in London. Astounded and shaking before such dignity, I was greeted by a kind of embrace of love by someone from whom it would have been a great thing merely to be looked at" (Ep 8).

It seems possible, however, as both Burton and Jean Truax have suggested, that the two men had met much earlier, when Aelred was a young man at the court of King David,[74] or later, perhaps at Henry's court. Some earlier acquaintance between them would help to explain Aelred's report of the warmth of a meeting in London, after Foliot's episcopal promotion. After (according to the fourteenth-century *Peterborough Chronicle*) having helped to persuade Henry to

---

[71] Young Henry died in 1183, six years before his father.

[72] Knowles, *Episcopal Colleagues*, 97–101.

[73] Squire says, "Aelred's relationship with the austere opponent of Thomas of Canterbury is not quite clear, his letter, in spite of its effusions about love and friendship, being almost as enigmatic on this question as the character of the bishop himself. . . . It was evidently to the friendship of the Gilbert who, whatever his political affiliations, had the reputation of being a good monk, that Aelred aspired" (*Aelred of Rievaulx*, 134). See also Truax, *Aelred the Peacemaker*, 94–95.

[74] Pierre-André Burton says that if Gilbert was indeed the son of Robert, "it is difficult to see how they would not have crossed paths at some point prior to 1163, since Robert served as steward to David while David was still Count of Huntingdon" (*Aelred de Rievaulx*, 537). See also Truax, *Aelred the Peacemaker*, 94.

support Alexander III in the papal schism that ended in 1161,[75] Aelred was invited to write a new life of Edward the Confessor and, according to Walter Daniel, to preach at the translation of his relics in 1163. He and Foliot could hardly have failed to meet on that occasion.[76]

In referring to the two men's meeting in London, Aelred sets the tone for the favor he writes to ask. He begins with warm praise for Foliot, acknowledging Foliot's busy workload while declaring his desire for Foliot's friendship. He goes on to recall the divine love that led to the incarnation and the purpose of the incarnation itself, so that "as though on a kind of middle ground, wretchedness and mercy could meet, strength could unite itself to weakness, the Word and the soul could be in one flesh, and, among these three, there could be one person, both God and human being" (Ep 3). Thus he articulates the grand theme of God's love that runs throughout the homilies.

Aelred then boldly descends from this theological exordium to ask Foliot to serve as an outside reader on his manuscript, offering it "to your consideration and discernment" (Ep 6). He explains that the homilies he encloses are currently incomplete, an introductory sample of a fuller work to be written if Foliot approves, but to be discarded if Foliot rejects them: "I have put down my pen [*suspendi calamum*] until judgment comes forth from your countenance on the things that I have written and your eyes have taken account of them all. Thus, according to the decision that you reach, everything I have written will be destroyed, corrected, or confirmed" (Ep 7).

[75] *Chronicon Angliae Petriburgense*, ed. J. A. Giles, Caxton Society 2 (London, 1845), 98. See also Vita A 32; CF 57:121; and Peter Jackson, "*In translacione sancti Edwardi confessoris.*"

[76] See for Aelred's presence at the translation, James Craigie Robertson, ed., *Materials for the History of Thomas Becket, Archbishop of Canterbury*, 7 vols., Rolls Series 67 (London: Longmans, 1875–1885), 3:57 n. 1. Knowles reports that at the end of the event Becket took Saint Wulfstan's gravestone, "to which, it was believed, St Wulfstan of Worcester's staff had adhered when he was unjustly threatened with deposition by a Westminster synod, driven by William the Conqueror. It might defend him too against enemies, traitors and tyrants" (*Thomas Becket*, 95). Aelred tells the story about Wulfstan's staff in *Vita Sancti Edwardi, Rex et Confessoris* XXXVI (CCCM 3A:164–68; CF 56:220–25). See Marsha L. Dutton, "The Staff in the Stone: Finding Arthur's Sword in the *Vita Sancti Edwardi* of Aelred of Rievaulx, *Arthuriana* 17, no. 3 (2007): 3–28.

Though it is common to refer to Aelred's epistle as dedicatory, in fact Aelred does not dedicate the homilies to Foliot, with a letter like those preceding many of his other works.[77] Instead, he writes to ask Foliot to read and evaluate his lengthy work—essentially to serve as its editor. He also acknowledges that Foliot will have to sacrifice spare time to do so: "Therefore, although it may be a great thing for a wise person to have at least a little time to give to leisure, I beg you not to be annoyed, my lord, to lose a moment to trim what is excessive, add what is lacking, or destroy all of what we have written. . . . According to your judgment, I am ready either to stop here or to continue further" (Ep 9).

While the graceful theological paragraphs that precede Aelred's request help to mute its audacity and obscure the unlikelihood that Gilbert will agree, the request is unmistakably presumptuous, as Aelred himself declares (Ep 8). The suggestion that the superbly busy bishop of London would have the time or interest to read thirty-two lengthy and difficult sermons written by a presumably slight acquaintance of inferior rank of both birth and position simply astonishes. Moreover, the claim that after having written such a lengthy commentary Aelred would be prepared either to destroy it at a word from Foliot or to continue writing on the eight remaining burdens is similarly unconvincing. In practical terms, the thirty-one existing homilies on three Isaian burdens would have required roughly another eighty homilies on the remaining eight, adding up to almost two-thirds of the number of his surviving liturgical sermons.

The most striking aspect of this letter, though, is that which initially seems least surprising: Aelred's powerful paragraphs on the incarnation, with particular emphasis on the way Christ's descent from glory into human life equalized human relationships, with the high and the low meeting together. Rhetorically, this passage attempts to justify Aelred's reaching out to Foliot, as Dietz points out: "it is

---

[77] Five of his treatises begin by stating that he writes in response to a request, another three volunteer advice or information, two lack such letters but purport to record a conversation initiated by one or more monks, and one addresses an audience gathered for the translation of relics. Only *Homilies on the Prophetic Burdens of Isaiah* asks anything from the addressee.

surprising to notice with what ease Aelred shifts from one level to another: the real purpose of this beautiful and deep passage was to justify the fact that a lowly abbot dared to send his work to such an eminent prelate!"[78] But, more important, it establishes the central theme of the homilies that follow: God's love for his creation, the love that "is common to God, angels, and human beings" and that links all "for whom there is one faith, one hope, one charity" (Ep 4).

So Aelred here for the first time declares the subject of his work, rendering the theological exordium not merely a rhetorical exercise but the thesis of all that is to follow, linking this letter substantively to the homilies themselves. White makes just that point: "The introductory *Epistola ad Gilbertum* is thematically integral to this series of homilies. . . . The letter focuses on the unity of opposites, a theme to which homily thirty-one, the last in the collection, dramatically returns."[79] It also not so incidentally departs from the argument of Aelred's two principal sources. For while Isaiah and Jerome both proclaim the doom that God proclaims to the nations, with only occasional glimpses of rescue for his people, Aelred turns that proclamation on its head. Citing the incarnation as precedent and evidence, he proclaims God's love for his people, God's desire to show mercy to sinners, and God's promise of salvation to those who hear and respond. Indeed in the epistle itself Aelred gives no hint of the darker side of the homilies: the damnation of the proud who refuse God's mercy, followers of Satan and the Antichrist and unyielding in their apostasy.

This letter raises three questions of its own. What was Aelred's goal in writing it? What did he actually expect of Foliot? And what in fact did Foliot do? No correspondence exists recording whether he politely rejected the request or simply ignored it, and the autograph manuscript that he presumably received apparently no longer exists. Clearly, however, Aelred neither destroyed what he had written nor added to it, perhaps an indication that Gilbert recommended neither course to him, whether through expressed approval or silence. Or of course perhaps Aelred simply ignored Gilbert's decision, whatever it was.

---

[78] Dietz, "Ambivalence Well Considered," 80.

[79] White, "*Bifarie itaque potest legi*," 420.

The Sermon for the Coming of the Lord

Aelred's sermon for Advent follows the epistle to Foliot. It too focuses on the entry of God's love into the world in the incarnation. It begins with the proclamation of the Day of the Lord: "It is time, dear brothers, *for us to sing to the Lord of mercy and judgment.* For it is the coming of the Lord, of *the Almighty, who came and is to come*" (Adv 1).[80] It is a long sermon, much longer than most of Aelred's liturgical and miscellaneous sermons, and it seems unlikely to have been preached in this form. It is also, as Pierre-André Burton has shown, a conscious and effective introduction to the thirty-one homilies that follow,[81] in part by pointing to the essential ambiguity of human destiny as defined in 1 Thessalonians 5. This theme resonates in both content and argumentative structure throughout the homilies, echoing Paul's explication of the Day of the Lord as both darkness and light, promising "sudden destruction" to the "children of darkness" and salvation through Christ for "the children of light, children of the day."

After the initial proclamation of Christ's coming, the sermon returns to the grand theme of Christ's mercy: "he showed himself humble in his humanity, powerful in his miracles, strong in overcoming the demons, and gentle in taking on our sins. And all of this came forth from the fountain of mercy" (Adv 6). Aelred then introduces Isaiah's prophecies, continuing the theme of Christ's power over evil, now expressed with violence as his cross destroys the yoke that has burdened his people: "*the Lord* raised his *rod over the sea and* raised *it in Egypt's path*" (Adv 7). The rest of the sermon deals with the victory of the cross. After listing Isaiah's eleven burdens, Aelred explains the meaning of the word *burden* in simple terms but with a dual effect: "And what is a *burden* except a kind of weight that pulls the soul down to the earth, making it pay attention to base things and ignore the things above?" (Adv 10).

---

[80] Squire gives the title "Darkness and Light" to his seventh chapter, which discusses the homilies (Squire, *Aelred of Rievaulx,* 129). This sermon also appears in the Durham Collection, as number 47 of Aelred's complete sermons ("In Annuntiatione Dominica," CCCM 2B:98–105). The following sermon also anticipates the themes and language of the homilies.

[81] Burton, *Aelred de Rievaulx,* 545.

The sermon then addresses each of the burdens in turn, explaining their meanings and exemplifying the way they are characteristically experienced, regularly extending that experience to monks. So of the burden of Babylon Aelred writes, "This is a burden that weighs down many, curving them down toward lower things. . . . Oh brothers, what king does not laboriously acquire what he covets? What king is so safe that he fears no one? What king loses something without pain? But let us turn this idea back on ourselves. Does none of us, I ask, sigh under the weight of this burden? Does no remnant of worldly love remain in us?" (Adv 12–13).

Again, after defining Dumah (Isa 21:11) as meaning *silence,* Aelred notes first that "silence burdens and stillness weighs down many people. . . . their head aches, their stomach rumbles, their eyes cloud over, their kidneys trouble them. But everything pleases them when they go out, wandering here and there" (Adv 24). He then turns to monastic behavior: "So if you see a monk living in the cloister who looks in all directions, constantly yawning, stretching his hands and feet, setting aside his book only to take it up again, finally running about from place to place and from auditorium [*auditorio*] to auditorium as though something had stung him, do not doubt that he sighs under the burden of Dumah" (Adv 24).

As the sermon approaches its end, Aelred directs his listeners to the ways in which they must respond to their burdens. He speaks pastorally, reminding each monk of his own trial and offering guidance in resisting and rejecting it: "If the burden of Egypt rests upon you, cast off the works of darkness and equip yourself with arms of light" (Adv 40). And "if on account of the burden of the beasts of the south your desire fades from weariness, reflect and know that if you reject the burden of charity you will justly bear the burden of damnation" (Adv 41). He concludes the sermon with a return to Christ's mercy, to culminate when Christ comes in Judgment: "Thus, brothers, *let us sing to the Lord of mercy and judgment,* the mercy we experience and the Judgment we await. Let us embrace the former and fear the latter, that we be found devout here, and free from care there, by the favor of our Lord" (Adv 44). So he again associates the Day of the Lord with both mercy and Judgment, still offering hope and trust in God's generosity.

This juxtaposition of mercy and Judgment echoes a long passage in Aelred's treatise *The Formation of Anchoresses*, directing the contemplative audience to Christ sitting in Judgment. Aelred here points out that those who will be damned see only a face of anger, while those who stand on Christ's right see the same face they had seen in life.[82] This double vision is precisely that to which Aelred points in the Advent sermon and the thirty-one homilies, with the darkness of Christ's gaze turned upon the arrogant, the apostates, and the followers of the Antichrist, and the amiability of his gaze upon those who endure the suffering of the world while looking to and welcoming his mercy, coming finally to harmony in his love. Aelred concludes this sermon with that same opposition: "Whoever neglects the time of mercy should fear the time of Judgment, because he who redeemed us through mercy will judge us through justice. . . . Let us embrace the former and fear the latter, that we may be found devout here, and free from care there, by the favor of our Lord" (Adv 44).

This lengthy sermon is in every way a monastic discourse, abundantly full of doctrinal explication, scriptural interpretation, and pastoral guidance. It represents Aelred's preaching at its best, showing both rhetorical range and clarity of thought and language. It is long but never tedious, and it speaks to both non-monastic and monastic men and women as it celebrates the coming of the Lord in the new season. It is no wonder that Aelred's monks should have asked him for more of the same.

The Thirty-One Prophetic Homilies

The thirty-one Isaian homilies are neither so straightforward nor so explicitly pastoral as the Advent sermon. Aelred presents the work in two ways, as both a series of only loosely related homilies in three parts and a treatise with a single source and purpose: to instruct the faithful and so to reform them to wisdom, their original likeness to God. The discontinuous homiletic form allows him to explore a variety of concerns and address a variety of audiences, whether monks whom

---

[82] Inst incl 33; CCCM 1:678–79; CF 2:99.

he guides through moral and spiritual progress or princes and prelates whom he seeks to chastise and correct. Aware of the complexity of his subject, and writing in such a way as to make that complexity inescapable, Aelred takes particular care from beginning to end of the homilies to clarify what he is doing. Raciti notes that he sought "to weave a sort of vast medieval tapestry . . . , but a clearly defined global plan, a text supplemented by numerous clarifications, . . . orients the reader through a work whose weft does not lack complexity."[83]

Despite having described the work to Foliot as containing nineteen homilies (well over half of the work) on the burden of Babylon, Aelred actually devotes the first two of these nineteen to establishing the subject, purpose, structure, and method of the work. He begins with a powerful theological exordium defining God as the cause and end of all things, as being itself, with all his creatures participating in that being: "just as God is the being of all things that exist, so too is he the life of the living and the wisdom of all the wise" (H 1.2). He begins with this truth, he explains, because humankind then "began to be foolish and to live foolishly" and continues to live in that foolishness until God himself brings about reformation. The work thus begins with God, Creation, the Fall, and the way men and women may be led back from unlikeness to likeness through instruction. Giving that instruction in faith, hope, and love, with the help of Scripture, is Aelred's stated purpose.

Having spelled out the theological underpinnings and the purpose of the work, Aelred goes on to explain his source and method. He first introduces Isaiah: "I will now take up the book of Isaiah to examine a small portion of it with you. Although you may be quite familiar with it from the commentaries of the saints, I think it is highly useful for us to repeat what they said, if not differently, at least in another fashion. Let us bring to light just as God provides what they passed over as obvious or insignificant, gathering seeds from their reasoning" (H 1.7). A little later for a first time he identifies Isaiah's own purpose as fundamentally Christian, saying that "He reveals in prophecy . . . things about Christ and the church's mysteries [*sacramenta*]" (H 1.9).

---

[83] Raciti, Introduction, VI.

Aelred goes on to identify his method of interpreting by multiplying meanings as grounded in Scripture and informed by the Holy Spirit, with proper discernment requiring awareness of those meanings' correspondence to faith, hope, and charity. Only in the final portion of the homily does he move to the announced subject of the work, again identifying and defining his key terms, *burden* and *Babylon*.

Rather than advancing as expected into exposition of the burden of Babylon, however, the second homily again digresses to consider how Isaiah saw the burdens with which God would afflict the nations, and asking what made his visions prophetic. Aelred answers these questions by narrowing the visionary taxonomy that Augustine had offered in *Genesis according to the Letter*. Augustine had defined three categories—*corporalia, spiritualia*, and *intellectualia*—with the third containing both reason's grasp of things like mathematics and logic, and the experience of divine things, which Guglielmo Scannerini calls mystical.[84] Aelred divides these three into six—sensory, imaginative, phantasmal, spiritual, rational, and intellectual—with the last two equivalent to Augustine's single *intellectualia*. So he divides understandings that are natural to the human mind from what can be known through God alone, without participation of the senses, imagination, or reason, as meaning is received "in the very light of truth" (H 2.14). Only those understandings, those sights, he says, are prophetic.

In a narrative that ends this second homily, Aelred offers an exemplum of such prophetic visions, in it echoing his previous explanation of God as being. He tells of the Gilbertine nuns who after leaving behind things of earthly experience and devotion are "taken up by a kind of inexpressible and incomprehensible light," therein seeing "nothing except that which is and 'is the being of all things'" (H 2.18). So he narratively prepares his audience for what is to come in the remaining twenty-nine homilies.[85]

---

[84] Augustine of Hippo, *De Genesi ad litteram libri duodecim*, in *Sancti Aurelii Augustini Opera*, ed. Joseph Zycha, CSEL 28.1 (Vienna: F. Tempsky, 1894), 12.6–37.

[85] For a helpful discussion of Aelred's treatment of the Augustinian taxonomy, see J. Stephen Russell, "Vision and Skepticism in Aelred's *De Oneribus*," CSQ 49, no. 4 (2014): 485–91; and Scannerini, "Mystica o misticisimo?" 146–50. Both

Having identified Isaiah's visions as prophetic, Aelred now reinterprets them, transforming their figurative language into more familiar explanations. He never implies that his commentary is more truthful than Isaiah's, but rather simpler and more accessible to his contemporary audience, implicitly recognizing that verbal signification is by its very nature multileveled, complex, and varying over time and space.

Thus although the Advent sermon serves as the prologue to the work, establishing both the theme of God's conjoined deeds of mercy and Judgment and introducing Isaiah's eleven burdens, these first two homilies provide a further theological preface to the work that follows. Taken together, the sermon and the homilies manifest the themes initiated in the Epistle and the Advent sermon: the incarnation as the manifestation of God's love and the way in which faith, hope, and love enable men and women to experience that love now and always—trusting in God's promises, hoping for their fulfillment, and loving God in heart and deed.

Aelred's use of the traditional patristic senses of Scripture in his interpretation are vital to his purpose in this work, allowing him to transform Isaiah's prophecies of nearly universal darkness and devastation into an opportunity for salvation for many. He explains that the damned and the blessed live together in the world Isaiah saw: "the prophet described the world in general with the name of Babylon. He understood the world to be divided between the chosen and the condemned, and that each would be either weighed down or crushed" (H 20.1).

Aelred thus repeatedly expands the Isaian lens by providing different ways of understanding each of the divine punishments Isaiah promises to the people, complicating the prophecies by multiplying their meanings, alternating between warnings of impending divine punishment and promises of redemption through the cross of Christ. These constant expansions and alternations emphasize the importance of his method, often rendering the homilies difficult to parse. White explains the effect of the persistent and incremental multiplication of possibility: "because it is confusing, perhaps it also seems

---

authors also consider the relationship between Aelred's distinctions and the Gilbertine exemplum.

to be confused. It somehow manages to be about everything, even contradictory things. With bewildering regularity, Ælred carefully interprets a verse of Isaiah's burdens only to contradict himself a few lines later."[86] But the approach is neither inadvertent nor truly confusing. For just as Aelred takes care to signal his shifts between exegetical levels and from one to another of the three foreign nations, he also makes clear his intentionality in offering multiple ways of understanding names, terms, and images, as when he writes of Moab, "because we explained above that Moab could be spoken of in two ways, according to the conversion of some and the turning away of others, this verse seems to explain which Moab is being talked about" (H 31.6).

In this way Aelred repeatedly points to the cosmic reality that defines his work, recalling throughout the opening line of the Advent sermon that Christ's coming means both mercy and Judgment, and that his cross means both redemption and damnation. For the lived reality of these homilies is just that: that since the Fall men and women have lived in a world characterized at all times by both misery and grace, it is simply not always possible to tell which is which, but in all times God's love pierces through the darkness.

THEMES AND ARGUMENT

In the course of the homilies Aelred identifies light with both divine and human activity and understanding. In the Advent sermon, he refers first to "the works of light" and "the arms of light," then moves to "the shining light of wisdom" and "the light of the Scriptures," opposing these phrases to "the works of darkness," "those who hate the light," and "children of darkness" (Adv 27, 40, 43, 20). In the homilies too he uses light sometimes for human seeking and effort as guided by God and sometimes of God's illumination. Of the community's fervor in prayer, he writes, "the lifting up of the voice can express that fervor that is so necessary for an assembly of brothers. This fervor leads to that interior fire spreading everywhere

---

[86] Lewis White, *"Bifarie itaque potest legi,"* 395.

through the sound from the mouth. The brothers can thus raise one another up and light a spark in one another, until one flame springs from the many" (H 5.10). Of Augustine's words on the fall of Lucifer, he says, "With the light of so great an authority leading the way, we may thus examine the deep abyss of this part of Scripture all the more securely for being more brightly lit" (H 16.3). Linking apostates with Lucifer, he writes, "after works of light, after a good beginning to a good monastic life, [they] turn back from the fellowship of the saints to *works of darkness* as though falling from heaven" (H 17.25). Regarding the role of faith in comprehending "Christ's incarnation and, following from it, humanity's restoration," he cries out, "If only that light would at least shine for me through a small chink I could then at least explore that heavenly secret with one eye, drawing for myself at least a small droplet of divine sweetness and a pleasant memory of the delight explored" (H 26.16). Ultimately the light that he describes as reaching and guiding believers in this life is the light of God: "After abandoning the darkness of error and ignorance, they must be bathed in saving light and say with the prophet, *The light of your face is imprinted upon us, Lord*" (H 28.4).

While Aelred most often links darkness with worldly cares, ignorance, wickedness, and sin, with the outer darkness into which the wicked are cast, and with the prince of darkness, Satan, he sometimes also connects it with the darkness where God is (H 4.14) or with the obscurity of certain portions of Scripture (HH 3.18; 27.2). But in almost every case he counters even this darkness with light: the light of faith (H 4.14), the light of truth (e.g., H 22.13), saving light (H 28.4), and the inaccessible light in which God dwells (H 28.9). He weaves the evangelical emphasis on God's light overcoming the darkness within his interpretive commentary, moving from Babylon, enslaved by ignorance and confusion, to the Philistines, dominated by pride, to Moab, the worldly wise. The upward movement offered by God's mercy to these three nations, he shows, is one of spiritual progress into the light, not through human self-sufficiency and pride, the overarching sin of the three nations, but through the conquering cross of Christ, raised over and illuminating the dark mountain of Babylon (HH 4 and 5).

Aelred exemplifies this theme of a dark world constantly experiencing God's presence with recurrent homilies on the history, contemporary state, and future of the church. For the church, like the world in which it lives, contains both darkness and light, populated not only by the chosen but also by the condemned, caught in the shadows of postlapsarian human experience. In this work, therefore, it embodies the experience of Christians, upheld by God but struggling toward the light.

Aelred examines the historical church in about half of the homilies as a motif translating the individual's journey from conversion to contemplation into the journey of the body of Christ, with the two journeys—individual and corporate—interwoven. Names of popes and events in church history occur alongside summary categorizations of the ages of the church, sometimes four but more often three. Aelred interprets Isaiah 13:10 (*Because the stars of heaven will not shine forth their light*) as prophesying four ages, from the beginnings to Judgment: "We can thus understand that the prophet, learned in the Spirit, ordered his prophecy to treat first the preaching of the apostles, then the persecution of the church, after that, the conversion of the nations and the tranquility of peace—and so also, the repentance of the fallen and the dread of death—and finally, the time of the Antichrist, with the reward of the righteous and the damnation of the wicked" (H 9.23).

In the final homily Aelred returns to the theme as a fulfillment of Isaiah 16:14, but this time stopping short of Judgment: "The prophecy describes three periods of the church: the times of calling, of trial, and of consolation. The church was called by the preaching of the apostles, tried by the persecution of the martyrs, and consoled by the conversion of rulers" (H 31.16). This list thus culminates with a hoped-for time within history (H 31.16).

In other cases, however, Aelred considers the history of the church more particularly. He explains the Isaian promise that "*the Lord . . . will still choose from Israel*" (Isa 14:1) as foretelling the conversion of the Jews, a topic that runs throughout the homilies: "First he chose the apostles, disciples, and the crowd of believers from Israel, so that the early church might be founded. He will also *choose* many at the end of the world with whom the last times of the church will be adorned. But by *choosing*, we understand that not all the Jews found at that time will be saved" (H 13.25).

Aelred's treatment of the church is by no means incidental to his overall purpose, but a conscious embodiment of his concern with a world divided between darkness and light. Scholars have in fact identified this topic as a dominant theme in the work. Burton links the recurring homilies on the history of the church to Aelred's Christology, pointing to the way that the listing of the three ages of the church "derives from the three comings of Christ," with Christ standing "at the center of this theology of history." He thus argues for reading the work as "a general interpretation relating to the formation of Christ in history."[87]

Just as Aelred uses the church both to insist on Christ's presence in the world and to exemplify the lived experience of the condemned and the chosen, he also approaches the subject through insistent attention to human vice and virtue, urging conversion to virtue through God's aid. Aelred addresses the theme more or less insistently in thirty of the thirty-one homilies, with vices defined early on as those things that hold the citizens of Babylon captive (H 3.5), other times as relevant in terms of human relationship to God:

> So virtue and its reward of blessedness are the region of likeness. The region of unlikeness is vice and wretchedness. Humanity first became unlike God through vice, so that it could rightly become unlike him through wretchedness. For this reason, we must first become like him by virtue, so that someday we may be made like him in blessedness. Furthermore, the more full of vice we are, the more we are unlike God, and therefore more distant from him. But the more virtuous we are, the more similar we are to God, and therefore closer to him. (H 7.14)

Several scholars have explained this dynamic as designing a spiritual and essentially monastic journey to God through abandonment of vices and adherence to the theological and cardinal virtues. Molac interprets the homilies as explaining "the monastic way as the imitation of Christ himself in his spiritual combat in the desert,"[88] and Renna writes of the way Aelred's homilies guide monks to correct the vices represented by Babylon, the Philistines, and Moab (love of the world, pride and vainglory, and worldly wisdom) by adhering

---

[87] Burton, *Aelred de Rievaulx*, 563.
[88] Molac, "Théologie de l'histoire," 92.

to the virtues characteristic of the monastic life. He emphasizes that Aelred "never lets his audience forget that he's talking about virtues appropriate to the cloister: vigils, fasts, contrition, with the monk in a constant state of conversion."[89]

In allegorical terms that reach beyond the cloister, however, Aelred shows the journey defined by the history of the church and the struggle between vice and virtue all to be subsumed by the effect of the incarnation in the world, resisting the darkness of ignorance and worldly distraction that obscures God's light, overcoming the pride and despair of grace that results in "heaping vice upon vice" (H 21.7), and finally piercing through and incorporating even the world's wisdom into divine teaching (H 29.7). Thus throughout the homilies Aelred calls his audience back to God through reliance on faith, hope, and charity and the teachings of Scripture as he guides them to restore humankind to wisdom.

While writing of God's power to transform, Aelred also insists on the aspects of the soul as created, with reason, memory, and will, that allow men and women to know, remember, and obey God. So he indicates that human abilities have a role to play in emerging from darkness into light. Pointing to the role of Scripture in teaching through the power of the Holy Spirit, he also commends reason, authority, and experience as human traits that feed the theological ones. Far from rejecting human abilities, he argues them to be God-given and essential to the nurturing of faith, hope, and charity (H 21.14).[90]

At the same time, though, he makes it clear in his allegorizing of the burdens of Babylon, Philistia, and Moab that because of the debasement of the soul through the Fall, human ability is ineffective on its own. Of the Philistines he writes, "All of Philistia is brought low when reason falls into error, the memory of God falls into forgetfulness, and the will falls into wantonness. All is brought low when the heart occupies itself with shamefulness, speech with duplicity, and works with base affairs and iniquity" (H 22.10). He reiterates this point when discussing Moab: "The three forms of sin—in

---

[89] Renna, "Aelred of Rievaulx and Isaiah," 258.

[90] For further instances of Aelred's treatment of this topic, see Aelred, Spec car 1.3.9; CCCM 1:16; CF 17:91–99; Anima 1.32, 36; CCCM 1:694; CF 22:50, 52–53.

thought, word, and deed—can also be called a fork in the road. The three powers of the soul, through which every sin occurs, namely, memory, will, and reason, can also fittingly be called a fork in the road. Therefore, those who give in to this triple concupiscence—those who do wrong in thought, word, and deed—have the wretched lot of living at Moab's fork in the road. Their memory is disfigured by thought, their will is corrupted by pleasure, and their reason is weakened by consenting to sin" (H 24.27).

Throughout, however, God controls and guides, with his light working through the darkness, and Aelred promises that that light will illuminate even the Day of Judgment. Though Isaiah and Jerome both promise that day to be one of cruelty for sinners, Aelred's explication of Isaiah's words moves rapidly from the perspective of sinners cast into darkness to that of the blessed, who experience it as a day of light:

> That day will be cruel, . . . Finally, when Judgment is given on the last day, they will be utterly crushed and driven down to hell.
>
> [The prophecy] continues, *because the stars of heaven will not shine forth their light. The sun will be dark when it rises, and the moon will not shine with its light* [Isa 13:10]. Indeed, on the Day of Judgment, when Christ appears in glory, this brightness will overwhelm all the stars. As a small lamp in sunlight seems not to give forth any light, so will onlookers perceive the stars to be dark on that day. (H 9:20, 21–22)

With this inversion of the Isaian curse he silently recalls to his audience the alternative revelation made to John the Evangelist: "The city does not need the sun or moon to shine on it, for the glory of God gives it light, and the Lamb is its lamp. The nations will walk by its light, and the kings of the earth will bring their splendor into it" (Rev 21:23, 24).

THE END

Although in the Epistle to Foliot Aelred described his work as unfinished, hinging on Foliot's response to determine whether or not he would continue it, the last five homilies consciously conclude it, showing it to be incomplete only in the sense that in this life the Christian's journey to God is incomplete. Beginning in homily 27 Aelred offers a vision of the end of the Christian experience in this life, tracing the culminating steps of the progression from darkness to light and then to celestial harmony, with God and humankind resonating in the unity of the cross. In these homilies he moves quickly through the history of salvation as seen through the incarnation into the vision of the God who dwells in light, linking the visions of Isaiah to those of John the Evangelist, bringing together the lamb, the spiritual marriage, the new wine of the kingdom, contemplative vision, and the harp with many strings. As he has done throughout the work, he interweaves scriptural images, now replacing those of darkness and damnation with those of radiant light and salvation.

Homilies 27 and 28 initiate this closing movement as Aelred once again proclaims the coming of Christ. Here Christ comes as the lamb promised by God to Isaiah but also as light, emerging from the darkness of language, allegory, and Scripture:

> *God will come from the south, and the Holy One from a shady, dense mountain.* Behold, dear brothers, as our Lord Jesus bursts forth from this dense forest of allegorical words. He was hidden in its shady thickness up to the point where the prophet says, *Send forth the lamb, O Lord, the ruler of the land, from the rock of the desert to the mountain of the daughter of Zion* [Isa 16:1]. Truly, *my beloved stands behind our wall, looking through the windows, peering through the lattice.* [Song 2:9]
>
> Is there anyone who has heard the Lord Jesus saying in the gospel, *Examine the Scriptures,* etc., who does not know that we must seek him in the Scriptures? But the darkness of these very Scriptures, the riddles of words, and the narrative's allusions are like a kind of wall between us and him. In fact, those spiritual craftsmen who raised this wall for us installed windows and lattices in it, through which the beloved often lets his lovers see him. Thus no one may doubt that he whom the clear parts of Scripture plainly show is also to be found everywhere in the obscure parts. (H 27.1–2)

Here Aelred accomplishes two purposes, one theological and the other pedagogical. He proclaims the coming of the Lord now as literal rather than figurative or allegorical, and he acknowledges his own role in that proclamation, instructing his audience in order to re-form them into wisdom, tacitly once again pointing out the relationship between himself and Isaiah as his prophetic predecessor. A little later he connects the Isaian prophecy to Jeremiah, to John the Baptist, and to the whole history of the church, now reaching back even to the synagogue: "The apostles came from this synagogue and brought the lamb *who took away the sins of the world* to the Gentiles with their preaching. In this way, the lamb could reign over the entire world. The church would thus be born from the synagogue as though it were Zion's daughter, whose mountain is the height of faith, the grandeur of hope, and the more excellent way of charity" (H 27.6). So Aelred eliminates the old division between synagogue and church, acknowledging Jesus' ancestors and the Jewish prophets as ancestors of the church. Just as he originally insisted on Babylon as "the whole world," enslaved in darkness, now he declares the whole world—Jew and Gentile alike—to be governed in faith, hope, and charity through Christ.

In the next homily Aelred again points out the literal fulfillment of the prophecies. But now he adds John the Evangelist's image of Christ as bridegroom to that of the lamb:

> A clear prophecy concerning the Lord should neither be wrapped up in allegorical layers nor diminished by moral allusions. For nothing nourishes faith or builds up morals more than to read that the holy prophets foretold what we now perceive to be so clearly fulfilled. For what is clearer than to hear the blessed Baptist point out the lamb, of whom we read in the prophet that he would come? The prophet said, *Send forth the lamb, O Lord, the ruler of the land,* whereas the Baptist cried out, *Behold, the lamb of God, who takes away the sins of the world.* The same Baptist says elsewhere of him, *He who has the bride is the bridegroom.*
>
> Who is this bride? It is she whom the Father addresses in the psalm: *Listen, daughter, and see, and bend your ear, and forget your people and your father's house* [Ps 44:11]. (H 28.1–2)

Both the traditional liturgical use of Psalm 44 for Vigils of the feast of the Annunciation and the first line of the Rule of Saint Benedict ("Hear, oh son, the teaching of your master, and bend the ear of your heart") resonate in this passage, though Aelred mentions neither.[91] With them, however, he introduces the Virgin Mary as bride, the church as prefigured in Mary, and perhaps also the monk who hears. So he again signals the movement from the world of confusion and darkness into the light so long foreseen, inviting his hearers not only to hear but also to respond, to bend, to incline toward the lamb and to join in the mystical marriage with Mary and the church, the mother and bride of Christ. The richness of the language and imagery here is enhanced by Aelred's insistence in both homilies 27 and 28 that what he declares is a matter of neither allegorical nor moral teaching, but the literal truth.

A little later Aelred introduces the Moabites, the figurative subject of the last nine homilies, finally readying themselves to approach the lamb and enter into the spiritual marriage. As Isaiah had prophesied that they would suffer for only three years, Aelred invites them now in the third age of the church, which he has defined as both consolation and contemplation, to rise from their sin through Christ's cross and to ascend to God: "So Moab's daughters must climb from the lower to the higher to be joined in saving marriage to that lamb *who,* sent forth *from the rock of the desert,* takes away *the sins of the world.* After abandoning the darkness of error and ignorance, they must be bathed in saving light and say with the prophet, *The light of your face is imprinted upon us, Lord*" (H 28.4).

A little later Aelred writes again of "the daughters of Moab" as they move toward light, now on a spiritual journey: "When they then strive to cross over from carnal to spiritual love as though *from darkness to light, . . .* they must first flee both the vices and occasions for vice. Thus, growing feathers first in the nest of discipline and later in the nest of wisdom, they may climb from the lower to the higher, from the human to the divine, and from the earthly to the heavenly" (H 28.17). This then is the route for all who hear Christ's call, first to abandon the darkness of ignorance and to be illuminated by God's light, then to mature in wisdom, to cross to spiritual light, and finally to climb to the heavenly realm.

Finally Aelred invites the daughters of Moab to take flight, enabled by the goal itself: "Like an eagle that, borne on the wings of

---

[91] *Obsculta, o fili, praecepta magistri, et inclina aurem cordis tui* (RB Prol. 1).

contemplation, flies in the highest heaven, they may thus open their eyes to gaze fixedly on the splendor of the very sun near at hand" (H 28.16). This is the spiritual journey that he has limned throughout, from darkness to light, from earthly blindness to full vision and to love:

> As you were formed for life, so too may you be illuminated for knowledge. When you learn from the Scriptures to refer everything that lives and perceives to the love of God and neighbor, you will climb the mountain of contemplation borne on two wings, namely, knowledge and love. You will then learn to form the structure of this earthly tabernacle according to the heavenly one, and you will hear with Moses, *Look, make everything according to the pattern that was shown to you on the mountain.* (H 28.20)

This journey upward does not go uninterrupted, though, for as Aelred has written elsewhere, in this life even spiritual progress is inconsistent, unstable.[92] As he writes of the spiritual development of the daughter of Moab in homily 28, he recalls the dangers to those who "would rather remain safely below than attempt what is above" (H 28.19). The double possibility, as he has made clear throughout the homilies, is always before the one called to the vision of God, so that those who trust in themselves rather than God are likely to fall short: "Seeking sustenance by their own effort, they sometimes climb the heights of heaven in flight, and sometimes they sink down with tucked wings" (H 28.10). Just after the repeated lyrical passages inviting the audience to the spiritual marriage and contemplation of God's light, then, Aelred steps back from celestial anticipation to warn against human sin, juxtaposing the invitation to heavenly light in the previous homily with its absence from "those who, blinded by sin, persevere in the darkness of their errors" (H 29.1).

In the next homily, however, Aelred again looks toward beatitude, now introducing the various kinds of wine available to the seeker, from the wine of love to the wine of rejoicing, the wine of wisdom, and finally the wine that, "squeezed from the vineyard of

---

[92] See, e.g., Inst incl 31; CCCM 1:667, 673; CF 2:85, 92; *De Iesu puero duodenni* 30–31 (hereafter Iesu); CCCM 1:276–77; CF 2:37–39.

Scripture . . . makes glad the entire city of God" (Ps 45:5; H 30.8). Again, however, he steps briefly backward, acknowledging that even as one continues to approach God, the taste of divine experience may be alloyed by the wine of bitterness, the wine of lust, the wine of compunction, all of which distract and afflict humans in this life. After recalling "the wine of doctrine from the vineyard of the knowledge of Scripture" (H 30.8–9), he completes the discussion with another kind of wine, not, however, the anticipated wine of the experience of the kingdom, but one useful in this life that continues, a wine that converts and inspires those who drink of it: "Finally, there is the wine of the evangelical and apostolic teaching, *the new wine*, which, coming down from the heavenly storeroom into the apostles' hearts, begets virgins throughout the entire world and makes the hearts of the faithful drunk with the desire for perfection" (H 30.9). With this imagery he again declares Christ's power in this world and indicates the desire that leads his followers forward as they here taste what they will drink in time to come.

Although the audience may hope that the work will conclude with contemplation like that of the Gilbertine nuns if not with the experience of beatitude, it ends instead with a return to the church.[93] But Aelred now at last depicts the church not as riven by ambition and discord, but as harmonious, defined by Saint Paul's image of the variety of spiritual gifts, celebrated as a musical celebration of "the conversion of many after Christ's gospel shone forth" (H 31.1). The church and the chosen thus remain harmoniously in the present, still waiting to sing the anthem of the church triumphant.

At this point again Aelred emphasizes that Isaiah speaks not from a pre-Christian misunderstanding of the visions he has received but as Christ himself. The image Isaiah offers seems inept, bathetic, but Aelred appropriates and redeems it by insisting on it, quoting it in three of the first five sentences of the homily and crediting it not only to Isaiah but also to Christ: "*On this account,* he says, *my belly [venter] will sound forth to Moab like a harp* [Isa 16:11]. This is the voice of the

---

[93] Of Aelred's works only Inst incl concludes in heaven, at the Last Judgment (Inst incl 33; CCCM 1:677–81; CF 2:97–102); like these homilies, Iesu leads the contemplative back from gazing on heavenly mysteries to exercising care for the neighbor (Iesu 29–31; CCCM 1:275–78; CF 2:36–39).

prophet, or of Christ speaking in the prophet" (H 31.1). Aelred goes on to offer two ways of understanding this image—the church as Christ's belly, and God's belly as Scripture, and he links both to the cross. So he brings his constant concern with the church and Scripture into a final unity through Christ, and he incorporates both into his explanation of human blessedness:

> There [in the belly] the heart provides a living impulse for the entire body, there the liver feeds the body's heat and distributes life-giving blood to all the limbs, there reside the other interior organs, each with its appointed function for the body's nourishment. So it is in the church, where the Lord has appointed *some apostles, some prophets, some pastors and teachers in the work of ministry, in building up the body of Christ.*
>
> There are also many strings on the harp, each with its own sound. Yet all are arranged by certain proportions and calculations in such a way that all agree in one harmony, and one beautiful tone arises from them all. So too in Christ's church there are various ranks and various orders, each with diverse gifts of virtues. Yet all are founded in one charity. Through charity, they compose one beautiful tone by bringing together many virtues. (H 31.2–3)

A little later he reprises the image, now declaring this harmony to reside in the relationship between what is hidden and what is known:

> . . . every holy person has a spiritual belly. . . . Just as the belly's contents are locked up in a prison from everyone's eyes and concealed from everyone's knowledge, so *no one knows what is worked in a person except for* that *person's* conscience *that is within.* Happy the soul in which all things have been arranged and ordered like the strings of a harp, in which the virtues agree with one another and the inner corresponds to the outer. (H 31.7)

Finally, however, Aelred insists that human achievement, even in the journey toward God, is impossible through human effort alone. The virtues he writes of here are not those in which the Philistines and Moabites trusted in their pride, but are essentially Christ's, part of his cross: "Virtues are like spiritual strings, which, stretched between two pieces of wood, the upper and the lower, represent the mystery of the cross" (H 31.8). So he concludes as he began, with the incarnate God, with Christ who came into the world to save his people, with the cross that overcomes the dark confusion of Babylon rather than being overcome by it. From beginning to end, that is the message of this work.

Conclusion

Aelred presents his work on Isaiah's prophecies as dual, both a three-part series of only loosely related homilies and a treatise with a single source and end: to instruct the faithful and reform them into their original form of wisdom—their likeness to God through Christ. The homiletic form allows Aelred to explore a variety of concerns and to address a variety of audiences, from monks to princes and prelates, and the treatise allows him to develop a complicated but ultimately unified argument about the man or woman loved, sought, and redeemed by Christ's incarnation. Like light itself, the work exists throughout as both particle and stream, its separate insights always comprising a single whole.

Throughout his life as a writer Aelred had experimented with different forms for different audiences; this late work can be recognized as one more instance of his writerly expression and experimentation, one last opportunity to put down in pen and ink—with his own hand—some of the things he had thought about while he was mostly housebound in his late years, while the kingdom was experiencing a new kind of internal conflict as the great bishops of the English church battled one another. The homilies thus also serve to link Aelred's ascetic, historical, hagiographical, and homiletic works, gathering up the fragments of his life and thought into one great final vision.

The monks of Aelred's community are present in almost every one of the homilies as he greets them and sends them off to bed, acknowledging his own prolixity and their fatigue, insisting on his love for them as he prepares to leave them and again when he returns, even tacitly associating them with both the Virgin Mary and Moab in the culminating rise to spiritual marriage and contemplative vision. The deep commitment he has to his community thus resounds clearly here as in all his works. At the same time, his frustration with and despair at the enduring pride, arrogance, and apostasy among prelates and princes—all of which had over the decades of his life led England and the church to conflict, schism, and persecution—recurs in homily after homily. That too was after all a lifelong concern.

Above all, however, Aelred proclaims the incarnation, Christ's coming to bring God and humankind together and, through faith, hope, and love, to reform God's people. He writes of the light that came into the world in Creation and again in the incarnation, and of the possibility that men and women both lay and religious might come to drink of the wine of love and rejoicing, to embrace the bridegroom, and to gaze toward the light as though borne on eagles' wings.

Marsha L. Dutton

Christmas 2017

Bibliography

Primary Texts

Aelred of Rievaulx. "Abbot Aelred of Rievaulx's Letter to Gilbert, Venerable Bishop of London." Trans. R. Jacob McDonie. CSQ 45, no. 2 (2010): 119–24. Rept. in Jean Truax, *Aelred the Peacemaker*. CS 251. Collegeville, MN: Cistercian Publications, 2017. 242–49.

———. *De anima*. See *Dialogue on the Soul*.

———. *De institutione inclusarum*. See *A Rule of Life for a Recluse*.

———. *Dialogue on the Soul*. Trans. C. H. Talbot. CF 22. Kalamazoo, MI: Cistercian Publications, 1981.

———. *Genealogia Regum Anglorum*. In *Opera Historica et Hagiographica*, edited by Domenico Pezzini. CCCM 3. Turnhout: Brepols Publishers, 2017. 1–56.

———. *Genealogy of the Kings of the English*. In *The Historical Works*, edited by Marsha L. Dutton; translated by Jane Patricia Freeland. CF 56. Kalamazoo, MI: Cistercian Publications, 2005. 71–122.

———. *The Historical Works*. Ed. Marsha L. Dutton. Trans. Jane Patricia Freeland. CF 56. Kalamazoo, MI: Cistercian Publications, 2005.

———. *Homeliae de oneribus propheticis Isaiae*. Ed. Gaetano Raciti. Aelredus Rievallensis Opera Omnia V. CCCM 2D. Turnhout, Belgium: Brepols Publishers, 2005.

———. *Homélies sur les fardeaux selon le prophète Isaïe*. Trans. Pierre-Yves Emery. Pain de Cîteaux 25, 3rd series. Oka, Québec: Abbaye Notre-Dame-du-Lac, 2006.

———. *In translacione sancti Edwardi confessoris*. Trans. Tom Licence. In Peter Jackson, "*In translacione sancti Edwardi confessoris*: The Lost Sermon by Aelred of Rievaulx Found?" CSQ 40, no. 1 (2005): 45–83. Rept. in Jean Truax, *Aelred the Peacemaker*. CS 251. Collegeville, MN: Cistercian Publications, 2017. 260–73.

————. *Jesus at the Age of Twelve*. In *Treatises and the Pastoral Prayer*. CF 2. Kalamazoo, MI: Cistercian Publications, 1971. 1–39.

————. *The Life of Saint Edward, King and Confessor*. In *The Historical Works*, edited by Marsha L. Dutton; translated by Jane Patricia Freeland. CF 56. Kalamazoo, MI: Cistercian Publications, 2005. 123–243.

————. *Lives of the Northern Saints*. Ed. Marsha L. Dutton. Trans. Jane Patricia Freeland. CF 71. Kalamazoo, MI: Cistercian Publications, 2006.

————. *Mirror of Charity*. Trans. Elizabeth Connor. CF 17. Kalamazoo, MI: Cistercian Publications, 1990.

————. *Opera. B. Aelredi*. In Bibliotheca Patrum Cisterciensium, V. Ed. Bertrand Tissier. Bono-Fonte, 1662. 229–93.

————. *Opera Omnia, I. Opera Ascetica*. Ed. Anselm Hoste and C. H. Talbot. CCCM 1. Turnhout: Brepols Publishers, 1971.

————. *Opera Omnia IIA, B, C, D*. Ed. Gaetano Raciti. CCCM 2A, 2B, 2C, 2D. Turnhout, Belgium: Brepols Publishers, 1983, 2001, 2005, 2012.

————. *Opera Omnia III*. Ed. Domenico Pezzini. *Opera Historica et Hagiographica*. CCCM 3. Turnhout: Brepols Publishers, 2017.

————. *Opera Omnia IIIA*. Ed. Francesco Marzella. *Opera Historica et Hagiographica: Vita Sancti Edwardi regis et confessoris*. CCCM 3A. Turnhout: Brepols Publishers, 2017.

————. *Patrologia Latina*. Ed. J.-P. Migne. Vol. 95. Paris, 1855. 361–500.

————. A *Rule of Life for a Recluse*. In *Treatises and the Pastoral Prayer*. CF 2. Kalamazoo, MI: Cistercian Publications, 1971. 41–102.

————. *Sermones de oneribus*. Edited by J.-P. Migne. PL 195. Paris, 1855. 361–500.

————. *Spiritual Friendship*. Ed. Marsha L. Dutton. Trans. Lawrence Braceland. CF 5. Collegeville, MN: Cistercian Publications, 2010.

————. *Treatises and the Pastoral Prayer*. CF 2. Kalamazoo, MI: Cistercian Publications, 1971.

Augustine of Hippo. *De Genesi ad litteram libri duodecim*. In *Sancti Aurelii Augustini Opera*, edited by Joseph Zycha. Corpus Scriptorum Eccesiasticorum Latinorum 28.1. Vienna: F. Tempsky, 1894.

Choisselet, Danièle, and Placide Vernet, eds. *Les Ecclesiastica Officia cisterciens du XIIème siècle*. La Documentation Cistercienne 22. Reiningue: Abbaye d'Œlenberg, 1989.

Chronicon Angliae Petriburgense. Ed. J. A. Giles. Caxton Society 2. London, 1845.

Daniel, Walter. *The Life of Aelred of Rievaulx*. Trans. Maurice Powicke. CS 57. Kalamazoo, MI: Cistercian Publications, 1994.

———. *Vita Ailredi Abbatis Rievall'*. Ed. and trans. Maurice Powicke. Oxford: Clarendon Press, 1950.

Gregory the Great. *Moralia in Iob*. Ed. Marcis Adriaen. 3 vols. CCCM 43, 43A, 43B. Turnhout: Brepols, 1979.

———. *Moral Reflections on the Book of Job*. Trans. Brian Kerns. 6 vols. CS 249, 257–261. Collegeville, MN: Cistercian Publications, 2014–2017. Vols. 5–6 forthcoming 2019, 2020.

Jerome. *Commentaire de Jérôme sur le prophète Isaïe, I–IV, V–VII*. Ed. R. Gyson, et al. Vetus Latina: Aus der Geschichte der lateinischen Bibel 23, 27. Freiburg: Verlag Herder, 1993–1994.

———. *Commentariorum in Esaiam*. Ed. Marcus Adriaen. CCSL 78. Turnhout: Brepols, 1968.

———. *Commentariorum in Isaiam prophetam libri duodeviginti*. Ed. J.-P. Migne. PL 24.

———. *St. Jerome: Commentary on Isaiah*. Trans. Thomas P. Scheck. New York and Mahwah, NJ: The Newman Press, 2015.

Mansi, Johannes Dominicus. *Sacrorum conciliorum . . . collectio*. Florence, 1775.

RB 1980: The Rule of St. Benedict in Latin and English with Notes. Ed. Timothy Fry. Collegeville, MN: Liturgical Press, 1981.

Richard of Hexham. "History of the Church of Hexham." In *The Priory of Hexham*, edited by James Raine. 2 vols. Surtees Society. Durham, UK: Andrews, 1864. 2:1–62.

Robertson, James Craigie, ed., *Materials for the History of Thomas Becket, Archbishop of Canterbury*. 7 vols. Rolls Series 67. London: Longmans, 1875–1885.

Studies

Barlow, Frank. *Thomas Becket*. Berkeley and Los Angeles: University of California Press, 1986.

Bell, David N. "The Commentary on the Lord's Prayer of Gilbert Foliot." *Recherches de théologie ancienne et médiévale* 56 (1989): 80–101.

Brooke, C. N. L. "Gilbert Foliot, c. 1110–1187." *The Dictionary of National Biography*, *http://www.oxforddnb.com.proxy.library.ohio.edu/view/article/9792?docPos=1*.

———. "Gregorian Reform in Action: Clerical Marriage in England: 1050–1200." *Cambridge Historical Journal* 12 (1956): 1–21.

Burton, Pierre-André. *Aelred de Rievaulx (1110–1167): Essai de Biographie Existentielle et Spirituelle*. Paris: Les Éditions du Cerf, 2010.

———. *Aelred of Rievaulx (1110–1167): An Existential and Spiritual Biography*. Trans. by Christopher Coski. CS 276. Collegeville, MN: Cistercian Publications, forthcoming 2020.

———. "Bibliotheca aelrediana secunda supplementa." In *A Companion to Aelred of Rievaulx (1110–1167)*, edited by Marsha L. Dutton. Brill Companions to the Christian Tradition 76. Leuven: Brill, 2017. 295–324.

———. "Une lecture 'aux éclats' du Cantique des cantiques. Les enjeux de l'herméneutique biblique selon saint Bernard. Un commentaire du *Sermon 23 sur le Cantique*." *Cîteaux* 57 (2006): 165–241.

Dietz, Elias. "Ambivalence Well Considered: An Interpretive Key to the Whole of Aelred's Works." CSQ 41, no. 1 (2012): 71–85.

———. "L'ambivalence bien réfléchie." In Intentio Cordis: *Temps, histoire, mémoire chez Aelred de Rievaulx: Collectanea Cisterciensia* 73 (2011): 13–26.

Dumont, Charles. "Autour des sermons 'De Oneribus' d'Aelred de Rievaulx." *Collectanea Cisterciensia* 19 (1957): 114–21.

Dutton, Marsha L. "Aelred of Rievaulx: Abbot, Teacher, and Author." In *A Companion to Aelred of Rievaulx (1110–1167)*, edited by Marsha L. Dutton. Brill Companions to the Christian Tradition 76. Leuven: Brill, 2017. 17–47.

———. "The Conversion and Vocation of Aelred of Rievaulx: A Historical Hypothesis." In *England in the Twelfth Century*, edited by Daniel Williams. London: Boydell, 1990. 31–49.

———. "The Staff in the Stone: Finding Arthur's Sword in the *Vita Sancti Edwardi* of Aelred of Rievaulx." *Arthuriana* 17, no. 3 (2007): 3–28.

Fremantle, William Henry. "Hereclius (23)." In *A Dictionary of Christian Biography, Literature, Sects and Doctrines*, edited by William Smith and Henry Wace. Vol. 2. London: John Murray, 1880. 904.

Hallier, Amédée. *The Monastic Theology of Aelred of Rievaulx: An Experiential Theology*. Trans. Columban Heaney. CS 2. Shannon, Ireland: Cistercian Publications, 1969.

Jackson, Peter. "*In translacione sancti Edwardi confessoris*: The Lost Sermon by Aelred of Rievaulx Found?" CSQ 40, no. 1 (2005): 45–83.

Knowles, David. *The Episcopal Colleagues of Thomas Becket: Being the Ford Lectures Delivered in the University of Oxford in Hilary Term 1949.* Cambridge: University Press, 1970.

McGuire, Brian Patrick. *Brother and Lover.* New York: Crossroad, 1994.

Molac, Philippe. "Théologie de l'histoire chez Aelred d'après les sermons *De oneribus.*" In Intentio Cordis: *Temps, histoire, mémoire chez Aelred de Rievaulx. Collectanea Cisterciensia* 73 (2011): 86–98.

Morey, Adrian, and C. N. L. Brooke. *Gilbert Foliot and his Letters.* Cambridge: University Press, 1965.

———. *The Letters and Charters of Gilbert Foliot.* Cambridge: University Press, 1967.

Nouzille, Philippe. *Expérience de Dieu et Théologie Monastique au XIIᵉ Siècle: Étude sur les sermons d'Aelred de Rievaulx.* Paris: Les Éditions du Cerf, 1999.

Pezzini, Domenico. "La théologie politique chez Aelred de Rievaulx d'après ses œuvres historiques." In Intentio Cordis: *Temps, histoire, mémoire chez Aelred de Rievaulx. Collectanea Cisterciensia* 73 (2011): 56–85.

———. "The Sermons of Aelred of Rievaulx." In *A Companion to Aelred of Rievaulx (1110–1167),* edited by Marsha L. Dutton. Brill Companions to the Christian Tradition 76. Leuven: Brill, 2017. 73–97.

Raciti, Gaetano. Introduction, in *Homeliae de oneribus propheticis Isaiae.* Ed. Gaetano Raciti. Aelredus Rievallensis Opera Omnia V. CCCM 2D. Turnhout, Belgium: Brepols Publishers, 2005. V–XXI.

Raine, James, ed. *The Priory of Hexham.* 2 vols. Surtees Society 44. Durham, UK: Andrews, 1864.

Renna, Thomas. "Aelred of Rievaulx and Isaiah." In *The Joy of Learning and the Love of God: Studies in Honor of Jean Leclercq,* edited by E. Rozanne Elder. CS 160. Kalamazoo, MI: Cistercian Publications, 1995. 253–68.

Riyeff, Jacob. Introduction. In *Saint Aethelwold of Winchester: The Old English Rule of Saint Benedict with Related Old English Texts,* edited by Jacob Riyeff. CS 264. Collegeville, MN: Cistercian Publications, 2017. 1–26.

Russell, J. Steven. "Vision and Skepticism in Aelred's *De Oneribus,*" CSQ 49, no. 4 (2014): 483–97.

Scannerini, Guglielmo. "Mystica o misticismo? Un approcio patristico ad Aelredo di Rievaulx, *De oneribus S. 2 (3).*" *Analecta cisterciensia* 54, no. 1–2 (2002): 134–85.

Sommerfeldt, John R. *Aelred of Rievaulx: On Love and Order in the World and the Church*. Mahwah, NJ: Paulist Press, 2006.

Squire, Aelred. *Aelred of Rievaulx: A Study*. CS 50. 1960; Kalamazoo, MI: Cistercian Publications, 1981.

Thibodeaux, Jennifer D. *The Manly Priest: Clerical Celibacy, Masculinity, and Reform in England and Normandy, 1066–1300*. Philadelphia: University of Pennsylvania Press, 2015.

Truax, Jean. *Aelred the Peacemaker*. CS 251. Collegeville, MN: Cistercian Publications, 2017.

White, Lewis. "*Bifarie itaque potest legi*: Ambivalent Exegesis in Aelred of Rievaulx's *De Oneribus*." CSQ 42, no. 3 (2007): 299–327; rept. CSQ 52, no. 3 (2017): 395–423.

Letter from Aelred, Abbot of Rievaulx to the Most Reverend Bishop Gilbert of London

1. To the beloved and loving holy father Gilbert,[1] bishop of London, who is worthy to be embraced with all the sweetness of devotion, Brother Aelred of Christ's poor who are at Rievaulx renders due obedience with all affection.

2. I have heard, most blessed father, that among the countless tasks that either the royal majesty's authority or the needs of pastoral care impose on you, you are a cultivator of wisdom, a friend of peace, eager for spiritual knowledge, attentive to reading, and that, among the sweet delights of prayer, you lighten the trouble of encroaching cares by frequent meditation on the Holy Scriptures. I have thus become eager for you,* not only desiring knowledge of your serenity, but also—because I am speaking foolishly*—daring to desire your very friendship.

*Oner 15.28
*2 Cor 11:21

3. For, forgetting both your loftiness and my lowliness, I rely on the laws of love,* in which nothing is lowly, nothing lofty. This love brought heaven to earth's level and planted the Lord of heaven in earthly members, so that the Word became flesh and dwelt

*amor

---

[1] Gilbertus Foliot, ca. 1110–1187. Abbot of the monastery of St. Peter of Gloucester 1139–1148, bishop of Hereford 1148–1163, bishop of London 1163–1187.

*John 1:14
*Luke 1:52
*Ps 84:11
*2 Cor 12:9; 13:4
*Gen 2:24;
Eph 5:31

among us.* This love pulled God down and raised humanity up.* Thus, as though on a kind of middle ground, wretchedness and mercy could meet,* strength could unite itself to weakness,* the Word and the soul could be in one flesh,* and, among these three, there could be one person, both God and human being. What is lofty, then, that love does not pull down, or what is base that it does not lift up, making them one in himself? Conserving rather than confusing each nature's properties, with the soul so wonderfully serving as a mediator, he joined heaven to earth, God to flesh, and spirit to dust.

4. Further, I see in every creature, whether irrational or senseless, a kind of vestige of love, through which what is diverse is joined, what is incongruent is brought into harmony, and what is contrary is united. For the likeness of love appears in other creatures, but

*Aelred, S 68.3-4;
Aelred,
Spec car 1.21;
Aelred, Spir
amic 1.53–55

it is in the rational mind that love's truth is at work.* Loving is common to God, angels, and human beings. Love, therefore, not directed toward something beyond nature, joins nature to nature, so that there is one heart and one soul in those for whom there is one

*Acts 4:32;
Eph 4:4-5

faith, one hope, one charity.*

*Ezek 1:12

5. Likewise, my mind, following the impulse of love,* in a kind of spiritual movement passes beyond everything that is yours but not you, and beyond everything that is around you but is neither yours nor you. Subtly passing through even the body's mass, it pours itself entirely into the very bosom of your mind, blending yearning with yearning, perception with perception, and spirit with spirit. My spirit may thus be renewed by taking part in your spirit; from the light of your perception, my perception may obtain the light of knowledge; and my affection may be fostered by the sweetness of your affection. There I see how good you are, there I embrace and perceive how wise you are, there I delight and taste how worthy of love you are.

6. So it is, most loving father, that I have come to the conclusion that I should submit my learning in holy letters, if I have such a thing, to your consideration and discernment. Thus your authority may confirm what I have perceived rightly, the truth may shine forth for me by your teaching where I have wavered, and your holy severity may correct me where I have strayed. Although I once discussed the prophetic burdens of Isaiah briefly, touching on each of them in the gathering of the brothers, many asked me to address them at greater length. And so I yielded to the desire of those whose progress I am bound to serve.

7. Therefore, beginning with the burdens of Babylon and from there moving on through the burdens of the Philistines to the secrets of the Moabite burden,* I have *Isa 13:1–16:14 written thirty-one homilies. Lest by chance I should run, or have already run, in vain,* I have put down *Gal 2:2 my pen until judgment comes forth from your countenance on the things that I have written and your eyes have taken account of them all.* Thus, according *Ps 16:2 to the decision that you reach, everything I have written will be destroyed, corrected, or confirmed. Therefore, although reading these things may appear unworthy of such wisdom, yet the eagerness of love dares to demand it. This is the love that embraces charity in such a way that it throws itself almost irreverently at majesty.

8. Furthermore, the memory of your humility together with your kindness encourages me, you who came before me in the blessings of sweetness when I was in London.* Astounded and shaking before such *Ps 20:4 dignity, I was greeted by a kind of embrace of love by someone from whom it would have been a great thing merely to be looked at.* From there this presumption *Acts 9:6; has arisen, most blessed father, of desiring the fulfill- Mark 5:33 ment of the acquaintance of your favor toward me that began at that time, and of not losing hope that my mind, knocking on the gates of your friendship, could be led into the inner room.

9. Therefore, although it may be a great thing for a wise person to have at least a little time to give to leisure, I beg you not to be annoyed, my lord, to lose a moment to trim what is excessive, add what is lack-ing, or destroy all of what we have written.* Therefore, to the sermon that was written previously, which gave us the occasion of writing the others, we have attached nineteen homilies on the burden of Babylon, three on the burden of the Philistines, and nine on the burden of Moab. According to your judgment, I am ready either to stop here or to continue further.*

*Oner 31.26

*see also
Oner 31.26

Sermon for the Coming of the Lord: On the Eleven Burdens

1. It is time, dear brothers, *for us to sing to the Lord of mercy and judgment.** For it is the coming of the Lord, of *the Almighty, who came and is to come.*† But how or to what place will he come or did he come? It is clearly his voice that says, *I fill heaven and earth.** But how could he have come to heaven or earth if he fills heaven and earth? Listen to the gospel: *He was in the world, and the world was made through him, and the world did not know him.** He was, therefore, both present and absent. He was present because he was in the world; he was absent, because the world did not know him.

2. *He is not far,* says Paul, *from any one of us. In him we live, move, and are.** And yet *salvation is far from sinners.** He was near in terms of his essence, but far in terms of his grace. How could he not be far, since he was neither recognized, believed, feared, nor loved? He was far from sinners: he did not call back the wandering, raise up the downtrodden, ransom the captives, or raise up the dead. He was far, I say, when he neither bestowed a heavenly reward upon the righteous nor openly imposed eternal damnation on the wicked.

3. The unrecognized one came so as to be recognized; the unbelieved, to be believed; he who was not feared, to be feared; the unloved, to be loved. Thus, he who was essentially present came mercifully, so

*Ps 100:1;
1 Pet 4:17;
Exod 15:1, 21
†Rev 1:8; 1:7
*Jer 23:24

*John 1:10

*Acts 17:27-28
*Ps 118:155

5

that we might recognize his humanity, believe in his
divinity, fear his power, and love his kindness. *His
humanity appeared* in the taking up of our weakness,*
his divinity in performing miracles, his power in over-
throwing the demons, his kindness in welcoming
sinners.

4. From his humanity he was hungry;* from his divinity he fed five thousand people with five loaves of
bread.* From his humanity he slept in the boat;† from
his divinity he commanded the sea and the waves.§
From his humanity he died;‡ from his divinity he
raised up the dead.# Likewise, from his power he
threw the Pharisees out of the temple,≈ and from his
kindness he ate with tax collectors and sinners.◊ From
his power the demons trembled;∞ from his kindness
he forgave the woman caught in adultery.° Finally,
from his power he threw to the ground those seeking
to bind him;Δ from his kindness he restored his persecutor's severed ear to its place along with his health.⊕
And we should attribute everything that pertains to
his first coming to his mercy.

5. Consider, if you will, what God is, and why he
laid aside such majesty, why he emptied himself of
such power,* why he weakened such strength, why
he brought low such loftiness, why he made a fool of
such wisdom.* Is this human righteousness? Far from
it. *Everyone turned aside, all were made useless; there* was
no one who did *good.** What then? Did he lack anything? Not at all. *His is the earth and its fullness.** Or did
he by chance need us for something? By no means.
He is *my God,* and he does not need *my goods.** What
then? Truly, Lord, it is not my righteousness, but your
mercy; not your lack, but my need.* For *you said,
"Mercy will be built in the heavens."** This is clearly so,
for wretchedness abounds on earth. Therefore, of your
first coming, *I will sing to you of mercy, Lord.**

6. For it was from mercy that, having become
human, he took *our weaknesses* on himself.* From

Marginal notes (left column):

* Titus 3:4;
Matt 8:17

* Matt 4:2; 21:18
and parallels

* Matt 14:17-21
and parallels
† Mark 4:36-38
and parallels
§ Matt 8:26;
2 Macc 9:8
‡ Matt 27:50
# Matt 27:52
≈ John 2:15
◊ Luke 5:29-32
and parallels
∞ Matt 8:29 and
parallels
° John 8:11
Δ John 18:6
⊕ Luke 22:51

* Phil 2:7

* Aelred, S 50.18

* Ps 13:3

* Ps 49:12

* Ps 15:2

* Aelred, S 50.18
* Ps 88:3

* Ps 100:1

* Matt 8:17

mercy he instilled faith in his divinity by miracles.* It
was just as much from mercy that he revealed the
demons' shrewdness to us and emptied their power.*
From mercy, he did not reject the prostitute's touch,
but approved her devotion.* Thus he showed himself
humble in his humanity, powerful in his miracles,
strong in overcoming the demons, and gentle in taking
on our sins. And all of this came forth from the fountain of mercy, all flowed forth from the depths of goodness. And therefore, in this your first coming, *I will
sing to you of mercy, Lord.** Rightly, because *the earth is
full of your mercy.**

7. Behold the oil that rotted the yoke of our captivity,
as holy Isaiah says: *On that day his burden will be taken
away from your shoulder and the yoke from your neck, and
the yoke will rot from the oil.** What is this day, what is
this burden, what is this yoke? Listen to what the
prophet had just said: *The Lord will raise the scourge
over him*—over the king of Assyria—*according to the
blow of Midian at the rock of Horeb and his rod over the
sea, and he will raise it in Egypt's path.** For after the
devil, who is *the king of all the children of pride,** was
scourged and beaten, *the Lord* raised his *rod over the
sea and* raised *it in Egypt's path.**

8. The sea is the world, the rod is the cross, and
Egypt's path is that *broad and wide way that leads to
death.** Thank you, Lord Jesus, for raising your *rod over
the sea,*† for laying low the pride of the world before
your cross and subjecting *powers and principalities* to
it.* Truly, Lord, your cross weighs down the world's
waves; it calms persecutions' storms and lessens
temptations' hurricanes. You also raised your cross *in
Egypt's path,** blocking *the wide road that leads to death*
and pointing out the narrow, constricted way *that leads
to life.**

9. Or do you not know? Have you not perceived it?
Have you not experienced it?* Sometimes, the ardor
of concupiscence boils in the flesh, anger rages in the

*Mark 16:20

*1 Cor 15:24

*Luke 7:37-50

*Ps 100:1
*Ps 118:64

*Isa 10:27

*Isa 10:26
*Job 41:25

*Isa 10:26

*Matt 7:13;
Prov 12:28
†Isa 10:26

*Col 2:15

*Isa 10:26

*Matt 7:13;
Prov 12:28

*see Isa 40:28

mind, and offended bitter words break out at every moment. A person's entire inner world is put to confusion like the sea stirred up by a violent wind.* But when Jesus lifts his cross above this sea, everything grows calm, everything grows quiet.* Furthermore, my brothers, what led you into this narrow, constricted path of salvation?† Was it not the example of the Lord's passion and cross that he *lifted in Egypt's path?§*

10. Rightly on this day, that is, at the time of grace, at the time of mercy, at the time when the cross is raised up, when the world is subjected to Christ, when *the prince of this world is cast out,** on this day, I say, at this moment, *his burden is taken away from your shoulder.** What burden? We read about many kinds of burdens in the Scriptures. For instance, holy Isaiah describes eleven burdens to us in his prophecy: *The burden of Babylon,** the burden of the Philistines,† the burden of Moab,§ the burden of Damascus,‡ the burden of Egypt,# the burden of the desert of the sea,≈ the burden of Dumah,◊ the burden in Arabia,∞ the burden of the valley of vision,° the burden of Tyre,Δ and the burden of the beast of the south.*** And what is a *burden* except a kind of weight that pulls the soul down to the earth, making it pay attention to base things and ignore the things above?

11. Such a burden sometimes comes to us from love of the world, and this is the burden of Babylon; sometimes from allowing unclean spirits in,* and this is the burden of the Philistines; sometimes from a kind of natural and unavoidable need, and this is the burden of Moab; sometimes from the darkness of ignorance, and this is the burden of Egypt; sometimes from our natural weakness, and this is the burden of Damascus; sometimes from the persecution of evildoers, and this is the burden of the desert of the sea; sometimes from a hidden mental agitation, and this is the burden of Dumah; sometimes from the consideration of death and the dread of our final destiny, and this is the burden of Arabia; sometimes from vanity when we make

*Job 1:19

*Isa 10:26;
Matt 8:26
and parallels
†Matt 7:14
§Isa 10:26

*John 12:31

*Isa 10:27

*Isa 13:1
†Isa 14:28
§Isa 15:1
‡Isa 17:1
#Isa 19:1
≈Isa 21:1
◊Isa 21:11
∞Isa 21:13
°Isa 22:1
ΔIsa 23:1
⊛Isa 30:6

*Ps 77:49

progress, and this is the burden of the valley of vision; sometimes from distress at what we must bear, and this is the burden of Tyre; and sometimes from charity when we wish to benefit others, and this is the burden of the beast of the south.

12. First, then, we need the burden of Babylon to be taken away from our shoulders.* Babylon means *the world*, whose love is cupidity. This is a burden that weighs down many, curving them down toward lower things. It burdens its wretched victims in three ways: by labor, by fear, and by pain. We laboriously attain what we covet, we possess it fearfully, and we lose it painfully. Oh brothers, what king does not laboriously acquire what he covets? What king is so safe that he fears no one? What king loses something without pain?

*Isa 10:27

13. But let us turn this idea back on ourselves. Does none of us, I ask, sigh under the weight of this burden? Does no remnant of worldly love remain in us?* Why is it that certain people who have abandoned their possessions do not fear to seek those of others? For the sake of such possessions, labors weary them, pain tortures them, and fear crushes them. What about those who, although they brought little or nothing to the monastery, do not cease taking whatever they can from the monastery in order to give to others? They demand rudely, become angry if they do not get what they want, are pained if they are corrected, and go into a rage if they are summoned. Are they free of this burden?

*Aelred, Spec car 1.29.85; Oner 5.3; 19.10

14. What about those whom parental affection binds to such an extent that they do not hesitate to sacrifice religion and undergo many labors for them, and on account of this spend empty days and sleepless nights?* What shall I say of those who seek honor? What burden do they sustain? At times they fawn, at times they slander, at times they go mad because of others' success, at times, frustrated in their hope, they

*Aelred, S 53.14; Esth 6:1

rise up with curses even against their own parents. So, brothers, all such people conform themselves to *Rom 12:2 this age.* We therefore say that they belong to Babylon's name, to be miserably crushed by that burden of punishment that the prophet describes concerning Babylon.

*Isa 14:28 **15.** The burden of the Philistines follows,* whose *Jerome, Nom 6 name means *falling down from drink.** The Philistines represent those who, drunk on pride, have fallen from *Isa 14:12; their heavenly dwelling.* They weigh down wretched 2 Cor 5:2 people, sometimes by temptation, sometimes by affliction. They burdened the Egyptians by many great plagues, just as you read in the psalm: *He sent the anger of his displeasure upon them; displeasure, anger, and *Ps 77:49 trouble, brought in through evil angels.** They burdened the heart of Judah with avarice, the heart of the Pharisees with envy, and the heart of Pilate with foolishness. They burden the hearts of the faithful with many temptations, insulting the heart that consents to them, *Isa 51:23 saying, *Bow down so that we may pass over.**

*Isa 15:1 **16.** The burden of Moab comes next,* which means *Jerome, Nom 6 *from the father,** expressing those natural needs that a father always pours into his son by generation. These include the unavoidable need to eat, drink, and sleep, and other needs that pertain to bodily care. What sort of burden is this, dear brothers, that, after *the brightness *Acts 26:13 of the sun,** compels us to return to the care of this flesh as to a rotting corpse? What sort of burden is this that compels us to attend to the stomach's burdens after the spiritual food of the mind? What sort of burden is this that demands daily payment of wretched subjection from us? This burden will compel us tomorrow to fill the empty stomach that we fill today!

17. What shall I say? How many cares and concerns do these needs impose on wretched mortals? This *Phil 3:19 burden is such that some people's *God is* their *stomach.** They are even willing to sell off righteousness and divine doctrine for the sake of the stomach's pleasure,

or rather, its burden! *For people such as this*, as Saint
Paul says, *serve their own stomachs rather than the Lord
Jesus Christ.** Further, what a burden we bear in dif-   *Rom 16:18
ferentiating between foods, desiring some and reject-
ing others. Some foods knot the stomach, others
aggravate the head, others clog the chest, still others
weigh down the heart with corrupt humors!

18. But what shall I say of those whom this need
compels sometimes to murmur, sometimes to disparage, sometimes even to quarrel? They grow sad if the
food is plainer, if simpler drinks are served, if the food
is prepared later or with less care.* We can call broth-   *Aelred, S 63.28
ers such as these *Moab*. They live carnally according
to carnal generation, and the weight of punishment
that the prophet recounts in the burden of Moab will
burden such unhappy brothers.

19. The prophecy of the burden of Damascus follows.*   *Isa 17:1
Damascus means *shedding blood*,* expressing that inborn   *Jerome, Nom 41
corruption in us that somehow draws and attracts us
against our will to sin.* This is the law in our *members*   *Aelred, SS 63.28;
that fights against *the law of* our *mind* and *leads* us *captive*   72.15; Jas 1:14-15
to the law of sin that is in our *members.** Every vital faculty   *Rom 7:23
in the body comes from blood, but the vital faculty in
the soul comes from reason. You know how sin's
natural movement sometimes nearly absorbs reason's
very power by a kind of power of pleasure, bleeding
the entire soul dry, as it were. But some have this sensation and do not consent; they are attacked, but not conquered; they are burdened, but not brought down. Such
people sustain the burden from Damascus, but they are
not Damascus. But those who consent and offer their
members as *arms of iniquity to sin* are indeed Damascus,*   *Rom 6:13
shedding their own blood and killing themselves with
their own hands. They surely know that they will be
crushed by the weight of punishment that is described
in the burden of Damascus.

20. Then follows the burden of Egypt.* Egypt means   *Isa 19:1
darkness.* There are two types of darkness: the dark-   *Jerome, Nom 73

ness of ignorance and the darkness of iniquity. Oh brothers, this burden that we carry from our ignorant blindness is not easy. In many situations, we do not know what is useful, what is not useful, what we should praise, and what we should reject. So we often call *evil good and good evil.** But *we also do not know what to pray for as we should*[†] and we walk forward in the light of the Scriptures *feeling our way as though it were night.** Such people are burdened by Egypt, but they are not burdened with Egypt, with those, namely, who are Egypt, that is, *darkness, children of darkness.** The Lord says this about them in the gospel: *All who do evil hate the light.** And the apostle says, *Those who sleep, sleep at night, and those who are drunk, are drunk at night.** Such people are weighed down by the same weight of punishment with which the holy prophet teaches that Egypt will be punished.

21. The burden of the desert of the sea follows.* The deserted sea is the crowd of the condemned, who, abandoned by God and separated from the company of the saints, weigh down the holy church with a load of persecutions. They will be punished later by the weight of punishments that the prophet designates in this burden.

22. Further, the sea represents those people who are shaken by the various storms of passions and vices, who are always in motion, "who are always wandering and never stable,"* *never remaining in the same place.** Sometimes they are puffed up with pride, sometimes they boil with anger, sometimes they are sad, sometimes frivolous, sometimes weighed down by silence, and sometimes falling apart from laughter. *They overstep the commands of their elders* and disturb the peace of the brothers.* Yet as long as they fear, as long as they feel pain, as long as they accept correction and do not avoid making amends, they are not the deserted sea. But if, falling into the depth of evil, they show contempt, if they loudly complain when

*Isa 5:20; Aelred, SS 55.22; 83.13
†Rom 8:26

*Job 5:14

*1 Thess 5:5

*John 3:20

*1 Thess 5:7

*Isa 21:1

*RB 1.11
*Job 14:2

*Matt 15:2; RB 23.1

corrected, if they respond in a way that lacks honor, peace, and order but, filled with pride, rise up with angry words against the very person who corrects them so that they must be abandoned to themselves, you should not doubt that they should be called a deserted sea.

23. Woe to those who, abandoned by God and humanity, are left *to the desire of their heart,* to walk *in their own devices!** The Lord speaks to them through the prophet, saying, *I will take my zeal away from you and will not grow angry anymore.** You know, dear brothers, what a heavy burden such people place on the shoulders of the saints. The prophet groaned under this burden, saying, *Sinners built on my back.*† Truly, such people have built on our back, burdening us with their daily disturbances.* They add sin upon sin and join insult to insult.* They are insolent, proud, *detractors, hateful to God,** disobedient toward their elders, not adapting to their peers. Such people know that they will meet with the weight of the punishments contained in this burden.

24. After this, the prophet describes the burden of Dumah.* Dumah means *silence.*† You know, brothers, that silence burdens and stillness weighs down many people. All things are burdensome to such people when they are silent or at rest: their head aches, their stomach rumbles, their eyes cloud over, their kidneys trouble them. But everything pleases them when they go out, wandering here and there* and talking. They forget their pains, and all of their members work properly. O, how great is the power of the tongue, which brightens the eyes, soothes the head, makes the kidneys function properly, and strengthens *the weakened knees!** It makes the weak tireless in their work, gives patience to those fasting, readies us for journeys, makes us quick to obey. So if you see a monk living in the cloister who looks in all directions,* constantly yawning, stretching his hands and feet, setting aside

*Ps 80:13

*Ezek 16:42;
Aelred, Spec
car 1.26.75; Oner
1.15; 6.5; 21.11
†Ps 128:3

*RB 65.7
*Isa 30:1
*Rom 1:30

*Isa 21:11
†Jerome, Nom 26

*Judg 15:5; 1
Sam 23:13

*Isa 35:3

*Judg 15:5;
Exod 2:12

his book only to take it up again, finally running about from place to place and from auditorium to auditorium as though something had stung him, do not doubt that he sighs under the burden of Dumah.*

*Aelred, S
43.24–25

25. There is yet another kind of silence that leads to a severe punishment for many people. This is the silence arising from shame and confusion,* which hinders confession and prevents the forgiveness of sins. The prophecy does not fail to describe the burden of punishment that such silence deserves.

*Ps 70:13

26. It is here that the prophet adds the burden in Arabia.* Arabia means *evening*,† which is the end of day and the beginning of night. I think this fittingly represents the hour of death, which places a heavy weight of fear on almost all mortals. For who can avoid this burden, to which even the Savior freely submitted himself as an example? For when death drew near, as the evangelist says, *he began to fear and grow sick*.* The entire human race lives under this burden of fear,* unless perhaps there is someone who is certain of a blessed life after death, someone whose desire or gaze does not feel even the bitterness of death.

*Isa 21:13
†Jerome, Nom 21

*Mark 14:33
*Heb 2:15

27. Further, evening, which as we have said is the end of day and the beginning of night, expresses the fall of those who, after works *of light*, begin performing *works of darkness*.* Their *last state turns out worse than before*,* and the weight described in this burden of Arabia surely crushes them.

*Rom 13:12
*Matt 12:45 and
parallels

28. The burden of the valley of vision follows.* *Vision* refers to contemplation, and *valley* to humility or a casting down. For some people's contemplation is humble, others' is downcast. The saints' is humble, the philosophers' is downcast. For if virtue grows, make sure that humility is preserved. If vanity burdens you, you know the kind of battle that the soul making progress must sustain. Otherwise, the acclamation of human praise will sneak in, flattery will

*Isa 22:1

undo your progress, and the heart will swell within. The more the saints advance, the heavier the burden of vanity that wearies them. And so they climb higher, only to be unwillingly pulled back down at times.

29. But these people—*because what was known of God was shown forth in them**—who saw *the invisible things of God through created things, vanished in their own thoughts and their foolish heart grew dark.** They fell from the mountain of contemplation to the valley of error. Therefore *they changed the glory of the incorruptible God into the image of a corruptible person, beasts, and snakes.** And if you wish to know what sort of burden such people deserve, listen to what follows: *Because of this, God handed them over to disgraceful passions,* and *God handed them over to the desires of their hearts,* and *God handed them over to their false perception.**

*Rom 1:19

*Rom 1:20-21

*Rom 1:23

*Rom 1:26, 24, 28

30. Those whose warped intention twists the knowledge of Scripture or heavenly instruction toward human praise or temporal gain also belong to the valley of vision. This is because vision signifies knowledge, and valley represents an earthly intention. The prophecy declares how great is the punishment that all such people should expect.

31. Next comes the burden of Tyre,* which means *narrowness.** This burden consists of the bitterness of repentance, the labor of continence, and bodily sickness. What then? Is there no burden in bodily practices and in the observation of the Rule? What of the labor of continence? What is more laborious, what is more difficult, what must be kept amid more dangers, what is more easily lost?

*Isa 23:1

*Jerome, Nom 30

32. There is another kind of narrowness of heart that self-will produces, which is the opposite of the breadth of heart that the love of God and neighbor brings about. Self-love grows out of self-will. Those who love their own will are burdened by the will of others. Such people therefore seek *what is theirs, not what* pertains to others.* They are ready to do everything that their

*Phil 2:21

own will suggests but sluggish and reluctant to do
"that which is imposed on them."* Of such people the
apostle says, *People will be lovers of themselves.** They
will not escape the weight of punishment described
in the burden of Tyre.

33. The burden of the beasts of the south is last.*
The south wind, which is warm, represents the Holy
Spirit. So you read in the Song of Songs, *Arise, north*
wind, and come, south wind, blow through my garden.*
Happy the soul that is the beast of this south wind,
that is governed, in other words, by the bridle of its
moderation, that in all things is brought under its will!
Happy of course is the soul over which the Holy Spirit
rules, directing all of its works, arranging its thoughts,
ordering its movements, and regulating its habits! It
is written of such souls, *Wherever the impulse of the Holy*
Spirit led, there they went when they walked.* And the
prophet says of them, *You made a path for your horses*
in the sea.†

34. Paul was a beast of this south, saying, *We did not*
receive the spirit of this world, but the Spirit who is from
God, that we might know the things given to us by God.*
You see how he is governed everywhere like the beast
of the south by the bridle of its master: he is forbidden
by the Spirit to preach in Asia,* he is advised by the
Spirit to visit Macedonia,* he is roused by the Spirit
to preach to the Athenians,* and obliged by the Spirit,
he hastened to Jerusalem.* You see how the Holy
Spirit sits upon him like his beast. Sometimes the
Spirit tightens the reins so that he cannot go where he
wants; at other times he spurs him on so that he has-
tens where the Spirit wills.*

35. What do we think, my brothers? Do beasts of
this sort carry no burden? But as beasts of the south,
their burden is also from the south. What sort of burden, you ask? Listen to the apostle: *God's charity was*
poured out into our hearts through the Holy Spirit, who
was given to us.* So in this charity, what kind of burden

did Paul bear? He himself would say, *Who is weak, and I am not weak? Who is scandalized, and I do not burn?** And again, *I am greatly saddened and my heart aches constantly for my brothers and sisters according to the flesh.** Whoever is a beast of the south is burdened by others' weakness, others' needs, and others' perversity. The beast of the south's burden is the hunger of the poor, the oppression of the needy, the wretchedness of the sick, the temptation of those advancing, the fall of the weak. They are also burdened by the people's distress, the abandonment of orphans, the groaning of widows, the affliction of captives.* Does not blessed Paul, as though weighed down by this burden, come down from the secrets of heaven to the bed of the weak?*

*2 Cor 11:29

*Rom 9:2-3

*Gregory, H 5 on the Gospel 3; Aelred, Inst incl 28

*2 Cor 12:2-4

36. But you too, brothers, have fled from the midst of Babylon in the north* and now *live in the land of the south.** *Bear one another's burdens, and so,* like the beasts of the south, *you will fulfill Christ's law.*† Whoever fails to carry a brother's burden is certainly not a beast of the south. Which burdens must you carry? *The sicknesses of body or mind** that we have recounted in these burdens as best we could.

*Jer 51:6

*Isa 21:14; Gen 24:62
†Gal 6:2

*RB 72.5

37. We could also say, brothers, that the beasts of the south represent those who obtain the Holy Spirit's gifts through their office rather than through merit.* These gifts include prophecy, healing, and others of this sort.* Whomever they ordain is ordained, whomever they curse is cursed, whomever they bless is blessed, whomever they bind is bound, and whomever they absolve is absolved.* But this is only insofar as they do all this according to the laws of the church rather than by their own initiative. So it is that Balaam blessed the people of God,* wicked Caiaphas prophesied,† and wicked Judas performed miracles like the other apostles.§ So it is that many will come *on that day,* saying, *Did we not prophesy in your name and perform many miracles in your name? And then I will say to*

*1 Cor 12:7-10

*1 Cor 12:28

*Matt 16:19; John 20:23

*Num 23:11-12, 25-26; 24:10-13
†John 11:51
§Matt 10:1 and parallels

*Matt 7:22-23;
John 11:47;
Aelred, Spec car
2.9.22; Oner 4.9;
Jerome, In Matt 1
†Rom 16:18;
Phil 3:19

them, says the Lord, *I never knew you.** Such people should be called beasts rather than people, because *they serve their own stomachs rather than the Lord Jesus Christ.*† They desire earthly things and condemn the heavenly. These people are wretchedly weighed down by that burden with which Isaiah terribly threatens certain beasts of the south.

38. We have broken this barley loaf as best we

*Matt 14:19 and
parallels;
John 16:9
†Matt 20:6
§John 6:12

could,* but in our haste, we have dropped many fragments. You who are at leisure,† therefore, whom Christ has kept free from cares, *gather what is left of the fragments so that they are not lost.*§ Each of you should look carefully at yourself to see what burden you are bearing now and if there are any you fear to bear in the future.

39. Those under Babylon's burden should hate it and cast it off. If you are conformed to its works, you will not be free from its punishments. If you are under the burden of the Philistines, do not let their drinks intoxicate you. If you do, you will become like them first in blame and later in punishment. If you feel you are laboring under that burden of Moab, concern yourself with fulfilling your bodily needs in such a way that Nebuzaradan does not destroy the walls of Jeru-

*2 Kgs 25:8, 10;
Gregory, Mo
30.XVIII.59

salem.* Nor should you satisfy your needs in such a way that you forever burn with them. If the burden of Damascus weighs upon your shoulders, be careful that you do not harm yourself, and so sowing *in the*

*Gal 6:8

flesh, you do not reap *corruption from the flesh.**

40. If the burden of Egypt rests upon you, cast off the works of darkness and equip yourself with arms

*Rom 13:12

of light.* If here you freely hand your mind over to inner darkness, you will someday unwillingly be tor-

*Matt 8:12

mented by outer darkness.* Further, if the burden of the desert of the sea attacks you with evil persecutions, do not grow weak, do not let yourself be broken, or you will impatiently suffer what they maliciously inflict. But if the burden of Dumah makes you impatient of silence, or if shame or confusion hinders confession, beware the weight of punishment with which the prophet threatens such silent ones. If you are weighed down by the burden of Arabia, if you fear natural death, behave in such a way that your conscience is not the reason for your fear. Otherwise, not only will Arabia weigh you down, but the burden of eternal damnation will also crush you with Arabia.

41. If you are sighing under the burden of the valley of vision and fighting against vanity, be careful not to fall from the mountain of contemplation into the valley of error. There you will be overwhelmed with that weight that the prophet describes in the burden of the valley of vision. If under Tyre's burden your soul sinks into a timid hopelessness because of present *labors and pains,** beware above all else the narrowness of self-will. Thus you will joyfully advance with expanded heart through all the difficulties of this life* and so escape *the eternal weight* of misery that Tyre threatens.† Finally, if on account of the burden of the beasts of the south your desire fades from weariness, reflect and know that if you reject the burden of charity you will justly bear the burden of damnation.

*Sir 14:15; Ps 89:10

*Ps 118:32; RB Prol 49
†2 Cor 4:17

42. It seems to me that even the very order in which the burdens are presented is not lacking in mystery. It is not without reason that the burden of Babylon is placed first, the burden of the Philistines second, and so on. For we know that cupidity is the burden of Babylon and *the root of all evil.** If we do not first cast cupidity from our hearts, we will by no means be able to turn aside or conquer the other burdens, nor advance to the peak of the virtues. Cupidity is cast out either by those who completely renounce the world or by those who *use this world as though they did not use it,** *as having nothing and possessing everything.*† After we have conquered or driven away cupidity, then *we do not struggle against flesh and blood, but against the rulers of the world of darkness, against spiritual evil in the*

*1 Tim 6:10

*1 Cor 7:31
†2 Cor 6:10

*Eph 6:12

*1 Cor 10:13

*heavens.** But when he who does not allow us *to be tempted beyond* our ability but also provides *a way out with the temptation, so that* we *can* bear it,* either lightens or casts aside this burden, the needs of the flesh will burden us, whose limits, being difficult to know, are impossible to keep.

43. Once the fire has been lit, natural stings necessarily wear us out. Unless we resist bravely, they lead to all sorts of forbidden acts. If all of the preceding burdens are overcome—if the Philistines are restrained, if Moab's bodily needs are brought within limits and sobriety is restored, and if Damascus's burden, the stings of the flesh, grows quiet—then immediately, errors and blasphemy like the darkness of Egypt cloud the eyes of the heart. But then the darkness withdraws before the shining light of wisdom, and immediately the envy and ill-will of the desert of the sea, that is, of the perverse, take its place. After this has vanished, when everything appears quiet, the quiet itself cannot remain quiet from the spirit of *acedia,* Dumah's burden. After constant work, prayer, and reading have warded off *acedia,* the burden of Arabia, that is, the fear of death, presses upon us. But after this too is overcome by the virtue of a good conscience and faith, vanity will grow burdensome to the person close to perfection. If deep humility conquers this vanity, nothing remains except to be burdened by the needs of others as a beast of the south.

44. What we have said about these burdens should be enough for the moment. Christ takes some of these burdens from our shoulders during this time of grace. He moderates others, others he diminishes, and others he arranges. *He does all this according* to the abundance of this mercy,* in whose presence, as though *in the presence of oil, the yoke* of the devil's rule rotted.† Whoever neglects the time of mercy should fear the time of Judgment, because he who redeemed us through

*1 Cor 12:11;
Ps 50:3
†Isa 10:27

mercy will judge us through justice. Thus, brothers, *let us sing to the Lord of mercy and judgment,** the mercy we experience and the Judgment we await. Let us embrace the former and fear the latter, that we may be found devout here, and free from care there, by the favor of our Lord.

*Ps 100:1; Exod 15:1, 21

Homily 1

1. God is the primary and efficient cause of everything that was, is, or will be; he is also the end of all things. For since he is, so to speak, being itself, all things have what they are from him. This is because it is only from being that they have what they are.* Humans and angels certainly exist. But being is one thing; being a human or an angel is another, since something can exist and not be a human or an angel. Think, if you can, not of the existence of a human or an angel, but of being itself, apart from humans or angels. Existence pertains not only to humans or angels, but also to all things that are.

*Aelred, Anima 2.50; Ps-Dionysius, Cael Hier 4.1

2. Therefore God is without a doubt being itself. Being does not belong specifically to this or that thing, but commonly to all things that exist, or, to put it more clearly, to the essences of all things. But just as God is the being of all things that exist, so too he is the life of all the living, and the wisdom of all the wise. Rational creation was created according to this form, having not only being and life from him, but also the capacity to be wise and live wisely. But wretched humanity, removing and separating itself from this form, *was made like the foolish beasts.** We began to be foolish and live foolishly. Yet we did not cease being and living. We can return to the original form when he who formed us reforms us.*

*Ps 48:13

*Aelred, Spec car 1.4.11; Aelred, S 67.14–15

3. That form is wisdom, and the way that leads back to it is instruction. All true instruction, by which we are led back from this deformity to that form, is threefold: faith, hope, and love. Thus we will know what to believe, what to hope, and what to love. So knowing, we will be able in fact to believe, hope, and love. For this purpose, wisdom *communicates itself to holy souls and makes friends of God and prophets.** Through them, it provides us with Holy Scripture, which is, as it were, the source of all instruction. Of course, the Spirit himself, who so prudently established Scripture, arranged it to be broad enough for countless meanings. He reveals some meanings to one person and others to another. Scripture is always fresh, thus training abilities and driving away boredom.* It always delights by a kind of renewal.

*Wis 7:27

*Augustine,
Civ Dei 17.3.2

4. But so that we can discern human error or demonic suggestion by careful examination and the Holy Spirit's revelation, the rule of faith has been established, the promise of hope has been written, and the precepts of charity have been announced. You should always ascribe any meaning occurring to the mind that does not correspond to these three either to demonic deception or to human error. But you should not doubt that any meaning drawn fittingly from the sacred pages, if it instructs in faith, raises up in hope, or kindles in charity, was included by the Holy Spirit and revealed to you by him.

5. The meanings spoken or written once concerning Scripture are enough, and more than enough, for those who are hindered by the darkness of worldly affairs or are caught in the nets of necessary tasks. The bonds of their countless cares and troublesome concerns curb wandering, base mental digressions. Scripture's meaning is so unfamiliar to such people that it always seems new. But you, beloved brothers, have renounced this world's works. You are free of every worldly care and concern.* You have joined battle with unclean spirits and your own thoughts.† For you, there is

*Aelred, Spec car
2.19.59; Aelred,
Inst incl 4
†RB 1.5

another reason for meditating on Scripture, as well as

Bernard, SC 1.1 a different need.

6. Because many of you grow bored with the same sermon and the same reading repeated again and again, we need to renew what seems old and familiar, either by adding certain ideas or at least by changing

*Augustine, Civ
Dei 10.20 the words.* In this way we can rouse the attentiveness that we seek and call the heart back from its useless and vain digressions to what is useful. So the mind that in its boredom had fled the familiar can, after being renewed by the sweetness of a reading or sermon, beneficially return to that from which it had been unconsciously distracted.

7. With that, I will now take up the book of Isaiah to examine a small portion of it with you. Although you may be quite familiar with it from the commentaries of the saints, I think it is highly useful for us to repeat what they said, if not differently, at least in another fashion. Let us bring to light just as God provides what they passed over as obvious or insignificant, gathering seeds from their reasoning. Thus, whoever does not dare aspire to the solid bread of

Heb 5:14 their perfect interpretations can, though a dog, approach the crumbs that we will collect from under

*Mark 7:28;
John 6:12 their table with the help of your prayers.* So in this way, beloved brothers, let us redeem the time, or

*Eph 5:16 rather outwit the time, *because the days are evil.** Let us, by means of saving words and holy meditations, defend our mouths from idle talk and our hearts from

*Aelred, Spec car
3.40.113; Aelred,
Inst incl 20 empty thoughts.*

8. This holy prophet is so deep in meaning, so lofty in mysteries, so clear sighted in foretelling future events, so delightful in moral instruction, that at times it seems as though he were carried to heaven itself to lay bare the secrets of divine wisdom. At other times he is sent down in swift flight to the lower regions of the firmament to make known heavenly mysteries. Then he flies lightly down to us to stroll in the moral fields. At times it is as though he were taken up *to Paradise*, returning to us again to relate ineffable *words that no human being may speak.** *2 Cor 12:4

9. He reveals so plainly in prophecy all these things about Christ and the church's mysteries* that he seems not so much to have foretold future things as to have narrated the past. All this is pleasing and delicious enough on its own, yet the wonderful charm of his eloquence renders it even more pleasing and sweeter. But by your leave we are bypassing the rest for a moment, putting forth for your instruction whatever the Holy Spirit supplies concerning the eleven burdens,* which the prophet treated by means of the same Spirit's dictation. *sacramenta; Eph 5:32

*1 Cor 14:3; Eph 4:29

10. I recognize my obligation to your progress in all respects,* because of my office, of course, but mostly because of my affection for you. But *necessity* also *compels me. Woe to me if I do not preach the gospel,** especially since I do not doubt that whatever progress I make in spiritual teaching or in understanding of the Scriptures is not so much for me as it is for you, given through me. Nothing should be attributed to my merits, since I am a sinner, nor to scholarly training, since, as you know, I am mostly uneducated;* nor to my zeal or diligence, since I am rarely at leisure and frequently busy. Everything, therefore, is from God, entrusted to me and passed on to you, *so that all who boast should boast in the Lord.** *Rom 1:14

*1 Cor 9:16

*Aelred, Spec car, Prol. 2; Aelred, SS 64.1; 79.1

*1 Cor 1:31

11. Be present, then, good Jesus, and pour forth the grace of your blessing on the bread that we have offered,* that the *poor* may *eat and have their fill,†* and say with the prophet, *How sweet in my throat is your eloquence, sweeter than honey in my mouth.§* Behold, I apply my hand, lend your assistance, because *without* you I *can do nothing.** You who inspired holy Isaiah to write, inspire me too, I beg, to understand what he wrote. You have already inspired me to believe, for unless we believe, we do not understand.* *Matt 14:19 and parallels †Ps 21:27 §Ps 118:103

*John 15:5

*Isa 7:9 LXX

12. What, then, do we take this *burden* to mean? There is a burden that weighs down, and a burden that crushes. Sickness weighs down; iniquity crushes. Temptation weighs down; damnation crushes. The first burden considered is Babylon,* after which follow the burden of the Philistines,* the burden of Moab,† and the burden of Damascus.§ The burden of Egypt comes next,‡ and then the burden of the desert of the sea.# Then follow the burden of Dumah,≈ the burden of Arabia,◊ then the burden of the valley of vision∞ and the burden of Tyre,° and finally the burden of the beasts of the south.△

13. Holy Isaiah shows a sinking down of certain cities or peoples, or rather of those represented by these cities and peoples. Nor is he silent regarding the extent, causes, and nature of the sinking itself. He also includes a word concerning the happiness of those whom this sinking burdens not for ruin, but for salvation. And everywhere it is clear that the power is God's, and yours, Lord, mercy; *because you render to all according to their works,* dividing *day from night, light from darkness.* Thus the darkness appears even thicker when compared to the light, and the light shines more abundantly by the gathering darkness.

14. And who judges and divides them if not he who says, *The Father does not judge anyone, but has given all judgment to the Son?* And again, *I came to the world in judgment, so that those not seeing might see, and those seeing might be blinded.* Therefore, the coming of our Lord and Savior brought about this dividing of good from evil, with the sinking of some and the deliverance of others. It is well known that the prophet's main subject throughout the whole book is the coming of the Lord. Saint Simeon says of this, *Behold, here is one placed for the fall and resurrection of many in Israel, and as a sign that will be contradicted.* What Isaiah calls a *burden*, Simeon calls a *fall*.

*Isa 13:1
*Isa 14:28
†Isa 15:1
§Isa 17:1
‡Isa 19:1
#Isa 21:1
≈Isa 21:11
◊Isa 21:13
∞Isa 22:1
°Isa 23:1
△Isa 30:6

*Ps 61:12-13
*Gen 1:14, 4

*John 5:22

*John 9:39

*Luke 2:34

15. He describes these burdens so as to make clear that God weighs down some but does not crush them; he crushes others but does not weigh them down; others he both weighs down and crushes. He weighs down those whom he afflicts; he crushes those whom he abandons. He therefore afflicts some but does not abandon them, as it was written, *The Lord scourges every child whom he accepts.** This is why the psalmist says, *I will punish their iniquities with the rod and their sins with blows; but I will not scatter my mercy from him.** He abandons but does not afflict those of whom the prophet says, *They have no part in human work, and they will not be scourged with others.** And again, *I left them to the desires of their heart.** Another prophet says, *I will not punish their daughters when they fornicate, nor their wives when they commit adultery.** There are still others whom he afflicts and abandons, about whom he himself speaks through the prophet: *I wore them away, and they refused to accept instruction.*†

*Heb 12:6

*Ps 88:33-34; Oner 19.17; 21.9

*Ps 72:5

*Ps 80:13

*Hos 4:14; Aelred, Spec car 1.26.75; Oner Adv 23 = Aelred S 47.23; Oner 6.5; 21.11

†Jer 5:3

16. Of course, when we begin discussing the burdens themselves, God willing, it will become clear how or in what ways this affliction or abandonment comes to pass. But the burden of Babylon, or of the Philistines, or of Moab, can be understood as the burden with which they weigh down others, or as the burden by which they themselves are weighed down. This also applies to the other prophecies. Now, with your leave, let us look at the title of the following narrative.

17. *The burden of Babylon, which Isaiah, son of Amos, saw.** As you well know, beloved, the name *Babylon*, which means *confusion*, represents the world.* The world is surely the place where all things are confused. Here the good live with the wicked, the chosen with the condemned. Here the grain is with the chaff, the oil with the dregs, and the wine with the seed. Here, insofar as temporal things are concerned, the righteous

*Isa 13:1

*Jerome, In Isa 6.2

and the ungodly are alike. Here a person has no advantage over the beasts, since here neither do those who live as rational human beings get a reward, nor are those who become beasts through carnal vices punished according to their deeds.*

*Ps 48:13, 21; Luke 23:41

18. We usually understand Babylon as only being the city of the wicked with their king, to which city none of the chosen belong and from which none of the condemned is excluded. We can divide the condemned into three groups. The first still share in the fellowship and works of the chosen. The second are separated from these works and from the communion. The third, having been stripped of their bodies, are handed over to eternal punishment. Thus, all these together, each of these groups and the individual persons of each group, are rightly regarded to belong to the name *Babylon*.

19. It is clear that the chosen, too, can be divided into three classes. For some have not yet been called, such as Jews or pagans. Others are called but not justified, such as Christian sinners. Others are justified but not yet glorified, such as the saints still subject to the miseries of this life.* Thus the chosen who have not yet been called still carry the name of Babylon. Although predestination will separate them from Babylon, Babylon's errors still blind them. So too for those whose hateful works distinguish them from the chosen. Although both calling and predestination join them to the chosen, the disgrace of the Babylonian name overpowers them.

*Rom 8:30

20. And so Babylon applies to all humanity, in which the same errors and vices entangle both the chosen and the condemned. *The twisted and unsearchable heart* is also Babylon,* because it is confused with vices and passions. That society of the condemned for whom eternal confusion is prepared is also called Babylon. But there is also a burden of Babylon that destroys the confused mass of people, separating one from another.

*Jer 17:9

It is also the burden of Babylon that constantly inflicts temporal evils upon this crowd of people. It is the burden of Babylon that knocks down the edifices of faults and wicked passions in the city of confusion of each person's heart. The burden of Babylon is also that which will burden the city of confusion alone with eternal punishments from above after this life. And this is *the burden of Babylon which Isaiah, son of Amos, saw.** *Isa 13:1

21. How did he see it? Ah, brothers! Those whom we now call *prophets* were once called *seers* for their superior and more godly kind of vision, if I may phrase it so.** But the time is short, and the tasks at hand do not permit us to speak of this vision now. Let us reserve this reflection for another sermon. Meanwhile, pray that, following the Spirit's wisdom, we may describe these burdens in such a way that we can more bravely sustain those that weigh us down, that we can be careful of those that would crush us, and that we can escape those that would condemn us, by the help of him who wanted to be burdened by our burdens for us,** our Lord Jesus Christ, who with the Father and the Holy Spirit lives and reigns as God forever and ever. Amen.

*1 Sam 9:9; Jerome, In Isa 1.2

*Isa 53:4; Matt 8:17; 11:28

Homily 2

1. You know, dear brothers, that in speaking of the burdens, I myself am undertaking a heavy burden. For this reason, let us call upon the Spirit. May he who first placed the burden of charity on us lighten every burden so as to advance your progress,* until the infusion of his light brings to fruition the desire that he gave. Yesterday we explained as best we could the burden of Babylon insofar as the title is concerned. But when it says, *The burden of Babylon that Isaiah, son of Amos, saw,** it seems we should ask how Isaiah saw this burden. This is particularly the case because there are many kinds of vision, and because prophets are called *seers* because of a kind of superiority of their vision.*

2. Following are the types of vision: sensory vision, imaginative vision, phantasmal vision, spiritual vision, rational vision, and intellectual vision.* Sensory vision is that by which the bodily senses perceive physical things. The imaginative vision forms interior images of things that the body has perceived, or creates new images never experienced on the basis of previous physical perceptions. The phantasmal vision holds the specter of physical things up either to the eyes or to the mind. With spiritual vision, meaningful images of visible things take shape in a person's very spirit.* With rational vision, we separate the true from the false and virtues from vices. With intellectual

*see Matt 11:30

*Isa 13:1

*Oner 1.21; 1 Sam 9:9; Jerome, In Isa 1.2

*Aelred, Anima 3.9; Augustine, C Adim Man 28.2

*Augustine, Gen ad litt 12.22

vision, by contrast, we do not separate the true from the false, but we regard Truth itself in what is true.

3. Thus, sensory vision is in the body, including all the bodily senses with their nature and powers. We say, for example, "Look how white it is," or *Taste and see how sweet it is*,* "Listen and see how loud it is," "Smell and see how fragrant it is," "Touch and see how soft it is." Therefore, every experience that comes to us through the physical senses can be called sensory vision.* This vision can indeed be prophetic, but it does not actually make anyone a prophet.

*Ps 33:9; 1 Pet 2:3

*Augustine, In ev Ioann Tract 121.5

4. The vision of the bronze serpent that *Moses held aloft in the desert*,* by which the children of Israel were cured from the serpents' bites, was certainly prophetic, but it did not turn those looking at it into prophets. It was also sensory vision with which *Abraham saw the three men coming down on the road*.* He himself, who *saw three but adored one*,† did not doubt that it was prophetic. But it was not sensory vision, though prophetic, that made Abraham a prophet. Another kind of vision allowed him to perceive that his sensory vision was prophetic. Therefore, he who explained the writing engraved on the wall of the Babylonian royal hall was more of a prophet than he who watched the hand and fingers writing.*

*Num 21:9

*Resp Dum staret in Dom Quinq, Hesbert 4.6563; Augustine, C Max Arrian 2.7; Gen 18:2
†Gen 18:2

*Dan 5:5; Augustine, Gen ad litt 12.11; Augustine, C Adim 28:2

5. The imaginative vision is that with which we see images in the mind of physical things already perceived by the senses. These images do not come to us from elsewhere but from ourselves, having entered through the senses. We imagine them interiorly just as we saw them exteriorly. Or sometimes we form other images based on sensory perceptions.* Having seen a four-legged deer with my eyes, I can imagine it interiorly. I can then imagine a six-legged deer, which I have never seen.* But this kind of vision is never prophetic, nor does it ever make someone a prophet, unless it could perhaps be called prophetic

*Augustine, Gen ad litt 12.12, 24

*Augustine, Trin 11.10

because prophetic sensory things can be imagined in the mind.

6. The phantasmal vision sometimes arises from the body, sometimes from the soul, and sometimes from a spirit of another nature. It comes from the body during sleep or illness. While our bodies are asleep, our souls, which cannot sleep, engage the specters of physical things in the meantime. This occurs naturally, because the senses normally occupy the soul with real perceptible physical things while awake. During times of illness, "when poor health disturbs the senses,"* we perceive visions "resembling physical things."† Obviously this often happens to the delirious. The phantasmal vision clearly comes from the soul itself when it dwells constantly on a thought while awake. It then sees semblances of the same thought while asleep.*

7. Another kind of spirit forms this vision when empty specters fool the physical eyes,* when evil spirits show the semblances of things to the souls of the sleeping or sick, or when a soul is torn from its sense, despite the body's being healthy and awake. For we certainly know that many eyes have been deceived, believing that a person was an animal, that there was running water when there was not, that fire raged where there was none, and many other phenomena of this sort. It is not unbelievable to anyone that demons form many dreams.

8. It can happen that harmful spirits put forward many visions to the minds of the mentally ill or those affected by other diseases, although many visions also occur in times of health. Whenever an evil spirit "tears the soul from its senses," as though in a sort of ecstasy, it renders the deluded person "demonic, raving, or a false prophet."* So we should clearly distinguish between this phantasmal vision and the prophets' role.

9. We call that vision *spiritual* that one spirit works in that of another. It takes place either in dreams or

*Augustine, Gen ad litt 12.19
†Augustine, Gen ad litt 12.12

*Aelred, Anima 3.10

*Augustine, Gen ad litt 12.12, 19

*Augustine, Gen ad litt 12.19

in ecstasy.* It happens in dreams when good spirits form the images of physical things in the mind of the sleeper. This vision, although it may be prophetic, does not make someone a prophet. For the Patriarch Joseph's vision was prophetic when he saw *the sun, moon, and eleven stars adoring him.** Yet he would not have been a prophet from this vision if he had not understood the mystery of the vision itself. Nor do we call the Pharaoh a prophet because we read that he had foreknowledge from his dreams of a future bounty and subsequent famine. Rather, it was Joseph who was the prophet, him to whom God revealed the secret of his purpose through that dream.* Nor do I think that Nebuchadnezzar deserves the name *prophet*, him to whom the statue appeared in his dreams. Rather, it is Daniel to whom it was given to understand the dream itself and the dream's power.*

10. "There is another kind of vision that takes place in a healthy body when the senses are not lost in sleep. A certain hidden spiritual work draws the soul into visions similar to physical things."* This is called ecstasy or flight. In this vision, hidden things are revealed and future events are shown. When the intellectual vision, which we will discuss afterward, complements this vision, it makes the person seeing such things a prophet who speaks mysteries, lays bare hidden things, or foretells what is to come.*

11. *In an ecstasy of the mind,* Peter saw a vessel coming down *from heaven* in which were all kinds of reptiles and animals, and it was said to him, *Kill and eat.** At the time he did not understand this vision, or rather command, but only after the intellectual vision was added to it, when he said, *In truth I have discovered that God is not a respecter of persons,* etc.* Furthermore, we read that the holy prophet Ezechiel saw in the spirit, not in the flesh, many mysteries† of Christ and the church under the guise of a city placed on a mountain.§ Seized by

*Augustine, Gen ad litt 12.12

*Gen 37:9

*Gen 41:1-7; 25-36; Aelred, Anima 3.11

*Dan 2:1, 31-45; Augustine, Gen ad litt 12.9; Augustine, C Adim Man 28.2

*Augustine, Gen ad litt 12.21

*Augustine, Gen ad litt 12.19

*Acts 10:10-13; 11:5-7

*Acts 10:34-35; Augustine, Gen ad litt 12.11
†*sacramenta*
§Ezek 40:2; Eph 5:32; Matt 5:14

ecstasy, he was taken to Jerusalem, and his prophetic
eye discovered the Jews' terrible abominations.*

*Ezek 8:9

12. But whether it could ever happen that good
spirits could deceive a person's senses, like the eyes
of those prevented from recognizing Christ,* I do not
wish to offer a hasty opinion.* I take it to be uncertain
whether it was through good or evil spirits that the
Syrians were struck with blindness so that they would
not recognize Elisha or Samaria.*

*Luke 24:16
*Aelred, Spec
car 1.14.41

*2 Kgs 6:18-20

13. By rational vision, we apprehend what is true
and what is false by sure reasoning, we distinguish
between vices and virtues, and we prove the calculations of numbers, weights, and measures.* We do this
without any support from the physical senses. We
perceive nothing so surely by the physical senses as
we do in the mind when we see that the number three
cannot be divided into two equal parts.

*Wis 11:21;
Aelred, Anima
1.44; 2.18, 39

14. Therefore, we perceive physical things by
sensory vision, we imagine physical things by imaginative vision, the phantasmal vision deceives us
through physical images, by spiritual vision the spirit
is instructed through physical likenesses, by rational
vision the mind is trained in invisible things, and by
intellectual vision the mind is led into Truth itself.*
For we call that vision *intellectual* by which the mind,
transcending all matter and all physical images and
likenesses, rests in the very light of Truth. Here all
things past, present, and future are true and truly are.
Future things are no different from past, nor the
present from past or future, but all things are always
and in the same way together. Whatever Truth reveals
is contemplated by an inner gaze.

*Aelred,
Anima 3.9

15. This is why the Lord says in the gospel, *I have
many things to say to you, but you cannot bear it now. But
when the Spirit of Truth comes, he will lead you into all
truth.* What is *all truth*, except the one Truth of all?
Certainly whatever is, is true, for what is false does
not exist.* Person, stone, wood, horse, bird: all these

*John 16:12-13;
Aelred, Anima 3.9

*Augustine,
Conf 7.15.21

are and are true. But a picture of a person is not a person and for that reason is not a true person. Yet it is a true image or picture and therefore is not without truth. Therefore the apostles are led into all truth, that is, into that very Truth in which all things are and which is in all things. In Truth there is nothing false, nothing doubtful, nothing deceitful. What is true is only perceived by the heart, not by the flesh.

16. *I have many things to say to you,* he says. He had many things to say to them, not in the many nor through the many, but in the one and through the one, where many are not many but one. *But you cannot bear it now,* he says. Busied by sensory vision on account of the sweetness of his presence, and physically intent on his physical words, they were not able to rise to that intellectual vision that excludes the memory of all physical things, where pure Truth itself speaks. Therefore, he says, *It is good for you that I go,** so that *John 16:7 after this physical vision and physical conversation is taken away, the Spirit may speak to the spirit brought into the light of Truth.

17. I know of a monastery of virgins serving under the venerable and deeply respected holy Father Gilbert* where they daily send the rich fruit of their *Gilbert of modesty to heaven. There was a certain virgin— Sempringham perhaps she is still there—who, when she shut out from her breast all love of the world, carnal affection, care for the body, and exterior concern, began with burning mind to feel distaste for earthly things and a desire for the heavenly.* *Aelred, Spec

18. It happened once that, when she devoted herself car 3.6.17 to her customary solitary prayer,* a kind of wonderful *RB 4.56 sweetness overcame her. This sweetness extinguished from her mind every disturbance, every mental digression, and even every spiritual affection that she had for her friends. Soon her soul, as though saying good-bye to everything in the world, was seized above itself* *Aelred, and taken up by a kind of inexpressible and incompre- Iesu 3.22; Aelred, Mira 3; Aelred, Spec car 3.6.19

*1 Tim 6:16
*Oner 1.2;
Aelred,
Anima 2.50;
Augustine, Gen
ad litt 12.31

hensible light.* She saw nothing except that which is
and "is the being of all things."*

19. Nor was it a physical light or the likeness of
something physical. It had neither extension nor dif-
fusion; thus it could be seen everywhere. Nor was it
contained, but it contained all things in a wonderful
and inexpressible way. It contained them just as Being
contains whatever is, and Truth whatever is true. Permeated by this light, she began to know *Christ* himself

*2 Cor 5:16

not according to the flesh, as she had before, because
the spirit before her face, *Christ* Jesus, led her *into the*

*John 16:13;
Lam 4:20;
Aelred, S 57.22
†Bernard, SC
23.15; Aelred,
Iesu 3.23

truth itself.*

20. After she had passed not a little time in this
ecstatic state,† her sisters disturbed her. But she was
barely able to return to the physical senses she had
abandoned. And since this happened to her frequently,
and since the others often asked her to explain this
form of ecstasy, many began to imitate the excellence
of this vision. Removing themselves from every care
and worldly concern, many shared in the same grace
with tears and continual prayer. Even at the sisters'
gatherings, they were often bathed in this light, even
unwillingly.

21. There was a certain virgin there, a woman of
great discernment, who, knowing that one should not

*1 John 4:1

believe in *every spirit,** thought that all of this should
be attributed to sickness or phantasmal illusions. Insofar as she could, she dissuaded her sisters from the
company of such visions. When she asked their superior why nothing of the sort had happened to her, she
was told, "Because you do not have faith in us, nor do
you love the virtue in others that you yourself do not
possess." "Ask God," said the first sister, "that, if this

*1 John 4:1

is from him, it may also happen to me."*

22. When they had prayed for a few days without
result, she asked the superior again. She replied, "You
must renounce all your affections for this world and
for every mortal thing, and occupy yourself with the

memory of God alone." "Why should I not pray for my friends and benefactors?" she asked. "At the time you want to climb to higher things by mental contemplation, you must commend and entrust everything you love to God. Be like someone about to leave the world, and bid a decisive farewell to every created thing. Yearn for the face of your beloved." Still unbelieving, the discerning sister asked that, with the help of her interlocutor's prayer, she might be worthy to have her desire fulfilled, if such things really were from God.* "Yet I do not wish," she said, "that my soul should be thus seized and taken from my body. I do not wish that my memory of all things, especially my friends, should be erased from my mind. But it is enough for me to know whether these things are from God."*

*1 John 4:1

*1 John 4:1

23. Thus, on Good Friday, restless with anxious thoughts,* suddenly she began, bathed in light, to be drawn on high in an inexplicable way.† But her weak eye was unable to bear that *inaccessible light* shining within her.§ She asked to be called back, if possible, to the vision of the Lord's passion.* Having suddenly seen, as it were, being itself,* she descended from the higher to the lower. She is brought to that spiritual vision and sees in the spirit Jesus hanging on the cross, attached by nails, pierced by the lance, with blood flowing from the five wounds, kindly gazing at her.* Then, returning to herself and breaking into tears,† she believed the sisters and regarded herself as less fit for this light.§

*Aelred, Spec car 1.30.86
†Augustine, Gen ad litt 12.26
§1 Tim 6:16

*Aelred, S 57.22

*Exod 3:14

*Bernard, SC 62.6; Aelred, S 57.23; Aelred, Iesu 1.1
†Aelred, Iesu 3.22
§2 Cor 2:16

24. Perhaps this story has a purpose here. We should understand that only the intellectual vision makes someone a prophet, as we read that wisdom *communicates itself to holy souls; it makes friends of God and prophets.** Whatever we perceive in the other visions is either doubtful or confirmed by faith rather than by knowledge. But that which is perceived in the Truth, in whom whatever will be is made,* is both bright and certain.* Therefore, when the intellectual vision works

*Wis 7:27

*Oner 17.11; 19.3

*Augustine, Gen ad litt 12.25–26

*Isa 45:11 LXX

*Augustine, Gen
ad litt 12.8–9,
19, 24

*Isa 39:4

*Isa 39:4

*Isa 39:6; 2 Kgs
20:15-17

*Isa 6:1; Aelred,
Anima 3.11;
Augustine, Gen
ad litt 12.26
†In Isa 6.2
*Hos 12:10

in the sensory or spiritual vision,* there is no doubt
that the gift of prophecy is present.*

25. Who can easily say by which vision—only intellectual, or also sensory or spiritual—*Isaiah, son of
Amos, saw the burden of Babylon*? For we can tell from
the book itself that he foresaw many things by each
of these visions illumined by the intellectual vision.

26. He composed his prophecy from sensory vision
when he rebuked King Hezekiah by his prophetic
authority for showing the treasury to the Babylonian
messengers. *What did they see in your house?** he asked.
And the king answered, *There is nothing that I did not
show them.** Then the prophet responded, *Behold, the
days will come, says the Lord, when everything that your
ancestors gathered will be taken off to Babylon.** But it is
with spiritual vision that he says, *I saw the Lord sitting
on a high and lofty throne,** along with what follows.

27. With whichever of these visions he saw the burden of Babylon, it is certain that he saw it with his
mind, not with the flesh.† He revealed it who said, *I
have given comparisons into the hands of the prophets.** But
since the distinction between these visions has detained us for a considerable time, let us postpone
beginning this prophetic vision until tomorrow.

Homily 3

1. When the fullness of time came, God sent his Son
made from a woman, made under the law.* What is
this fullness of time? The Lord speaks of it in the gospel, saying, *Lift up your eyes, and see the fields, because
they are already white for the harvest.**

2. We say that the time is vacant and empty when the
seeds in the ground dry up under the harsh sun* or rot
from rain floods. *Famine* consumes everything,* leaving
vacant fields to the harvesters. *Ten acres of vineyard* yield
one vessel, and sixty gallons of seed yield *six gallons.** On
the other hand, the time is full when all things abound,
when the earth answers its tiller with an abundant crop
and the harvester races about naked in the field. The
time is full when the call is sung out everywhere in the
vineyard,* when the *storehouse* is filled *with grain, and
when the presses* overflow *with wine.**

3. Let us call to mind the Savior's parable of the
grain and the tares, and let us pay attention to what
he says is the wheat and what are the tares: *The good
seed are the children of the kingdom; the tares are the wicked
children.** He calls those whom his mercy *predestined*
to life children *of the kingdom.** The wicked children
are those for whom his justice foresaw punishment.

4. Before the coming of our Lord, the wicked children occupied almost the entire face of the earth. There
were very few children of God's kingdom hidden
among them. Famine for God's word was everywhere,* and the vacant, empty time left the spiritual

* Gal 4:4

* John 4:35

* Gen 1:2
* Gen 41:30

* Isa 5:10

* Jer 48:33
* Prov 3:10;
Joel 2:24

* Matt 13:38
* Rom 8:29-30

* Amos 8:11

39

Gen 1:2   workers nothing for their labor. But *the fullness of time came* when the land abounded everywhere with those
Gal 4:4   who were to be separated from the Babylonian errors. Once separated, they would be justified, and once
Rom 8:29, 30   justified, glorified. The Savior says of them, *The harvest is great, but the laborers are few.*
*Matt 9:37

5. Babylon, the city of confusion, used vices and errors to hold the chosen ones in captivity together with those who were condemned. But Babylon would be invaded through the Lord's coming, and would be destroyed by the chosen ones' separation from the condemned. And this is the first burden, *the burden of*
*Isa 13:1   *Babylon that Isaiah, son of Amos, saw.* He began to describe prophetically how it would be destroyed as follows: *Raise a sign over the dark mountain, lift up your*
*Isa 13:2   *voice, raise up your hand, and let the leaders enter the gates.*

6. Who is speaking? Who is spoken to? I think we should note that the holy prophets foretell the future in various ways: by narrating, praying, blessing, or almost cursing, performing an action, and often as though by commanding. Here is an example of narration: *In the last days, the mountain of the house of the*
*Isa 2:2   *Lord will be prepared on the mountaintops.* An example of praying: *Show us, Lord, your mercy, and grant us your*
*Ps 84:8   *salvation.* And another: *Break forth from the heavens and*
*Isaiah 64:1   *come down.* And another from holy Moses: *I beseech*
*Exod 4:13   *you, O Lord, send the one whom you will send.*

7. Here is an example of the prophet almost cursing: *Scatter them in your power and cut them off, my protector,*
*Ps 58:12   *O Lord.* And: *Just as wax melts before the fire, so may*
*Ps 67:3   *sinners perish before the face of God.* And elsewhere the prophet says, *Give to them, O Lord. What will you give*
*Hos 9:14   *to them? A womb without children and withered breasts.* We have an example of blessing when Isaac blesses his son: *May God give you dew from heaven, and abundance from the richness of the land, of the grain, the wine, and the oil; may the tribes serve you and the peoples adore*
*Gen 27:28-29;   *you, et cetera.* An example of performing an action is
Ps 4:8

Jacob's setting up a stone and anointing it.* Another   *Gen 28:18
is *Moses' raising up a bronze serpent in the desert*.* An-   *John 3:14;
Num 21:9
other is Isaiah himself going about *naked and with bare*
feet.*   *Isa 20:3

8. An example of a command occurs later in this
book, where it says, *Go, swift messengers, to a torn and*
wounded nation.* If he had been narrating, he would   *Isa 18:2
have said, "Swift messengers will go." The present
passage is also a command: *Raise a sign over the dark*
mountain.* The prophet saw that, after the Lord and   *Isa 13:2
Savior came in the flesh, the apostles' ministry and
the preachers' instruction would overthrow the city
of confusion. He orders them on his authority, or
rather on that of the Lord, to do what he saw that they
were going to do.

9. *Raise a sign over the dark mountain*.* We can rightly   *Isa 13:2
interpret *the dark mountain* to be Babylon, that is, the
world as Christ found it. One can call it a *mountain*
because of its pride and *dark* because of its error. The
Roman Empire was like a mountain at that time, towering over the entire world. The more its pride inflated it, the darker it grew from its many errors,
especially the ignorance of God. Did not a kind of
horrible darkness—*idolatry*, the philosophers' vanity,
the temples' superstition, and unchecked lust—cover
the world?*   *Aelred, S 72.25;
Wis 14:27; 1
Cor 10:14

10. *Raise a sign over the dark mountain*.† What sign?   †Isa 13:2
Listen to the gospel: *Behold, this one was placed for the*
ruin and resurrection of many in Israel, and as a sign who
will be contradicted.* This is the sign of the cross, which   *Luke 2:34
human pride clearly contradicted. Jews and Gentiles
with their kings and chiefs, with the wise and prudent
of the world, fought against it. But the little ones lifted
it up over the dark mountain.* For *you hid* the myster-   *Aelred, S 72.25
ies of your cross, O Lord Jesus, *from the wise and the*
prudent, and you revealed them to the little ones.* The   *Matt 11:25
apostles and apostolic men are little or humble in this
way. They are commanded to raise *a sign over the dark*

*Isa 13:2
*Jerome, In
Isa 6.3

*Exod 25:18-22
*Gen 29:10

*Matt 11:29

*Phil 2:8-10

*Luke 11:21-22;
Matt 12:29

*Isa 13:2

*mountain,** thus teaching the entire world to submit to the Lord's cross.*

11. One object placed on top of another weighs it down, closes it up, or rises above it. Two cherubim are placed above the ark of the covenant to make them more prominent;* a rock is placed on a well to close it up;* a beam is placed on a winepress to weigh it down. The banner of the cross is lifted up *over the dark mountain* to weigh down the power of this world by its power, to close up the mysteries of our redemption from the proud, and to rise above all worldly glory in the presence of the meek and humble.*

12. Hear blessed Paul describe how the cross weighs down: *Christ was made obedient to the Father unto death, death on a cross. Because of this God exalted him and bestowed on him the name above every other name, so that at the name of Jesus every knee should bend in the heavens, on earth, and in hell.** See how heaven, earth, and even hell itself are subjected to the mystery of the cross, and how the Babylonian king's power is everywhere weighed down, his might emptied.

13. *When an armed strong man guards his hall, his possessions are at peace. But if someone stronger comes upon him and defeats him, then his vessels are stolen, his arms taken away and the spoils distributed.** The armed strong man is the devil; his hall is the world; his vessels, the wise of the world; his arms, the kings and chiefs; the spoils, the common people. Behold Babylon with its king and riches. Before the strong person came, this king was at peace, that is, he reigned without anyone speaking against him. But after someone stronger overcame him, a heavy burden, a conquering burden, a plundering burden is placed upon him.

14. This burden of Babylon is the cross of Christ. The cross conquered the devil and invaded Babylon. It plundered the Egyptians and enriched the Hebrews. These are the Hebrews to whom it is said, *Raise a sign over the dark mountain.** Thus he *who rescued us from the* *power of darkness and transferred us to the kingdom of his son, who is his splendor,** seizes the spoils of Babylon or Egypt by the power of his cross preached to all nations. He chose the little ones, that is the humble; the Hebrews, that is, those leaping across;* those despised of this world yet above the world; the weak of the world but stronger than the strong of the world; the foolish of the world but wiser than the wise of the world.*

*Col 1:13; 1:11; Phil 3:21

*Aelred, SS 1.56; 2.40; 10.13, 16; Jerome, Nom 35

*1 Cor 1:25

15. For *God chose these foolish things of the world to confound the wise. God chose the weak things of the world to confound the strong. And God chose the insignificant and contemptible things of the world, and the things that are not, to destroy those that are.** These are the ones who look down on themselves, regarding themselves as little out of humility, who leap over everything of this world, just like the Hebrews. They raise up the cross and trample down riches and pleasures contrary to the cross. They judge *the reproach of Christ to be better riches than the Egyptians' treasure house.**

*1 Cor 1:27-28

*Heb 11:26; Phil 3:7

16. Hear how the preaching of the cross, with a voice raised above all the world, closes up the depth of divine power and wisdom. *We,* says Paul, *preach Christ crucified, a stumbling block to the Jews and foolishness to the gentiles.** Therefore the foolishness of the cross hid God's wisdom; the stumbling block of the cross truly closed up God's power. But to whom? To the Jews and Gentiles, of course. Yet not to all, but to those of whom he wrote elsewhere, *The word of the cross is foolishness to those perishing, but to those being saved, that is to us, it is the power of God.** *We preach Christ crucified, a stumbling block to the Jews and foolishness to the Gentiles, but to those who have been called, Jews and gentiles, the power of God and the wisdom of God.** Paul teaches how the cross could stand above all the riches and honors of the world for those called, saying, *Far be it from me to boast, unless I boast in the cross of our Lord Jesus Christ.**

*1 Cor 1:23

*1 Cor 1:18

*1 Cor 1:23-24

*Gal 6:14

17. But if you think that the *dark mountain* should be interpreted in a positive sense, call to mind what Isaiah says: *Go up a high mountain, you who preach the good news to Zion.** Consider that if someone's teaching is lofty, that person's life should also be lofty.* Those whose tongues abide in heaven should not crawl with their hands in the dirt, nor should those who rise above themselves in speech lie below themselves in base things. For we can appropriately call the evangelical teaching itself a *dark mountain*, because like a towering mountain it rises above all worldly wisdom. Like fog on a mountain, the evangelical teaching hides higher realities from the eyes of the unfaithful or weak under the veil of the mysteries.

18. We can also call the Old Testament writings a *dark mountain*. In another place, the Old Testament is referred to as a shadowy and thick mountain, lofty according to the spirit but dark according to the letter.* The darkness of the letter hides the secrets of the heavenly mysteries. These mysteries are revealed through the Gospel by him of whom it is written, *The voice of the Lord, preparing stags, will reveal dense things.** For this reason the prophet says, *Dark water in the clouds of air.*† This is also why Solomon says, *The Lord said that he would dwell in a cloud.** This is also the reason that *Moses* was able to enter *the darkness where God was.**

19. The preachers who announce the burden of Babylon are thus commanded not to wallow in base things but to prepare *ascensions in their heart.** Those who would preach the things from above should taste *the things above.** Those placed on a mountain, not cast below into a valley, should *raise a sign; lift up your voice.** Or else it says this because the first heralds of the truth had been chosen from the remnants of the children of Israel, instituted by legal decrees and accustomed to the mysteries of the letter. So the Holy Spirit orders them to cross over from the law to the Gospel, from the letter to the spirit,* and to climb up

margin notes:

*Isa 40:9

*Jerome, In Isa 6.4

*Hab 3:3 LXX; 2 Cor 3:6

*Ps 28:9; Aelred, S 69.6
†Ps 17:12

*1 Kgs 8:12

*Exod 20:21; Jerome, In Isa 6.3

*Ps 83:6

*Col 3:2

*Isa 13:2

*Rom 7:6; 2 Cor 3:6

from the valley of carnal observance to the mountain of spiritual precepts. Or else they are ordered to prove that the Gospel they preach fulfills what the ancient writings foretold. As the Savior says, *Examine the Scriptures; it is they that give witness to me.** And he says to the apostles, *Everything written about me in the law of Moses, the prophets, and the psalms must be fulfilled.**

*John 5:39

*Luke 24:44

20. There are two ways to read the following prophecy: *Raise a sign over the dark mountain.** Either the raised sign is over the dark mountain, or they themselves standing on the dark mountain raise the sign.

*Isa 13:3

21. *Lift up your voice, raise your hand.** And elsewhere you have, *Lift up your voice in strength, you who preach the good news to Jerusalem.** This is that lifting up of the apostolic voice about which holy David spoke: *Their sound went forth*, he says, *to all the land, and their words to the ends of the earth.** Holy David foretold what he saw would happen in the future by using the past tense, as though it had already taken place. Isaiah, or rather the Lord himself speaking through Isaiah, commands this same future event to be done. *Lift up*, he says, *your voice.**

*Isa 13:2

*Isa 40:9; Jerome, In Isa 6:4

*Ps 18:5

*Isa 13:2

22. For throughout the entire world *the vessels of anger*, defiled by Babylonian wantonness, were to be changed *into vessels of mercy.** For this reason, the voice of those preaching the Gospel rang out with such power that none could object that they had not heard the word of God.** This is why the apostle said, *Faith comes from hearing, and hearing through the word of Christ. But I say: Did they not hear? Indeed, their sound went forth to all the land and their words to the ends of the earth.** Therefore, just as we say that the raising up of a sign represents the mystery of the Lord's cross, so too the lifting up of the voice prophesies the apostolic preaching's excellence and power. It is as Jesus said to his disciples, *Go to the entire world and preach the gospel to every creature.**

*Rom 9:22-23

*Ps 28:4

*Rom 10:17-18; Ps 18:5

*Mark 16:15

23. Still other meanings for the lifting up of the voice come to mind, but time compels us to move on to other tasks. Let us take up these ideas, God willing, at the beginning of tomorrow's sermon. But you who are now moving on from sermon to reading and from reading to prayer, knock devoutly with your prayers on Jesus' kind ears. Ask him to uncover our *eyes* to consider the *wonders of* his *law*,* who lives and reigns with the Father and the Holy Spirit, and is God, forever and ever. Amen.

* Ps 118:18

Homily 4

1. You have not forgotten, dear brothers, where we were to take up today's sermon according to yesterday's promise.* As we said, the preachers of the truth are told to lift up their voice. The apostolic preaching should thus make known to all lands everywhere the salvation that *the Lord worked in the midst of the land*.* In this way, *all the ends of the earth* will remember *the Lord* and turn to him,* *and in the far-off islands* they will say, "Our Savior has come!"* The holy prophet, wishing to distinguish carefully between the heralds of the Old and New Testaments, urges the latter to lift up their voice by preaching.

2. You know that earthly happiness was the promise to the Jewish people, a carnal people that tastes only earthly things.* This promise consisted of an abundance of bread and wine, of milk and honey,* as it is written, *If you wish it and you listen to me, you will eat the good things of the land.* And also: *If you walk in the Lord's commandments and cling to him, the Lord will scatter all nations before your face. Everywhere your foot treads will be yours.* And from the prophet Amos: *The plowman will overtake the harvester, and the crusher of grapes the sower.* There are many other verses similar to these.

3. Those who promised earthly things did not lift up their voice. They preached lowly things to a people lying low; they offered passing rewards to those who loved passing things. But the voice of those whom

*Oner 3.23

*Ps 73:12

*Ps 21:28
*Jer 31:10;
Isa 62:11

*Col 3:2; Phil 3:19
*Deut 8:8; Num
16:14; Exod 3:8
*Isa 1:19

*Deut 11:22-24

*Amos 9:13

47

Christ established as evangelists of the New Testament is lifted up. They teach us to desire heavenly things and reject earthly things. They promise their listeners no recompense in this age, but instead they promise labors and struggle here, and crowns and rewards in the future.

4. Paul certainly lifted up his voice when he said, *Seek the things that are above, where Christ is seated at the right hand of God; taste the things that are above, not those on the earth.** And again, *That which in the present is momentary and light in our tribulation works exceedingly for us above for an eternal weight of glory.** The holy evangelist John also raises his voice and dreadfully shouts as a voice of thunder over Babylon,** saying, *Do not love the world, nor what is in the world,** and, *The world is passing away with its desires.** Even the first preacher of evangelical grace, John the Baptist, began his preaching not with an earthly kingdom but with a heavenly one, lifting up his voice and saying, *Repent, for the kingdom of God will draw near.** Those who lift up their voice preach the spiritual, speak of the divine, and promise the heavenly.

5. *Lift up the voice; raise up your hand.** One raises up hands in prayer, in good works, and in performing miracles. It is the duty of preachers to pray for those to whom they preach. They should pray that they first listen, then believe, and finally persevere in faith and good works. Yet it is also the preachers' duty not to act in a manner contrary to what they teach.** Their mind, voice, and hands should be in harmony with their intention, words, and actions.**

6. We can also rightly interpret the raising up of hands to be *the signs and wonders worked among the people through the apostles' hands.** With these words is fulfilled what the Lord's command foretold in the gospel: *Go,* he said to his disciples; *preach, saying: The kingdom of God will draw near.** This is the same as what Isaiah had said, *Lift up your voice.** And the Lord

*Col 3:1-2

*2 Cor 4:17

*Mark 3:17
*1 John 2:15
*1 John 2:17

*Matt 3:2

*Isa 13:2

*RB 2.13

*RB 19:7

*Acts 5:12

*Matt 10:7
*Isa 13:2

added, *Cure the sick, raise the dead, cleanse the lepers, cast out demons.** And this is why the prophet says, *Raise up your hands.**

7. But I do not think it is out of place to say that the lifting up of hands or the lifting up of the voice signifies an upright intention. If the intention alone is twisted and sinking to lower things, then God will judge both words and works as lowly, however lofty they may appear. Paul speaks of those who preached the Gospel of God insincerely, for an exterior motive rather than for the truth, saying, *They all seek their own interests and not those of Jesus Christ,** and, *People like this do not serve the Lord Jesus Christ, but rather their own stomachs.** Such people neither lifted up their voice nor raised up their hands. Their worthless and twisted intention brought low absolutely everything that sounded sublime in their words or appeared lofty in their miracles.

8. This is why the prophet says, *They turned aside their victims into the depths.** The preaching of the truth, *the affliction of the flesh,** the relief of the poor, constant and attentive prayer: all these are saving sacrifices. But those who abandon their intention of heavenly rewards and twist their victims down to the lower regions of present convenience certainly turn them aside into the depths.** For this reason, the Lord says in the gospel, *See that you do not do your righteous works in the presence of others in order to be seen by them,* etc.**

9. Therefore, those who waste the office of preaching, or the gift of prophecy, or the grace of miracles, or righteous works, or the light of knowledge on the vanity of human praise or avarice for *foul profit,** do not lift up their voice or raise up their hands. Nor do heavenly rewards await them, but rather eternal punishment.** We can easily confirm that many misuse even these higher gifts, namely, prophecy and miracles, by referring to the prophecy of Balaam and the miracles of Judas.** But our main proof is the Savior's

*Matt 10:8
*Isa 13:2

*Phil 2:21

*Rom 16:18

*Hos 5:2
*Eccl 12:12

*Gregory, Hiez 1
Hom 4.4
*Matt 6:1

*1 Cor 12:9-10;
Titus 1:7;
1 Tim 3:8; Jude 16

*Oner 8.11

*Num 23:11-12,
25-26; 24:10-13;
Matt 10:1

terrible judgment in the gospel: *Many will come on that day, saying: Did we not prophesy in your name, and in your name did we not perform many signs? And then I will tell them, I never knew you.**

10. O, dear brothers, *strive for the better gifts:*† humility, patience, and charity. These gifts are certainly better, because they are more useful. The Lord will not say *on that day, I never knew you* to the humble, the obedient, or those who love *one another in charity.** We know he will say this to many prophets and miracle workers. Therefore, let none of you, brothers, regard yourself as less acceptable to God because you do not perceive yourself to be glorious with miracles. Judge, rather, according to the three things that we just mentioned, *never doubting* this to be pleasing in God's presence.* For *God resists the proud but gives grace to the humble;** and, *In your patience you will possess your souls,** and, *In this they will know that you are* Christ's *disciples, if you love one another.**

11. Christ *sent* the holy apostles and apostolic men *into the world* to conquer the *strong man's hall.** There are four ways that these men lifted up their voice: by preaching the kingdom of God, by promising the good things of heaven, by despising present things, and by stretching themselves toward what was to come. *Oh how beautiful on the mountains* of the virtues *are the feet,* that is, the affections, *of those preaching the Gospel of peace to people of good will,** to those rejecting earthly goods in favor of the heavenly.**

12. Beautiful indeed are the feet to which not even the dust sticks. Either Christ himself washes such feet in a basin of water* or else, following the Lord's command, the dust is shaken off against those on whose account it had gathered.* Any dust of worldly dispositions that preachers or superiors gather because of their office is either washed away, with Christ's help, by that charity for which it was gathered, as it is written, *Charity covers a multitude of sins,** or else it is

Marginal notes:

*Matt 7:22-23;
John 11:47;
Aelred, Spec car 2.9.22; Adv 37;
Jerome, In Matt 1
†1 Cor 12:31

*Matt 7:22-23;
Rom 12:10;
Eph 4:2

*Jas 1:6

*Jas 4:6

*Luke 21:19

*John 13:35

*Luke 11:21;
John 10:36; 17:18

*Luke 2:14

*Isa 52:7;
Rom 10:15

*John 13:5

*Matt 10:14

*1 Pet 4:8

certainly shaken off against those for whom they work if they are ungrateful or disobedient. Everything will be reckoned not to the preacher, but rather to those for whom he worked.*

*Aelred, S 78.28

13. Having carefully considered all of this, let us briefly summarize the text's meaning.* The voice of the prophet, or rather the voice of the Lord speaking through the prophet to the apostles, says, *Raise a sign over the dark mountain.** It is as if he had said, "Against Babylon, that is, the world, exalted like a mountain and dark with error, raise up the sign of faith and the Lord's passion." In this way the cross's humility will conquer the world's pride, and the light of faith will drive away the darkness of errors. Nor should this be done in one place or in one region only. Rather, *Lift up your voice,* and let its *sound* go forth *to all the land and your words to the ends of the earth.** *Raise up your hand,* so that the doctrine of truth is gladly heard, easily believed, and devoutly received. *Raise up your hand,* so that what you teach by words, you may confirm by miracles. All this was fulfilled when *the disciples went forth and preached everywhere, with God's help confirming the word with signs.**

*sensum litterae

*Isa 13:2

*Ps 18:5

*Mark 16:20

14. We can also read it as follows: You preachers of the word of God, ascend from the valley to the mountain, from the letter to the spirit,* from the fleshly ceremony of the law to the lofty mysteries† of the Gospel. Standing on that dark mountain where God is,§ that is, standing on the knowledge of the Scriptures, *raise a sign,* etc. Or thus: You whom I command to preach lofty realities, climb up to lofty realities in your mind. Learn on the mountain of contemplation what you teach in the valley of this world. Stationed in lofty action and contemplation, raise a sign by preaching the mysteries of the cross. Lift up your voice by promising the heavenly rather than the earthly. *Raise pure hands everywhere* for those to whom you preach by praying or doing good works with an upright

*Rom 7:6; 2 Cor 3:6
†sacramenta
§Exod 20:21

*1 Tim 2:8
*Luke 11:22;
Matt 12:29

*Isa 9:3
*Isa 13:2

*1 Cor 16:9

*Song 5:2;
Rev 3:2

*Acts 13:46;
Luke 9:60

*Acts 7:55-57

*sacramenta

intention.* Thus the sting of the cross will pierce Babylon's walls, its *spoils* will be taken,* and what the prophet wrote will be done: *They will rejoice in your presence like those who rejoice at the harvest, as victors rejoice after taking the booty when they divide the spoils.*

15. *Let the leaders enter the gates.** In everything that has been said, the gates of the city open and the leaders enter. One of the leaders boasts at the gates' opening, saying, *A great and evident door was opened to me, and many opponents.** The leaders discover Babylon's closed gates wherever God's word has no access to human hearts. Unfaithfulness and ill-will have locked all these gates. They hear the preacher's voice *knocking at the door,** but they do not welcome the doctrine of truth. The Jews were like this, to whom Paul said, *We had to announce the kingdom of God to you first, but because you rejected it and judged yourselves unworthy of eternal life, behold, we are turning to the pagans.** Those who *held their ears* upon hearing Stephen preach the glory of the Lord Jesus also shut the door to these leaders.*

16. The preachers are called leaders of the Word because they lead the Word of God into their listeners' hearts. They entered the city's gates when the pagans received them, and they governed the church built from the Gentiles as directors and leaders. The mysteries* of faith can also be understood as *gates.* Faith must lead the way, and then the entrance lies open to the understanding. One could say that the leaders enter when their listeners' hearts receive them through faith. They then pour the light of a higher and more secret teaching into their hearts.

17. But I also think that the firstfruits of believers deserve the name *gates.* Through the first believers, the apostles had easier access to convert others, and they entered the city well equipped with heavenly arms. I think it is for this reason that the apostle said, *I will remain in Ephesus until Pentecost, for a great and*

*evident door was opened to me, and many opponents.** *1 Cor 16:8-9
Indeed, *the crowd of believers* was like a door through
which Paul entered the city of confusion to confront
his opponents.* Their number was not small; he had *Acts 5:14
to fight against many at close quarters. We can understand in all of this the burden of Babylon, which we
said above was overthrown by the separation of many
through Christ's coming.* *Oner 1.20; 3.5

18. But let us conclude this sermon here.* We would *Oner 19.36;
not wish to stand in the way of equally necessary tasks 21.28; 26.34
in our desire to serve your progress here. Let us pray
before tomorrow's sermon, in which we will repeat
what was said today allegorically, but with a moral
explanation. Pray, therefore, that the construction of
good works can be added to the foundation of faith
already laid,* to the praise and glory of our Lord Jesus *1 Cor 3:10
Christ, who lives and reigns forever and ever. Amen.

Homily 5

1. Remember, dear brothers, that we said that you could aptly take the name *Babylon* to be the soul confused by wicked passions and vices.* For *Babylon*, as you know, means *confusion*.* And what is more confused than such a soul? At times, pride raises it up, at times anger lays waste to it, at times timidity casts it down, at times sadness hems it in, at times rage rides it,* at times cruelty bloodies it, at times lust defiles it, and at times gluttony disgraces it. We can surely call such a soul *a dark mountain*; pride raises it up and lust darkens it. For a kind of dark gloom envelops the eyes of people of this sort. Thus they cannot distinguish between the light of the virtues and the darkness of vices. They flee the former and wallow delightedly in the latter.

2. The burden of this Babylon is the cross. Raised up now throughout the world, the cross is a burden *to those who are perishing, but to those who are saved** it is a useful and pleasing comfort. For what, my brothers, is so burdensome to the lovers of the world as the cross?* For the cross commends contempt for the glory that they seek. It commends affliction of the flesh, from which they desperately flee.* It commends putting to death one's self-will, an act that they despise. And it commends nakedness and stripping away of temporal things, which they curse.

3. But so it is for us, too, brothers! The more the remnants of Babylon seize us, so much the more does the cross burden us, as we are taught by daily experience!* For the more the delight of the flesh pleases us, so much the more does its affliction torment us. The more pleasing we find honor, the more burdensome we experience lowliness. The more praise lifts us up, so much the more does slander cast us down. If riches are loved, poverty afflicts. If wantonness seems sweet, chastity is found difficult. Hence it is that *many of* Christ's *disciples turned back* upon hearing the mystery of the cross *and did not walk with him anymore.** Let us make sure then, my brothers, that we drive whatever remnants of the world that are in us from our hearts, and erase all traces of Babylon, if this is possible.* Then we can experience how much sweetness is in the cross, how much safety and glory. For there is nothing sweeter than the love it brings forth, nothing safer than the martyrdom it elicits, and nothing more glorious than the contempt for the world that it produces.

4. *Raise up a sign over the dark mountain.** I think this voice is addressed to the angels whom the Lord commanded to be the guardians of our souls.* The Lord orders them to place the memory of the cross in the hearts of those whom the world still delights or tempts. He commands them to set the pertinent virtue of the cross against each corresponding vice that ravages or attacks the soul. *These are the ministering spirits, sent to minister to* us.* They are with those chanting psalms, they stand by those in prayer, and they are present to those reading or meditating.* They oppose the unclean spirits. They hold up the example of the Lord's passion against those urging the world's enticements, they bring forth the goodness of the Lord's patience against those wishing to inflame the mind with anger, and they suggest that we imitate the humility of the humble Jesus against those urging haughtiness or pride.*

5. Therefore, dear brothers, stand in the church *with reverence* and fear. *Honor God,* and give *thanks* to these

*Aelred, SS 7.4; 72.26; RB 59.6

*John 6:67, 61

*Aelred, Spec car 1.29.85; Oner, Adv 13 = Aelred, S 47.13; Oner 19.10

*Isa 13:2

*Jerome, In Isa 5.3

*Heb 1:14

*Ps 137:1; RB 19.5-6

*Matt 11:29

*Heb 12:28; Acts
12:23; Rev 14:7

blessed and kindly spirits.* May they never depart from you, offended by inconstancy on your part or by some disdain toward your neighbor. Without them, the wicked angels would have free access to your heart.

6. Happy is the soul that, while chanting psalms, is inflamed with desire for that of which it chants. With affection stirred up and tears welling, such a soul addresses those whom it senses to be present in spirit: *Daughters of Jerusalem, declare to the beloved that I have*

*Song 5:8; Ant
Anima mea in
Ass (Hesbert
3.1418)
†Song 2:8

*grown weak with love.** These blessed spirits seem to respond with a happy expression and a cheerful voice, saying, *Look, it is he who comes leaping in the mountains and jumping over hills.*† And turned toward him who even now is drawing near to the soul that he loves, they say, *This is she, the beautiful one among the daughters*

*Ant In comm
Virg (Hesbert
3.3415–16)
†Isa 7:23, etc.

*of Jerusalem.**

7. Unhappy and wretched are those who, like thorns and briers,† prick such a soul with unrestrained signs or speech. Lacking the sweetness we described above, they are handed over to the demons to be mocked. But beyond that, they also become Satan's servants, exposing others to his darts and persecutions as much as they can. O, what a pleasant show do such people

*Matt 10:1

put on for the unclean spirits!* They unhappily tear away their voice, their tongue, their mouth, and finally their heart itself and their whole night's labor from

*Luke 5:5

the hands of the most holy angels,* who had already taken all of this to that heavenly temple to be placed

*Rev 8:2-4
*1 Cor 10:20

on the divine altars *in God's presence.** Thus *they sacrifice* everything *to the demons, and not to God.** Therefore, they deserve to hear, *My soul hated* your new moons, your sabbaths, and your sacrifices; *they have become*

*Isa 1:13-14

*offensive to me.**

8. O you, holy soul, friend of God, bride of Christ, and dwelling place of the Holy Spirit, bear patiently

*2 Macc 7:17;
1 Pet 2:20

with such people.* If they attack you and you bear them patiently, they will not overcome you. If they try to entice you, they will not lead you astray. Nor will they be able to turn you away from yourself and toward them, making you like them and unlike those holy spirits who stand by you. Rather, may your bridegroom boast of you, saying, *As a lily among thorns, so is my friend among the daughters!**   *Song 2:2

9. So, dear brothers, if you are spiritual,* do not   *Gal 6:1
grow angry when you see someone like this. Rather, pray for such a person. Speak to your intimate friends the blessed spirits who are with you. Pray that they raise *a sign over* this *dark mountain** so that, held back   *Isa 13:2
by the memory of the Lord's passion and cross, such people are *put to shame and blush** and so return to the   *Ps 82:18
unity of heart and voice.*   *RB 19.7

10. Then it adds, *Lift up your voice, raise up your hand.** And so, because we have come upon a passage   *Isa 13:2
from the Night Office, the lifting up of the voice corresponds to chanting the psalms, and the raising of the hand is appropriate to prayer.* And lest we com-   *Ps 140:2
pletely neglect the letter here, the lifting up of the voice can express that fervor that is so necessary for an assembly of brothers. This fervor leads to that interior fire spreading everywhere through the sound from the mouth. The brothers can thus raise one another up and light a spark in one another, until one flame springs from the many, lighting those *rich burnt offerings* that the angels bring to the divine altars *for a pleasing odor.**   *Rev 8:3-4;

11. The raising up of the hand also recommends   Lev 17:6; Eph 5:2;
purity of prayer, as the apostle says, *Raising pure hands*   Ps 65:15
everywhere without anger or argument.* Those whose   *1 Tim 2:8;
consciences rejoice in the memory of good works   Jerome, In Isa 6.4
when they pray lift up pure hands in prayer. Such people raise themselves in a kind of confidence and offer themselves to the divine gaze. This confidence must come forth from innocence or repentance. One must either do what need not be mourned, or weep as befits one's acts.

12. But when, you ask, can I assume that I have worthily and sufficiently repented? Absolutely never. From where, then, does such confidence arise? O, dear brothers, we are comparing *the spiritual to the spiritual.** *All the best gifts and every complete gift is from above.** Is it in our power, I ask, to pray as we like? Is it the case that when we want it we break down in tears, or burn with devotion, or are raised up in confidence, or inflamed with charity, or raised on high in contemplation? You know from experience that none of these is in our power. *God* sends *his Son's Spirit into* our *hearts, crying, Abba, Father.**

*1 Cor 2:13
*Jas 1:17

*Gal 4:6

13. Therefore, this *Spirit* distributes these dispositions in prayer, *dividing to each as he wishes.** He himself pours out a saving groan into the hearts of those praying to such an extent that he can even be said to intercede *for us with inexpressible groans.** Inexpressible, I say. For who can express the variety of ways that the mind is influenced in prayer? At times, shame makes us groan for our sins. At other times, we groan with fear at the prospect of punishment. Sometimes, devotion provokes a groan out of our longing, and then love makes us groan for our desire. But we also often feel remorse from the consideration of our present unhappiness or weakness, and we groan with disgust at this life.**

*1 Cor 12:11

*Rom 8:26, 34

*2 Cor 5:2, 4

14. Sometimes we consider the sins that we have committed, the punishment that we fear, and the kingdom that we hope for, and we remember the boundless kindness of God all around us. Despite these meditations, no sense of sadness moves us, no fear pricks us, and no desire for heavenly blessedness raises us up. Often, while not imagining any of these things, we are suddenly seized into all of it. We pass from emotion to emotion in an inexpressible way, and a shower of tears floods us.

15. Why is this? Certainly because the *Spirit blows where he wills, and you hear his voice and you do not know*

where he comes from or where he is going.* You know
when he comes, because he does not let himself go
unnoticed when he blows. You know when he goes,
because lukewarmness takes the place of the fading
fervor, making you notice that he has stopped blow-
ing.* But you do not know where he comes from or where
he is going.†* Where could the Spirit come from, *or where
could he go,* since he fills *the entire world?§* For this
voice is none other than his: *I fill heaven and earth.‡* And
yet he comes, and you do not know where he comes
from; and he goes, and you do not know where he is
going.

16. You certainly do not know where he comes from:
from the chamber of mercy, the tribunal of justice, the
abyss of judgments,* or the storehouse of wisdom.†
For we can say that he comes forth from the chamber
of mercy when he comes to arouse the lukewarm,
sting the sinner, or console the afflicted.* When he
rewards the good worker with the sweetness of spiritual compunction, we say that he has come down to
us from the seat of justice. But sometimes he breathes
profitable feelings into the minds of those for whom
all things work together for the worse.* These people,
ungrateful for the kindnesses shown to them, are set
aside for punishments. Both good and evil work together for their torment. In such a case, do not doubt
that the Spirit has arrived from the abyss of judgments.* But trust that he has come out of the storehouse of knowledge if the soul, cleansed by his visit,
becomes more luminous and able to examine the secrets of divine knowledge.*

17. *But you do not know where he comes from,†* since
you do not know *if* you *deserve love or hatred.§* You cannot know whether he is granting you mercy, bestow-
ing a reward on you, or exercising Judgment against
you. *You do not know where he is going,** whether he
remains close by and will return shortly, or whether
he is going far away, not to come back for a long time.

*John 3:8

*Bernard,
SC 74.5–6
†John 3:8
§Wis 1:7
‡Jer 23:24;
Oner, Adv 1 =
Aelred, S 47.1

*Ps 35:7
†Rom 11:33;
Col 2:3

*Aelred, Spec car
2.8.20; Aelred,
S 80.14

*Rom 8:28

*Ps 35:7;
Oner 19.33

*Rom 11:33;
Col 2:3
†John 3:8
§Eccl 9:1

*John 3:8

You do not know if he is offended, leaving never to return. And so he blows when he wants, *where he wants*, and just as he wants, *distributing to each* what he wants, *in the way he wants.**

*John 3:8; 1 Cor 12:11

18. Whenever the Spirit raises the mind of someone praying to a kind of confidence, do not doubt that this person's hands are raised on high. After everything that had clouded the conscience is erased, the Spirit casts out absolutely every fear and every concern for transgressions from the heart. He makes this person certain of salvation at that moment in a wonderful and inexpressible way. Because this happens with the holy angels' help, the following can be taken as referring to them: *Raise up your hand.**

*Isa 13:2

19. There are three kinds of sins that we commit, namely, of thought, word, and deed. The prophet demands three things of us against these three kinds of sins: *On the dark mountain, raise a sign, lift up your voice, raise up your hand.** For our heart, since it is lofty by nature and unsearchable in its depths,* can be called a dark mountain. We must always fortify ourselves with the memory of the cross so that we do not sin in thought. And we are ordered to lift up our voice so as not to sin in word. This command is necessary, especially now, when nearly everyone's tongue busies itself all day with base and harmful affairs. Rare is the person who lifts up the voice on high.*

*Isa 13:2
*Jer 17:9

*2 Chr 5:13

20. O, dear brothers, it is shameful to speak of how, when a group is gathered together, slander sounds forth on all sides and judgments boil up.* I will remain silent about the lovers of the world,* whose every word concerns profit or filth. What shall I say of those who have supposedly renounced worldly affairs, whose every dispute or conversation, nearly, is about their stomach? I will not say that they speak in favor of its pleasure, but rather, its burden.* Now they are reeling with anger, now cast low by sadness, now afire with hatred, now weighed down by murmuring, now losing control in conflicts. Their minds always

*1 Cor 11:20
*1 John 2:15

*Aelred, S 51.16

resemble their intestines and stomach, from which they derive either their joy or their pain. They certainly do not lift up their voice, but shamefully cast it down. The same can be said for those who spend the entire day about other people's business, those who boast of their own works, those who disparagingly discuss the conduct of others, and those who announce what is empty and superficial while passing over what is serious and useful.

21. Against all of this, the prophecy orders us to lift up our voice so that our speech treats heavenly things. It should instill the fear of God, pour forth love, increase wisdom, or regulate conduct. We are also ordered to raise up our hands and store our treasure *in heaven, where neither rust nor moth will destroy it.** We should thus send all our works to heaven, not performing our *righteous works in the presence of others to be* seen.** *Matt 6:1

*Matt 6:20

22. *And let the leaders enter the gates.** Everything that we have said, brothers, about raising the sign, lifting up the voice, or raising up the hand, is a kind of a gate, if I may put it thus, through which the virtues are led into the soul. The virtues are like a heavenly army that can completely drive out the vices that had formed Babylon, the city of confusion. Thereafter it can be called a holy community, *a faithful city.** Let us understand the *leaders* of this army to be the main virtues: prudence, temperance, fortitude, and justice. If our thoughts are holy, if our words are good, and if our works are pure, these leaders will enter the gates and subject the entire soul to their authority, filling it with virtues and preparing a dwelling for the Holy Spirit. *Isa 13:2

*Isa 1:26; 48:2; Rev 21:2

23. This sermon has occupied us longer than we had thought it would. Would that it were as useful as it is long! Let us wait for another time to examine and discuss what follows, imploring him *who has the key of David, who opens and no one can shut, who shuts and no one can open,** that he may deign to open whatever is shut in his Scriptures, Jesus Christ our Lord, who lives and reigns forever and ever. Amen. *Rev 3:7

Homily 6

1. As you remember, beloved, we have already completed five sermons on the burden of Babylon. In those sermons, we discussed as best we could the dark mountain, the raising of a sign, the lifting up of the voice, and the raising up of hands. It may seem unlikely that these verses were, as we claimed, prophetically addressed to the preachers of the New Testament.* But the words of the Lord speaking in the prophet express the same thing. For he says, *I commanded my sanctified ones and I called my strong ones in my anger, those rejoicing in my glory.**

*Oner 4.1

*Isa 13:3

2. For he had ordered that all his commands be carried out, but he did not specify who should perform them. It is as though someone approached him and asked, "Lord, to whom are you entrusting such great and lofty tasks?" He answers, *I commanded my sanctified ones,* etc. It seems to me that these words refer to three orders of preachers. He calls the first order *sanctified,* the second the *strong ones in* his *anger,* and the third *those rejoicing in* his *glory.* Three stages of the church are also mentioned here: the first of election, the second of persecution, and the third of peace. For *sanctification* can refer to election, *anger* to persecution, and *glory* to peace.*

*Oner 10.2

3. First, then, Christ chose the apostles and disciples, whom he calls *sanctified.* It was especially for them that, after his final discourse at the supper, he poured out his prayer with a wonderful and inexpressible

yearning to the Father. *Father,* he said, *I do not ask you
to take them from the world, but to keep them from evil.
Father, sanctify them in truth.** And later, *I sanctify myself
for them, that they also may be sanctified in truth.**

4. The ones who were truly sanctified in truth, then,
are those who were all the more fruitfully sanctified
the nearer they were to him. For they were sanctified
by the presence of his body, by the doctrine of his
sweet mouth, by the commendation of his powerful
prayer, and, finally, by the fresh *outpouring of* his holy
*blood.** The prophet says quite aptly, *I commanded,* that
is, I ordered, *my sanctified,†* so that you understand that
here he is talking about those who received the ministry of preaching and the office of apostle from his
own honeyed mouth. But because persecutions were
to harass and temptations test the church founded by
the apostles, he continues, *I called my strong ones in my
anger.**

5. God's anger is understood in many ways in the
Scriptures. For it is said that God is angry when he
afflicts, when he restrains himself, when he resists
people's desires, and when he shows favor. It is said
that he was moved against Job, whom he allowed to
be afflicted. For God himself says to Satan, *And you
have moved me against him in vain.** But to those whom
he spared despite being angry, he says, *My zeal will
withdraw from them, and I will not grow angry with them
anymore.** Although angry, he left some *to the desires of
their heart,** and again, angry, he fenced in the paths of
many *with spines,* so that they would not find *their
lovers* whom they sought.† And thus the affliction with
which he permits his own to be afflicted is also called
anger.

6. He also allowed persecutors to wear out his
church. He allowed this not so that the church would
lose virtue, but so that it would amass a reward. Yet
this punishment is not wrongly called God's *anger.*
This is not on account of the providence of the one

*John 17:1, 15, 17
*John 17:19

*Heb 9:22; 1
Pet 1:2
†Isa 13:3

*Isa 13:3

*Job 2:3

*Ezek 16:42

*Ps 80:13; Aelred,
Spec car 1.26.75;
Oner, Adv 23 =
Aelred, S 47.23;
Oner 1.15; 21.11
†Hos 2:6-7

allowing it, but on account of the pain and perception of those experiencing it, because they did not know what would come of it in the future. However, this anger could truly refer to those who, at the time of persecution, left the faith and did not return by the weeping of repentance. He was truly angry when he allowed these people to be afflicted; their temporal punishment was the occasion of eternal damnation. For *it would have been better for them not to have recognized the way of truth than to have turned back after recognizing it.**

*2 Pet 2:21 var

7. We can also see God's anger raging against the persecutors of the holy ones. As was said of Pharaoh, these persecutors were roused up for the very purpose of God's showing forth his strength in them and making *known his power.** He allowed them to be hardened lest they believe,† blinded lest they see, and stirred up to kill the believers. For this reason it was written in this same book of Isaiah, *Blind this people's heart and stop up their ears and close their eyes, lest by chance they see with their eyes and hear with their ears and understand in their heart and are converted and I cure them.**

*Ps 105:8; Rom 9:17; Exod 9:16
†Exod 9:12

*Isa 6:10

8. The holy martyrs proved themselves strong before this anger of God, which punished the chosen to crown them and the condemned to make them known, and allowed sovereigns to rage so that they might be damned more completely and unhappily.**

*Josh 6:20; Isa 13:2

9. In a wonderful way, just as princes had conquered the world for themselves by battle, so the martyrs conquer it for Christ by suffering. The sign is truly raised* when the cross is placed on a king's crown for glory,* the same cross that before had been a terror for punishment, a disgrace for abuse. The glory of Christ began to appear even to the world when throughout the entire earth temples were overthrown, idols were trampled, and martyrs were crowned. Christ's holy preachers rejoiced in this glory of Christ. The prophet said of these preachers, *I called my strong ones in my anger, those rejoicing in my glory.**

*Isa 13:2
*Hab 2:16

*Isa 13:3

10. Thus, he commanded his sanctified ones and called his strong ones, or those rejoicing. He gave orders to his sanctified ones, whom he cheered with his presence, whom he instructed with the teaching of his own mouth. Ascending to heaven, he entrusted them with the office of preaching and the administration of the sacraments, saying, *Go, teach all the nations, baptizing them in the name of the Father and of the Son and of the Holy Spirit.** He called others to be either martyrs or doctors when he was *physically absent* but *present* in his divinity.* He justified those whom he called and sent those whom he justified to call and instruct others.*

* Matt 28:19

* 1 Cor 5:3

* Rom 8:30

11. As long as there are heralds of the truth, the prophet can call them *sanctified* for their chastity, *strong* for their charity, and *rejoicing* for their hope. For nothing is holier than perfect chastity, nothing stronger than charity, and nothing more delightful than the hope of heavenly things. And these are the virtues that faith sought, that persecutions tested, and that Christ's shining glory strengthened. Thus faith conferred sanctity, anger tested love, the contemplation of glory strengthened hope. But let us too, beloved brothers, be sanctified in his grace, *strong* in his anger, and *rejoicing in* his *glory.**

* Isa 13:3

12. General scriptural usage suggests that *sanctification* refers to chastity. For when the children of Israel are told, *Be sanctified tomorrow,* or *on the third day,* they are forbidden physical union for a certain period of time.* This explains the story of David seeking bread from the priest. The priest told him that there was not any *lay bread* there, but *only the bread of the proposition.* When the priest asked if the *boys* were pure, *especially from women,* David *answered: As far as women are concerned, we have refrained from yesterday and the day before yesterday, and the vessels of the boys are holy.** This is why the apostle says, *Each one should know how to keep the vessel in sanctification and honor and not in the passion of desire.**

* Josh 7:13;
Exod 19:15

* 1 Sam 21:3-6

* 1 Thess 4:4-5

13. We must recognize that there is a physical chastity, a chastity of the senses, and a spiritual chastity. Physical chastity concerns restraining one's will from every forbidden defilement. The chastity of the senses consists in keeping all the sense organs free from every forbidden pleasure. Spiritual chastity involves driving away all unclean dispositions and impure thoughts from the eyes of one's heart and casting them out before they seize the flesh and the desires.

14. O beloved, a kind of temporal sanctification was shown to that carnal people, to whom only carnal things had flavor.* This sanctification is of the flesh alone, only preventing lust in the lower members. We are not only ordered to observe that continual carnal sanctification, but additionally a more sacred law of punishing all our senses is imposed upon us. It is in this way that we may be cleansed also *from every defilement of flesh and* spirit,* and thus, sanctification may be brought to completion in us. This complete sanctification does not subdue one member of our bodies to the laws of chastity, but places all the senses of the interior and exterior person under itself by a constant claim.*

15. And so, brothers, let us not allow the time to pass negligently. Let us carefully consider if some impurity is still in our eyes, if empty and poisonous words pollute our ears, if our hands are clean, if our nostrils are pure, if our speech is holy, if our palate is restrained, if our face is free from inconstancy, and if our gait is free from vanity. Let us then cut loose everything that is contrary to our sanctification, so that a kind of sweet fragrance may arise from each of our members and senses,* and thus our *burnt offering may be rich.** From there, let us climb to that spiritual chastity that is more excellent than the other kinds. Let us set free all the desires and movements of the heart not only from every uncleanness but also, insofar as this is possible, from every wandering pleasurable

*Rom 8:5

*2 Cor 7:1

*Exod 29:28

*Exod 29:18, 25
*Ps 19:4

impulse.* Thus uniting interior continence to exterior,   *Cassian,
Conl 14.11
let us pour out one sacrifice to God as an offering from
the union of the two. Happy, happy are those who,
whether they eat, drink, listen, speak, *or whatever else*
they do or think, do everything for the glory of Christ.*   *1 Cor 10:31
Such people are sanctified by Christ and sanctify
themselves for Christ. Thus sanctified in the truth,*   *John 17:19
they may participate in the secrets of the heavenly
commandments as one of those of whom he says, *I
commanded my sanctified ones.**   *Isa 13:3

16. Then comes strength, which is necessary in
temptations. For it is impossible to preserve that fullness of sanctification so pristinely in this life that
temptations never spoil its serenity. Our Lord seems
to be sweet, friendly, and agreeable during times when
everything is peaceful and quiet. But when he leaves
us unprotected from the temptations of the flesh or
the demons' suggestions, or afflicts us with this
world's troubles, or crushes us with persecutions, it
seems to us that he is somehow stern and angry. And
happy are those who are strong in the face of his anger.
At times they resist, at times they fight, at times they
despise their trials, and at times they flee. Thus, they
are not found weak or feeble, giving in or losing hope.

17. And so, brothers, whoever is not found strong
in the face of his anger will not be able to rejoice in his
glory. Therefore, if we pass *through fire and through
water* without the fire burning us or the water drown-
ing us,* to whom does this glory belong? Is it ours to   *Ps 65:12;
Isa 43:2
rejoice in as though it were our own? Not at all! How
many people, brothers, rejoice when others praise
them, seeking their own glory from God's gifts and
not rejoicing in God's glory!* Seeking *their own interests*   *John 7:18; 12:43;
Isa 13:3
†Phil 2:21
and not those of Jesus Christ,† they both lose what is
theirs and do not obtain what is Jesus Christ's. And
so those *who do not seek* their own *glory*, but Christ's,*   *John 7:18; 8:50
rejoice in Christ's glory, understanding that there is
nothing to boast of in ourselves, since nothing is ours.

18. The city of confusion thus collapses in each individual if chastity casts out lust, strength conquers temptations, and humility shuts out vanity. Furthermore, we receive sanctification in faith and the sacraments of Christ, strength from Christ's charity, and rejoicing from hope in Christ's promises. Therefore, let us do as much as we can so that faith sanctifies us, charity strengthens us, and hope brings us joy in our Lord Christ Jesus, *to whom be the honor and glory forever and ever. Amen.**

*Rom 16:27

Homily 7

1. Immediately following the prophetic verses we discussed yesterday come those that we will take up with you for explanation today: *The voice of the crowd in the mountains like a numerous people, the voice of the din of kings and of nations gathered.** We must first ask whose *voice* this is: the prophet's or the Lord's. Then we must ask whether it belongs to the preceding lines as a continuation of that idea or whether this *voice* is the beginning of another prophecy, which a change in meaning marks off from what came before.

*Isa 13:4

2. These seem to me to be the words of the prophet rejoicing and lifting himself up in a joyful shout of the mind for what he saw in the spirit, which clearly fits with the passage before it. For he perceived that the kings and princes of the world would turn to Christ after the long and hard dangers of the persecution. He saw that Christ's church would shine throughout the entire world and would rejoice in his glory.* A great crowd of saints, who had hidden in caves and caverns at the time of persecution,* would run about everywhere with wonderful ardor, freely and boldly preaching God's word. The secular powers would hold back the remnant of Babylon by dread of their authority. When the prophet had seen all of this, he broke forth in a voice of exultation *from the fullness of his heart,** crying, *The voice of the crowd in the mountains!*† This should be read with wonder, as though admiring and rejoicing.

*Isa 13:3

*1 Sam 13:6;
Heb 11:38

*Matt 12:34 and
parallels; Ps 41:5;
Isa 48:20
†Isa 13:4

3. It seemed to the prophet that in the spirit he heard the voice of those preaching and rejoicing, teaching and correcting, and he said, *The voice of the crowd in the mountains!** *Mountain* means clarity, because *a city placed on a mountain cannot be hidden,** nor can someone who stands on a mountain remain concealed, nor can the voice of someone speaking on a mountain remain inaudible. Thus, after the church began to rule through the emperors, it could no longer lurk in the darkness. After the saints could preach openly and instruct whomever they wished in the evangelical teaching, the church could no longer whisper in nooks.*

4. Therefore, he said, *The voice of a crowd in the mountains like that of numerous peoples.** For the number of preachers at that time was so great that it seemed comparable to a crowd of peoples. But if you prefer to interpret the crowd of numerous peoples as the crowd of believers,** your interpretation is not without reason. On such a reading, countless common folk had long wallowed in the valleys of the vices. But when the church gained peace and the saints were free to preach, the common people ascended the mountains—that is, the teaching of the apostles and prophets—*in a voice of rejoicing and confession.** The psalmist says of them, *May the mountains take up peace for the people.** And elsewhere, *Its foundations*—those of the church, undoubtedly—*are in the holy mountains.** These are the mountains to which we raise our eyes, and from which help will come to us,** their wisdom enlightening us and their example teaching us.

5. *The voice of the din of kings and of nations gathered.** One can perceive great fear in the din with which the kings believing in Christ ordered by royal edict that the temples be torn down, the idols smashed, and the godless sacrifices abolished. So it is that the prophet spiritually heard the sound of the din, that is, of their great fear concerning Babylon: *The voice,* he said, *of the*

*Isa 13:4
*Matt 5:14

*Oner 16.15

*Isa 13:4

*Acts 5:14; 4:32

*Ps 41:5

*Ps 71:3
*Ps 86:1

*Ps 120:1

*Isa 13:4

*din of kings.** We know that the lowly converted to the catholic faith by the example of their superiors: the poor by the example of the rich, the weak by the example of the strong, the simple by the example of the wise, and the nations by the example of their emperors. It is for this reason that the prophet added, *and of nations gathered.*

6. How were they gathered, and from where? There was surely not one place where the people might be gathered to allow them all one voice and one will in the same judgment and desire. And yet *they were gathered,* called, of course, *from the east and the west, from the north* and the south.* Thus kings and nations coming together in one catholic and apostolic church might cry *to the Lord from the ends of the earth,[†] together with one mouth praising* and honoring *God, the Father of our Lord Jesus Christ.** The prophet then seems to repeat this same meaning with the following words: *The Lord gave the order to the army of war, to those coming from a distant land.**

7. He calls the kings and nations an *army of war.* This is the war for which he roused the might of kings, the glory of the rich, the diligence of the wise, and, finally, the faith of the nations to conquer the city of confusion and its princes, the powers of the air.* This is the army that came from a distant land, unlike the one that came from nearby, which the Savior himself in the flesh chose from the Jews for the first defeat of the devil-worshiping city.*

8. For the people who had *the covenant, the law, the allegiance, and the promise, from whose fathers Christ came according to the flesh,[†]* seemed to be nearby. They were near, worshiping the one God and living under the mysteries of Christ's future incarnation. For they believed that the incarnation would come to pass in the same spirit of faith with which we believe that it has already taken place. But the nations were far off, without the law, without faith, *without God in this world.**

*Isa 13:4

*Isa 43:5, 9;
Ps 106:2-3;
Luke 13:29
†Pss 60:3; 3:5

*Rom 15:6; Luke
2:20; Jerome, In
Isa 6.8

*Isa 13:4-5

*Eph 2:2; 6:12;
Cassian,
Conl 8.12

*1 John 4:2;
Augustine, Conf
8.2.4; Aelred,
Spec car 1.26.73
†Rom 9:4-5

*Eph 2:12-13

They were far off, those whom vices dominated, those from whom the virtues were far away in exile, those for whom there was no hope of heavenly things, no expectation of things to come. Therefore, the prophet aptly says, *to those coming from a distant land.** From *land*, of course, that is, from earthly, muddy works, from earthly affections and cupidity, from the desires and stains of this world.

9. As to where it says, *The Lord gave the order to the army of war,** the word *order* emphasizes the power of divine virtue and grace. By this power, he roused the nations inwardly with an unspeakable inspiration to hear, he enlightened them to believe, and he instructed them to come and recline *with Abraham, Isaac, and Jacob in the kingdom of God.** For we can interpret the *kingdom of God* to be the church. In the church, the nations were taken up to share in the *lot* of the patriarchs.** Cut off from the *wild olive tree* of unfaithfulness, they were grafted *onto the good olive tree** and made sharers of *the root and fat.** They obtained the promised blessedness of Abraham, Isaac, and Jacob, sharing with them in the merits of one and the same faith.

10. But also today, dear brothers, Christ leads some from nearby and others from afar to the spiritual army. He *makes those of one custom dwell in a house,** those whom he clothed *in the armor of God, so that* they could *stand against the snares of the devil.** Therefore, the psalmist says, *Let those whom the Lord redeemed speak, those whom he redeemed from the hand of the enemy, those whom he gathered from the regions.** For there are both neighboring and remote regions. From these he gathered his saints and chosen ones, who had placed *his covenant above sacrifices.**

11. It was *a distant region* to which *the younger son* went forth *and there* wasted *all* his *possession by living wantonly.** But since the father is understood as God, how could the son withdraw from him or return to him who is everywhere? What region is distant for

*Isa 13:5

*Isa 13:4

*Matt 8:11;
Luke 13:29

*Acts 26:18

*Rom 11:24

*Rom 11:17

*Pss 67:7; 132:1

*Eph 6:11

*Ps 106:2

*Ps 49:5;
Matt 24:31

*Luke 15:13

him outside of whom nothing exists? But the distant region is unlikeness, just as likeness is proximity.* And so the Father is near to him who resembles the Father completely. Although he himself is not the Father, yet he is just what the Father is. It is said of this likeness, "As the Father is, so too is the Son."

* Aelred, Spec car 1.4.11; 1.7.23; Augustine, Conf 7.10.16

12. The Son can neither approach the Father nor withdraw from him. He can be neither more nor less like the one who is the very same as he himself is, because he cannot be other than him. For he was not made *in the image and likeness* of the Father,* but he himself *is the image* and likeness of the Father,* begotten from his substance,† and not from any other. But that son who was not born but made, and made *in* his *image and likeness**—that is, he himself is not made to be the image and likeness *of God,** but made to have the *image and likeness of God* impressed on and expressed in his being*—can both withdraw, because he is able to be unlike God, and return, because he is also able to become like him.

*Gen 1:26

*2 Cor 4:4; Col 1:15 †Heb 1:3

*Gen 1:26

*2 Cor 4:4; Col 1:15

*Gen 1:26; 5:1

13. We must consider two specific categories that, although they are one in the Creator, are two distinct things in creation. These categories are nature and virtue. Immortality and incorruptibility belong to nature; wisdom and love belong to virtue. These are one in God, because these properties in God are not anything but God himself. Human beings, on the other hand, possessed immortality and incorruptibility according to the nature in which they were created. They also possessed both wisdom and love, which were superimposed on them. But because human beings are not in themselves immortality, incorruptibility, wisdom, or love, they could separate themselves from these qualities and become unlike God. They could also return to them through grace and become like him again.

14. So virtue and its reward of blessedness are the region of likeness. The region of unlikeness is vice and wretchedness. Humanity first became unlike God through vice, so that it could rightly become unlike him through wretchedness. For this reason, we must first become like him by virtue, so that someday we may be made like him in blessedness. Furthermore, the more full of vice we are, the more we are unlike God, and therefore more distant from him. But the more virtuous we are, the more similar we are to God, and therefore closer to him. In fact, for as many virtues as exist, there is an equal number of regions, each belonging to that region of likeness that contains all the virtues. Likewise, for as many vices as exist, there is an equal number of regions, each belonging to that region of unlikeness in which all the vices exist.

15. For individual vices or virtues exist in their regions, outside of which one can scarcely or never find or possess them. Thus chastity is a virtue whose region can be called abstinence, but also labor and keeping vigils, and above all, interior solitude. Chastity dwells in this region. Let the conscience of each of you examine whether chastity could also be found outside of this region. But on the other hand, fornication is a vice whose region is gluttony, sleepiness, idleness, and above all the dwelling together of disorderly people. So too charity, which is a virtue, dwells in the region of voluntary poverty, but avarice, which is a vice, dwells in the region of the love of temporal things. It is easy to perceive how this also pertains to other vices and virtues.

16. Of course, those who do not surpass the limits of marriage are near to chastity; but those who are stained by fornication, adultery, or open lewdness are far removed from it. Similarly, those who lawfully use what is theirs without plundering the goods of others are near to charity, while those who neither mercifully distribute what is theirs nor abstain from seizing what belongs to others are far removed from it. After you carefully examine how this applies to other vices and virtues, consider how many come from far away and how many from nearby to join this army to which you have sworn obedience.*

* Isa 60:4; Jer 25:26; Matt 8:11

17. Therefore, those who climbed from the dung heap of the vices to the mountains of the virtues came from a far-off land. In these mountains, one voice is heard from all those chanting psalms as one, living as one, praising as one, and desiring the one. Hearing this voice in the spirit, the prophet said, *The voice of a crowd in the mountains like that of numerous peoples, the voice of the din of kings and of nations gathered.**   *Isa 13:4

18. For in this spiritual army, some are kings and others are common folk. It is the kings who rule and the common folk who obey, or else the kings are the perfect and the common folk the imperfect. The kings are a terror to the people, just as the perfect are to the imperfect and superiors to their subjects. This is why it said, *The voice of the din of kings.* So, brothers, *may thanksgiving and a voice of praise sound forth* in your mouth and *in your hearts.** For you have gone forth not only from the vices but also—and this is given to few people—from the regions themselves of vices. You have stood in the mountains of the virtues, and from the likeness of God that you possess in the virtues, you hasten to that blessedness that is still absent.   *Isa 51:3; Song 2:14; Eph 5:19-20

19. But if you wish to interpret the kings and common folk as the vices and virtues, remember what I said to the brothers in chapter on Epiphany.[1] On the occasion of the three Magi who *came from the east,** we discussed as best we could the vices and virtues and their regions. Indeed, you can fittingly apply that sermon here, if you refer the kings, nations, regions, and the journey they made to Christ, to what was written here.   *Matt 2:1

20. But bypassing all of this,* let us restore ourselves with both prayer and silence for the next topics that we will investigate and discuss. May Christ himself remove the veil from our eyes to consider the *wonders of his law,** he who with the Father and the Holy Spirit lives and reigns as God, forever and ever. Amen.   *RB 1.13

    *Ps 118:18

---

[1] Aelred is referring to what is apparently a lost sermon.

Homily 8

1. In few words but with deep meaning, the prophet has thus far described Babylon's burden in the following sense:* it was destroyed through our Lord's coming in his holy preachers, who separated many people from that city. Now the prophet's word turns to those who either *did not accept the truth of the Gospel, that they might be saved,** or corrupted the truth of the faith they received with wicked works: *From the height of heaven the Lord and the vessels of his fury, to destroy all the land.** It is not the land we tread that he claims will be destroyed.* Rather, he wants us to understand *the land* to be those people who taste nothing but the earth,* who put the divine promises after earthly desires, who prefer temporal things to eternal, and who spurn the truth of the Gospel and become entangled in the vanity and errors of the world.* The prophet's judgment cited above declares that these people must be destroyed.

2. We should recognize that sinners can be destroyed in two ways. They are destroyed when, turning to the Lord in repentance, they cease to be what they were and begin to be what they were not. Such is the case where it says, *Turn the wicked, and they will not be.** And they are certainly destroyed when, falling from bad to worse, they are finally delivered over to eternal torments. Let no Christian doubt that the Lord himself, who shows mercy on whom he will,* brings about the first kind of destruction for his own people.

*Oner 21.1

*2 Thess 2:10 var; Gal 2:14

*Isa 13:5

*Deut 1:36; 28:23
*Phil 3:19

*2 Thess 2:10

*Prov 12:7; Aelred, S 82.9

*Exod 33:19; Rom 9:18

Scripture's authority shows that his judgment brings about the second kind of destruction, but through the service of the evil spirits. For the devil put it in Judas's heart first to betray the Lord* and then to hang himself,* and the Lord *sent* the Egyptians *anger, displeasure, and distress, brought in through evil angels.* *John 13:2 *Matt 27:5 *Ps 77:49

3. Let us recognize that the reason for all this—why one person should be taken up and another abandoned,* why this one should be converted to be healed, while another should be handed over to the demons to be hardened or punished—belongs to the hidden judgments and deep purposes of God.* Therefore, it says, *From the height of heaven the Lord and the vessels of his fury, to destroy all the land.* It seems to me that *the height of heaven* is the lofty and blessed Trinity. From the Trinity comes forth the immutable judgment that our Lord Jesus, *the son of man,* to whom God the Father *gave the power to judge,* should destroy some through repentance and others through punishment. Repentance comes about through Christ himself, that is, by his interior inspiration; punishment, through vessels of his fury that have received power to rage against the godless. Therefore, *From the height of heaven the Lord and the vessels of his fury, to destroy all the land.* Understand *the vessels of his fury* to be the opposing powers at work *in the faithless children.* Thus, the one *who is in the dirt may still grow dirty,*† the one who is blinded may still be blinded, and the one who is hardened may still be hardened.

*Matt 24:40 and parallels

*Rom 11:33-34

*Isa 13:5

*John 5:27

*Isa 13:5

*Eph 2:2; Jerome, In Isa 6.9 †Rev 22:11

4. Perhaps you think that this phrase should be joined to the one above it. Thus, the preceding phrase, *The Lord gave the order to the army of war, to those coming from a distant land,* would be explained by the words that follow, where it says, *From the height of heaven the Lord and the vessels of his fury.* If this is so, then we should interpret what follows consistently with the meaning that came before. Not only did *the Lord give the order to the army of war, to those coming from a distant*

*Isa 13:4-5

land, so that what was foretold might come to pass. Additionally, *The Lord himself came down from the highest heaven* so that through the vessels of his fury he might destroy those who did not believe in his vessels of grace.* Yet I prefer to think of this as the beginning of another section. Thus in the previous verse we find a description of how the faith of kings and nations overthrows Babylon. In the following verse, we find a prophecy of the conversion or damnation of those who did not believe, or of those who, believing, fell. We should also read what follows according to this double meaning.

5. It follows, *Wail, for the day of the Lord is near.** The prophet announces wailing to sinners, whom he foresaw would wail either in punishment or repentance. For *wailing* aptly represents crying out in profound mourning. Either torments wrench this wailing from the wretched or repentance draws it forth from sinners' hearts. For what do we think, my brothers? After the persecutions came to an end and the church reigned in a state of peace, how great was the confusion of those who had fallen away? How much contrition was in their hearts, how dreadfully did their conscience roar within them,* how tearfully did they lament! *Wail,* it says, *for the day of the Lord is near.** The prophecy calls the Day of Judgment *the day of the Lord.* On that day, the Lord appearing in power *and majesty will render to each according to their works.** That day, of course, begins for each of us when we leave the body.† We will then receive either the firstfruits of beatitude in rest, or the beginning of damnation in the soul, which we will later also receive in the body.

6. This day *will* certainly *come as desolation from the Lord.** From the Lord, of course. For truly, Lord, *the number of* our *months is in your presence* and *you established* our *limits that cannot be exceeded.** *As a desolation it will come from the Lord.** For what will that day not lay waste? *Naked I came forth from my mother's womb,*

* Ps 18:7;
John 3:13;
Rom 9:22-23

* Isa 13:6

* Job 3:24; Ps 37:9
* Isa 13:6

* Matt 16:27;
Ps 61:13;
Luke 21:27;
Matt 25:31
† Jerome, In
Isa 6:10

* Isa 13:6

* Job 14:5
* Isa 13:6

said a certain holy man, *and naked I will return there.**   *Job 1:21
Where, then, is the wealth, where are the pleasures,
where are the heaps of gold or silver, where are *the
crammed storehouses, flowing from here to there?* Where
are *the fruitful sheep* and *the fattened cattle,** where the   *Ps 143:13-14
silk garments and the warhorses? All things are
brought to nothing for the dying person. For *when
people die, they do not lay claim to anything, nor does their
glory go down with them.** That day overtakes and de-   *Ps 48:18
vours whatever strength was in their body, whatever
enjoyment in their flesh, whatever pleasure in their
senses, and whatever pleasing in their habits.

7. Happy is the mind from which the memory of
this day does not fade. Solomon bears witness to how
useful it is to meditate on death when he says, *Child,
always remember your last moments and you will never
sin.** For who would take pleasure in sinning if that   *Sir 7:40 Vulg
hour were always before their eyes? Therefore, wail
in repentance, O sinner, so that you are not compelled
to wail in punishment. May the Lord's Day in your
memory make you bitter against the world's pleasures
so that it does not make you bitter in experience. And
may you hear what follows: *Because of this all hands will
grow slack, and every human heart will waste away and
crumble.** *Hands* should be understood as activity.   *Isa 13:7-8

8. O, brothers, just as the Lord says, we *must work
while it is day. The night will come when no one can work.**   *John 9:4
*Blessed are the dead who die in the Lord. From this point
forward, the Spirit says, they may rest from their labors.**   *Rev 14:13
Therefore death is the night, *when no one can work.** For   *John 9:4
we will either rest in our good works or be punished
in our evil works. Therefore, on that day of the Lord,
*all hands will grow slack.** On that day, some will be sent   *Isa 13:7
into the outer darkness *with their hands and feet bound;**   *Matt 22:13
others, after six days' work,* will be received by the   *Exod 20:9-10
sabbath,* which is rest, and admitted to inner delights.   *Gen 2:2
For *from this point forward, the Spirit says, they may rest
from their labors.** Therefore, *Do whatever work your hand*   *Rev 14:13

is able, because there is neither work nor reason in the hell to which you hasten.* For *all hands will grow slack.*† And what do you say, you who trust *in* your *virtue and* boast *of the extent of your wealth?**

*Eccl 9:10
†Isa 13:7
*Ps 48:7

9. Understand this, dearly beloved. Some do almost no works, some do evil works, some do good works badly, and some do good works well. That wicked and lazy servant who buried the money he received in the ground did almost no works.* He neither cheated anyone from what he received nor profited from it. Those like him are lazy and lukewarm. It seems to such people a great thing just to refrain from crimes, although they do not devote any labor or persistence to acquiring virtues. It is, therefore, as though they were without hands. What will they do at night, *when no one is able to work?** Clearly *their works* will not *follow them.* Therefore they will not rest.* They have no works in which they could rest. *All hands will grow slack* and will thus not have the strength to work.* What will remain, then, except that the useless servant also be cast out *into the outer darkness?**

*Matt 25:18, 26

*John 9:4
*Rev 14:13

*Isa 13:7

*Matt 25:30

10. Those who work well send their good works before them to God. After they die, they may rest and boast in their works with slack hands. Likewise, those who work badly send their evil works before them to hell, where they will be forever punished. For *torments will powerfully afflict* those who are *powerful* in evil here,* the cruel will be cruelly tormented, the stench of sulfur will plague those stinking of lust, the Tartarean flames will burn those whom avarice kindles, and never-dying worms will feed on those whom gluttony and drunkenness defile. Pay attention to yourself, O human!* For as often as you sin, you send before you to hell the material for punishment with which you could be tormented. You yourself light the fire that will torment you, you provoke the stench that will torture you, you bring to life the worms that will consume you,* you prepare the darkness that will blind

*Wis 6:7

*Sir 13:16

*Mark 9:43, 45, 47

you. Then your *hands will grow slack,** so that they are neither fit to work nor strong enough to resist, but can only passively suffer.

11. What about you who do good badly, you who are not *like other people: robbers,* fornicators, *adulterers,* or *this tax collector?** You are not a lazy servant;† you fast *twice a week and* give *a tenth part of what you* have.§ You labor, you work, you gather many things. But where do you send it all, where is it kept, and where will it be found? Certainly, *the day of the Lord is near,** and then *night* will follow, *when no one can work.** I ask, where is everything you gathered? *All hands will grow slack.** From this point forward it is not the time for working. Indeed, *from this point forward, the Spirit says, they may rest from their labors.** This clearly concerns those of whom it is added, *For their works follow them.** Will your works thus follow you after you have sold them or scattered them *with every wind?** Whatever good works you gathered you sold for the cheap price of human praise, you spent them on the gain *of base profit,** or you allowed the winds of vanity and pride in your soul to blow them away. And you believe your works will follow you? When you have nowhere to be consoled, what is left except to suffer torment?*

12. This applies to you, too, beloved, who do good works well. I do not want you to trust *in* your *virtue* or to boast *in the extent of* your *wealth,** though it be spiritual, because at that time *all hands will grow slack.** How, you ask? Because *all our righteousness is like a menstrual rag in his sight.** For *no living being will be found righteous in his sight.*†

13. Therefore, everyone must wail. The wicked must wail to avoid the damnation that comes from continuing in their wickedness. The lazy and lukewarm must wail so that God does not spit them out of his mouth because they are neither hot nor cold.* So too those who do good badly, so that they do not enter *the land by two roads.** But those who do good well should also

*Isa 13:7

*Luke 18:11
†Matt 25:26
§Luke 18:12

*Isa 13:6
*John 9:4

*Isa 13:7

*Rev 14:13
*Rev 14:13

*Sir 5:11

*Titus 1:7; 1 Tim 3:8; Jude 16

*Oner 4.9

*Ps 48:7
*Isa 13:7

*Isa 64:6;
1 Cor 1:29
†Ps 142:2; Jerome, In Isa 6.10

*Rev 3:16

*Sir 2:14

wail, so that the hidden Judgment of God does not condemn them. Thus, the prophet says, *Wail, for the day of the Lord is near; as a desolation it will come from the Lord,** so that the good may fear and the wicked may mourn upon glimpsing death nearby. May those who do not wish to wail in punishment thus learn to wail in repentance.

14. It may seem that this verse addresses everyone. Yet according to the order of the prophetic message, it especially threatens either those who fell in times of persecution or those whose wicked deeds disgraced them in times of peace. The prophecy both encourages repentance and threatens punishment to such people, who have the ability both to be converted and to act well while they live. This ability of course is taken from all upon their death. For then *All hands will grow slack, and every human heart will waste away and crumble.**

15. O brothers, rotting flesh gives rise to decay. It will not stop oozing until it is completely rotten. Decay brings with it both horror and stench. Let us all look at our heart, let us see on what foods it feeds.

16. God's word, of course, is a food of the soul. This food never goes bad, nor does it produce decay or corruption in the person eating it. Good works are also a food of the soul, as the Lord says in the gospel: *My food is to do the will of the one who sent me.** Saving compunction is also a food of the soul, as the prophet says: *You will feed us with the bread of tears.** And again, *My tears were my bread, day and night.** Devotion to God is also a sweet food of the soul, like the grain's fat that fills Jerusalem. As the psalmist said to the city, *And he fills you with the grain's fat.** These kinds of food provide life-giving nourishment to the soul of the person eating them. They transform the soul into the food itself, making it a sharer in its own eternity.

17. There are other very harmful kinds of food that foster decay and induce rotting. These are pigs'

*Isa 13:6

*Isa 13:7-8

*John 4:34

*Ps 79:6
*Ps 41:4

*Ps 147:14

husks.* The soul often greedily desires and feeds on *Luke 15:16
them with such delight that they cause disgust for
heavenly food and provoke nausea for manna, the
angelic food.* This is *meat that rots in a sinful people's* *Ps 77:25;
teeth, those who are wretchedly buried *in the tombs of* Num 11:6, 20
concupiscence,* consumed by the very decay that they *Num 11:33-34;
themselves created. Deut 9:22

18. And so *fornication, adultery, theft, blasphemy,** and *Matt 15:19
things of this sort are pigs' husks,* that is, the food of *Luke 15:16
the demons. Although they may taste delicious in
human hearts, they are the source of decay and rot. A
person will either healthily perceive their stench and
horror in repentance or will perceive them as a punishment in the conscience when death approaches. For
*every human heart will decay and crumble** when the flu- *Isa 13:7
ids of uncleanness and the filth of the vices ooze from
all the crannies of the conscience.* That *worm* that *does* *Jerome,
not die is conceived and the *fire* that *is not put out* is In Isa 6.10
kindled from such material.* These are the worms that *Mark 9:43,
make those hearts crumble in punishment that have 45, 47
not here been crushed in repentance.* *Ps 50:19

19. *Every human heart*, it says, *will decay and crumble.** *Isa 13:7
Every human heart refers to the heart of someone living
according to human standards. The apostle said of
such people, *Since there is rivalry and strife among you,
are you not human?** In the previous verse when the *1 Cor 3:3, 4
prophet said, *all hands will grow slack,** he did not *Isa 13:7
qualify it with *human*. This is because both good and
evil works cease with death, but only the heart and
conscience of those who live according to human standards crumble. Therefore, dear brothers, do not let
this hour fade from your memory. If it has been a cause
of fear, may it later become a gate of salvation,* *Matt 7:14
through Jesus Christ our Lord. Amen.

Homily 9

1. Speaking for the church, Hezekiah deplores these unhappy times on which this our age has fallen, saying, *Behold, in peace my bitterness is very bitter.** Truly, brothers, this is so. Persecution seemed bitter, but in persecution itself there was no small consolation for good people, for everyone standing in the ranks of the good, both subjects and superiors. Then there was no room for deception, no time for idleness or negligence.* Then a kind of happy necessity compelled nearly everyone to be perfect. But once that fear was taken away, negligence was born and ambition grew. Now honors and riches are preferred to virtue and pleasures feed the vices.

2. After the prophet Isaiah described the apostolic preaching and the martyrs' courage, he saw that many would fall into a worse state in times of peace, after the persecutions came to an end. He instilled a healthy fear of the coming disaster in them, saying, *Wail, for the day of the Lord is near; as a desolation it will come from the Lord. Because of this all hands will grow slack, and every human heart will decay and crumble.** We discussed this yesterday, as you know, brothers, and explained, just as the Lord provided, how it could pertain either to the repentant or to the dying.* It follows, *Torments and pain will seize* them,* referring to those whose hands are slack and whose hearts are decaying and crushed. *Torments* pertain to the belly, *pain* to the limbs.*

*Isa 38:17

*Aelred, Spec car 2.17.43

*Isa 13:6-8

*Oner 8.5–19
*Isa 13:8

*Jerome, In Isa 6.11

3. O brothers, all shame starts with the belly, but the other limbs carry out wicked deeds. Gluttony, which results in a full belly, provokes the stings of lust. From lust, fornication and all kinds of uncleanness arise. On the other hand, *blasphemy* is uttered with the tongue, and *theft, murder,* and the like are committed with the hands,* with the help of the eyes to investigate, the ears to hear, and the feet to approach.† Therefore, understand *torments* to mean the mental anxiety that arises from the memory of shame as death draws near. But *pain* is the anxiety born from the memory of wicked deeds.

*Mark 7:21-22;
Eph 5:3
†Aelred, S 53.10;
Augustine, Doct
chr 3.10.16

4. For what great sadness will shameful people endure, my brothers, when they see that they deserve eternal punishments from the festering of such trivial and brief pleasure!* And what anxiety will overcome the evildoers, whose cruelty is repaid with most cruel torments! What do you think, beloved? Will these insipid foods that you eat yield no flavor at that hour? Happy are those for whom the pleasures of the stomach do not prepare such torments, whose members are circumcised here so that they do not later feel such pain!*

*Oner 13.6

*Rom 2:29;
Phil 3:3
†Isa 13:8

5. *Torments,* it says, *and pain will seize* them.† How much more useful it is to have torments come before torments, to have pain keep pain at bay! Thus, let us suffer all this—or rather, let us suffer much less—by repenting, and so not be compelled to suffer such things by dying! And so you undergo spiritual torments insofar as the memory of the pleasure you have experienced afflicts your mind and rouses desire, provoking loathing and horror at this plain food.* But these torments allow you to escape those torments that many experience at death. You will rejoice to hear the holy patriarch's judgment between the purple-clad rich man and the poor Lazarus as though it were addressed to you: *You received good things in your life, and Lazarus bad things. But now he is consoled, and you are tormented.**

*Aelred, SS
72.25, 82.13

*Luke 16:25

6. It continues, *As though giving birth they will suffer pain.** O brothers, there is no *pain as of one giving birth.*† But there is a physical birth, a spiritual birth, and a punitive birth. And certainly, *a woman is sad when she is in labor, because her hour has come.** Pain takes hold of her members; death, her eyes; and fear, her conscience. She does not know how it will turn out.

7. A spiritual birth takes place when the holy ones give birth to spiritual children by instruction and care. One such holy person said, *My little children, with whom I am again in labor.** And this birth is not *without pain.*† For such a person must *rejoice with those rejoicing,* weep *with those weeping,*§ be weak with the weak, burn with the scandalized,‡ and much more. It is also a spiritual birth when the *barren* and *unfruitful* soul conceives *by fear* of the Lord.# Turned toward the Lord, such a soul gives birth to the beginnings of good works. And what pain lies in this birth when the flesh resists the spirit and habit resists the will!* One moment, the mind desires good works, and the next it does not; one moment it fears, and the next it trusts; one moment, desire for the good impels it, and the next, the pleasure of evil pulls it back!

8. A harmful birth takes place when a person conceives *pain and* gives birth to *iniquity,** when it conceives from a desire* to acquire and gives birth by carrying out* that desire. This is why the Lord said in the gospel, *Woe to you who are pregnant or nursing!** Woe indeed to those conceiving and giving birth in this way. Even if now they exult *when they do evil* and rejoice *in wicked things,** as though giving birth they will suffer pain when death draws near.* For just as a woman who conceives in pleasure suffers great pain when she is in labor, so too the soul, corrupted by pleasures and vices, is crushed by sadness and pain when the wages of corruption begin to appear at death.* When the soul's belated repentance is turned back on itself, it will begin to feel what is written: *Walk*

*Isa 13:8
†Ps 47:7;
Lam 1:12

*John 16:21

*Gal 4:19
†Ant et Resp
Nesciens mater In
Nat Dom
(Hesbert 3.3877;
4.7212)
§Rom 12:15
‡2 Cor 11:29
#Exod 23:26; Isa
26:18 var
*Gal 5:17

*Ps 7:15
**affectus*
**effectus*
*Matt 24:19

*Prov 2:14
*Isa 13:8; 42:14

*Rom 6:23

*in the light of your fire and in the flame that you lit for yourselves.** *Isa 50:11

9. We can call a birth *punitive* when someone dies in a condition of punishment as though giving birth. The dead receive the punishment they conceived by sinning, as though giving birth to a most unhappy progeny. How much more happily does a person conceive repentance for sins from the fear of God and give birth to conversion of life!* This birth, although not without pain, prepares joy in tranquility of conscience, because *when she gives birth to the child, she does not remember her distress anymore on account of her joy,** and *whoever sows tearfully will reap joyfully,** and *Blessed are those who mourn, for they will be consoled.** Therefore, everyone who abandoned the faith—whether overcome by torture during persecution or corrupted by vice during peacetime—*as though giving birth will suffer pain,** either by profitably repenting or unhappily dying.

*Isa 26:18 var; RB 58.17
*John 16:21
*Ps 125:5
*Matt 5:5
*Isa 13:8

10. *They will all gape at their neighbor.** Look at this, my beloved brothers. *Neighbor** can refer to many kinds of relationships, such as that of place, time, nature, family ties, similarity, love, and compassion. It can refer to place, as when one place is said to be the neighbor of a nearby place. To time, as when one person immediately succeeds another. It can refer to nature, in that all people are one another's neighbors. This is why it is said, *You will love your neighbor as yourself.** No Christian doubts that this refers to every person. It can refer to family ties, as the relationship of a child to a parent, a sibling to a sibling, or a relative to a relative. It can refer to similarity, as a good person to a good person or an evil person to an evil one. Even if time or place separates them, we regard them as neighbors because of their similarity to one another. Further, love joins people and makes them neighbors. In this way, there was *one heart and one soul of the crowd of those believing* in the

*Isa 13:8
*proximus

*Matt 22:39 and parallels

*Acts 4:32

Lord.* It can refer to compassion, as when the gospel bears witness that the Samaritan *was a neighbor to the person who fell upon thieves,* because *he was merciful*

*Luke 10:36-37, 33

to him.

11. Likewise, anyone living in a *just, sober, and godly* manner is a neighbor of anyone else living in the same

*Titus 2:12

way.* An angel is also a neighbor, favorably inclined to one living thus. God himself is also a neighbor, giving the grace to do well to anyone living in this way. And so too, any wicked person is the neighbor of any other, whether human or spirit. For the spirit of fornication is called the neighbor of fornicators; the spirit of pride, the neighbor of the proud; and the spirit of

*Aelred, S 54.8

blasphemy, the neighbor of blasphemers.* We all clothe ourselves with a likeness through our vices or virtues, and we deserve our proximity to our neighbors. We must believe, therefore, that both good and evil spirits are present to the dying. The good spirits take up the good, and the evil spirits torment the evil.

*Isa 13:8

12. Therefore *they will all gape at their neighbor.* For anyone dying in filth cannot help but gape when the demon of fornication appears. For what had seemed alluring and pleasant at the moment of enticement turns bitter when the rebuke comes. Such wretches gape to find hard and severe what they had often experienced as agreeable. It is important for us, brothers, to make neighbors for ourselves who will be a consola-

*Resp *Libera me* Pro defunct (Hesbert 4.7091)

tion and not a terror to us at that dreadful hour.* Happy are those who deserve to have the angelic spirits as neighbors through a clean life and honorable habits. Thus these spirits will be like friends and neighbors standing by those going forth, rejoicing in them as in a familiar acquaintance.

13. We read in history books that angels have often stood by those with a worthy faith. The saints, too, have often been present in time of urgent need to those who had revered them with a special devotion. But we also know of evil spirits with fearful visage and flaming eyes, and armed with hellish instruments, appearing to those who had contaminated themselves with vices and crimes by living according to their suggestions. And therefore, wonder and astonishment strike the holy ones going forth from the body to such brightness, and anxiety confounds the condemned departing for such horror. And so *they will all gape at their neighbor.** *Isa 13:8

14. It then follows, *Their faces will have a burnt aspect.** I think this refers to the condemned alone. People perceive one another through each one's face or expression, and it is by a certain appearance that individuals recognize one another. Moreover, it is customary to brand the face of those condemned of certain crimes. In this way, the criminal cannot hide; one cannot hide one's face, and so neither can one hide the crime that the face's deformity makes known. It seems to me that the soul's face is its conscience, which is the witness of all its actions, words, and thoughts. For whatever someone is like cannot be hidden from that person's conscience. Indeed, the conscience is like the mirror of the soul. We perceive our progress or failure in this mirror, and we recognize in it the full condition of our interior person.* *Rom 7:22

15. O dear brothers, let no one be careless! We sin easily, transgress easily; we easily fall into whatever is idle and vain, and what is forbidden draws us on almost without our noticing it. As it is written, *Ephraim became like a loaf unturned under the ashes. Foreigners ate his strength, and he himself did not realize it; his hair turned gray and he himself did not know it.** Yet our sins do not blow away with the wind, nor are they consigned to oblivion. Rather, they are written in the conscience itself, whether we like it or not. The apostle says that certain people have a *branded conscience,** that is, a conscience burned by the flame of iniquity. This burn is often hidden from us while we live, but it will not escape either our notice or that of the spirits present

*Isa 13:8

*Hos 7:8-9

*1 Tim 4:2

at death. Rightly therefore it says, *Their faces will have*

*Isa 13:8
*a burnt aspect.**

16. For after the hands have grown slack and the heart has crumbled, amid the *torments and pain* that

*Isa 13:8
sinners will bear when death draws near,* anything still unhealed by the medicine of repentance or by the ointment of contrition will burst forth in the open. Many things that now appear quite healthy will then reveal themselves as burnt. Labor, keeping vigils, fasting, generosity: these are magnificent works. If a corrupt intention distorts these works, they do nothing to adorn the conscience. Rather, the accuser of thoughts chars the conscience with flame.

17. Of course, someone may request that we apply this verse to those who repent. Among the pains mentioned, we can fittingly understand the pain the repentant suffer through the memory of their sins. While they carefully explore all the crannies of their consciences and brood in fine detail over every act they committed, the conscience discovers that many things appear charred by the fire of concupiscence that before had seemed clear and healthy.

18. We should categorize as *Babylon* both those who live immoderately in the church and those who have fallen from the church or the faith. Therefore, the prophet described both the *burden* that would weigh down those who turned to the Lord through repentance, and that which would crush the dying who continued in their evil ways. The prophet continues, mystically describing that wretched time in which

*Matt 24:12
iniquity will abound and *charity will grow cool.** In this way, those to whom that worker *of error* is sent will be

*2 Thess 2:3, 10
worthy of him, who is *the person of sin, the child of ruin,**

*Job 41:13;
Aelred, S 76.29
of whom it is written, *Want will go before his face.** The prophet is not silent about this *want* in the passage that follows. He first composes a prophecy about the Day of Judgment, so that out of fear we may more easily avoid the vices that will abound at that time

and more nobly bear the torments that the blasphemer will inflict on us.

19. It therefore continues, saying, *Behold, the day of the Lord is coming, cruel and full of displeasure, anger, and fury.** After the previous verse addressed each person's last day, the prophetic discourse aptly enough turns to all humanity's last day insofar as this present life is concerned. Thus, whoever does not fear the former will dread the latter. The prophet lists the following four clear signs of the coming disaster: cruelty, displeasure, anger, and fury. Cruelty is when a punishment exceeds proper boundaries; displeasure, when the baseness of a person who acted unjustly somehow becomes known; anger usually manifests itself in the voice or facial expression; rage, in action.

20. That day will be cruel, because a show of cruelty will appear on that day more than on any other, *when a fire's heat will melt the elements,** and *in the* Lord's *sight fire will burn and around him a powerful storm.** It will be a day full of displeasure, when the divine majesty and human frailty will become known, and everyone will clearly see how such great weakness raged against such great power. It will thus escape no one's notice how greatly *the king of glory* should be displeased to have suffered such an injustice from such lowly dust.* And it will be a day full of anger, when that dreadful voice is heard: *Depart from me, cursed ones, to the eternal fire that was prepared for the devil and his angels.** The rage of the one who afflicts follows this Judgment. There will then be no way to escape, no hope of fleeing for those headed for the eternal burning.

21. *To place the land in solitude,* it says, *and to crush sinners from it.** Whether you interpret *land* as the world or as that earthly city of Babylon, it is certainly clear that it will then be placed *in solitude.* For after some have been carried to heaven and others assigned to hellish punishments, *the land* will remain *without inhabitants,* that is, a world *without people.** That

*Isa 13:9

*2 Pet 3:10, 12
*Ps 49:3

*Ps 23:10

*Matt 25:41

*Isa 13:9

*Isa 6:11

forsaken city will be left alone, without the company of any good person. Then too, the sinners of the land will be crushed from it. The sinners of heaven are de-

*Ps 16:3

mons; as soon as *iniquity was found in* them,* they were crushed from heaven, *and there was no place for them*

*Rev 12:8

there *anymore*.* But the sinners of the land are those who sin daily and yet continue to dwell in the land. Finally, when Judgment is given on the last day, they will be utterly crushed and driven down to hell.

22. It continues, *Because the stars of heaven will not shine forth their light. The sun will be dark when it rises,*

*Isa 13:10
*Col 3:4

*and the moon will not shine with its light.** Indeed, on the Day of Judgment, when Christ appears in glory,* this brightness will overwhelm all the stars. As a small lamp in sunlight seems not to give forth any light, so will onlookers perceive the stars to be dark on

*Jerome, In
Isa 6.13

that day.*

*1 John 2:18

23. But I think we can also refer what we have briefly said about the Day of Judgment to the time of the Antichrist.* We can thus understand that the prophet, learned in the Spirit, ordered his prophecy to treat first the preaching of the apostles, then the persecution of the church, after that, the conversion of the nations and the tranquility of peace—and so also, the repentance of the fallen and the dread of death—and finally, the time of the Antichrist, with the reward of the righteous and the damnation of the wicked. But because the hour has already passed, let us address what needs to be explored at another time, when we can gather together without interruption and open our mouths in unison *in the praise and glory* of our Lord Jesus Christ, who with the Father and the

*Phil 1:11; Deut
26:19; 1 Cor 11:20;
Oner 18.27

Holy Spirit lives and reigns as God forever and ever.* Amen.

Homily 10

1. *Behold, the day of the Lord is coming, cruel and full of displeasure, anger, and fury.** As you remember, beloved, we said that these words of the prophet could refer to the time of the Antichrist, although they could also fittingly be taken to refer to the last day. But in applying it to the time of the Antichrist, we can understand that holy Isaiah not only foretold the various conditions of the church but also preserved the order in which they were to take place.*

2. The prophecy began by presenting the apostolic preaching, saying, *Raise a sign over the dark mountain*, etc.* It then foretold the persecution that would crown the martyrs, saying, *I commanded my sanctified ones*,* and what follows. Beginning from *The voice of the crowd in the mountains*,* it announced the peace that the conversion of the kings and nations bestowed upon the church. It went on to speak of the ruin or conversion of those who fell away by yielding to persecutions, or who disgraced themselves with vices during times of peace, saying, *From the height of heaven, the Lord and the vessels of his fury*, etc.* Then, striking them with the fear of death, it added, *Wail, for the day of the Lord is near*, etc.* Finally, the prophet saw that, in a time of growing wickedness, almost the entire human race would be on the verge of abandoning the truth and forsaking charity, entangled in vices and errors. This is why he composed the prophecy about the time when the worker *of error* will be sent to such people,

*Isa 13:9

*Oner 9.23

*Isa 13:2
*Isa 13:3

*Isa 13:4

*Isa 13:5

*Isa 13:6

so that they believe in a lie and so that all are judged who

2 Thess 2:11-12; do not believe in the Gospel of God.
1 Pet 4:17

3. And it is for this reason, or so it seems to me, that the prophet uses the phrase *the day of the Lord* to refer to that time. The wicked one will come forth like a sword of God's fury from the abyss of his Judgment as *from a sheathe for the punishment of evildoers, but for

1 Pet 2:14; Ezek the praise of the good. The prophet calls this day cruel,
21:4; Ps 35:7   because such *will be the distress as had not existed since

Matt 24:21;   the nations had begun to be until that time. He calls it *full
Dan 12:1   of displeasure,*† because the proud one will grow angry
†Isa 13:9   with the holy ones* throughout the land.§ Then he will
§Dan 7:21   see that the poor despise him as rich, the humble despise him as lofty, the weak despise him as strong, and the lowly despise him as glorious. He will see that they do not wish to yield to his rule, but rather wish to resist his decrees and to go against his commandments.

*Isa 13:9   That time will also be full *of anger and fury.* He will express his anger in threats and his fury in torments. For *this is how* the beast's *anger will rage against* Christ's worshipers: sitting *in God's temple as though* he himself

2 Thess 2:4;   were God, he will frighten Christ's worshipers with
Num 16:22   threats, deceive them with miracles,† and compel them
†2 Thess 2:9;   with torments to consent to his wickedness. God's just
Jer 23:32   judgment will permit the beast to do all this *to place

Isa 13:9; Wis   the land in solitude, and to crush sinners from it.
16:18; 2 Thess 1:5

4. We should take *the land* here to represent Christ's church, of which it was said, *The Lord's is the land and

Ps 23:1   its fullness. It was also said to Moses about this land,
*Exod 3:5   *The place where you are standing is holy land.* In this land, the good live together with the evil, the humble with the proud, the drunk with the sober, the chaste with the lustful, and false Christians with true ones. Therefore, at that time the Lord will bend that wretched one's wicked will to his own most righteous severity. He will use that wretch's dominion as a winnowing fork to thoroughly cleanse his own threshing floor. The wind of the evil one's persecution will make

the chaff fly off the floor, separating it from the grain.* *Matt 3:12;
The holy land will thus maintain a kind of healthy   Job 21:18
solitude for the few good people still remaining in it.*   *Exod 3:5;
However, we could also interpret this solitude accord-   Isa 13:9
ing to the opinion of those who will consider Christ's
church to be lowly and trampled at that time, *as though*
*reduced to nothing.** Then certainly *its sinners* will be *Job 17:7
crushed *from it.**   *Isa 13:9

5. This is also the case for those in Christ's church
whom pleasures and wantonness deform, whom ambition crushes, to whom poverty is a burden and the
Gospel an object of ridicule. We should realize that
they will either despise the promises or suffer torments for Christ. For now, *the mystery of iniquity is*
working in them.* Because the church now reigns in   *2 Thess 2:7
faith, many of them publicly preach it, although they
secretly disparage it. They argue in the schools as
though they were in favor of faith, but they mock the
same faith in the bedroom and in hidden nooks. They
use their profession of faith to obtain a full pantry, a
stuffed pocketbook, and privileged *greetings and the*
*highest seats.** But when it comes to the perfuming   *Luke 11:43
room and chalices, to the bedrooms and *hidden dis-*
*graceful things,** they casually dismiss the catholic faith, *2 Cor 4:2
they explain away the resurrection of the body as impossible, they mock the Last Judgment, and they excuse lust as a natural need. Thus they either proceed
to that blasphemy of the foolish—*The foolish said in*
*their heart: There is no God**—or certainly to that audac- *Pss 13:1; 52:1
ity of the wicked, which the psalmist mentioned, say-
ing, *Why did the wicked one trouble God? For he said in*
*his heart, He will not ask.**   *Ps 9:34

6. Before, every perversity among the Jews, which
was the cause of their eventual desolation, as it were,
took its beginning from the scribes and the Pharisees.
They possessed the key of knowledge and handed the
decrees of the law to the common folk. In the same
way, we clerics and monks, we who seem to be *lights*

*Matt 5:14; Phil 2:15; Gen 1:16

of the world*—it pains me to say this—are now sowing the origins and causes of future evils. Concerning this, it follows, *Because the stars of heaven will not give forth their light, the sun grows dark when it rises, and the moon*

*Isa 13:10

will not shine forth its light.* It seems to me that these are signs of a future disaster, of which the Lord says in the gospel, *There will be signs in the sun, the moon,*

*Luke 21:25

and the stars.* If you want to know which signs, listen to the prophet Joel: *The sun will turn to darkness and the moon to blood before the great and clear day of the Lord*

*Joel 2:31;
Acts 2:20

comes.*

    7. O, brothers, *God made two great lights: the greater*

*Gen 1:16

light to rule the day, and the lesser light to rule the night.* God also created two great lights in the holy church's firmament: priesthood and royalty, king and bishop, prince and cleric. Day means spiritual; night, worldly. So the greater light, the priesthood, is to rule the day, that is, the things of the spirit; the lesser light, royalty, is to rule the night, that is, the things of this world.

    8. It is against nature for the sun to rule the night or for the moon to rule the day, for princes to take it upon themselves to perform the sacraments or for priests to cloud the bright sky of their consciences with the darkness of worldly affairs. For *none of God's soldiers*

*2 Tim 2:4

entangle themselves in worldly affairs.* After King Uzziah presumptuously entered the Holy of Holies as though

*2 Chr 26:16-21;
Eccl 6:9

he were a priest, he was struck with leprosy.* Covetousness blinded the prophet Balaam, who indulged the desire of the ungodly king against God's will after

*Num 24:16

the prophetic light had opened his eyes.*

    9. O, how fitting were these two lights, how brightly they shone forth from this spiritual firmament, how excellently did they divide the *days, months, times, and*

*Gal 4:10

years.* The king and priest confined themselves to their spheres: the king's power served only the peace and tranquility of his subjects, and with his wisdom and teaching, the priest was on guard to drive the darkness away from souls and pour in the light of truth! Woe to us who have fallen on these unhappy times in which the sun seems to have turned to darkness! What darkness, you ask? I do not want to say, brothers, I do not want to say, lest I should seem to place my mouth in heaven. It is for them to say.

10. Let them call to mind those whose office they bear, whose chairs they occupy, in whose insignia they boast. Let them consider what rays of knowledge, what lights of virtues, what sparks of charity, what bolts of spiritual correction Gregory, Augustine, Ambrose, Hilary, Martin, and thousands of others gave forth in their times. Let them reflect on how more recently our Cuthbert, Wilfrid, John, Dunstan, and hundreds of others shone forth in their times. Did not all of them make the priesthood radiate with an incomparable light throughout the entire world like one great sun? Let them see now how these saints shone brightly from their chair. Let them see whether they themselves shine forth as much or more or less, and so compare their times to ours, their merits to ours, their character to ours, and let them judge according to *the witness of their conscience* whether the *sun* has turned to *darkness.** Happy are the times in which a wicked person is so rarely found as a good person is today!

*Joel 2:31; Acts 2:20; 2 Cor 1:12

11. And now, what shall we say of royal power, which we thought should be compared to the moon, which rules the night?* For it shone forth its light when kings and princes were a consolation for good people and a terror to the wicked, driving away the darkness of this night, that is, the darkness of wickedness and unrighteousness. They were the fathers *of orphans and* judges *of widows,** defenders of the churches and bulwarks against injustice, high in power but low in humility, desiring *to do good rather than to rule.** Such was Constantine, such was great Theodosius, and there were many others besides.

*Gen 1:16

*Ps 67:6

*RB 64.8

12. But *the moon will turn to blood* when the princes' *hands* will be full of blood,* spilling the guts of the

*Joel 2:31; Acts 2:20; Isa 1:15

*Job 16:4

wretched with taxes and tolls,* *justifying the ungodly for bribes and* taking the *justice of the just* away *from*

*Isa 5:23

*them.** They devour the people like prey, showing themselves to be tyrants rather than kings, destroyers of the poor rather than counselors. They confuse and interchange the just and the unjust, the permitted and the forbidden, following not duty and fairness but

*Aelred, S 64.15

their own lust and stomachs.*

*Matt 24:29
*Gen 1:16

13. *And the stars will fall from heaven,** it says. The stars are not said to rule the night.* But because they too give it light, I think we should take them to be those who, renouncing the world, live in heavenly

*Ant et Resp *Iste sanctus digne* In comm Confess (Hesbert 3.3432; 4.7009); John 14:2; Phil 3:20
†Gen 1:16; Matt 5:14; Phil 2:15
§Phil 3:8

dwelling places in their thoughts and desires.* They were truly *lights of the world* at that time,† elevated above the entire world by their lives, customs, love, and contemplation. They despised all earthly and time-bound things, thinking of riches and honors *as dung.§* They were chaste in body, pure in mind, and unmoved by the humiliations and wrongs brought upon them. They subjected themselves to their superiors by humility and obedience. They were satisfied

*Jas 1:19

with little food of low quality, slow to anger,* ready to serve, reluctant to receive, and never seeking their

*1 Cor 13:5; Phil 2:21

own but *what is Jesus Christ's.**

14. What can I say, dear brothers? What can I say? What are we? Where are we? Are we in heaven? Are we in the same place that formerly Anthony, Macarius, Hilary, and many others were? Or rather, have we not

*Matt 24:29; Rev 9:1; 6:13
†Phil 3:19
§1 Cor 11:16
‡Jude 16; RB 4.39
#Gal 5:15
≈Jas 4:11; Gal 5:26; Oner 18.5

fallen *from heaven to earth,** we who taste almost nothing but earth,† love the earth, think of the earth, speak of the earth, we who are contentious,§ argumentative, murmuring,‡ biting at and devouring one another,# envying and disparaging one another?≈ What are market days without monks? What is the public square? What are assemblies? I will be silent concerning the many who are so absorbed by the earth that neither land nor sea would be enough for their gluttony. They turn aside from nothing that pleases them. They

trouble and torment the wretched over whom they
rule like Pharaoh's overseers,* wrenching away
money more cruelly than any worldly leader. Fattened
by the blood of the poor, bloated, extended,* they
burst forth even to the point of buying and selling
sacred objects.

15. After foretelling the time of the Antichrist as
follows—*Behold, the day of the Lord is coming, cruel,*
etc.*—the holy prophet immediately explains why
they deserve the Antichrist to either deceive or crush
them, saying, *Because the stars of heaven will not shine
forth their light.** What light, I ask, will darkened people
shine forth, those who have transformed themselves
from stars to coal, crashing from heaven into the filth?
*The sun grows dark when it rises.** O brothers, many
shine at the beginning of their priesthood. They have
an irreproachable life, an upright intention, and were
well chosen. Yet their lifestyle changes and they grow
dark. But when the time of the Antichrist draws near,
greed and ambition will rule over human minds in
such a way that even the beginning of their vocations,
like the sun's rising, will be full of darkness. A wicked
life will precede their elevation, and a twisted intention and poor start will follow. So the *sun* will grow
dark *when it rises and the moon will not shine forth its
light** when, as we said earlier, *the sun will turn to darkness and the moon to blood,* so that *the great and clear day
of the Lord* may follow.*

16. But some may prefer to interpret the *stars* to be
the perfect of that time, those who *will not shine forth
their light,** that is, their knowledge and miracles, in
the darkness of persecution and deceit occupying all
things. We will not reject this understanding if what
follows fits with it. If indeed it is correct to interpret
the name *sun* as the Antichrist, on account of Satan
who *changes himself into an angel of light,** then what
the prophet says is clear: *The sun grows dark when it
rises.** As soon as his rule begins to rise, pride will

*Exod 5:14

*Deut 32:15

*Isa 13:9

*Isa 13:10

*Isa 13:10

*Isa 13:10

*Joel 2:31;
Acts 2:20

*Isa 13:10

*2 Cor 11:14

*Isa 13:10

blind him and errors will darken him. The smoke of ill-will and concupiscence will enshroud him. Then *the moon,* which is the church, *will not shine forth its* *Isa 13:10 *light,** because, after every earthly power has cast it down, the nations will trample it *for a time and times* *Rev 12:14; *and half a time.** Dan 7:25

†Isa 13:11   **17.** It follows, *And I will visit evil on the cities.*† I think *cities* should be interpreted as the congregations living in different places, under different rules and with different customs, yet sharing in the one catholic faith. For just as many citizens come together in the same city under one law, so those who come together under *Oner 18.3, 26 one order in one society form one city, as it were.** So around that time the corruption will be so great in communities of this sort that it will seem that they were formed not to worship God, but only to fulfill their desires and concupiscence. The blessed apostle said of this state of affairs, *Dangerous times will threaten* *in the final days, and people will be lovers of themselves,* *desirous, puffed up, lovers more of pleasure than of God,* *having indeed the appearance of goodness, but denying its* *2 Tim 3:1-5 *power.** There are many like this today. They wear the habit, chant psalms, and bear the tonsure. They put *2 Tim 3:5 forth *the appearance of godliness,** but they do not have its power, which lies in charity, chastity, humility, and despising pleasures. So the Lord will visit *evil on cities* *Isa 13:11 of this sort,** exacting revenge and laying bare their *Isa 47:2-3; disgrace.** They will thus either be corrected when Ezek 16:37 they are worn down by persecutions, or, if they go beyond shameful acts to infidelity, eternal punishments will crush them with Babylon when God's judg- *Wis 16:18 ment comes to light.**

    18. I see you are still eager to hear the many things that still remain. But have patience with me, for I have grown tired from such a long sermon. Let us pray that we may be found adequate for what remains to be explored, through our Lord Christ, *to whom is the honor* *Rom 16:27; *and glory forever and ever. Amen.** Heb 13:21

Homily 11

1. I confess, dear brothers, that things have not worked out as I had thought. For it seemed to me that we could deal with the mysteries of our discourse's burdens in a few sermons. But this first burden, which we still have in our hands, has already detained us for many days. And it begins once more to open a great abyss of mysteries to us here, where the Lord says through the prophet, *And I will visit evil on the cities and against the ungodly for their iniquities. And I will silence the pride of the unfaithful, and I will humble the arrogance of the strong.** But if we reflect on what we have already said in the other sermons, all this will be sufficiently clear. So let us touch on these matters lightly with a brief epilogue.

*Isa 13:11

2. At the time of the Antichrist, the Lord will visit *evil on the cities*—the cities of those who *keep up the appearance of goodness in* hypocrisy*—by dispersing their *assemblies.*† He will visit *against the ungodly for their iniquities*§ by punishing with torments or errors those who are found to be openly wicked. He will *silence the pride of the unfaithful* by bringing down the powerful of the world, those to whom the Christian faith has lost its value. He will also humiliate the arrogance of the strong,* using temptations and persecutions to put a stop to those who boast in their own virtues.*

*1 Rom 1:18; 2 Tim 3:5
†Ps 15:4
§Isa 13:11

*Luke 1:52

*Ps 48:7

3. For there are some who, because of their religious habit and participation in the common life, act publicly

101

as though they were good but are secretly wicked. We take *the cities* to represent such people. There are others who do not blush to appear evil even in the presence of others; we judge that the prophet refers to them as *ungodly* and wicked.* There are also many who are estranged from the Christian faith, even proudly mocking the faith itself. We think that such people should be called *unfaithful*. There are others who are not only faithful but also diligent in the virtues. But because they *trust in their own power and boast in themselves rather than in the Lord,* we are not wrong to call them arrogant. The heavenly oracle declared that all these people would either be completely crushed on the Day of Judgment or handed over at the time of the Antichrist.

4. It continues, *A man will be more precious than gold, and a person more precious than pure gold.* The word *man** comes from the word *virtue.†* And so the prophet points out the scarcity of virtues, saying, *A man will be more precious than gold.§* All rare things are precious, but easily acquired goods are rotten.‡ But those eager for the virtues—those who do manly or strong deeds,# who prefer a bitter death to this life's forbidden acts, who would rather be condemned by the world and tormented by an executioner for Christ than enjoy this world's pleasure—such people will be rare at that time. Thus *a man will be more precious than gold,** that is, less common. And *a person*—someone who lives according to reason, not according to physical sensation like an animal—*will be more precious than pure gold.**

5. But we can also correctly take the *gold* or *pure gold* to be the perfect ones in the primitive church.* We know that they have been tested and tried *like gold in a furnace,* and are nobly included *in the gold-embroidered clothing* worn by *the queen,* who *stands at the right of* Christ.* But the one who is found to be a *man* during that last persecution—not shrinking before torments,

*Isa 13:11

*Ps 48:7;
1 Cor 1:31

*Isa 13:12
*vir
†virtute; Aelred,
S 58.2; Isidore,
Etym 10.74;
11.2.17
§Isa 13:12
‡Jerome, In Isa
6.16; Jerome,
Ep 130.16
#Aelred, S 5.9

*Isa 13:12

*Isa 13:12

*Phil 3:15;
1 Cor 2:6

*Wis 3:6; Ps 65:10

*Ps 44:10;
Matt 25:33

nor agreeing to promises, nor believing signs and wonders*—will shine forth among the saints with a special kind of privilege in the way that gold exceeds other metals in its value and beauty.* Of course, when it says, *and a person more precious than pure gold,** it is repeating itself. What the prophecy first called *a man* it then calls *a person,* and what it first called *gold,* it later calls *pure gold.*

6. It goes on to say, *For this reason I will disturb heaven, and the earth will move from its place.** Heaven is the church of that time, or whoever in the church is regarded as perfect. The prophecy says they will be disturbed, because they will see the ungodly and the wicked battling against the holy ones with a triple weapon:* with promises to allure them, miracles to deceive them,† and torments to break them. Who, I ask, can be so perfect that such great temptation will not disturb them when *false apostles and false prophets rise up and produce signs and wonders to lead even the chosen into error, if such a thing were possible?**

7. *And the earth,* it says, *will move from its place.*† What earth? Perhaps *earth* refers to that part of the church that longingly clings to the earth. Its *place* now is either faith or the church itself. But it will move from its place by avoiding torments, admiring wonders, or assenting to allurements. It will either abandon the faith, withdraw from the church, or hide somewhere *until the iniquity passes away.** This is because many people whom *false signs* deceive will abandon the faith,* many whom torments conquer or errors fool will withdraw from the church, and many shrinking from danger will settle for any hiding place.* All such people are aptly called *earth* when compared to those who, bravely confronting every danger, are called *heaven.*

8. There will be so few learned people, and their misfortune will be so great at that time, that there will not be enough of them to gather those who are scattered, raise up the fallen, correct offenders, or console

*2 Thess 2:9; Matt 24:24

*Aelred, S 75.25
*Isa 13:12

*Isa 13:13

*Dan 7:21; Isa 13:11
†Jer 23:32

*Matt 24:24; 2 Cor 11:13
†Isa 13:13

*Ps 56:2
*2 Thess 2:9

*1 Macc 1:56

*1 Thess 5:14
the fainthearted.* It immediately follows, *And they will be like a doe running away, like a sheep, and there will be*
*Isa 13:14
*no one to gather them.** The prophet is speaking of the earth here, which will be *like a doe running away, like a sheep.* The doe is a timid animal; the sheep, a simple
*Isa 13:13
one. So *the earth will move from its place;** afraid of persecution or deceived by its own simplicity in the face of miracles, it will run away from fellowship with the perfect.

9. Therefore it says, *And they will be like a doe running*
*Isa 13:14
*away, like a sheep.** For the *doe* runs away frightened and quivering from barking dogs and pursuing hunters. In the same way, many people with timid hearts
*1 Sam 18:17
will be unable to fight in *the Lord's wars* at that time.* They will avoid the impending dangers either by withdrawing from their *place* or by conspiring with
*Isa 13:13
their persecutors.* Likewise, when the shepherds have fled or been struck and beasts attack the flock, the
*Zech 13:7; Matt 26:31 and parallels; John 10:12; 1 Chr 10:7
sheep run away, scattered *here and there.** The simple ones in the church behave in the same way. After the learned are cast out or killed, the simple will wander aimlessly and be brought to wastelands of errors, because there is no one to guide them, to *gather* those who are scattered or lead back those who have
*Isa 13:14
strayed.*

10. It follows, *And all will turn to their own people,*
*Isa 13:14
*and they will each run away to their own land.** O brothers, there are two peoples, two nations, and two kingdoms: the good and the wicked, the wise and the foolish, the chosen and the condemned. But at the time in which all things are mingled together and confused, one cannot detect to which nation or people any given person belongs. This is because many people are good insofar as outward appearance goes but are wicked in the depths of their conscience. As we said yesterday, many praise the faith verbally because they dare not do otherwise, but they attack it
*Oner 10.5
with their corrupt way of life.* And when the time of

winnowing comes,* *all will turn to their own people,*† *Matt 3:12 and parallels
†Isa 13:14
chaff to chaff, grain to grain, good to good, and
wicked to wicked. For the *thoughts of many hearts* will
be revealed when those who are now goats appear
just as they are in the company of goats, and those
who are now sheep are brought into the fellowship
of the sheep.

11. For as you heard today when the gospel was
read, *When the Son of Man comes to the seat of his majesty
and all the angels with him, all the nations will be gathered
to him, and he will separate them from one another.** Then *Matt 25:31-32
*all will turn to their own people.** For it is as though those *Isa 13:14
who will sit and judge with the Lord are one people;* *Matt 19:28
another people is that of the angels obeying the Lord;
another is that of the sheep who will be rewarded by
the Lord;* another is that of the goats, who will hear *Matt 25:34
the Lord say, *Depart from me, cursed ones.** This will *Matt 25:41
begin to take place at the time of the Antichrist. Then
the weak will appear weak, the wicked will be found
wicked, and, when persecution breaks out, *the strong
in faith* or firm in good works will show themselves
to be perfect.* *1 Pet 5:9

12. *And they will each run away to their own land.** It *Isa 13:14
seems to me that the same meaning is repeated in
different words. For whereas before it had said *all*, it
here repeats the same meaning using *each;* those
whom *people* represented are here rendered by the
word *land*, and what before the prophecy called *turning*, it here calls *flight*. But if some wish to explore these
matters in more detail, let us humor them. Let us say
that there is a land of the living and a land of the
dying; a land of the saints and a land of the ungodly.
The land of the living is Paradise, the land of the dying
is the world, the land of the saints is the church, and
the land of the ungodly is Babylon.* *Aelred, S 7.3

13. *I believe I will see*, said the prophet, *the good things
of the Lord in the land of the living.** For in Paradise, no *Ps 26:13
one dies; there, life is in the truth and truth is in

eternity. But this present world is quite appropriately called the land of the dying. Here nothing is stable, nothing is eternal,* and a person's very life is a shadow of death.* Christ's church is the land of the saints, of which Scripture says, *Let us have mercy on the ungodly, but they will not learn to act righteously; they have worked iniquity in the land of the saints.** Rightly is the land of the saints the church, outside of which there is no holiness, no righteousness, and no sanctification in this life. The saints' flesh can also be called their land, of which it is said, *Blessed are the meek, for they will possess the land.** Similarly, although we can call the city of confusion the land of the ungodly, their flesh is also their land.

14. Now while the church reigns, *the mystery of iniquity** does not dare to come forth from the dark caverns of many hearts. But when persecutions begin to crush the church, this iniquity will boldly burst forth. Those who are now hiding in the church will then openly run away from it, *each to their own land,** joining to themselves partners in their errors. But where will those who run away from the land of the saints go if not to the land of the ungodly, which is the city of Babylon, the city of confusion? There, various tenets and errors are found. Some pursue the desire of the flesh as the highest good, some worldly honors, some riches and delights, some the freedom of their own will. And so the wanton people's land is the enjoyment of the flesh; the land of the ambitious, desire for honors; the land of the greedy, riches; the land of unstable wanderers, their own will.* Just so, those abandoning the church and shrinking from the tribulations from which the church will then suffer will gather together in the city of ruin, each running away to their own land, that is, using their flesh for their own pleasure.

15. After the Antichrist receives dominion, he will find many entangled in Babylonian errors, and he

*Aelred, Inst incl 31
*Job 3:5; 8:9; 14:2; Ps 43:20

*Isa 26:10

*Matt 5:4

*2 Thess 2:7

*Isa 13:14

*RB 1.11

will gain possession of many who separate themselves from the fellowship of the saints as though *arriving*. It therefore rightly goes on to say, *Everyone who is found will be killed, and everyone who arrives will fall by the sword.** For the condemned whom the Antichrist finds in the city of confusion will be killed, that is, entangled in his errors and wicked teaching. *Those who arrive*, that is, who flee to him from the church, will fall from the faith they seemed to have, struck down by the sword of his mouth.* And because many of these people will have *small children, houses, and wives*,* it says, *Their small children will be smashed before their eyes, their houses will be plundered, and their wives raped.**

16. O, my brothers, it is not only the ignorant common folk who will be entangled in the errors of that most ungodly one. Many of those to whom the leadership of the churches was committed will also yield to him.* The simple can be called the leaders' *small children*, to whom they administered the sacraments of the church; the *houses* are the churches that they led; their *wives* are the teaching of the prophets and the Gospel, from which they fathered children in Christ's faith.* But when these leaders turn from true faith to error, *their small children will be smashed before their eyes.** That is to say, the simple ones will see their leaders' consent and be persuaded by the Antichrist's disciples, who mock our Lord's teaching and faith as worthless and lowly. They will then stumble *on the obstacle stone and the stumbling block, as it is written:* Whoever falls on this stone will be crushed.†* Indeed *many will fall on this stone and be crushed* when, falling from Christ's faith, they *are scandalized* by Christ.* And so *their houses will be plundered** when many are taken away from the churches that they had governed, *and their wives raped* when Christian doctrine,* which to that point was simple and pure, is stained by that wretched one's foul errors.

*Isa 13:15

*Rev 2:16; 19:21;
2 Thess 2:8

*Isa 13:16

*Isa 13:16

*Acts 20:28

*1 Cor 4:15

*Isa 13:16

*Rom 9:33;
Isa 8:14
†Matt 21:44

*Matt 24:10
*Isa 13:16

*Isa 13:16

17. If you are asking who will do these things, the Lord, speaking through Isaiah, answers, saying, *Behold, against them I will rouse the Medes, who do not seek silver or desire gold but will kill the little ones with arrows and will not show mercy to the sucklings in the womb, and* *whose eye will not spare the children.** I think that *Medes* refers either to hostile spirits or to the Antichrist's heralds. For it is clear that the deceitful powers do not seek the riches of this world, nor long for heaps of precious metals, since they are intent only on deceiving and killing souls. The contempt for gold or silver can also represent the hypocrisy of the Antichrist's disciples. Skilled in all manner of counterfeiting and disguising, they will regard gold as mud* and silver as worthless clay,* solely devoted to killing *the little ones with arrows.** For they have the arrows of logical words and shrewd arguments. With these, they can turn the small ones aside from an upright faith, those simple ones who lack *the sharp arrows of the powerful with destructive coals.**

18. *And they will not show mercy to the sucklings in the womb,** it says. The sucklings in the womb are the faithful recently formed in the womb of mother church, *those who* still *need milk* instead of *solid food.** Neither false teachers nor the demons will have mercy on their tenderness. Rather, taken from the milk of maternal charity, these sucklings are given the venom of error to drink, which kills them. No wonder, since the *eye* of the Medes does *not spare their own children,** namely, those whom they begot in errors. They always cast them down from bad to worse, drive them from smaller vices to greater ones, drag them from one evil deed to another, until falling *into the depth of evils,** they burst out in contempt for the divinity itself.

19. The Lord is said to rouse them,* which of course confirms that God's just permission arises from his most severe judgment. As it is written, *I will give them kings in my fury.** For this reason it is fitting that the

*Isa 13:17-18

*Job 14:21
*Wis 7:9
*Isa 13:18

*Ps 119:4

*Isa 13:18

*Heb 5:12

*Isa 13:18

*Prov 18:3

*Wis 16:18

*Hos 13:11

word *Medes* comes from *Medai*,* which means *from the*   *Gen 10:2
powerful, strong, or *measuring.* The strong and powerful
God assigns opposing powers or wicked people in his
just judgment.* In this way, just as he repays the good   *2 Thess 1:5
for their good works through good messengers, so too
he renders to the evil *according to their works* through
evil messengers.* This is why he establishes for the   *Ps 61:13; Rev
ungodly a certain measure not to be surpassed for   22:12 and
tempting the good or punishing the evil. Or *Medes*   parallels; Jerome,
means *measure* because the measure of punishment   In Isa 6.19
corresponds to the measure of blame, just as the repay-
ment of good *will be measured* to us *in the measure* that
we measured the fruits of good works.*   *Matt 7:2 and
   parallels

20. Of course, you can largely understand our explanation based on what we have already said about
the rousing of the Medes. But because it is not right
for me to cheat your eagerness, these same prophetic
words will be briefly repeated with a fuller explanation. But this is more suitably kept for the beginning
of another sermon. Meanwhile, the things we have
said can impress themselves fully on your souls by
constant meditation, and silent rest can prepare your
souls beforehand for the dreadful divine judgments,
through Christ the Lord our Savior, *to whom is the honor
and the glory, forever and ever. Amen.**   *Rom 16:27;
   Heb 13:21

Homily 12

1. When our Lord and Savior ascended into heaven and brought his physical presence to an end, he promised his spiritual presence to us, a presence that is not temporal but eternal, saying, *Behold I am with you every day until the fulfillment of the world.** Let no one think that the Lord will withdraw his presence at the time of the Antichrist. Rather, he will bestow great virtue on his people at that time. Not only will they despise all of the Antichrist's shrewd arguments and mock his torments, but they will even boldly go forth armed with faith to meet the beast.* They will restore many whom the beast had seduced by errors and flattery, bringing them back from every depravity to the catholic truth.

2. It therefore says, *Behold, against them I will rouse the Medes,* etc.* We can call the fully learned people of that time *the Medes*. These are the people whom Christ's power makes powerful, whom the strong one makes strong.* They do not cease supplying *a measure of wheat,** that is, of spiritual teaching, to their fellow servants,* to those laboring under temptations never before experienced. Roused by the Lord against the Babylonians—against the false Christs and false prophets*—these learned ones will despise all the temporal goods offered to them, which are represented by the price of gold or silver.* Or the silver and gold represent the worldly splendor of wisdom and eloquence of which the teachers of perverse doctrine

*Matt 28:20; Aelred, SS 9.1; 60.1; Aelred, Spec car 3.24.56

*Rev 19:19-20

*Isa 13:17

*Oner 11.19
*Luke 12:42
*Matt 24:49

*Matt 24:24 and parallels

*Isa 13:17

110

boast.* Our Medes will not seek such wisdom for themselves nor fear it in others; their greatest care will be the eagerness *to cure* souls' *wounds* and *to prepare for the Lord a perfect people.**

3. They will therefore go forth, armed with sharp arrows, against *deceitful lips and an arrogant tongue.** With these *arrows they will kill the little ones* of the ungodly,* following what Peter was told, *Kill and eat.*† For then the perfect will make sure that the witness of the Scriptures, like arrows of wholesome compunction, wound those recently led astray like little ones,* until they regain the life of faith they lost from that which killed them.

4. We should call those to whom nothing harsh or difficult is given *sucklings of the womb.** They are treated thus to hold them closer and pleasantly soothe them. What is pleasurable and pleasant is provided to them as though it were healthy, and they are given the sweetness of milk to drink rather than the bitterness of wine. But the learned will show no mercy on them so that they may thus show greater mercy.* The more affectionately zealous these learned are for their salvation, the more eagerly do they heap up whatever frightens them, whatever inspires fear, and whatever instills a wholesome pain. They will not spare even their own children,* those who are entrusted to their care, visiting *their iniquities with the rod and their sins with blows.**

5. O brothers, let us turn back to ourselves. Three things must be maintained in every good work: the virtue of discretion, the purity of intention, and the foundation of humility. Discretion pertains to the bounds of moderation, intention to the cause, and humility to the fruit. *If you rightly offer but do not rightly divide, you have sinned,* says the Lord.* Those who do good offer rightly, but they do not divide rightly if they surpass the bounds of moderation. But if you have performed good works well, consider their

Margin notes:

*Jerome, In Isa 6.19

*Luke 1:17; RB 46.6

*Pss 11:4; 119:4

*Isa 13:18
†Acts 10:13; 11:7

*Jerome, In Isa 6.19

*Isa 13:18

*Jerome, In Isa 6.19

*Isa 13:18

*Ps 88:33

*Gen 4:7 LXX

cause, with what intention you performed them, and to what end. If it was so that others might see you,* if it was to acquire some material advantage, if it was to serve your *pleasures* more freely,* then this *little bit of leaven ruins all the dough* of your work.* But if an upright intention is followed by an upright work performed with discretion, be careful lest that twisted snake—pride—should raise its head.* While you must be careful of pride *always and everywhere,*[†] this is especially so when it comes to good works.[§]

*Matt 23:5

*Titus 3:3

*1 Cor 5:6; Gal 5:9

*Job 26:13;
Isa 27:1
†Phil 4:12
§Aelred, S 54.41

6. For what if a field is perfectly tilled, if the seed is wisely scattered, if rain provides adequate water, if the stalks grow, if the heads are fruitful, if, ripening under the right amount of sun, the fruit begins to invite the eager harvester? What profit is all of this if just then a sudden storm comes, as though snatching everything from the harvester's hands? So then, what if you labor, fast, keep watch,* keep silence, are still, and persevere in works of mercy? Pride alone empties the fruit of all of these, haughtiness alone consumes them all. For this reason we should fear nothing so much as that God should abandon us on account of pride, and that *the day of the Lord* should come to us, *cruel and full of displeasure, anger, and fury.**

*2 Cor 6:5

*Isa 13:9

7. Take it as you like, but I judge that nothing crueler could befall us than to be abandoned by the Lord and left *to the desires of our heart* and *go according to our own devices.** What cruelty comes forth from God's displeasure! Because God hates and detests ingratitude above all other vices,* his displeasure rises up mainly against those who boast in themselves for their good works. O despicable pride, mother of ingratitude, moth of the virtues, and parent of the vices! You provoke the Judge's cruelty against wretched mortals, you rouse up his displeasure, you sharpen his anger, you kindle his rage. Therefore, that day when God abandons a person because of pride is a *cruel* day, *full of displeasure, full of anger and fury.**

*Ps 80:13

*Prov 6:16

*Isa 13:9

8. *To place the land in solitude,* it says.* For God
abandons the proud heart as though it were a condemned land and very near to being cursed.* What
before had seemed good and fertile land is reduced
to solitude,* sprouting *the thorns and briers* of sins and
accessible to the wild beasts of the vices.* *And to crush
sinners from it.** Look, my beloved brothers. When true
humility reigns in our breast, we are always roused
up to remember our sins, we are always provoked to
examine carefully even the good that we do. But when
pride consumes everything related to humility, it
thrusts from the sanctuary of our heart the thoughts
that used to make us feel compunction arising from
the memory of what we had done. And this is what it
means for sinners to be crushed from the land: the
memory of faults is erased after haughtiness has entered in.

9. Understand the moon to be faith; the sun, charity;
and the stars, the other virtues.* If the darkness of
pride shrouds all these heavenly bodies, they will produce no light, no grace, nothing that could please God,
nothing that could be profitable. Rather, this darkness
will fill the soul's substance with an ungodly and unfaithful dread. Hearts of this kind are like cities opposing the Lord,* closed up behind a wall of
stubbornness and fortified by towers of pride. For this
reason it is necessary that the Lord visit such hearts
with the evils that they have done,* *taking vengeance
on all their designs** and visiting *their iniquities with the
rod and their sins with blows.** For the proud and the
unfaithful are also called *ungodly,** not raging so much
against other people as against God himself.

10. Notice what a destructive evil it is that arose
from offending the divinity. This is what made an
angel into the devil and drove humanity from Paradise; the former strove for equality with the divine
power while the latter aimed at equality of knowledge.
And so, brothers, *those who think they are something*

*Isa 13:9

*Heb 6:8

*Gen 3:17
*Gen 3:18
*Isa 13:9

*Isa 13:10

*Isa 13:11

*Isa 13:11
*Ps 98:8
*Ps 88:33
*Isa 13:11

*Gal 6:3; Jas 1:26

when they are nothing deceive themselves. Those who think that they know something do not yet understand how they

*1 Cor 8:2;
Jas 1:26
†Ps 88:33
§Isa 13:11

should know. May the Lord visit anyone who is like this with the rod of his correction,† silencing *the pride of the unfaithful and* humbling *the pride of the strong!*§

11. And so it is helpful to the proud, as a certain

*Augustine, Civ
Dei 14.13

saint said, "that they should fall into some open sin."* They are thus humbled, and what was written happens to them: *You will take away their spirit, and they*

*Ps 103:29

will fail, and they will return to their dust. A person's *spirit* here refers to the spirit of pride. After this spirit

*Ps 103:29

is taken from them, they return *to their dust,* that is, to a recognition of their own fragility. The Spirit of God, who does not rest *except over the humble, the silent,*

*Isa 66:2 LXX

and those trembling at his *words,* may thus be sent forth

*Jerome, In Ps
103.4.13–14; Ps
103:30

to them.* In this way, they are restored and renewed and can advance to *perfect maturity,* corresponding to reason in all things. They may thus become what was written here: *A man will be more precious than gold, and*

*Isa 13:12

a person more precious than pure gold. That this be done, it is necessary that the fear of God disturb heaven, that is, the soul, and that the land, that is, the body, be moved from its place by giving up its wicked habits and desires.

12. O my brothers, as many of you know from experience, it is difficult to depart from the *place* of wicked habit even with one's soul disturbed. It is difficult to unlearn a habit, difficult to pull off the skin

*Lam 4:8
*Aelred, S 72.10
*Isa 13:14

that sticks to meat and bones.* Yet humility arises from fear, and trembling from humility.* Then one *will be like a doe running away, like a sheep.* My brothers, every soul eager to withdraw from the place of its wicked habit needs two things. First, it needs to run away from the occasions of sin like a doe, shaking and fearful of

*Mark 5:33

its pursuers.* Then, like a sheep—a model of simplicity, which neither grows angry at the shearer nor opposes

*Isa 53:7

the slaughterer*—it must subject itself in simplicity to the one correcting it and sustain in simplicity the one rebuking it. And thus, after the city of pride has been destroyed and the stones of vices from which it had been built are scattered,* when the soul is founded on true humility, *there will be no one to gather* the stones again and raise up the ruins of the city.*

13. Then *all will turn to their own people, and they will each run away to their own land.** All *wicked spirits* are lovers of and inciters to all the vices.* Yet one is called the spirit of fornication because of its baser longing for the filth of lust; another is called the spirit of pride because it takes greater delight in the haughtiness of the human mind; another is called the spirit of avarice because it suggests that vice more frequently than the others; another is called the spirit of discord because it loves anger and strife more than the others; and another, which takes more pleasure in tempting mortal breasts with heresies and various errors, is called the spirit of blasphemy.* When these spirits are cast out of the heart of the one repenting through God's grace, *all will turn to their own people:** the spirits of fornication to the unclean, the spirits of pride to the proud, and so on with the others. *And they will each run away to their own land,** to those who, indulging their suggestion, *taste what is earthly,** looking for any sort of rest for themselves.†

14. Unhappy is the soul that prepares a place in itself for any demon that has been cast out from another! Such a soul receives its own enemy, who will wound it with the sword of iniquity. *Everyone*, it says, *who is found will be killed, and everyone who arrives will fall to the sword.** For who is so perverse as to have neither virtue nor the semblance of virtue? But the ancient enemy, when received in the heart, takes even the appearance of goodness,* so that *the person's last state turns out worse than before.** If some useful thought should arrive to such a person, the one who controls everything easily smothers it, lest it should bear *the fruit of salvation.**

*Lam 4:1

*Isa 13:14

*Isa 13:14
*Acts 19:12

*Aelred, S 54.8

*Isa 13:14

*Isa 13:14
*Phil 3:19; Col 3:2; Rom 8:5
†Matt 12:43 and parallels

*Isa 13:15

*2 Tim 3:5
*Matt 12:45 and parallels

*Sir 1:22

15. Therefore *their small children* are *smashed before their eyes;** in other words, a kind of hardness of heart comes over them, crushing their good but still delicate thoughts. And *their houses* are *plundered,** because wicked spirits pillage whatever is good in their conscience. Even their *wives,** that is, their affections, whom they enjoyed for the purpose of begetting children of good works as though in lawful marriage, are stained by foul loves and filthy thoughts.

16. Good Jesus, *when will you look* to restore *my soul from* this *evil,* and from these *lions my only one?** Would that you raised up the Medes—that is, the good angels—over us,** so that they would take up *arms and shield* and rise up *to help* us.** The Medes are strong from the strong one and powerful from the powerful one and can thus arrange all these trials for us *in proper measure,** not allowing us *to be tempted beyond* what we are able to bear, but creating *a way out with the temptation, so that* we might *withstand* it.**

17. You should bear in mind, brothers, that these Medes despise those who are inflated with worldly wisdom, and they hate those who boast in empty rhetoric, for they do not seek silver or want gold.** But they willingly visit those who kill *the little ones with arrows,** who do not show mercy *to the sucklings of the womb,* and whose *eye* does not spare *the children.** They joyfully help such people, willingly confronting those fighting against them. I take *little ones* to mean thoughts suggesting what is forbidden, *sucklings* to mean thoughts that take delight in these same forbidden things, and *children* to mean thoughts that are breaking out as forbidden acts even now through consent. But *blessed is the one who will seize and smash* these little ones *against a rock.** Blessed are those who kill harmful thoughts as they arise with the arrows of the fear of God; who do not have mercy on themselves, however often forbidden pleasure carries them off; who, if they have perhaps fallen into consent, prefer

*Isa 13:16
*Isa 13:16
*Isa 13:16
*Ps 34:17
*Isa 13:17
*Ps 34:2
*Wis 11:21
*1 Cor 10:13
*Isa 13:17; Jerome, In Isa 6.19
*Isa 13:17
*Isa 13:18
*Ps 136:9; as cited in Jerome, In Isa 6.19

to punish rather than to spare themselves. All of this takes place with the help of the blessed angels, who *are all ministering spirits* and are sent *for* us *who* are taking possession of *the inheritance of salvation.** *Heb 1:14

18. Understand the burden of Babylon in all of this as that which is destroyed in the hearts of many by the help of God's grace. In this way you will then be able to recognize by which burden Babylon will be weighed down in the condemned. But let us save this, if you will, for tomorrow, so as not to mix allegorical laws with the moral sense in which we toiled today. For if the mind is stretched toward many topics, it will be found darker in each. May the Lord Jesus be with us so that, examining the Scriptures, we may find him who *made comparisons in the hands of the prophets** and *Hos 12:10
was made known by the voices of the apostles, he who lives and reigns with the Father and the Holy Spirit, one God, forever and ever. Amen.

Homily 13

1. When we talked about the burdens in the beginning, we said that we could understand the burdens of Babylon, Philistia, or the other nations in two ways: as the burden that weighs down each particular nation, or as the burden by which each nation weighs down others.* Having described the burden of Babylon as the burden with which the devil's city will weigh down the city of God at the time of the Antichrist, the prophet now directs his speech to its own oppression, saying, *And Babylon, the glorious one among kingdoms, renowned among the Chaldeans in their pride, will be like Sodom and Gomorrah, which God destroyed.**

2. We have often said that Babylon represents the world. But here it means that world that is always impure, the world that *dwells in wickedness,** the world for which the one who overcame the world does not pray,* the world from which those who conquer the world are chosen:† *I do not pray for the world,* he said, *but for those whom you gave me from the world.*§ O unclean world, why are you proud?‡ It is true that now you are glorious *among the kingdoms,* now you are renowned *in the pride* of the demons or wicked princes.* For *Chaldeans* means *like demons.**

3. O brothers, how glorious will Babylon seem to itself, that city of confusion, that city of the condemned, when, at the time of the Antichrist, it will be granted the power of raging against the holy ones *among* all *the kingdoms* of the earth?* And how *renowned*

*Oner 1.16

*Isa 13:19

*1 John 5:19

*John 16:33 and parallels
†John 15:19;
1 John 4:4
§John 17:9, 6
‡Sir 10:9

*Isa 13:19

*Jerome, In Isa 6.20

*Dan 7:21;
Rev 13:7

will it be *in* the *pride* and grandeur of its supporters, the princes of the lands, who like demons seek not so much the destruction of bodies as the ruin of souls? But why do you boast, O Babylon?* Listen to the prophet, if you will: *And Babylon, the glorious one among kingdoms, renowned among the Chaldeans in their pride, will be like Sodom and Gomorrah, which God destroyed.**

*Ps 51:3

*Isa 13:19

4. It was said that Sodom and Gomorrah's region was *like God's Paradise before* the Lord destroyed it.* But their destruction was such that no trace of their former beauty remains in them.* Rather, they give a horrid impression of hellish punishments, with an unbearable stink of sulfur and pitch.* Let the fruit trees shrouded in smoke and the barren lake bear witness to the hateful horror of Sodomite wickedness.* Everything is unnatural in that place where we read that the law of nature first fell.* That stink against nature, that hateful sin, rightly left behind stinking and horrifying reminders, so that all such people—those whom smoke will blind, whom a foul odor will corrupt, whom the birdlime of uncleanness will trap like pitch in eternal bonds, whom the *devouring flame* will eat at without consuming—may see which punishments they will suffer in hell.*

*Gen 13:10

*Jerome, In Isa 6.20

*Gen 19:24

*Augustine, Civ Dei 21.5.8

*Gen 19:5

*Judg 20:48; Mark 9:43 and parallels

5. This is the end of all your delights, O Babylon, you who spread the sweetness of your venom for all wretched mortals in that place. From there, the eye looks away from the horror, the mind turns away from such shame, and speech falls silent before such ugliness. Every creature keeps to the natural order of its nature by the coming together of the opposite sexes for procreation. Only human beings lay open their own nature to such perversity in contempt for God, to their own shame, and in an affront to all things. As a result, they do not fear twisting everything that God has instituted, reason has proven, and custom has confirmed.*

*Aelred, S 28.29

6. Woe to you, city of confusion! You corrupt so many today with this corroding disgrace. The just

requiter rightly prepares Sodom and Gomorrah's destruction for you, so that you resemble Sodom and
Gomorrah in punishment, to whom you showed yourself alike in guilt! Therefore, like Sodom and Gomorrah, you will be destroyed. Your glory, your riches,
your power, and your unclean desires: you will remember none of it, except as a punishment. Rather, *a*
stink will be yours *instead of a pleasing odor,** worms
instead of reverence, a fire instead of lust, eternal punishment instead of fleeting pleasure.*

7. *It will remain uninhabited forever,* it says, *and it will*
*not be founded for generation after generation.** Let those
lying heretics be silent who say that the Lord will visit
Babylon in hell, though after much time has passed.
The ruin prophesied for Babylon is eternal. The prophetic authority clearly proves that Babylon will not
be inhabited further, nor can it be founded hereafter.

8. *The Arab will not pitch tents there, nor will shepherds*
*rest there.** *I will sing to you of mercy and judgment, Lord.*†
Now is certainly the *time of showing mercy;*§ the time
of judging will follow.‡ Now is the time of turning to
the Lord; the time of rewarding will follow. The Arabs
put their tents in Babylon. *Arab* means *western* or
*evening.** The Arab represents Christ, who pays in the
evening those whom he hires in the morning.†

9. For he did not *serve the good wine at first,* that is,
in the morning, *and in the evening, when they were drunk,*
*then serve the worse.** Rather, he reserves what is sweet
and pleasant for the evening, always offering what is
hard in the morning. *In this world,* he said, *you will have*
*affliction.** And, *The world will rejoice, but you will be*
*saddened.** This is *in the morning,* that is, *at first.* What
comes next? *Your sadness will be turned to joy.** When?
At evening, of course. Therefore, *Woe to the land whose*
*princes eat in the morning.** On account of the temporal
delights that they misuse now, they lose those delights
that will be distributed at evening, namely, at the end
of this day of time. He is also called *western,* not

Margin notes:

*Isa 3:24

*Oner 9.4

*Isa 13:20

*Isa 13:20
†Ps 100:1
§Ps 101:14
‡Oner 27.24

*Jerome, In
Isa 6.20
†Matt 20:1;
Ps 103:23

*John 2:10; Matt
20:1; Ps 103:23

*John 16:33

*John 16:20

*John 16:20

*Eccl 10:16

looking so much on our rising as our setting; not considering the beginning of a work, but always its end.

10. The *Arab* has a *tent* here now.* The tent represents the saints who sojourn in this world.* God's Spirit moves them here and there like a tent.† Here in this Babylon, where they are now situated like tents, they do not have *a lasting city, but* seek *a future one* that is in heaven.* But they are pitched here to conquer Babylon and cry out with the prophet, *Take flight from the midst of Babylon, all of you, and save your souls.** Here, too, shepherds now rest, boasting in the faith and good works of those who have turned to the Lord. Therefore, now is the time for taking flight from the midst of Babylon, now is the time for migrating to heavenly tents, now is the time, too, for submitting ourselves to the shepherds' teaching and laws. But after the city is finally destroyed in anger and the saints have been brought to the heavenly kingdom, *The Arab will not pitch tents there, nor will shepherds rest there,** because it is useless to give medicine when there is no hope for a cure.*

11. *But beasts will rest there, and their houses will be full of serpents,** etc. If we wish to refer this to the final destruction of Babylon, in which it will be cast down into a pool of sulfur with the false prophets, as is written in Revelation,* it seems that we should emphasize the literal meaning. We can thus show how in Babylon, after its condemnation, the beasts—we can understand them as either vices or wicked spirits—are able to rest. Or perhaps the demons are said to rest in the condemned, because, when the demons stop tempting the good or the wicked, they will rejoice in the punishments of those whom they now entice to agree to their will.

12. But if each person's house is the conscience, as we said above,* then *their houses will be full of serpents*† when vices that now seem pleasant and sweet present the image of a serpent to a person's conscience. The conscience will shrink before this serpent's face and

*Isa 13:20

*2 Cor 5:6;
Heb 11:13
†1 Sam 23:13

*Heb 13:14; 11:6

*Jer 51:6

*Isa 13:20
*Jer 46:11

*Isa 13:21

*Rev 20:9-10

*Oner 12.15
†Isa 13:21

be unable to bear the flame. For these beasts are said to have a frightful face and such a fiery nature that flames seem to shoot forth from them. Thus the vices and sins that seem delightful now will seem horrible to the damned, adding fuel to the eternal fire. Every single crime in which people pleasurably become entangled will twist the consciences of the wretched with a special reminder. This is why it is attested that *there ostriches* dwell, *shaggy creatures* dance, *owls* answer *one another, and sirens in the temples of pleasure.** Understand *ostriches* to be the pretense of hypocrites, the *shaggy creatures* the pricks of lust, the *owls* the whispering of slanderers or murmurers, and the *sirens* the deceit of flatterers.

*Isa 13:21-22

13. For although the ostrich has feathers, it cannot raise itself above the earth. Because of its body weight and lack of feathers, it gives the illusion of being able to fly without actually doing so.* Therefore, this bird's nature expresses the vices of hypocrites. Such people's countenances show signs of the virtues, but the weight of vices pulls them down in secret. Such people talk much but do little, prattle on about heavenly things but think about earthly things, shine forth with knowledge but neglect intention, and lift high their wings as though they would fly to the stars, but their minds, fettered by cupidity, drag the entire body down.

*Jerome, In Isa 6.20

14. The shaggy creature, which is also called an incubus, is a hairy, horned animal that always burns for intercourse.* It represents the stings of lust that spurred Esau, covered by the hair of vices,[†] to defile himself by his forbidden union with foreign women.[§] This was after gluttonous enticements led him to sell his birthright.* Offending both father and mother by his marriages,* he lost the blessing due to the firstborn.* Observe carefully, dearly beloved. First of all, as one devoted to hunting, Esau preferred the exterior to the interior, the trivial to the serious, and restlessness to quiet. Then he lost his rights as the firstborn

*Gregory, Mo 7. XXVIII.36
†Gen 27:11
§Gen 26:34

*Gen 25:29-33
*Gen 26:35
*Gen 27:35-36

by not restraining his gluttony. After that, he abandoned modesty in wronging both of his parents. Finally, he deserved to be excluded from his father's blessing.

If only we did not know of so many engaged in such behavior today! Such people grow tired of the spiritual sweetness that is only perceived inwardly.* They curiously chase after exterior consolations and wander about pointlessly. First, they subject themselves to the slavery of their belly.* For the sake of its pleasure, they cheat themselves of the glory of their birthright, namely, the benefits of renunciation. Thus, burned by the fire of sensual desire, they do not reach the Father's blessing awaited in the fruit of the virtues.

15. The text speaks of *owls* as big as a raven,* mottled, with stretched-out necks, sending forth a dreadful call or a shrill sound with their beaks fixed in the swamp. I ask: What is more mottled than detractors or murmurers? For detractors possess this very quality. They always mix just a little bit of praise in the criticisms with which they try to besmirch others. They thus mottle every word of their detraction with contrary opinions. What about murmurers? Do they not always excuse their murmuring with some pretext or another? At times they claim they are acting out of good zeal;* at times they lie, saying that they are speaking out not on their own account but for others; and at times they act as though they were showing compassion on the legitimate needs of others. Because they are not completely honest,* do they not leave at least dishonesty's defiling blemish? Such people, then, fix their beaks in the earth; having forgotten heavenly realities, they speak of what is earthly. They caw in nooks, whisper in the darkness, and inspire horror in those who listen to them.*

16. Further, flatterers are fittingly compared to sirens. They entice the ear of their listener with a pleasing but deadly sound. Unless you prudently plug your

*Ps 44:14

*Aelred,
S 44.2, 14

*Isa 13:22

*RB 72.2

*candidus

*Aelred,
Spir amic 3.43;
Oner 16.15

*Jerome, In Isa
6.20; Aelred,
S 83.8–9

*Ps 9:24 (10:3)

ears and pass them by, they will lure you onto the
rocks of pride or the Charybdis of presumption.* For
a sinner is praised by them *in the desires of the soul, and
the worker of wickedness is blessed.** Unhappy are they
who entrust themselves to such people and, having
abandoned the witness of their own conscience, ex-
pose themselves to be deluded by another's judgment.
*No one knows what is worked in a person except for that
person's spirit within.** *My people, those who call you*

*1 Cor 2:11
*Isa 3:12

*blessed deceive you.** Wretched are those whom the Lord
rebukes through the prophet, saying, *The prophets
prophesied falsehood, and the priests clapped their hands,*

*Jer 5:3

*and my people loved such things.** This is the people
whose speech is described elsewhere in this way: *You
see* empty *things in us and you speak pleasing things to*

*Isa 30:10

*us.** How much more uprightly did David say, *The just
person will correct me in mercy and will rebuke me, but the*

*Ps 140:5
*Matt 25:8
*Job 20:5

*sinner's oil will not anoint my head.** This is the oil that
ran out in the lamps of the foolish virgins,* because
*the praise of the hypocrite is brief.**

17. If, then, we refer all these things to the final destruction of Babylon, when it will be handed over to
eternal fire, our explanation will perhaps seem too
unreasonable and forced. How, I ask, when Babylon
is already exposed to the avenging flames, *will ostriches dwell* there, or *shaggy creatures dance,* or *owls
answer in its dwellings,* or *sirens in the temples of plea-*

*Isa 13:21-22

*sure?** Or is it because the vices are inflicted in some
way on the eyes and memory, to the confusion of those
who polluted themselves with them? Thus, just as
pain occupies the body, so too the sin for which they
are punished occupies the conscience. And just as
there will be eternal punishment in that condemned
city, there will also be an everlasting memory of the
sins that were committed.

18. And so ostriches will dwell there, that is, the
pretense that contorts hypocrites; the hairy creatures
will dance, because the base and violent movements

of lust that now impel people will not withdraw from their conscience. And the owls will answer. Whom will they answer? Perhaps they will answer the soul itself, which grieves and bewails its punishment. In this way, the soul remembers its slander and murmuring in the hidden places of its heart as *in its dwellings.* It is thus forced to admit that the punishment inflicted on it is just. Indeed the sirens' song, which had seemed sweet in the recesses of the breast as though in *the temples of pleasure* when it was heard from the flatterer, will appear highly bitter when the reality comes to light. This temple is a shrine to the demons, where they offered a kind of *semblance of goodness* while secretly engaged in the business of pleasure.* These breasts always cling to such pleasures. The fawning of the godless adorn them as though with virtues, although true vices always secretly stain them.

*2 Tim 3:5;
Aelred, Spec car
2.23.67; Aelred,
Inst incl 23

19. How does this seem to you? So far, this explanation is not so clumsy as we had thought. Yet let us not neglect another that comes to mind. Does it not seem plausible for us to say that the demons, already damned by the eternal fire, are able to take some comfort from the wretched company of those whom they have drawn to themselves? We can thus take these beasts to be those who provoke the vices already mentioned. They will gladly dwell like ostriches with the people in that lost city, or will happily dance like the shaggy creatures, or will give answer like owls or sirens to those burning. But do not take this as the dance of those clapping their hands, but of those moving from one punishment to another by a kind of compulsion. It is similar to where it says, *From snow water they will go on to too much heat.** For a liquid that is heated seems to jump, and in the English language, boiling water is said to *play.*[1]

*Job 24:19

---

[1] In Middle English, *pleien* means both *to play* and *to boil.*

20. But, following the established order, let us shift all of this to the time of the Antichrist. Let us imagine that condemned city, which certainly seemed *glorious and renowned among the kingdoms* of the world, boasting and rejoicing *in the pride* of the princes of this age.* Let us imagine it after that last persecution separates it from the good, when it is about to be destroyed *like Sodom and Gomorrah.** Handed over to the eternal flames and the stench of the vices, it will retain no trace of the virtues. Nor will good people continue to dwell there when the Last Judgment threatens. Nor will the holy preachers lay that *foundation that is Christ* any longer.* *The Arab will not pitch tents there;*† namely, Christ will not establish his tabernacle there, which is those perfect people who renounce the world. Nor will the holy angels find rest there, nor will perfect men, *the shepherds of* our *souls,** whose rest is the outstanding life of good people, the peace and harmony of their subjects. *But beasts* or serpents *will rest there, and ostriches will dwell there, shaggy creatures,* too, *will dance, and owls will answer one another, and sirens.**

21. Understand these beasts to be either the vices themselves, as we said above, or the demons. The demons will prevail greatly over the faithless at that time, claiming for themselves an unoccupied room in them, leaping unrestrained to shameful acts, answering one another. For in that corrupt company of the faithless, wicked angels—inciters of various forms of wickedness—will come together. Some of them will dwell in the same person, while others will move on to others with a nimble leap.* Still others will answer people, greatly encouraging them in everything they desire to carry out what they want, though it is clear that all these things can also take place in a single person. For when a soul, confused by passions and faults, is thrown down from every virtue and so deserves to be compared to Sodom and Gomorrah, all

*Isa 13:19

*Isa 13:19

*1 Cor 3:11
†Isa 13:20

*1 Pet 2:25

*Isa 13:21-22

*Lucretius, Rer nat 5.559

the wicked spirits enter it and make it the receptacle
of all the vices.

22. If someone should murmur about wickedness
flourishing for such a long time and complain that the
time when all things are fulfilled is far off, the prophet
continues, saying, *For his time is near at hand, and his
days will not be postponed.** Everything that seems long   *Isa 14:1
to us is quite brief for God, because *a thousand years
before* his *eyes are like yesterday, which has passed.** And   *Ps 89:4
certainly everything that passes is brief; brief is everything that an end limits at some point. Therefore, the
Holy Spirit wants us to fix our eyes on eternity, so that
we regard fleeting time as of no duration.**   *Jerome, In
                          Isa 6.20

23. *His time is near at hand,* it says.† Whose time? His,   †Isa 14:1
of course, of whom it was previously said, *Behold, the
day of the Lord is coming, cruel,* etc.* Therefore, the day   *Isa 13:9
of the Lord is the Lord's time, when the good will be
tried, the false will be made known, the perfect will
be crowned, and the condemned will be punished.
When will this be?* What is the cause of this delay? It   *Matt 24:3 and
is put off, of course, *until the fullness of the nations* en-   parallels
ters in, *and thus all Israel* may be *saved.** And so, before   *Rom 11:25-26
these things begin to take place, *the Lord will take pity
on Jacob and will still choose from Israel.**   *Isa 14:1

24. O brothers, that heavy sentence still stands over
Jacob, which the same prophet in an earlier part of
this book says that the Lord himself revealed: *Blind
the heart of this people, and stop up their ears, and weaken
their eyes, lest by chance they see with their eyes, and hear
with their ears, and understand in their heart, and be converted, and I cure them.** The day will come, it will come,   *Isa 6:10
when the veil will be taken away from them,* so that they   *2 Cor 3:16
themselves will see *with uncovered face the glory of* my   *2 Cor 3:18
Lord Jesus,* when it is announced to Jacob, *Your son   *Gen 45:26
Joseph is alive and rules all the land of Egypt.** And then,
waking from a deep sleep of unfaithfulness, he will
say *I will go and see him before I die.** *For the Lord will*   *Gen 45:28

Isa 14:1 — *take pity on Jacob,* on him whom he seems now to oppose in the faith of the nations, calling that which was not his people his people, and the unloved loved, and that which had not obtained mercy one that has obtained mercy.**

Rom 9:25; Hos 2:23-24

25. *The Lord will take pity on Jacob and will still choose from Israel.* Still choose,* it says. First he chose the apostles, disciples, and the crowd of believers *from Israel,** so that the early church might be founded. He will also *choose* many at the end of the world with whom the last times of the church will be adorned. But by *choosing,* we understand that not all the Jews found at that time will be saved. Some of them will welcome the Antichrist, as the Lord said in the gospel, *I came in my Father's name, and you did not accept me. Another will come in his own name; you will accept him.** If you want me to distinguish between Jacob and Israel, and between pity and choosing, understand *Jacob* to be the weaker ones on whom the Lord takes pity so that they do not perish, and the more perfect to be *Israel,* from whom the Lord chooses people to instruct and rule over others.

Isa 14:1

Acts 5:14 and parallels

John 5:43

26. It follows, *And he will make them rest on their own soil.** What is this soil? Is it that land of promise that was formerly theirs, from which they were cast out, scattered throughout the world? In the last times, after they become Christian, it could happen that they rest in that land. Some might dwell there physically, while the others would love those who dwell there as Christians loving Christians. But it is much better to understand *the soil* to be the church. The Jews, approaching by means of faith and morals, will then finally regard the church as *their soil,* rejoicing in its good things and resting in the abundance of its fruit.

Isa 14:1

27. But this applies to us, too, brothers, if we are Jacob. Babylon represents the love for the world in us, where spiritual beasts dwell, about which the prophet said, *Do not hand over to beasts the souls that* *confess you;* where serpents, namely, unclean spirits, *Ps 73:19; Jerome, abide, where pretense reigns, lust provokes restless-   In Isa 6.20 ness, slander inflicts wounds, and flattery dissipates. When Babylon is destroyed in us—when, I say, all these elements of worldly love have been cast out— the Lord will have mercy on us. For *Jacob* means *wrestler.*   *Jerome, In Isa 6.21;

28. What is this wrestling match? *The flesh has desires* Origen, In Ex 11.5 *against the spirit and the spirit against the flesh.* What   *Gal 5:17 wrestling match? *We do not struggle against flesh and blood, but against the rulers of the world.* What wrestling   *Eph 6:12 match? *The kingdom of heaven suffers violence, and the violent seize it.* What wrestling match? *Do not be amazed*   *Mat 11:12 *if the world hates you, for it hated me first.* Therefore, we   *John 15:18; have a wrestling match with the flesh, with the demon,   1 John 3:13 with the world, and with God. The first match is for beginners; the second, for those advancing; the third, for those who have been tested; and the fourth, for those being perfected. The first match is laborious, the second is dangerous, the third is wearisome, and the fourth is fruitful.

29. I ask, what is so laborious as to fight a battle within or even against oneself? There is a fire within that we must both encourage and beware. For if it is not encouraged, nature is overwhelmed, but if we are not careful, chastity is endangered. Hence the fear, hence the mourning, hence the tears for those who do not know the limits of necessity, for those frightened of the matter of pleasure, for those who dare not deny nature's due, and for those who wish to impose the bridle of sobriety on their palate. When they decide to care for necessity, they apply fuel to pleasure, and when they give up what they think is unnecessary, they suffer loss in other good things that they love equally.

30. The wrestling match *against the wicked spirits* is highly dangerous.* They have a thousand ways to   *Eph 6:12 inflict harm,* given that they have trained in such   *Virgil, Aen 7.338

dealings for so many thousands of years. Yet among all the snares and cunning tricks of the demons, the most dangerous is that by which they turn themselves into angels of light.* They disguise their vices under the likeness of virtues and give their wretched victims a golden chalice of poison to drink.* *We do not struggle against flesh and blood** when, after we have conquered the flesh, the demons' wicked shrewdness deludes us, urging vices through our virtues or else urging pride in our virtues.

*2 Cor 11:14

*Jer 51:7
*Eph 6:12

31. After this, this world fights against us with two arms, namely, prosperity and adversity. From prosperity comes an abundance of temporal goods, in abundance is peace, and in peace is security. We can likewise include human praise, the friendship of the rich, the goodwill and loyalty of peers, and the support and esteem of underlings. Some also reckon that both physical health and a sound body belong to prosperity. O brothers, who can easily say how much the world weighs us down with this arm, how violently it struggles against us, how often it casts down the wretched and incautious? How rare is the person who does not slacken the mind a little from its usual seriousness when prosperous, who is not even a little more indulgent in abundance, nor a bit more cheerful with human praise, nor a bit more puffed up by the goodwill of princes, nor in the esteem of friends a little more carefree, nor in the support of underlings a trifle haughtier, nor in bodily strength a bit harsher! Therefore, those who want to be a spiritual Jacob know that they must engage in a constant wrestling match against these dangers in times of prosperity.

32. The world's other arm, which we said was adversity, is more troublesome but less dangerous. To adversity belong a lack of material goods, slander, disgrace, persecutions from the rich, the hatred of

princes, the betrayal of friends, the rebellion of underlings, and bodily sickness. What a struggle we have
against all of these things, brothers!* Who is there who   *Eph 6:12
is not more timid in times of adversity, whom shame
does not move nor slander sadden? Who does not
become angrier in times of persecution, more downcast by the hatred of princes, less patient at the betrayal of friends, and crueler at the rebellion of
underlings?

33. Happy is the soul that triumphs in all these
things. May it be both sober in times of prosperity and
steadfast in times of adversity. Happy is the soul who,
although it cannot fully conquer these things, yet still
commits itself to fighting as best it can lest it be conquered! For *the Lord will take pity on Jacob,** that is, on   *Isa 14:1
the wrestler, so that, if one is not fully victorious in
this life, one may deserve an eternal crown in heaven
after the battle is over.*   *2 Tim 4:7-8; 2:5

34. Of course, those who emerge victorious in these
wrestling matches will begin to wrestle with God.*   *Gen 32:24-25
They will cross over from Mesopotamia to Mount
Bethel,* from the lower to the higher, from the human   *Gen 33:18;
to the divine, from the bodily to the spiritual. There-   35:1, 9
fore, raise up, O soul, your two arms of prayer and
meditation. Lift them toward the hidden places of
heaven, *where Christ is sitting at God's right hand;** *insist*   *Col 3:1
in and *out of season,** so that you may regard his *face,*[†]   *2 Tim 4:2
so that he may come down to you or draw you up to   †Gen 32:30; Exod
him, so that you may taste *how sweet he is* and experi-   33:13; Ps 26:8
ence *how mild and merciful he is.** And so, if the fire of   *1 Pet 2:3; Ps
heavenly desire breaks out in your prayer or medita-   85:5, 15
tion,* if the pricks of love should burst into flame, if   *Ps 38:4
heavenly feelings stir you, making you burn and gasp,
and you sometimes sense the presence of what you
love as though you possessed it, and at other times,
after it escapes from your hands, you ache and sigh
for its absence,* then this is the spiritual wrestling   *Song 5:6

match. This is what bestows upon you the name of Israel,* so that you may be regarded worthy not only of pity but also of election.†

35. *The Lord will take pity on Jacob and will still choose from Israel,*§ because those who, fighting against the vices, labor *with* their *groans* and wash their *bed with tears** are worthy to have mercy weighed out to them. Now those who, after the vices have been conquered, boast in the perfection of the virtues are brought to the heavenly storehouse like a cleaned and chosen grain.*

36. *And he will make them rest on their own soil.** A great blessing is promised here. Our soil is our flesh. Many are under it, many are in it, but few are *on top of* it. Those whom *the concupiscence of the flesh* rules are under it.* Those who always do and think about the things of the flesh are in it.† Those who punish the flesh with *labors, vigils,* and *fasts* so that it does not grow strong are on top of it.* The first condition is carnal, the second is animal, and the third is spiritual. Paul forbids us to be ruled by the flesh, saying, *Do not let sin rule in your mortal body, making you obedient to its desires.** What does it mean to be obedient to the desires of the flesh, if not to be under the flesh? Neither does Paul want us to be in the flesh. He says, *Do not be anxious about the flesh in its desires.** Listen to the person who is on top of the flesh, the one who courageously resists its desires: *I punish my body and reduce it to slavery.** As long as there is something to fight against, there is labor rather than rest. But if, when the vices have been extinguished and the passions overcome, we are on top of the flesh in such a way that there is no longer anything in it that weighs us down, then we will indeed rest *on our own soil.** This is the beatitude that the Lord promised to the meek, saying, *Blessed are the meek, for they will possess the land.**

* Gen 32:28; Gregory, Hiez 2.2.12
† Jerome, In Isa 6.21
§ Isa 14:1
* Ps 6:7

* Matt 13:30
* Isa 14:1

* 1 John 2:16; Rom 6:12
† Rom 8:5

* 2 Cor 6:5

* Rom 6:12

* Rom 13:14

* 1 Cor 9:27

* Isa 14:1

* Matt 5:4; Oner 11.13; 18.25; Jerome, In Isa 6.21; Bernard, OS 1.9

37. But we have come upon a part of Scripture that commends rest. Because we have already labored for a long time in speaking, it is right that, keeping still for a while in the refuge of silence,* we should restore both mind and voice. Thus we may be found more apt for investigating the mysteries of God and our Lord Jesus Christ, who lives and reigns as God, forever and ever. Amen.

*Cassian, Conl 24.26.19

Homily 14

1. Illuminated by the Holy Spirit, holy Isaiah describes the conversion of the Jews, which we believe will take place *in the last days:** *The Lord will take pity on Jacob and will still choose from Israel, and he will make them rest on their own soil.** And it follows, *The foreigner will be joined to them and will cling to the house of Jacob.** Understand *foreigner* to mean the people of the nations. After seeing the prophets' declarations fulfilled by the calling of the Jews, the nations will hasten to be joined to them, taking up the same faith. Or else that faithful people whom the Jews had greatly feared as foreign until that time will be joined to them in love. Then the two divided rods that were in the hand of the prophet Ezekiel *will be in union.** According to another prophet, Judah and Israel will make *for themselves one head and will come up from the land.** The people of the nations will thus cling to the Jewish people, that is, *to the house of Jacob*, so that there will be for them *one God, one faith, one baptism.**

2. *And the peoples will hold them,** that is, the Christians will hold the Jews. They will hold them in charity, they will hold them in the rules of discipline, they will hold them in care, and they will hold them in affection. *And they will lead them into their place,** that is, to the church. For the Christians' place is the church. The place of which the Lord spoke to Moses prefigured the church: *Remove your shoes from your feet, for the place where you are standing is holy ground.** The

*Isa 2:2; Oner 13.24-26

*Isa 14:1

*Isa 14:1

*Ezek 37:17

*Hos 1:11

*Eph 4:5-6

*Isa 14:2

*Isa 14:2

*Exod 3:5

134

prophet added about this land, *And the house of Israel will possess them as servants in the Lord's land.** For after the Jews have been received into the church, which is certainly the land of the Lord, the rejoicing of the Christian peoples will be so great, such wondrous devotion will surround them, that those whom the Jews now have as persecutors and masters they will then have in charity as servants and handmaidens. This is why the apostle says, *Serve one another in charity.** *Isa 14:2

*Gal 5:13

3. *And they will capture those who had captured them.** It seems to me that the prophecy describes the mutual love with which the Jews and Gentiles will capture each other, as though embracing one another with arms of love. Of this capturing Paul says, *Receive us.** Or, *they will capture those who had captured them** when, just as the gentile faithful will draw the Israelite people to the church's breast by the net of holy preaching,* so too these converts will subjugate many from the Gentiles to Christian laws by both word and example. *Isa 14:2

* *capite; 2 Cor 7:2

*Isa 14:2

*John 21:11

4. It therefore continues, *And they will subjugate their overseers.** We can understand the Christian people as *overseers,* to whom that wretched mass now pays tribute and before whom it always casts itself down in base servitude. But united to the faithful at the end of the world, they will hold subject in charity those who had troubled them before with many kinds of taxes. The unclean spirits are also now the Jews' overseers. These spirits drive the Jews, bound by various errors, to blasphemy, insults, and many kinds of vices. At the end of the world, armed by the sign of the cross, the Jews will subjugate these overseers, when they will also receive the power *to trample snakes and scorpions and all the enemy's power.** *Isa 14:2

*Luke 10:19

5. *And it will be on that day, after the Lord has given you rest from your work and from your confusion and from your hard slavery in which you served before, that you will take*

up this parable against Babylon's king, and you will say,
*Isa 14:3-4 *How has the overseer failed, etc.** The prophet has described the church's state up until the time of the Antichrist, the Antichrist's persecution, the destruction
of spiritual Babylon, and the Jews' conversion. He
now turns his mystic speech to the fall of the Antichrist, or rather to the fall of the devil in or with the
Antichrist, and to the saints' rest and exultation. He
who, speaking in the third person, had foretold difficulties for them, now speaks to them directly to announce their good fortune, saying, *And it will be on*
*Isa 14:3 *that day, after the Lord has given you rest.** We can fittingly apply this both to the church, which at that time
will consist of both Jews and Gentiles, and to the entire
company of saints that will arrive at that eternal rest.

6. *And it will be*, he says, *after the Lord has given you*
*Isa 14:3 *rest.** By *rest* we can understand the peace that the
church may have from the Antichrist's destruction
until the day of Judgment. Or we can understand that
1 Cor 15:26 peace after the last enemy, death, has been destroyed,
1 Macc 14:12-13 when there will be no one to attack or frighten us.
Three kinds of affliction that will subdue the human
race are noted here. These three afflictions are not easily escaped before the Antichrist's destruction: labor,
confusion, and slavery. Labor properly belongs to the
body, confusion to the mind, and slavery to both. For
at the time of the Antichrist the church will labor,
brought low amid other torments; it will be confused,
exposed amid other reproaches; afflicted by slavery,
it will be weighed down with tributes. But after you
rest from all these things, he says, after the death of
2 Thess 2:3 that son of perdition, *you will take up this parable*
*Isa 14:4 *against Babylon's king and you will say.**

7. Interpret the king of Babylon as the devil, whose
power will mainly appear in the Antichrist. So it is
that the Antichrist himself, whom the ancient enemy
chose as a unique dwelling for himself, can also be
called the king of Babylon. That name could also be

applied to the Antichrist in his own right on account of the dominion he will hold in those wicked ones who assent to him. Therefore the prophet describes his ruin as though in the words of those who, freed from his tyranny, will wonder at his sudden ruin after such great glory, saying, *How has the overseer failed, the tribute come to an end?* The chosen will be amazed that that cruel overseer has perished so suddenly and has been erased from the earth. Both he and his henchmen had plagued the world with various taxes,* plundering all things through torments and tributes and drawing them to conspire in his crime.

8. *The Lord has broken the staff of the ungodly, the rod of the rulers.** The Antichrist himself, on whom the ungodly lean, is called the staff of the ungodly. Thus, as though supported by his aid, the ungodly can exercise their wickedness among the good both more cruelly and more freely. He is also called the rod of the rulers, that is, their power. Whoever rules at that time will rule from the Antichrist's power. To them will be given the power of trampling the holy land,* that is, the church, *for a time and times and half a time.*† Therefore, the faithful who survive these evil ones will marvel at this power unexpectedly emptied out, saying, *How has the overseer failed, the tribute come to an end? The Lord has crushed the staff of the ungodly, the rod of the rulers striking the peoples in displeasure with an incurable blow.** This *blow* is eternal death, by which the Antichrist's strokes, that is, his persecution, will wound many. This blow is incurable, because there is no redemption in hell. There is no place of repentance where sin could be cleansed, nor cure of confession by which it could be healed, nor acceptable satisfaction by which it could be made right.

9. *That had subjugated the nations in fury and persecuted them cruelly,* it says.* Everything above where his persecution was described was laid out clearly enough, and we have explained it as best we could.*

*Isa 14:4

*1 Sam 19:11

*Isa 14:5

*Luke 10:19; Rev 11:2; Exod 3:5
†Rev 12:14; Dan 7:25

*Isa 14:4-6

*Isa 14:6

*Oner 11

10. It continues, *All the land took its rest and kept silent, it rejoiced and exulted.** When the Antichrist ruled, labor was everywhere, cries were everywhere, pain was everywhere. But after the divine power lays him low, all things will seem at rest, all things will keep silence, all things will exult, because *there will no longer be mourning, nor cries, nor any pain, because the earlier things have departed.**

11. *The fir trees also rejoiced over you, and the cedars of Lebanon.*† Interpret the fir trees as people lofty in wisdom, and the cedars as people with surpassing power. The historical books of Sacred Scripture reveal that wise Solomon used this kind of wood for the construction and decoration of the temple.* Just as that temple represented the church, understand the fir trees and cedars, which tower over other trees and have a more pleasant scent, to be the lofty people in the church, who become widely known by the scent of their good character. The stronger they are found at the time of persecution, the loftier they will be regarded then. They will surely boast over the Antichrist's destruction and rejoice in the long-desired peace.

12. The prophet then adds the voice of those boasting and exulting: *Since you have slept, no one has arisen to cut us down.** This sleep represents death.† After the Antichrist dies, there will be no one to cut down the cedars or fir trees. *No one has arisen.*§ *Arising* expresses pride, power, or prudence. You should thus understand that no one will arise after him with such pride or be raised up with such power or be skilled with such prudence. Thus no one will be able to cut down any of the perfect from the foundation of faith *in the paradise of God,** namely, the church, either by raging with pride, crushing with power, or seducing with prudence. It is therefore well said, *Since you have slept, no one has arisen to cut us down.**

13. It follows, *Hell below was confused at meeting you; it raised up giants for you.** Understand *hell* to be the

company of evil spirits, who, sensing God's coming
Judgment in the destruction of that wicked one, will
be thrown into turmoil, knowing that they have little
time.* Of course, if we believe that the infernal servants   *Rev 12:12
and chief spirits of punishment go to meet those who
lived corruptly in order to drag them down to their
due torments,* how much more does all of hell go to   *Jerome, In
meet the most corrupt of mortals after he has been   Isa 6.23
removed from this light? They raise up giants, that is,
the cruelest tormentors, so that the most wicked in life
will be the most excruciatingly punished.

14. *All the chiefs of the land rose up from their thrones,*
*all the chiefs of the nations.** I believe the *chiefs of the land*   *Isa 14:9
or *nations* should be interpreted as opposing powers,
each sitting like a chief on a throne at that time in individuals tasting earthly things or nations seduced by
the Antichrist.* Of all of these the most powerful, as   *Phil 3:19
their king and most distinguished of them all, will
claim the Antichrist's body and soul as his throne.
When these chiefs see Christ render void the effort
their king was making through his instrument,* they   *1 Cor 15:24
will flee in terror from their thrones, from those individuals in whom they ruled. Amazed by their king's
downfall, it is as though they will answer and say, *You*
too were wounded just as we were; you have become like
*us.** This is that painful wound by which the entire   *Isa 14:10
company of unclean spirits will be wounded. After
the Antichrist's dominion has been destroyed, their
final destruction will be at hand on the Day of Judgment. Nor will the one whom we call the first prince
of all evil himself be able to escape from that wound.
Therefore they say, *You too were wounded just as we were;*
you have become like us. Your pride has been dragged down
*to hell.** This means, the higher you exalted yourself,   *Isa 14:10-11
the lower you have fallen.

15. *Your corpse has fallen.** We can fittingly take the   *Isa 14:11
Antichrist to be the corpse of the prince of darkness,
because the devil will animate him with all forms of

his evil. With his wicked will as living breath, the Antichrist will carry out his villainy. His body will then fall when *the Lord Jesus Christ will kill* him *with the spirit of his mouth and will destroy him by the radiance of his coming.**

* 2 Thess 2:8

16. *The moth and rot will spread under you, and worms will be your covering.** The prophecy describes plainly enough the eternal punishment that will possess the entire being of the devil or the Antichrist.* From below the moth will lay him waste, from above the worms will gnaw him, and from within rot will consume him.* Understand the moth as frivolity, the worms as cruelty, and the rot as lust. Or the moth as forbidden speech, rot as forbidden thoughts, and worms as forbidden actions. Or the moth, which consumes in secret almost unperceived, is the suggestion of the devil; rot, which causes trembling and stench, is unclean pleasure; the worms, which openly destroy, are consent. All this gives birth to material for torment, either inwardly in the conscience or externally in punishment.*

* Isa 14:11

* Matt 6:19

* Job 13:28

* Jerome, In Isa 6.23

17. We have explained these things briefly, because the mind has already hastened to other things that must be said. For it is time* to take a journey that the Order's law demands of us, to which desire rouses us and affection invites us. But how will I be separated for such a long time from my heart's desire?* I will be separated, I say, *in the body,* but not *in the spirit.** And I know that I will be as present in affection and spirit as I am absent in body. *I am speaking humanly on account of the weakness of* my *flesh.** It is my will to lay down the tabernacle of my flesh in your presence,* to pour back my spirit into your hands,† that you may close the eyes of your father and under your eyes my bones may be laid. Pray then, O sweetness of my heart,§ that the Lord may grant me the desire of my soul.‡

* 1 Pet 4:17

* a uisceribus meis

* 1 Cor 5:3; Col 2:5

* Rom 6:19

* 2 Cor 5:4; 2 Pet 1:14

† Luke 23:46 and parallels

§ dulcia uiscera mea

‡ Mic 7:3

18. But think, beloved, of what was written of the Lord Jesus just when his physical presence was about to be taken from his disciples:* *Eating with them, he*

* Oner 12.1

ordered them not to leave Jerusalem.* We have already
gotten up from the table after our sweet banquet, and
in a little while we will depart. Following his example,
we command you, we beseech you, we remind you
not to leave Jerusalem. For Jerusalem means peace.*
We commend peace to you, we command peace
among you. May Christ *himself*, who *is our peace*, making *both into one*,* keep you in the unity of *spirit* and
in the bond of peace.* I commit you to his protection and
consolation under the wings of the Holy Spirit. May
he restore you to me and me to you in peace and
safety.

19. Now draw near, my sweet children, kiss your
father as a sign of the peace and charity that I commended to you.* Let us all pray together that the Lord
will make *the journey prosperous for us,*† and that he will
permit us to find you in this peace upon our return,§
he who lives and reigns forever and ever. Amen.

**Acts 1:4

**Jerome, Nom 50

**Eph 2:14
**Eph 4:3

**Aelred, Spir
amic 2.24
†Ps 67:20
§2 Pet 3:14

Homily 15

*Gen 46:2
†1 Cor 4:14
§Phil 4:1

*Aelred, S 68.1
†Ps 117:15, 24;
Song 3:11
§Luke 17:22;
John 8:56
‡Exod 2:22;
Ps 136:4
#Ps 9:38 (10:17)
≈Ps 106:9
*Ps 147:14

1. *Here I am,* my beloved and most desired* children,† *my joy and my crown* in Christ.§ *Here I am,* returned to you after many labors and a quite dangerous journey, returned by your prayers, returned by your longing, returned by your desires.* For me, today is a *day of joy and exultation,†* a day that I desired to see§ while I was *in a foreign land,‡* while I was exposed to winds and sea. And *the Lord heard the desire* of the poor one.# O love, how sweetly you burn those who are absent, how delightfully you feed those who are present. Yet you do not fill the hungry≈ until you bring peace to Jerusalem's borders and fill it with the grain's fat!*

*Ps 132:1; 1
Pet 2:3

*Oner 14.17–18

*Col 3:15

2. This is the peace whose firstfruits revive you, in which you taste *how good and how pleasing it is for brothers to live in unity.** This is the peace that I commended to you, as you remember, when the Order's law compelled me to be away from you for a time.* Returning to you now, thanks be to God, I find this peace among you. This is surely *Christ's peace,** which feeds you with a kind of foretaste of charity on the way, to be filled by its fullness in the homeland. O sweet brothers, everything that I am, everything that I experience, everything that I know and perceive, I offer for your progress, I dedicate to your use. Make use of me as you please, and do not spare my labor wheresoever it may serve your progress.*

*Aelred, S 68.1;
Aelred, Orat past
7

3. Let us return, if you will—or rather, precisely because you will—to the task that we left behind. Let us break open the heavenly storehouses that holy Isaiah hid under the husk of parables, since the Holy Spirit has poured forth the light of truth. For in describing the *parable* that the people would take up *against Babylon's king* once they were freed from his tyranny,* the prophet says, *And it will be on that day, after the Lord has given you rest from your work and from your confusion* (or *disturbance) and from your hard slavery in which you served before, that you will take up this parable against Babylon's king.** And so let us understand this parable as a parable, not judging it to be spoken against Nebuchadnezzar, prince of the earthly Babylon,* but rather against *the one from the north,*† the prince of confusion. But because we gave an allegorical interpretation in our last sermon with you concerning these matters,* let us continue with the moral reading of this same part.

*Isa 14:4

*Isa 14:3-4

*Jerome, In Isa 6.22
†Joel 2:20

*Oner 14.5–16

4. Therefore, if any of us, formerly caught in the confusion of vices and crushed by the yoke of wickedness, should now rejoice to rest from labor and to be free of confusion at what has happened before, if we should rejoice to have cast off the yoke of wicked slavery, then we should *take up this parable against Babylon's king.** Labor lies in the vices, but rest in virtue. Confusion lies in lust, but tranquility in chastity. Slavery lies in cupidity, but freedom in charity.

*Isa 13:4

5. For there is labor in the vices, labor because of the vices, and labor against the vices. There is labor in the vices when, in order to satisfy wicked desires, the ancient enemy imposes labor on many people. There is labor because of the vices when someone either willingly suffers the labor of repentance or is unwillingly afflicted for evil deeds committed. There is labor against the vices when various temptations wear down a person turned toward the Lord.

6. There is also confusion in the vices, confusion because of the vices, and confusion against the vices. There is confusion in the vices when someone, undone by wicked passions, is not governed by reason. Rather,

the commotion of the vices stirs such people into confusion. There is confusion because of the vices when
someone, caught and convicted of an offense, is put
to confusion. Or else saving confusion cleanses the
convict who repents and confesses the deed. Furthermore, there is confusion against the vices when a person turned to God resists temptations by the memory
of the confusion experienced in the past.

7. The Lord cries out in the gospel, *Come to me, all you*
*Matt 11:28   who labor and are burdened.** It is written elsewhere of
*Jer 9:5   certain people, *They have labored to commit evil.** What
labor it is for thieves and robbers to overpower a trav-
Luke 10:30   eler, or to break into a house and rob the householder!†
†Matt 24:43   What labor it is for adulterers or fornicators to win their
wickedly desired embraces! But so too for greedy
people who eye the fields or storehouses of others. They
have not a little labor, of the heart, if not of the body.

8. Confusion follows this labor, because just as there
is a beautiful order in the virtues, so too there is agitation and confusion in sin. But if the correct reading is
disturbance—which is found in many manuscripts—
those with experience know how the vices disturb
those whom they subjugate, surrounding their victims
and assaulting them from all sides.

*John 8:34   **9.** *Everyone who commits a sin is sin's slave,** says the
Lord Jesus. It is a hard slavery that often drives even
the resisting soul to the vices. The violence of bad
habit urges this soul to the vice that it even now hates.
In an amazing way, this soul would like to commit the
sin and thus does so, while at the same time it does
Aelred, SS 43.15; not want to commit the sin and thus weeps for it.
63.28; 72.10   When people are free from all of this, let them *take up*
this parable against Babylon's king and say, *How has the*
*Isa 14:4   overseer failed, the tribute come to an end?**

10. Hear our Lord Jesus address Peter in the gospel,
saying, *From whom do the nations' kings receive tribute?*
From their own subjects, or from someone else's? And
Peter answered, *From someone else's.* To which the Lord
*Matt 17:24-25 answered, *Therefore, the children are free.** There are,

then, three overseers demanding tributes: Caesar, the devil, and God. Caesar, like a demanding overseer, wrenches away his image printed on every coin,* an image that he imposed on humanity as a sign of his rule. The devil, a hard and cruel overseer, seeks his likeness by a payment of daily shamefulness, a likeness that he has implanted with the stake of depraved habit into the soul consenting to him by its longing for vice. God reasonably demands his image from his creature, an image that he has imprinted on the rational soul's nature.

*Matt 22:20-21

11. For humanity was created *in the image and likeness of God.** As long as we did not subject ourselves to another's power, we were not compelled to pay what we clearly did not owe. But just as a kind of likeness of God shines forth in the virtues, so the likeness of the devil is found in the vices. We are free of his image for as long as we do not render our misdeeds to him who urges us to consent. For consent depicts a kind of likeness to the devil in the soul by light brushstrokes, as it were. But when consent breaks out as action, we wretchedly impose his full image on ourselves by our desire to sin.

*Gen 5:1; 1:26-27

12. The devil thus gains power in us by means of sin. That unbearable *tax-collector* wrenches a daily *tribute* of sin from us when he crushes us under the yoke of bad habit.* But just as we read that Pharaoh, afflicting the Israelite people *with clay and brick,** had many overseers under him,* so too the prince of darkness appoints a different instigator to exact tribute from each person. These instigators assign them their labor, strike the reckless with suggestions and temptations, and force those oppressed by the hard slavery of sin to wear themselves out with filthy works.*

*Isa 14:4
*Jdt 5:10
*Exod 5:10

*Aelred, S 56.4

13. But whoever you are, O soul whom God's kindness has freed from this unhappiness, granting that *you rest from your work and from your confusion and from your hard slavery in which you served before,** you are surely amazed that continence, which seemed impossible be-

*Isa 14:3

fore, has become so easy for you. You are amazed that the yoke of fixed habit has vanished when, before, an inborn hopelessness had made you abandon every effort to be rid of it. You are amazed to despise the enemy's suggestion so easily when, up to this point, a kind of unavoidable necessity compelled you to obey it. Therefore, take up *this parable against Babylon's king.** Exult with trembling,* shout with astonishment, *How has the overseer failed, the tribute come to an end?**

*Isa 14:4
*Ps 2:11
*Isa 14:4

14. The spirit of fornication was in pursuit every day, demanding its tribute of filth and uncleanness. There was neither the ability to drive it away nor the virtue to resist it. *How,* then, *has the overseer failed, the tribute come to an end?** The spirit of anger rose up in me, it drove me time and again to words of fury. Sometimes it demanded bitter silence, sometimes furious shouting, and sometimes the trembling of quarrels and strife as though a service owed to it. But now, *How has the overseer failed, the tribute come to an end?** The spirit of gluttony, stirring up the appetite for forbidden and unavailable foods, demanding from me the coin of daily murmuring and criticism,* made me unmanageable to my teachers and impatient with my peers. And so now, *How has the overseer failed, the tribute come to an end?** The spirit of *acedia,* overturning every peaceful state within me and daily inflicting on me a dread of solitude and a hatred of quiet, compelled me to pay it with endless wanderings and useless or even harmful signs. But now, *How has the overseer failed, the tribute come to an end?**

*Isa 14:4
*Isa 14:4
*Wis 1:11
*Isa 14:4
*Isa 14:4

15. The spirit of sadness, devouring my soul's every joy, strove to impose a tribute of spite and hopelessness on me. *How,* then, *has the overseer failed, the tribute come to an end?** The spirit of pride invaded the innermost seat of my heart. At times, it made me impatient at being a subject, at times desirous of having power; at times it forced me to look down on others and walk *in great and wonderful things above myself;** at times it imposed a weight of daily pain and displeasure

*Isa 14:4
*Ps 130:1

on me, persuading me to prefer myself to my betters and to envy the progress of others. Now, *How has the overseer failed, the tribute come to an end?** Does this arise from my virtue? Does it come from my sword? Of course not!* How, then? Of course, *The Lord has broken the staff of the ungodly, the rod of the rulers.† The Lord, crushing wars, Lord is his name.§*

16. Thanks be to you, Lord Jesus, because you do not allow us *to be tempted* beyond our capabilities!* You did not put a sword in our enemy's hand, but rather a staff or a rod. For a sword kills, while a rod or staff afflicts. It is your voice, then, that spoke to Satan about blessed Job, saying, *Behold, in your hand is everything that he owns, but do not stretch out your hand against him.** Then, when he had given him power even over Job's body, God said, *But leave his soul.** A rod was given to him, a staff was given to him, but the sword was denied him. He was given a rod when he was permitted to seize temporal things. He was also given a staff when he was allowed to ravage Job's body. He was denied the sword when he was forbidden to destroy Job's soul.

17. He strikes with the rod when he affects things outside of us. He strikes with the staff when he afflicts the body itself. He strikes with the sword when he tears the soul from the body. With this triple temptation the devil raged long ago against the martyrs. With this triple temptation, too, the Antichrist will rage against the faithful by means of the devil at the end of the world. Against us who are situated, as it were, between the two eras, the devil attacks with the rod and the staff, because the sword has been taken away from him. And so, when we are struck by the loss of temporal things, it is the rod; when by bodily sickness or another physical affliction,* it is the staff. He also strikes with the rod when he persuades us to pleasure, with the staff when he draws us to consent, and with the sword when he compels us to take action. When we are set free from

*Isa 14:4

*Josh 24:12;
Ps 43:4
†Isa 14:5
§Jdt 16:3

*1 Cor 10:13

*Job 1:12
*Job 2:6

*Eccl 12:12

all this, this refrain will be ours: *The Lord has broken the staff of the ungodly, the rod of the rulers.** *Isa 14:5

18. The demons are the *ungodly*. They never cease to flog mortal humans, not out of a love for justice or a desire to correct our errors, but out of sheer ill-will. God's just judgment permits the demons to have mastery over humans either to purge them temporarily or to punish them eternally.* The prophet fittingly adds that the demons' ill-will *fell upon the peoples in displeasure with an incurable blow.** This incurable blow pertains to the condemned, who, murmuring, could be wounded by the blows of the staff or rod but could not be healed. And it follows, *that had subjugated the nations in fury and persecuted them cruelly.** For *the wicked spirit* subjects the nations to itself by many temptations.* It does this not out of a love for justice, but in fury. It persecutes them cruelly, not mercifully, as Christ does, who *strikes* to heal,* *puts to death* to give life, and *leads down to hell* to bring back up again.*

19. O dear brothers, *be on guard against murmuring and keep your tongue from slander.** Behold, the Lord visits our *iniquities with the rod and* our *sins with blows.*† The harvest has failed, and much of the livestock has perished. We may have to bear some loss of our accustomed consolation under this misfortune. Bear with patience, I beg you, the rod of the Lord.* For it is not mine, is it? Let us not delude ourselves, saying, "Far be it from me! We do not murmur *against the Lord,* but against those who should have been on guard against these things." Be on guard against yourselves, my dear children, guard yourselves in this respect! The *sons of Israel* were murmuring *against Moses and Aaron.** And they said, *you are not murmuring against us, but against the Lord. For what are we?**

20. Happy the soul that, passing *through fire and water,** is able to say, *All the land took its rest and kept silent; it rejoiced and exulted.** We are back to what was said before, *How has the overseer failed, the tribute come*

*Isa 14:5

*Wis 16:18; 2 Thess 1:5

*Isa 14:6

*Isa 14:6

*1 Sam 16:14; Acts 19:15

*Job 5:18

*1 Sam 2:6; Jerome, In Isa 6.22

*Wis 1:11; Matt 16:11 and parallels
†Ps 88:33

*Bar 4:25

*Exod 16:2-3
*Exod 16:7-8

*Ps 65:12
*Isa 14:7

to an end?* Then, the prophet answered his own ques-   *Isa 14:4
tion: *The Lord has broken the staff of the ungodly,* etc.* Not   *Isa 14:5-6
only does it say that *the overseer has failed* and that *the
tribute has come to an end,* but also that *all the land took
its rest and kept silent.*

21. In the land of our heart and in the land of our
flesh, when we grow weary of our many temptations,
how great is the disturbance, how great is the shout
of the vices shouting *to one another!** Happy is the soul   *Isa 6:3; Ezek 1:9
that does not hear this shouting within itself, that does
not hear *the leaders' exhortation and the army's howling!**   *Job 39:25
These are the leaders whom we called to mind a little
while ago, the inciters of the capital vices, those whom
an army of countless sins follows.* What great happi-   *Gregory, Mo
31.XLV.87
ness when *all the land* takes its rest and is silent,† when   †Isa 14:7
the stings of lust, the pricks of pleasure, and the spines
of unclean passions grow quiet in our flesh, when the
disturbance of thoughts, the suggestion of pleasures,
the swelling of pride, the onslaught of anger, the horror of murmuring, and the whispering of mistrust or
displeasure grow silent in the heart!

22. But when the shout of the vices rests and keeps
silent, the satisfaction and joy of the virtues follow: *it
rejoiced and exulted.** It says of the land that it *took its*   *Isa 14:7
rest and kept silent.* Therefore our flesh, which the text   *Isa 14:7
calls a *land,* is said to rejoice when it is quiet, because
it makes the soul to which it belongs rejoice and exult.
For we say that a day is joyful if it makes people joyful,
and we say that it is sad if it makes many people sad.
The prophecy says, *it rejoiced and exulted.** O, what joy,   *Isa 14:7
what exultation, when all things are joyful, when all
things are peaceful in a person's conscience, when the
soul boasts of the virtues alone after Satan has been
crushed underfoot and every stain has been removed
by the casting out of the vices!*   *Rom 16:20

23. It therefore continues, *The fir trees also rejoiced
over you, and the cedars of Lebanon.** You should inter-   *Isa 14:8
pret the fir trees and cedars, which are tall, fragrant

trees, as the virtues. Their crown reaches up to heaven, and their odor of good repute fills the world. The conscience truly rejoices in the virtues when they are both lofty from stretching forth to heavenly realities and fragrant with a sound character. This is what the apostle said: *Preparing good things not only in the presence of God, but also in the presence of human beings.** This happens when *the fir trees and the cedars* rejoice, that is, when the virtues take the place of the vices and flood the soul with saving joy: *Since you have slept,* they say, *no one has arisen to cut us down.**

*Rom 12:17

*Isa 14:8

24. This verse is addressed to *the king of Babylon,** that is, to the prince of darkness.* You fell asleep, O Satan, but you did not die. There is no safety, my brothers, there is no safety. The enemy sleeps, but he has not passed away. Whoever sleeps can easily wake up. There is peace, there is rest, because no one has arisen to cut down the virtues since Satan fell asleep. But this applies to the perfect ones, brothers. For them, there is no longer any *struggle against the flesh,* which often cuts down the virtues by its inborn concupiscence, *but against spiritual evil.** When this evil has fallen asleep, that is, when it is no longer a source of temptation, those who are perfect take their rest, not having anything to fight about in themselves that arises from themselves.

*Isa 14:4

*Eph 6:12

*Eph 6:12

25. Of course, you must know, my brothers, that this peace can be neither constant nor complete until *the last enemy, death,* is destroyed,* that is, the author of death, the devil.* When he sleeps no longer, but is as it were dead, the company of the saints will mock him, saying, *Where, death, is your victory? Where, death, is your sting?** Isaiah says the same thing in other words: *How has the overseer failed, the tribute come to an end?*†

*1 Cor 15:26

*Wis 2:24

*1 Cor 15:55;
Jerome, In
Isa 6.23
†Isa 14:4
§Isa 14:9

26. *Hell below was confused at meeting you; it raised up giants for you.*§ Once the saints have overcome the devil, the hellish throng—namely, the company of unclean spirits—comes to meet him. They raise up for

him giants, who are the strongest of their company, and return with them to the house from which they had been cast out. If they are permitted to reenter, they render *the person's last state worse than before.** *Matt 12:44-45

27. This alternation between temptation and peace continues in us until *all the princes of the land* and *all the princes of the nations,** fleeing from their thrones, mourn the destruction of their prince. *The princes of the land* are the chiefs of those pursuing earthly things,** and *the princes of the nations** are the Persian or Greek princes and kings, as you read in the book of Daniel,** or rather the chiefs of the vices. Their prince's corpse, that is, the entire company of the condemned handed over with him for eternal punishment, will be laid waste by moths, eaten by rot, and gnawed at by worms.**

*Isa 14:9

*Phil 3:19
*Isa 14:9
*Dan 10:13, 20

*Isa 14:9-11

28. Do not be amazed if I have kept you longer today than usual. Eager for you after such a long fast, I was not easily satisfied by your presence.** Nor should you think that I am satisfied now. I am ending this sermon because I am tired, not satisfied. *I will be satisfied when Christ's glory appears,** in whom I will now embrace you with great delight. I hope that I will happily enjoy you in him *whose is the honor and the glory, forever and ever. Amen.**

*Oner, Ep 2

*Ps 16:15; Col 3:4

*Rom 16:27; Heb 13:21; Phlm 20; Aelred, Spec car 3.9.28

Homily 16

1. Now that the holy feast of Christmas has come to an end, we return to the exploration of the prophetic vision's mysteries. In so doing, dear brothers, we do not forsake spiritual delights, but exchange them. But we do not even exchange them, since what we celebrate as having been fulfilled during these holy days we see foretold in the prophetic discourse. For the one Word of God feeds and nourishes us everywhere. It was for this reason that *he became flesh and dwelt among us,** so that fleshly beings could hear him. He could then instruct them by his words, strengthen them by his miracles,* draw them forward with his examples, and finally redeem them by shedding his blood.*

*John 1:14

*Mark 16:20

*Heb 9:12, 22; 11:28

2. We find that the prophet foretold his birth, passion, resurrection, ascension into heaven, the faith of the Gentiles, and the rule of the holy church, and we rejoice that all of this has been fulfilled. In the same way, no Christian doubts that the following will also be fulfilled: the Antichrist's tyranny, the persecution of the church in the last days, the destruction of that wretched one,* the future Judgment of God, and the ruin of the devil with all his members,† all of which the same Scriptures say will take place. And so, after describing the Antichrist's persecution, the prophecy continues up to his destruction, when both the power and dominion of Satan himself are cast down.* Still presented under the figure of the king of Babylon, he is attacked, as the prophecy goes on to say: *How did*

*1 Tim 4:1; 2 Pet 3:3 †Rom 2:2-3

*1 Cor 15:24

you fall from heaven, Lucifer, who were rising in the morning?*

*Isa 14:12

3. Concerning the matters that we are to discuss, dear brothers, I think it is useful to relate the words of blessed Augustine and what he thought appropriate to remark in this regard. With the light of so great an authority leading the way, we may thus examine the deep abyss of this part of Scripture all the more securely for being more brightly lit.

4. "It is spoken through Isaiah," he said, "*How did you fall from heaven, Lucifer, who were rising in the morning,** etc., which we understand to refer to the devil under the figure of the king of Babylon. Many of the things written about him correspond to his body, which he gathers from the human race, especially from among those who cling to him through pride, abandoning God's commandments. For just as the body of Christ, which is the church, is called Christ,* in the same way the body of the devil—that is, the crowd of godless people and especially those who fall from Christ or his church as though from heaven—is called the devil, and has the devil himself as its head. Many things are said figuratively that apply not so much to the head as to the body. And so we can understand Lucifer, who was rising early in the morning and fell, to be that group of people forsaking Christ or his church. Having lost the light they bore, they turn toward the darkness. In the same way, those who turn to God cross over from the darkness to the light, that is, those who were darkness become light."*

*Isa 14:12

*Col 1:24

*Augustine, Gen
ad litt 11.24;
Acts 26:18

5. And so, according to blessed Augustine, these verses refer not so much to the person of the devil as to his members. The prophet mystically describes not so much that first fall of the devil—of which the Lord said, *I saw Satan falling from heaven like lightning**—as the apostasy of those turning back from the church. Now because the Antichrist is said to be the most sublime and wicked of all the devil's members, during

*Luke 10:18;
Jerome, In Isa 6.24

whose time there will be a great crowd abandoning the faith, his ruin along with that of his followers is portrayed according to the prophet's arrangement. But because there is one body of evil ones, we should not doubt that whoever falls from the church never to return shares in this ruin. In all of them, the head of this body, the devil himself, is put to confusion, him whom the verse prophetically rebukes, saying, *How did you fall from heaven, Lucifer, who were rising in the* *Isa 14:12   *morning?**

6. The Antichrist can be called *Lucifer* for the brightness of his temporal glory, for his feigned holiness, for a kind of unique light of worldly wisdom that he will supposedly have, or for the false miracles that he will display. His rising, that is, the beginning of his manifestation, will shine forth in all of these things. For this *rising in the morning* announces the beginning of his manifestation. Or *in the morning* denotes this present life, which tends toward decrepitude like morning toward the evening, to be snuffed out when death overtakes it like night. This is why Solomon says about those people who, despising what is to come, can enjoy the delights of the present life, *Woe to the land*

*Eccl 10:16;   *whose princes eat in the morning!** The Antichrist's glory,
Gregory, Mo   then, will be temporal rather than eternal, brief rather
16.LIX.72   than lasting, and fleeting rather than stable. This is
               why it says, *How did you fall from heaven, Lucifer, who*
*Isa 14:12   *were rising in the morning?**

7. Understand *heaven* to be that temple of which the apostle, speaking in reference to the Antichrist, says, *He who opposes and is raised up above everything that is called God or that is worshiped, so that he may sit in God's*
*2 Thess 2:4   *temple, showing himself to be like God.** These words show that he will hold power in God's very church. He will perhaps first enter the church as though to guide it, but will in fact attack it. Let no one think it absurd that he should obtain a highly renowned seat in the church or a kind of royal dignity. Thus, gradu-

ally, first *by false signs and wonders,** then with the favor
of kings and princes, he will advance to great power,
glory, and reputation. Based on these, he will easily
persuade Jews and Gentiles that he is Christ, falsely
claiming that he is the son of God, *showing himself to
be like God.**

8. But whereas the apostle says, *He who opposes and
is raised up above everything that is called God,** holy Isaiah adds the proud thoughts with which the Antichrist
will desire superiority, prophesying, *He said in his
heart, "I will ascend to heaven."** This is the heaven from
which the prophet mockingly said that the Antichrist
had fallen: *How did you fall from heaven, Lucifer, who
were rising in the morning? You fell to earth, you who
wounded nations.** That the Antichrist will wound the
nations with a deep wound, a cruel *blow,** no one who
listens to the apostle can doubt: *Him whose coming according to Satan's power in every seduction, in false signs
and wonders, to those who are perishing.** *You fell to
earth,** it says. For brought low *by the spirit of* God's
mouth,* he will possess hell instead of heaven. His
body, sent to the earth, *will be corrupted by rot.** The
translators of the Septuagint translated it not as *you
who wounded nations* but as *you who sent to all the nations,** meaning that the Antichrist's messengers
would be sent to all the nations and would rage everywhere against Christ's church.*

9. It states, *He said in his heart, "I will ascend to
heaven."** We can understand these to be the words of
the devil speaking in the Antichrist and desiring to
subjugate Christ's entire city to himself through his
servant. The Antichrist, then, inspired by the devil's
spirit, will perceive that the prince *of darkness* has
given him power in worldly wisdom and *in signs* and
wonders.* He will then strive for that which is regarded
as most lofty in this world, namely, for leadership of
the church. When, as it says in the books of Revelation
and Daniel,* the beast receives power over all things—

*2 Thess 2:9

*2 Thess 2:4

*2 Thess 2:4

*Isa 14:13

*Isa 14:12
*Isa 14:6

*2 Thess 2:9-10
*Isa 14:12
*2 Thess 2:8
*Mic 2:10; Isa
14:11

*Isa 14:12

*Jerome,
In Isa 6.24
*Isa 14:13

*2 Thess 2:9;
1 Cor 2:6;
Eph 6:12

*Rev 13:1-10;
Dan 7:19-25

that is, when his rule shines forth through ten kings

*Ps 35:5 like ten horns—he will plot *wickedness in his bed.** He will say, *I will ascend to heaven,* that is, I will rule over the church, *over God's stars,* over those namely who shine forth like stars by the brightness of wisdom or the brilliance of religion. *I will raise up my throne,* sub-

Isa 14:13 jecting them to my decrees and judgments.

10. And it adds, *I will sit on the mountain of the cove-

*Isa 14:13 *nant, on the sides of the north.** The land of Jerusalem can be called the mountain of the covenant. Some think that the Antichrist will rule in that city's temple. The psalmist said of this mountain, *Mount Zion on*

*Ps 47:3 *the sides of the north, the great king's city.** All these things are better understood of Christ's church, which is certainly Mount Zion and the mountain of the covenant, whose sides the north—that is, the cold crowd of the condemned and persecutors—always surrounds. The mountain of the covenant can also be understood as denoting the more excellent and perfect members of the church, who place the New

*Ps 49:5 *Covenant over the sacrifices of the law,** in whom the ancient enemy will strive to prepare for himself a

2 Thess 2:3 seat through that son of perdition. Paul explains what is meant by *I will ascend to heaven* or *I will sit on*

*Isa 14:13 *the mountain of the covenant,** saying, *So that he may sit*
*2 Thess 2:4 *in God's temple.**

*Isa 14:14 **11.** *I will rise above the loftiness of the clouds.** The clouds are the preachers of the Gospel, of whom the Lord says through this same Isaiah, *I will command my clouds*

*Isa 5:6 *not to rain on that vineyard.** And elsewhere, *Who are*
*Isa 60:8; Jerome,
In Isa 6.25 *they who fly like clouds?** The devil boasts that he will rise above clouds of this sort through the Antichrist. Thus, being higher, he will rule the lower, and he will tempt the willing, deceive the reckless, force the un-willing, and punish the resisters, making them all give in to his will.

*Isa 14:14 **12.** It continues, *I will be like the Most High.** This is the same as what Paul said: *Showing himself to be like*

God.* But we can also fittingly apply all of this to any   *2 Thess 2:4
given heretic, and certainly to the category of heretics
as a whole. At first they are Lucifers, that is, bearing
the light* of knowledge. But they slip in the darkness   *lucem ferentes
of error and so fall from the firmament of the church.
They thus become teachers of perverse dogma. The
beginning of their apostasy is pride, by which they
strive to rule in the church as though climbing up *to
heaven.** By pride, they strive to preside over the holy   *Isa 14:13
ones, as though they were lifted up *over the stars.** By   *Isa 14:13
pride, they strive to subordinate whoever is loftier
than they, as though they sought to sit *on the mountain
of the covenant.** In their pride, they want to appear   *Isa 14:13
higher in wisdom than all the other preachers of the
truth, as though they were rising *above the loftiness of
the clouds.** In fact, the proud always want to rule in   *Isa 14:14
this way, so that they may refuse to be subordinated.
This is why, in their pride, they seek the likeness of
him who rules all things but is subordinated to
nothing.

13. Beware, dear brothers, beware of pride. It gives
me pain to say how many people are worthy of the
name *Lucifer.* Perhaps they see that they have advanced in the light of wisdom and have benefited
others by word and example. Thus, *early in the morn-
ing,* that is, at the beginning of their religious life,*   *conuersionis
they are regarded as brighter than those who share
the same life. At first, a hidden interior pride puffs
them up. They despise their superiors, at times accusing them of naiveté and ignorance, at others mocking and criticizing them for their involvement in
worldly affairs. They regard everyone as inferior to
themselves, having always before their eyes something that they find blameworthy in others. Even
when they find nothing, they pretend to have found
something. And calling to mind the praiseworthy acts
they themselves do in the sight of others, they feed
on their own inner vanity. Whoever is like this, then,

judging everyone unworthy of leadership, says, *I will ascend to heaven.**

14. *O Lucifer, who were rising in the morning,** you meditate on *iniquity on* your *bed!** What do you say? "Who is this person, or that other one, who would rule over us? An *uneducated* fool,** someone devoted to and entangled in earthly affairs, someone not known for eloquence, or well versed in the Scriptures, or distinguished in deed, or skilled in the spiritual art."* Saying these things in their hearts, such people, like Absalom, prepare to kill their father, saying, *Who will appoint me judge over this people?** I will ascend to heaven,** I who am worthy to rule *in the heavens,*† that is, in spiritual things, since my life is always in heaven.§ *Why such waste?‡* A waste, I say, of such wisdom, of such virtue and eloquence, which could be so useful. But because I sit below, these qualities are of no benefit. Therefore, *over God's stars,* like Lucifer, brighter than the others, *I will raise up my throne.** Sitting *on the mountain of the covenant* I will attain for myself the likeness of God by helping others.*

15. For since the Holy Scripture is called a *covenant,* it is not unfitting to say that the mountain of the covenant is love, which is the highest of the virtues and contains in itself the entirety of the law and the prophets.* Therefore, nothing is more arrogant and ambitious than to offer to rule in charity, all the while whispering everywhere against one's superior in nooks with accusations of hardheartedness and unkindness.* As though painting a picture before the brothers' eyes, such a one also describes *what kind of person the abbot ought to be,** how modest, how godly, how loving of one's subjects, how compassionate of their labors, how sympathetic to the sick. Then this proud monk establishes on the authority of the Scriptures how lovingly the refectory should be arranged, how mercifully the infirmary should be set up. In this way, the hearts of the listeners respond, "If only this

*Isa 14:13
*Isa 14:12
*Ps 35:5

*Acts 4:13

*RB 4.75

*2 Sam 15:4
*Isa 14:13
†Eph 1:20
§Phil 3:20
‡Matt 26:8

*Isa 14:13

*Gen 5:1

*Matt 22:40

*Oner 7.3; 13.15

*RB 2, title

person were abbot! What an abbot such a one would be! How wise, how eloquent, how merciful, and how kind!" And the ambitious monk, noticing this response, says, "*Who is like me in the clouds of heaven?** Who is as learned as I in the Scriptures? Who is more suited to preach? *I will rise above the loftiness of the clouds,** and, towering over the other preachers, *I will demonstrate my wisdom,** lest that which could benefit so many should remain hidden any longer. So in me the restored likeness of God will shine forth,* which likeness consists mostly in wisdom and charity."

*Ps 88:7, 9

*Isa 14:14
*Job 32:10

*Gen 5:1

16. When such people obtain their will and advance to the leadership that they sought either by their own scheming or by a faction of others, God's grace strips them of their pretended virtues and they fall into open vice. Hated by all, such people are cast out and thus deserve to hear, "*How did you fall from heaven, Lucifer, who were rising in the morning? You fell to earth, you* who boasted of your heavenly life.* It is now clear that you have not offered a remedy for others with your words, but rather you have inflicted the wounds of sins."

*Isa 14:12;
Phil 3:20

17. The prophecy is not silent about what kind of punishment all such people deserve, because it is certain that they belong to that wicked head's body. But because we have drawn this out into such a long sermon, let us save the things that follow to be discussed at another time, with the help of *him who is over all things, the blessed God forever. Amen.**

*Rom 9:5

Homily 17

1. Yesterday, brothers, we discussed as best as our limited capacity allowed the devil's fall, which he suffers or will suffer in his body. But many think that these prophetic words refer to the person of the devil himself and to his first fall. He fell from his heavenly dwelling and thus turned from an angel to a devil, from the morning star* to the evening.† If we are able to find something in this reading, I do not think I should rob you of it.

*Lucifer
†John 14:2; Jerome, In Isa 6.24

2. The prophet had described the destruction of either the devil or his members using the name of the king of Babylon, saying, *Your pride has been dragged down to hell; your corpse has fallen. The moth and rot will spread under you, and worms will be your covering.** Then, turning his eyes to the devil's original glory, with which he was formerly glorious *in the heavens,** and wondering at such a great and wretched change, the prophet said, *How did you fall from heaven, Lucifer, who were rising in the morning?**

*Isa 14:11

*Eph 3:10 and parallels

*Isa 14:12

3. It is believed that he is called Lucifer because, just as the *morning star* surpasses the other stars in the beauty of its light,* so too that archangel is thought to have been brighter than the other angels. The prophet Ezekiel said of him, *Every precious stone was your garment.** Then he added the names of nine stones. Some say this was to show that Lucifer was more highly decorated than the nine orders of angels, brighter than

*Sir 50:6; Rev 22:16

*Ezek 28:13

the others in wisdom, and more beautiful than the others.* ·····*Ezek 28:12; Gregory, Mo 32. XXIII.47; Gregory, Eu 34.7

4. As to the description of his rising *in the morning,*† I think this refers to that passage in the book of Job that we take to be about the devil: *He is the beginning of God's ways.** *In the morning,* that is, at the beginning of the day, means the *beginning of* all *creation.** It therefore says that he rose *in the morning* or at *the beginning of God's ways,* because, just as his nature appeared more worthy than the others, so too he preceded all the others in creation.* Another translation declares this more plainly, saying, *He is the beginning of his fashioning.** As to his falling from heaven, the Lord himself bears witness, saying, *I saw Satan falling from heaven like lightning.*†

†Isa 14:12

*Job 40:14

*Jas 1:18

*Gregory, Mo 32. XXIII.47

*Job 40:14 LXX; Augustine, Civ Dei 11.15.17

†Luke 10:18; Jerome, In Isa 6.24

5. It continues, *You fell to earth, you who wounded nations.** He calls *earth* that dark air that draws breath from the earth.* The apostle Peter plainly states that the demons were cast down there as though into a prison, saying, *He did not spare the sinning angels, but he handed them over to judgment, dragged down to the underworld by hellish ropes to be kept for punishment.**

*Isa 14:12

*Oner 20.16

*2 Pet 2:4; 1 Pet 3:19; Rev 20:7; Augustine, Gen ad litt 11.26

†Isa 14:12

6. *You fell to earth, you who wounded nations.*† If it does not seem ridiculous to you, we can understand *nations* to be that faction of angels that was struck by the spear of Lucifer's proud example. As sharers in his sin, they also became sharers in his punishment.

7. We have gone quickly thus far, making rapid progress in our explanation. What should I say about the parts that follow? *You said in your heart, "I will ascend to heaven. Over God's stars I will raise up my throne,"* etc.* We must first examine what *heaven* is, what *God's stars* are, what *the mountain of the covenant* is, what *the sides of the north* are, and what the likeness of God is. For since Lucifer is believed to have been in heaven before his fall—otherwise he did not fall from heaven—to which heaven did he desire to ascend?*

*Isa 14:13-14

*Jerome, In Isa 6.25

Even if the angels are to be understood as the *stars,*
how can he desire to raise his throne over them, since
it previously mentions that he was more excellent than
the others? These points are obscure; we will touch
upon them rather than explain them. And so let us
continue by offering opinions rather than stating facts.

8. We must first affirm that every creature was created as something changeable. For if the rational
mind, which surpasses all creatures, were not made
as something changeable, it would not need the help
of its Creator. If such were the case, it would not be
able to advance toward the better nor decline toward
the worse. Now the rational mind needed to be aware
of its changeability, so that it might learn by experience that without the Creator's help it could neither
stand in that good in which it was created nor climb
to anything higher. It would thus understand what is
written, *It is good for me to cling to God,** *so that every
mouth* might be silenced *and every* creature made subject *to God.**

9. Therefore, so that angels and humans could perceive the changeability of their natures, each had to
be tempted; and having been tempted, tried; and having been tried, confirmed. Grace would thus be
granted to those who conquered, and justice would
dawn for those who fell short because of their own
wickedness. For it was to the rational creatures' glory
that, from the grace of their Lord, some merit of their
own might lead the way to the fullness of blessing that
the Creator's kindness was to bestow upon them.
Happiness itself would thus be both a gift and a
reward.

10. And Sacred Scripture plainly declares the temptation of humanity. For *a beautiful tree, pleasing to the
eye and sweet to the taste,** was set before us, and we
were told not to touch it. This was the occasion of our
temptation; if we had conquered it, the cause for glory
would have been all the greater. Therefore, just as that

*Ps 72:28

*Rom 3:19;
Aelred,
Anima 2.50–51

*Gen 2:9; 3:3, 6

beautiful tree was set before humanity, so too something was perhaps set before the angels to tempt them. The temptation itself would thus both demonstrate the changeability of their nature and honor their free will, for which grace would bestow a reward upon some and justice would inflict punishment on others. Ask yourselves whether this heaven and this mountain of the covenant were not perhaps set before them as temptations. Only the one *who said in his heart,** I *will ascend to heaven,* etc.,* together with his followers, preferred his own rule to the love and obedience of his Creator. But what sort of heaven was this, and how was it set before him as a temptation?

11. O, my brothers, *He who lives forever created everything at once.** Of this it is also written, *He made the things that will be.** Listen to the blessed evangelist John: *In the beginning was the Word.†* And a little later, *What was made was life in him.§* Therefore, all things are present to the Creator as already made before they come to be in themselves. They are even said to abide* in the very Creator in a wonderful and inexpressible way. Places without place, times without time, and bodies without bodies exist there; there, all sensory things live free from the senses, all changeable things live without changing, all things liable to death live immortally. There this same Isaiah, gazing upon the incarnation of the Word, spoke of *what* had *not happened yet* as if it had,* saying, *A little one was born to us, a son was given to us.** There too, looking on his passion, he said, *We saw him, and there was no beauty.** And later it follows, *He handed his soul over to death and was considered one of the wicked.** There holy David remembered in the past tense the one who was pierced by nails, fed gall, given vinegar to drink, and many other such things.*

12. It would not be remarkable, then, if the recently created angels, whose nature was subtler and to whom God's nature was more present, saw in the Creator

*Ps 13:1

*Isa 14:13

*Sir 18:1

*Isa 45:11 LXX;
Oner 2.24; 19.3;
Augustine, In
Ps 104.11
†John 1:1
§John 1:3-4

*subsistere

*Isa 46:10

*Isa 9:6

*Isa 53:2

*Isa 53:12

*Pss 21:17-19;
68:22

himself some of the things that would take place as though they had happened already. Some might have proudly striven after what they saw, while others preferred obedience to their Creator above all this. Perhaps they saw there a small crowd of those who were chosen, humble, gentle, and dependent on their Creator in all things. Perhaps they also saw another opposing group, greater in number, proud of heart, fighting against God, bitterly attacking that smaller but more blessed group. The changeability of their free will thus tempted them to choose between being subjected to God in humility or ruling over such people in power.

13. For this reason, the most wicked one of all, the loftiest of all, *thought up wickedness in his bed,** saying, *I will ascend to heaven.** Just as he saw that that holy company in which God would reign would be called *heaven,* so too he arrogantly called those over whom he now longed to rule *his heaven.* But he also strives to ascend in that holy company, as though in God's very heaven. When he saw that the condemned would attack it, he himself decided to attack it in and through them.

14. *Over God's stars I will raise up my throne.** The devil calls *his throne* all the condemned who are lofty in this world, in whom he mainly rules. In this world, such people even receive power *over God's stars,* namely, the saints, whom they tempt, weigh down, pursue, and punish. Remember, my brothers, how small in number, how lowly, and how despicable the holy ones were when all the glory of the world, the kings and princes, with the Roman emperors above all, sacrificed to idols. Despising God and despised by God, they weighed down his few worshipers in Judea with *hard slavery.** Thus Lucifer saw in the spirit their grandeur and power, and also the small number and lowly condition of the holy ones. Seeing—that is, approving of—*every lofty thing,** and despising what was base, and striving for rule over the former and oppres-

*Ps 35:5
*Isa 14:13

*Isa 14:13

*Isa 14:3;
2 Macc 1:19

*Job 41:25

sion of the latter, he said, *Over God's stars I will raise up my throne.** *Isa 14:13

15. It is as though someone said to him, "What, then, will you do about the Jews, who are called the mountain of the covenant, who oppose your decrees?" He responds immediately with a godless thought: *I will sit on the mountain of the covenant.* And if not on the entire mountain, *on the sides,* that is, in the parts, *of the north,** in those people who will prepare a seat for me in their hearts with the northern cold of the vices.* The lofty figures Annas and Caiaphas dwell there,* as do the scribes and Pharisees, whom I will misuse to bring about my will. *Isa 14:13
*Ps 102:19
*Luke 3:2

16. Then he saw that the Lord would send his clouds to every place on earth that would oppose him. Trusting *in his own power and* believing *in his own great number* of tricks,* he said, "*I will rise above the loftiness of the clouds,** that is, of the preachers, whom he would weigh down or deceive, *and I will be like the most high.** God has his angels, prophets, and apostles, through whom he advises, rules, subordinates, and attracts his own to himself. In the same way, I, too, will have my angels, namely, the fugitive spirits, as well as my prophets and apostles—those whom we call false prophets and false apostles*—to draw my own people to me and subordinate them to my will in all things."* *Ps 48:7
*Isa 14:14

*Isa 14:14

*Matt 24:11;
2 Cor 11:13
*Jerome, In
Isa 6.25

17. He does not predict that these things will come to pass as a true prophet would. Rather, deceived by pride, he assures himself of such dominion by his empty thoughts. It is true that he said he would ascend *to heaven* and place his *throne over* heaven's *stars,** and other things of this sort. But if we cannot clearly and comprehensibly explain how this took place, we should understand that he did not foretell what would happen. Rather, seeing in the Creator those whom the Creator abandoned, and eager to rule them, he proclaimed boastful words. *Isa 14:13

18. Nor should you think that he spoke in his heart as we might, expressing what we wish through a kind of representation of words, nor was there any sort of delay between that vision of which we have spoken and his proud thought. But just as he saw in the Creator what he sought without any passage of time, so too he conceived in his mind everything represented by these words at once, without any delay. He thus fell without any passage of time. The prophet could not make all of this known to us without words written or produced with a certain delay. For of course the proud one was not able to remain in heaven, as indeed he might have done for some time if he had been allowed to think for a while after he had conceived his ambition.

19. If we accept the opinion of some that, dwelling in the lower parts or the firmament with those who fell, he aspires to that lofty heaven in which God dwells with those who did not fall,* then blessed Gregory's commentary will falter on Ezekiel's words: *You were a sign of likeness, full of wisdom and perfect beauty, you were in God's Paradise; every precious stone was your garment.** But if we assume that his commentary is correct, we must understand that he who fell ruled the other angels first. According to Gregory, God's likeness was more clearly stamped upon him,* especially because he is said to be *full of wisdom and perfect beauty.**

20. Let us also add that this same father, speaking on the very words we have in our hands, called the Jewish people the mountain of the covenant,* and blessed Jerome, commenting on this same prophecy, interpreted heaven's stars as those "who shine in the church" and the mountain of the covenant as the church itself.* How, then, dwelling in such great beauty before the Fall, could he have desired to rule over those who were shining in the church or to sit over the church itself, unless he had seen all these

*Jerome, In
Isa 6.25

*Ezek 28:12-13;
Gregory, Mo 32.
XXIII.47

*Gregory, Mo 32.
XXIII.47

*Ezek 28:12

*Gregory, In
Ezek 1.2.9

*Jerome, In
Isa 6.25

things beforehand in the place where they existed even before they were made? Furthermore, if we also accept the opinion that some fell from each of the nine orders, it is clear that all who shared the same rank had the same degree of perfection insofar as their standing at the time was concerned.

21. What was the sin of those who fell, then, if not pride? And where does this pride come from, if not from striving after something lofty that was not destined for them? And what was that, and where did they see it? If, according to the opinions of preachers, it was rule among the holy ones and in the church, where did they see these things that had not yet been created, unless in the place where these things were before they had been created, that is, in the Creator? But if those who were to fall saw these things, how much more did those who stood in the truth see them! Therefore they all saw them. How is it, then, that some fell and others stood firm? It must be that the former, lifted up by pride, preferred not to be subject to God, but to rule over what that they saw, while the latter preferred to be subject to God rather than to rule.

22. If we consider all these things carefully, we will notice that all were created to be equal according to their order's rank. The same temptation tried them all. But some, corrupted by pride, fell, while others were confirmed in that perfection in which there are now blessings. This was on account of the merit of their humility, which was tested and found worthy. Many things still occur to the mind concerning these matters. But because I lack the ability to explain such things in words, I entrust what I have said for you to ponder and examine. May we learn in this way according to the prophet's teaching what the end of this pride may be. After recording the devil's pride in the words he wished to use, or as best he could, the prophet added, *Yet you will be dragged down to hell, to the depth of the lake.**

*Isa 14:15

23. It is fitting retribution that he who arrogantly wanted to ascend to heaven should unwillingly be dragged down to hell. And not to just any part of hell, but it was fitting that he who sought the height of heaven should descend into the depth of hell. This is what *the depth of the lake* means.* We could say the same thing about his members, namely, the Antichrist and the others about whom we talked yesterday. After the glory of this world and their godless rule, they are to be dragged down to hell. Not to the higher parts, where the holy ones are said to have been before the Lord's incarnation,* but *to the depth of the lake,*† where eternal fire *was prepared for the devil and his angels.**

24. *Those who see you will lean down and look at you.** Truly, brothers, how could those who see with the eyes of the heart and carefully consider from what great perfection and glory the devil and his angels have fallen* and from what great sanctity the proud may fall daily into the abyss of shame, how could such observers not lean down, not humble themselves, not be afraid, not tremble, not place before their own eyes both the original glory or sanctity of those who have fallen and their current unhappiness? This is what the verse means: *Those who see you will lean down* in humility *and look at you* with constant recollection.*

25. Clearly when it says, *They will lean down over you,** it mainly refers to those who, after works of light, after a good beginning to a good monastic life, turn back from the fellowship of the saints to *works of darkness* as though falling from heaven.* The good lean over them out of a kind of compassion, mourning the loss of those who had demonstrated holiness. Remember, brothers, that wretched one who lived among you like Judas among the apostles, having *indeed the appearance of godliness* but fighting against the *virtue* of godliness.* Is there anyone who, remembering his outer appearance and now seeing his inner disposi-

*Jerome, In Isa 5.30

*1 Pet 3:19
†Isa 14:15
*Matt 25:41
*Isa 14:16

*Jerome, In Isa 6.27

*Isa 14:16; Jerome, In Isa 6.27

*Isa 14:16

*Rom 13:12

*2 Tim 3:5

tion, is not amazed that a wolf could hide in a sheep,* a lion in a lamb, a thief in a monk, for so long? Happy are those who, seeing such things, lean down, fearing for themselves and taking pity on him, and so wash *their hands in the blood of the sinner!** — *Matt 7:15

26. But let us return to the prophecy. *Those who see you will lean down and look at you.*† Next comes the discourse of those who mock him and wonder at his great wretchedness after such great happiness: *Is this the man who brought confusion on the land?** With your consent, beloved, let us postpone this until tomorrow, lest this burden should burden us too greatly. But because it does burden you somewhat, let us ask God that it may be understood and not be burdensome. May we comprehend what he wishes to be understood and be on guard against this burden, by the grace of him who lives and reigns forever and ever. Amen.

*Ps 57:11; Augustine, In Ps 57.21
†Isa 14:16

*Isa 14:16; Jerome, In Isa 5.31

Homily 18

1. As you recall, dear brothers, when we discussed the prophetic words figuratively spoken against the prince of Babylon,* we followed the prophecy's order. We first referred this prophecy to the Antichrist and the devil's body.* Then we examined how it could apply to the head itself.* We thus showed that the holy prophet had described the downfall of both. Keeping, then, to the same order for the parts that follow, let us say that the Antichrist is called a *man* not for his virtue,* but for his power: *Is this the man who brought confusion on the land?** Yet the prophet could have called him a man in rebuking him, as one might say of a lazy person, "What kind of man is he?"

2. *Is this the man who brought confusion on the land, who struck kingdoms?** The Antichrist certainly will bring confusion on the land and strike kingdoms when, as it says in the book of Revelation, the people *dwelling in the land will be amazed by the beast.** Kings and kingdoms, struck by a kind of terror, will tremble at his power. Or by *land*, understand the way of life of those who *do not taste the things that are above*, but rather *the things that are of the land.** Having seen the Antichrist's power, *they will stumble* on Christ's faith in their confusion.* Further, interpret the kingdoms of those kings as the dominion of those whose *heart* is *in God's hand*,* those of whom the Lord said, *kings will rule through me*,* those whose *life is in heaven.*† These are the saints and perfect ones of that time. They may indeed be

*Isa 14:12-16

*Oner 16
*Oner 17

*Isidore, Etym 10.274

*Isa 14:16

*Isa 14:16

*Rev 17:8, 12-13

*Phil 3:19, 20; Col 3:2

*Matt 24:10
*Prov 21:1

*Prov 8:15
†Phil 3:20

struck, but cannot be knocked down.* The Lord says
of this striking in the gospel, *False prophets and false
apostles will rise up and produce many signs to lead even
the chosen ones into error, if such a thing were possible.*

3. It follows, *Who made the world a desert, and destroyed its cities.* The prophet calls the church *the world.*
For it is written of the church, *And indeed he has set
right the world, which will not be moved.* After a fashion,
the Antichrist will make this world into a desert when
many will abandon it through him. In another translation it is written, *Who made the world to be like a desert.*
For the church, which will include so many perfect
people, will not really be a desert. But it will be like a
desert, because in comparison to the great number
who now inhabit it, it will seem abandoned and destroyed at that time. He will also destroy its *cities,*
which are the congregations of those who live in community. We clearly showed that they could be called
cities when we discussed the Antichrist's persecution.*
And so that wicked one will destroy the congregations
of the saints, dispersing the communities of the faithful either by subjecting them to his decrees or by persecuting them with torments and legal restrictions.

4. *Who did not open the prison for those whom he conquered,* that is, those of the world. The conquered of
the world are those who are in the church, but the
darkness of ignorance confines them, and the chains
of bad habit bind them. The prophet says of them, *The
ropes of sins have encompassed me.* The corrupt one will
not open the prison for these conquered people.† He
will not lead them out from error by teaching the truth
but will envelop them in the ever-thicker darkness of
his wickedness and treachery.

5. But if you wish to interpret the *man* as the devil
himself,* your interpretation is not baseless. He is
called a *person* in the psalms, the gospel, and many
other places in Holy Scripture. We thus read, *A person
who is against us* has done this.† And *Rise up, Lord, do*

*Jerome, In
Isa 6.27–28

*Matt 24:24;
2 Cor 11:13

*Isa 14:17

*Ps 95:10

*Jerome, In
Isa 6.27

*Oner 10.17

*Isa 14:17

*Ps 118:61;
Aelred, Ss
35.5; 63.10
†Prov 15:12

*Isa 14:16

*inimicus homo
†Matt 13:28

*Ps 9:20;
2 Chr 14:11;
Jerome, In Isa 6.27

*Phil 3:19

*Gal 5:15, 26;
Oner 10.14

*Gen 3:19

*Origen, In Jer 2.9

*2 Tim 2:12

*Jerome, In
Isa 6.27

*Ps 72:2

*Job 1:22; 2:10

*Gen 39:12, 15

*Isa 14:17

*Aelred, Spec
car 1.22.64
†Ps 11:9

*not let a person prevail.** And he has still not left off
disturbing *the land* and striking *kingdoms.* The lovers
of the world and pursuers of worldly glory can be
called *the land.* Anger, envy, ambition, wars, and strife
disturb them by turns. So too, brothers, if some of us
taste the earth or even love anything earthly,* we will
not be free from confusion. Rather, we will bite at,
devour, and envy one another.*

6. But if we lifted our heart from earthly things to
heavenly things, we would hear in the future not, *You
are earth, and you will go to earth,** but, "You are heaven,
and you will go to heaven."** If we lifted our heart in
this way, then our kingdoms, that is, the virtues
through which we already have begun to reign together with Christ,* could still indeed be struck, but
never knocked down.* That kingdom was indeed
struck that belonged to the person whose *feet were
nearly made to totter,* whose *steps nearly staggered.** Job
was struck, but not knocked down.* Joseph, too, was
struck when he *left behind his garment* with the adulter-
ess,* but he who preferred prison to defilement and
chains to adultery was not knocked down. And we
too are struck when we are tempted, but we are not
knocked down if we do not consent.

7. *Who made the world a desert.** We can interpret the
word *world* here to mean those who belong to the
world as though they were circling around the border
of a city, always laboring without ever reaching the
goal.* The prophet says of such people, *The godless
walk in circles,*† that is, in the world. Such people are
not only confused or struck, but even knocked down,
so that no trace of virtue remains in them. Thus, after
the virtues have been cast out, they will be filled with
vices as a wilderness is populated by wild animals.

8. Take note of the following three types of people:
the first type is confused, the second is struck, and the
third is knocked down. Opposing passions shake up
those of the first type and put them to confusion,

because they are *the land*.* Wicked spirits attack those
of the second type,† because they are kings.§ Unclean
spirits crush those of the third type, because they have
no constancy within them but are carried around *by
every wind of doctrine*.* The cities of this world are *their
assemblies of blood*.* These assemblies display the *appearance* of holiness but *deny its power and virtue*.* The
prince of darkness surely destroys such cities, overturning all their ramparts, that is, *the tools of the virtues*
with the virtues themselves.*

9. *Who did not open the prison for those whom he conquered*.* For *the ropes of sin* bind the conquered in such
cities.* The king of confusion brings them down to the
prison of despair, barring the door of confession to
them. Therefore the psalmist says, *Do not let the deluge
of water pull me under*, that is, do not let the power of
temptation bring me down, *nor the depth* of bad habit
swallow me up, nor the pit shut its mouth over me,* lock-
ing the door of confession with the bar of despair.*

10. The prophet then describes the end of the temptation itself. He describes the burden that in the last times
will crush the devil with punishment, along with those
whom he had crushed with sin, adding, *All the kings
of the nations have slept in glory, each one in his own house;
but you were cast out of your tomb like a useless stalk, defiled
and wrapped with those who were killed by the sword*.*

11. *Hear this, kings of the earth*,* you who, though
struck by Satan, could not be knocked down.† Here
there is fear, here there is labor, here there is groaning.
Here, constantly armed for war, *take up the armor of
God, so that you can stand against the devil's snares*.* For
there is a wage for your labor. What wage, you ask?
All the kings of the land will sleep *in glory*.* This is of
course the glorious sleep in which kings lie after victory.* Just as *precious in the Lord's sight* is *the death of his
saints*,* so too is it glorious. How gloriously that *great
king*, I mean Paul, went to his rest!† He joyfully took
up the repose of death crowned by so many victories,
winning a special place among those of whom it is

*Isa 14:16;
Gen 3:19
†Eph 6:12
§Isa 14:16

*Eph 4:14

*Ps 15:4

*2 Tim 3:5

*RB 73.6

*Isa 14:17
*Prov 5:22;
Jerome, In
Isa 6.27

*Ps 68:16
*Aelred, S 72.16

*Isa 14:18-19

*Wis 6:2; Pss 48:2;
148:11
†Jerome, In
Isa 6.28

*Eph 6:11, 13;
Jerome, In Isa 6.27
*Isa 14:18

*Isa 11:10

*Ps 115:15; Ant in
comm Reg
(Hesbert 3.4371)
†Isa 36:4

written in the book of Revelation, *Blessed are the dead who die in the Lord. From this point forward, the Spirit says, they may rest from their labors.**

12. *All the kings* will sleep *in glory.** It is a great thing, brothers, it is a great thing to fall asleep in glory. For some fall asleep in shame, others in mercy, and still others in glory. Those who persevere in their sins fall asleep in shame, those who repent fall asleep in mercy, and the martyrs and innocent ones fall asleep in glory. Those who die in their wicked deeds fall asleep in shame;* those who are washed of their wicked deeds by confession and repentant tears sleep in mercy; those who, made glorious by the wages of their many virtues, are brought to the heavenly realm by angelic hands sleep in glory. The rich man in the gospel fell asleep in shame *and was buried in hell;** Lazarus fell asleep in mercy and was brought to Abraham's breast, and Abraham himself, who was able to be a consolation not only to himself but also to Lazarus, fell asleep in glory. Judas, who *hanged himself with a noose,** fell asleep in shame; the paralytic whose sins the Lord forgave fell asleep in mercy;* Peter, who glorified Christ by his death, fell asleep in glory.†

13. *Each one in his own house,* it says.§ These houses are those *eternal dwellings* in which the perfect receive the imperfect, those namely who made *friends with the mammon of wickedness,** giving what is temporal to receive what is eternal. These houses are the most blessed *dwelling places in the Father's house,** in which there are different rooms for each of the variety of virtues.* Therefore, although all the perfect sleep in glory and they all arrive at the kingdom of heaven, yet *the sun's brightness is one thing, that of the moon another, and that of the stars is* yet *another,* and *star differs from star in brightness.** Therefore *all the kings* sleep *in glory,* yet *each one in his own house.**

14. In addition to these, there is also the shameful sleep of iniquity, the pitiful sleep of weakness, and the glorious sleep of charity. For Paul says to the person

*Rev 14:13
*Isa 14:18

*Josh 22:20

*Luke 16:22

*Matt 27:5

*Matt 9:2 and parallels
†John 21:19
§Isa 14:18

*Luke 16:9

*John 14:2

*Jerome, In Isa 6.28

*1 Cor 15:41
*Isa 14:18

sleeping shamefully, *Get up, you who are sleeping!** To
the one sleeping in weakness or laziness, the heavenly
word says, *How long will you sleep, O slothful one?** But
the bride, who sleeps *in the midst of lots,** boasts of the
bridegroom's embrace, saying, *His left hand is under
my head, and his right will embrace me.** She sweetly rests
between the bridegroom's *breasts, on* the bridegroom's
bosom,* on the bridegroom's *chest.*[†] The bridegroom
encourages this most blessed sleep of hers, saying, *I
implore you, daughters of Jerusalem, not to awaken my
beloved until she herself wishes it.**

    15. I ask, when would she want to wake up? When
would she want to do without these embraces, to be
torn from these breasts, to be separated from this
chest? When charity itself, which lulled her into this
heavenly sleep, wants to arouse her! Standing *at the
door and* knocking, it says, *Open for me, my sister, my
bride.** Hearing the friend's *head full of dew* and his curls
of *the nights' drops,*[†] she wakes up, rises, and opens the
door. Having abandoned the delights that she enjoyed,
she continues on under charity's promptings to his
hair. This hair represents those who cling to him in
faith* but, having caught something of the northern
chill from the night of ignorance, need to be instructed.
So it is that Paul preferred *to be accursed from Christ for
the brothers,** preferring the salvation of many to his
own desires, as lofty as they were.

    16. O brothers, *All the kings of the nations**—those
who rule the people in the church, or those who use
saving instruction to rule their own thoughts, feelings, and even impulses of anger and concupiscence,
as though these were different nations*—sleep *in
glory,* either receiving *the crown of life* in death[†] or resting in contemplation far from physical realities.[§] Another translation puts it thus: *A man in his own house.*[‡]
I think that these words indicate that each person will
find joy in the conscience,[#] not regarding the opinion
of others, but having *glory in oneself and not in
another.**

Marginalia (right column):

*Eph 5:14

*Prov 6:9
*Ps 67:14

*Song 2:6

*John 13:23, 25
†Song 1:12

*Song 2:7; 8:4

*Song 5:1-2;
Rev 3:20
†Song 5:2, 5

*Aelred, SS 36.19;
62.17; 63.22;
Oner 23.14

*Rom 9:3

*Isa 14:18

*Aelred,
S 28.10–11
†Jas 1:12
§2 Cor 12:3-4
‡Isa 14:18 LXX;
Jerome, In Isa
5.32, 6.28
#2 Cor 1:12

*Gal 6:4

17. What will happen, then, to the one who struck the kings who were sleeping thus? What will happen? *But you*, it says, *were cast out of your tomb like a useless stalk.** The tombs are the bodies of the Antichrist and all the condemned. Here the rot of the vices corrupts the soul,* and the fluid of all their filth makes it stink. They are cast out of their tombs when their souls, pulled from their bodies, are cast into the outer darkness.* Moreover, they are cast out *like a useless stalk*, which has no further end except for the fire.†

18. It also says that the Antichrist himself, or any other condemned person, is *defiled and wrapped.*§ They are defiled because of sin's pollution; they are wrapped because it is now impossible for them to correct their lives. Those who end their lives in their wicked deeds and are not consoled with any hope of escape are said to be wrapped in their sins. *You*, it says, *were cast out of your tomb like a useless stalk, defiled and wrapped with those who were killed by the sword, and they went all the way down to the depth of the lake.**

19. But that prince of all the wicked ones will also be cast out of his *tomb like a useless stalk.** All of the condemned are his tomb. He will be cast down from this tomb when he too, along with them, will be sent *to the everlasting fire which was prepared* for him *and his angels.** For he is permitted to work *now in the disobedient* children,* so that *those who are in the dirt may still remain dirty.** But after the sinners' iniquity is fulfilled,† and divine justice has inflicted punishment on the wicked, when there is no one else to whom he may counsel sin, he will be driven out from his tomb and cast down with the other lost souls *into the outer darkness.**

20. It says that he is both *defiled* and *wrapped.*† He is defiled by the blood of the many whom he has killed with the sword of iniquity, and wrapped with ill-will and despair so that he cannot be restored. Just as his ill-will is greater than the others', so too will his pun-

*Isa 14:19

*Mic 2:10

*Matt 8:12 and parallels
†Jerome, In Isa 6.28
§Isa 14:19

*Isa 14:19

*Isa 14:19

*Matt 25:41
*Eph 2:2
*Rev 22:11
†Lam 4:22

*Matt 8:12 and parallels
†Isa 14:19

ishment be more excruciating. For although he will
go down with the other lost ones to the bottom of the
lake, that is, to the depths of hell, yet in that depth he
will suffer harsher punishments.* For not only did he   *Jerome, In
Isa 6.28
sin without another's prompting, but he also encour-
aged others to sin.

21. For this reason, it follows, *Like a rotten corpse, you
will have no dealings even with those in burial.** This is   *Isa 14:19-20
the burial of that rich man clothed in purple.* As it is   *Luke 16:19
written in the gospel, *The rich man also died, and was
buried in hell.** Although this burial is for all of the   *Luke 16:22
condemned, not all will be equally tormented in it.
Rather, as it is written of the tares, *Bind them in bundles
for burning.** Thus, those who are alike in blame will   *Matt 13:30
also be made alike in punishment. But there is no one
who surpasses the Antichrist, or his prince, the devil,
in ill-will. Thus no one will have dealings with him in
burial. Comparing him to a rotten corpse serves to
describe his downfall, stench, and confusion.

22. Then, adding the cause for which he would suffer such things, it says, *For you ruined your land, you
killed your people.** The Antichrist's flesh is called his   *Isa 14:20
*land,** which he will either ruin by himself by the pas-   *Oner 11.13
sions of his vices or give over to spiritual beasts to be
ruined. Understand his *people* to be those who entrust
themselves to be ruled by him. He will not rule them,
of course, but destroy them; he will not give them life,
but kill them. Nearly all the manuscripts, though, have
only *land* and *people* instead of *your land* and *your
people.* We should thus understand that the devil or
the Antichrist will ruin those found clinging to the
land. But they will spiritually kill the *people*, that is,
the peoples of those ruled by reason and living more
honorably.

23. It follows, *The wicked ones' seed will not be called
forever.** This is that calling of which the apostle says,   *Isa 14:20
*Because we know that all things work for the good of those
loving God, for those holy ones who were called according*

*Rom 8:28   *to his purpose.** By this calling, *the wicked ones' seed will*
*Isa 14:20   *not be called forever.** This is of course the seed that *the*
*Matt 13:25, 27-28 *enemy planted over the wheat of the good householder.**
Christ himself explained this parable, saying, *The good
seed are the children of the kingdom; the tares are the wicked
*Matt 13:38   *children.** This seed is wicked or belongs to the wicked
ones, because wicked people come to be by self-will
Jerome, In   and the suggestion of those who are wicked. There-
Isa 6.30   fore, *this wicked seed will not be called forever,*[†] that is, it
†Isa 14:20 LXX   will not be counted among the number of the
chosen.

24. *Prepare your children for slaughter in their parents'*
*Isa 14:21   *iniquity.** To whom is this addressed? Of course, to the
wicked seed, that is, to the crowd of the godless. The
Antichrist or the devil did not create this crowd, but
scattered them throughout the world like seed. Just
as they are wicked, so too do they beget wicked ones
for themselves by their teaching and example. The
prophet addresses these wicked ones, saying, *Prepare
*Isa 14:21   *your children for slaughter.** This is a prophecy and not
a command, similar to what is written elsewhere,
*Amos 4:4   *Come to Bethel and act godlessly.** It is as if it said, You
*Oner 3.6, 8   will *come to Bethel and* you will *act godlessly.** So it is
that this prophet, perceiving that *the wicked seed* begot-
ten by the Antichrist or the devil would in turn beget
Isa 14:20 LXX   its own children by suggesting vices and errors, said,
*Prepare your children for slaughter in their parents' ini-
*Isa 14:21   *quity.** It is as if he said, "Just as you, begotten by the
ungodly, are destined for everlasting punishments, so
too you prepare children whom you beget for yourselves with your errors for the same slaughter, that is,
for damnation."

25. *They will not rise up, nor inherit the land, nor fill
*Isa 14:21   *the face of the world of cities.** I think these words should
be referred to the condemned. Prepared for the
slaughter by wicked teachers, they will not rise up
again. Rotting on the dung heap of their own flesh,
they will not be able to arrive at the possession of that

land of which the psalmist says, *May my portion, Lord, be in the land of the living.** For this reason, the Lord says in the gospel, *Blessed are the meek, for they will possess the land.*[†]

26. *Nor fill the face of the world of cities,*[§] that is, they will not fill the face of the cities that are in the world. We said above that *the world* represents the church. Its *cities* are the congregations of the faithful living together in a community. Their *face* is that outward appearance of holiness that shines forth in the presence of others by their habit, way of life, fasts, prayers, and so forth.* And so the prince of darkness will be *buried in hell* with his entire body.[†] When that takes place, these *wicked children* begotten by wicked fathers and now prepared for the slaughter,[§] that is, for final damnation, will not rise up through repentance, nor will they again aim for the outward appearance of holiness that they had put forth only for the eyes of others.*

27. I felt the need to finish this sermon, but we are already out of time. Let us therefore save what little remains for tomorrow's joy,* praying that we may be freed from Babylonian works in this life in such a way that everlasting punishments will not burden us with Babylon in the future. We ask this through Jesus Christ our Savior, who lives and reigns forever and ever. Amen.

*Ps 141:6; Ant in feria VI per annum (Hesbert 3.4316)
†Matt 5:4
§Isa 14:21

*Matt 5:16; 2 Tim 3:5
†Eph 6:12; Luke 16:22
§Matt 13:38

*2 Tim 3:5; Matt 6:1

*Oner 9.22; Aelred, SS 26.48; 67.34; 74.81; 76.33

Homily 19

1. Concerning the verse, *How did you fall from heaven, Lucifer, who were rising in the morning:** although you may think that what I have said is enough, another meaning occurs to me, one more briefly explained and more easily understood. Before we move on to other things, it is worth bringing it to light. You may then choose the meaning that you like, since it is the nature of the human mind to regard as more truthful that which better fits its capacity.

*Isa 14:12

2. So let us begin our explanation with the words of blessed Paul, who, composing his saving prophecy on *the law of sin and death,** says, *Death reigned from Adam to Moses even in those who did not sin, in the likeness of the transgression of Adam.** For the master of death,† the devil, ruled over humanity. He reigned without opposition before the law of Moses but still exercised tyranny even after the law had entered and sin had resisted the divine commandments. *For when there was no law, there was no transgression.** Therefore, *the law entered that sin might abound.**

*Rom 8:2

*Rom 5:14
†Augustine,
Conf 7.21.27

*Rom 4:15
*Rom 5:20

3. What, then, did Paul say to those deployed *not under the law, but under grace*? *Sin*, he said, *will not rule you, for you are not under the law but under grace.** It follows that sin did rule those who were *under the law*. Therefore, *from* the time of *Adam until* the time of Christ's grace, *sin* reigned, and *through sin*, sin's master,* staking claim not only to the condemned but even to the chosen not yet called, justified,* or redeemed *by*

*Rom 6:14

*Rom 5:12-14
*Rom 8:30

180

Christ's blood.* Whoever is aware of the power of predestination, in which what will be is made,* reckons
that the elect who have not yet been called can aptly
be called *heaven* by the prophet.

4. The prophet saw that the kingdom of the devil *in
the morning*—that is, having arisen at the beginning of
the world—had seized almost the entire world. It had
defiled kings, princes, and every sort of person except
a very few with idolatry. It had even attacked the chosen
and predestined. And the prophet marveled that
Christ's virtue had overthrown so great a power: *How
did you fall from heaven, Lucifer, who were rising in the morning?** He is called *Lucifer* because he seemed to bear the
light of knowledge when he said, *Taste and you will be
like gods, knowing good and evil.** He fell from heaven and
tumbled to the earth when, cast out of the chosen and
shut up only in the condemned as in a prison,† he de-
voured dirt like a snake.§ It was he who once wounded
the nations, piercing mortals with the arrow of sin.

5. *He said in his heart, I will ascend to heaven.** Christ's
coming was now at hand, but the devil saw that the
entire human race subjected to him tasted nothing but
the earth.* He saw that only very few of the Jews medi-
tated on heavenly things, clinging to God with faith and
good works. Puffed up with pride, he was sure he could
rule them, saying, *I will ascend to heaven.** We read about
this in blessed Job: *He will devour the river and not be
amazed; he will believe that the Jordan will flow into his mouth.**

6. *Over God's stars I will raise up my throne,*† that is,
over the holy people who were in Judea. *I will sit on the
mountain of the covenant, on the sides of the north,*§ so that
just as they offer sacrifices to my majesty in all the
temples of the world, so also in Jerusalem's temple they
will worship my majesty as divine.* For it is written of
Jerusalem's temple, *On the sides of the north is the great
king's city.** *I will rise above the loftiness of the clouds,*† that
is, I will surpass the preeminence and reputation of all
the prophets. *I will be like the Most High,** so that, just as

**1 Pet 1:18-19
*Isa 45:11 LXX;
Augustine, In ev
Ioann 68.1; Hiez
1.10.26; Oner 2.24;
17.11*

*Isa 14:12

**Gen 3:5 as
widely cited by
Augustine
†1 Pet 3:19;
Rev 20:7
§Gen 3:14*

*Isa 14:13

*Phil 3:19; Col 3:2

*Isa 14:13

**Job 40:18;
Gregory, Eu 26.9;
Gregory, Mo 33.
VI.12
†Isa 14:13
§Isa 14:13*

**Jerome, In Isa
5.29; 2 Thess 2:4*

**Ps 47:3
†Isa 14:14*

*Isa 14:14

heaven is God's, so all the land will be mine once Judea is subject to me. This is why he presumed lordship over the entire world when he tempted the Lord, saying, *I will give all this to you if you fall down and worship me.** *Matt 4:9

*Prov 16:18; 18:12   **7.** Scripture says it best: *The heart is exalted before a fall.** At the very moment when he expected more for himself, he lost even what he had. It is as though a *well-armed strong man* were dwelling safely *in a hall.** But someone *Luke 11:21-22
stronger, the Lord, *the strong and mighty in battle,** over-comes him, and the former is bound in chains and cast into hell. About this, it says, *Yet you will be dragged down to hell, to the depth of the lake.** The Lord speaks of his fall in the gospel, saying, *Now is the judgment of the world, now the prince of this world will be cast out.** *Ps 23:8

*Isa 14:15

*John 12:31

8. Those who with the eyes of faith see you cast out in this way will bend down in humility, and they will look on you.** In other words, they will recognize, so that those who had previously thought you strong and great will know you to be weak in comparison with Christ.** Is this the man who brought confusion on the land, who struck kingdoms,† making nation rise up against nation, kingdom against kingdom?§ Is this the one who made the world a desert for God's tillers,** who destroyed so many cities, who bound so many people in chains?** No one who reads the historical books is unaware that all this came about at his instigation before the Lord's coming. *Isa 14:16

*Jerome, In Isa 6.27
†Isa 14:16
§Matt 24:7; Luke 21:10
*John 9:31
*Isa 14:17

9. After the devil had been cast out of the chosen ones and locked up in the hearts of the condemned as in a hellish prison,** he stirred up his subjects to persecute the preachers and worshipers of Christ, concerning whom he adds, *All the kings of the nations have slept in glory,** etc. Understand all of this in the way we explained it above.** Let us continue from where we ended yesterday's sermon. *Isa 14:15; 1 Pet 3:19; Rev 20:7

*Isa 14:18
*Oner 18:10-26

10. *And I will rise over them*—that is, over the wicked children begotten by wicked parents—*and I will destroy the name of Babylon, remnant, shoot, and offspring, says*

*the Lord.** Babylon's name is the glory of the world;   *Isa 14:22, 20-21
Babylon's remnant, love for the world; its shoot, desire
to sin; its offspring, the deliberation and consent to
sin. For people desire above all a great name,* which   *2 Sam 7:9
the Babylonians acquire for themselves by means of
riches, foolish power, or worldly knowledge. When
they are unable to acquire what they seek or when
they lose what they have acquired, they carry a kind
of remnant in their heart. This remnant is love for the
world, which comes from the harmful shoot of a
wicked desire.* Wicked thoughts are their offspring,   *Aelred, Spec car
like the children of Babylon's daughter,† of whom the   1.29.85; Oner,
psalmist says, *Wretched daughter of Babylon, blessed is*   Adv 13 = Aelred,
                                                            S 47.13; Oner 5.3
the one who will seize and smash your children against the †Jerome, In
rock.§ The Lord will destroy them all at the end of the   Isa 6.30
world, when there will be no glory in Babylon's name,   §Ps 136:8-9
no delight in its love, no desire to sin—when, accord-
ing to the psalmist, even *all their thoughts will perish.**   *Ps 145:4

11. Next it says, *I will give it over to the hedgehog and*
*to swamps.** Therefore, at the end of the world, hedge-   *Isa 14:23
hogs and swamps will inhabit the city of confusion.
The spine of sin will thus always prick the conscience,
and wantonness and pleasure will obscure it, giving
off vapors and stench like a muddy swamp.

12. *And I will sweep it, wearing it down with a broom,*
*says the Lord of Hosts.** Just as a broom cleans and emp-   *Isa 14:23
ties a house,* so too will I destroy every glory of Baby-   *Matt 12:44
lon, all its riches and pleasures. I will wear it down
with torments and crush it with afflictions.

13. But let us, too, beloved brothers, from whom the
devil has been cast out by the Lord's coming,* let us   *John 12:31
prepare the children of the wicked seed for slaughter.*   *Isa 14:20-21
Thus may the sword of the Lord, which devours
flesh,* kill all carnal affections and illicit desires. May *Deut 32:42;
it kill even depraved thoughts born from carnal desire   Jer 12:12
as though from a wicked seed, so that they may not
rise again, nor inherit *the land* of our heart, *nor* fill *the*
*face of the earth with cities.**   *Isa 14:21

14. Understand *cities of the world* as the mind's activity. The mind can certainly be compared to the world, because whatever the world can contain physically, the mind can grasp mentally.* Now the face of the world or of the cities is the intention of our thoughts. He from whom nothing is hidden will judge everything we do or think according to our intention.*

15. Come, then, Lord Jesus, and rise up in your merciful severity *over the children of Babylon,* that the name of Babylon may perish from my soul.* May it be known by the name of *Jerusalem* after every confusion has been wiped out. But be pleased to destroy, too, the remnants of former confusion, that is, the images of vices that linger in the chamber of my mind even after the vices themselves have been cast out.* In this way, neither will the shoot remain from which the vices appear, nor will the shoot's offspring arise again, namely, wicked thoughts and desires.*

16. *I will give it over to the hedgehog and to swamps.*† Lord, may my heart be like a hedgehog covered with spines, pricked by the memory of each of my sins as though by spines. Just as vices had occupied my entire soul, so let saving compunction seize it entirely.* And so by the remembrance of its wantonness, how it was mired with foul swamps, so to speak, let it be worthy to bring forth the *fruit of repentance.**

17. Next, it says, *I will sweep it, wearing it down with a broom.** The broom that wears it down is contrition of heart, by which the Babylon in our soul is worn down and crushed, and all its filth removed. *For the Lord is near to those who* have crushed their hearts,* because *the crushed and humbled heart God does not reject.** But one could also call the *scourge* of God a broom that wears down,* whereby he punishes our *iniquities with the rod and* our *sins with blows.*† He crushes vices to bring in virtues, so as *not* to scatter his *mercy* from us.§

18. *Wicked seed* can also mean hypocrisy, whose children are the feigned virtues that a hypocrite prepares for slaughter rather than for reward.* These children

*Aelred, Anima 2.5–7

*Job 42:2

*Jerome, Nom 3 and *passim*

*Aelred, Spec car 3.3.6; 3.39.109

*Jerome, In Isa 6.30; Isa 14:21-22 †Isa 14:23

*Augustine, In Ps 103; Aelred, S 3.18

*Luke 3:8

*Isa 14:23

*Pss 33:19; 144:18
*Ps 50:19

*Jdt 8:27; Isa 10:26 †Ps 88:33 §Ps 88:34; Oner 1.15; 21.9

*Isa 14:20-21 LXX

are unable to rise up, because depraved intention plunges them into the depths. Nor can those feigned virtues, which are able to empty but not fill the soul or the soul's conscience, inherit the land of the living.* *Isa 14:21; Ps 26:13

Over these children, then, the Lord rises up *for evil and not for good,** to destroy the name of Babylon—that is, *Jer 44:27

the reputation acquired by false virtues—remnant, shoot, and offspring.* Hence neither does the appear- *Isa 14:22

ance of virtue remain nor is the desired fruit of human praise secured.* Rather, such hypocrites will utterly *2 Tim 3:5

lose whatever they sought by this kind of pretending.

19. Then such a person is given *to the hedgehog and to swamps.** Hypocrites most often fall, by God's judgment, *Isa 14:23

into two vices: avarice and lust. For according to the Savior's words, riches and worldly cares are like spines.* *Matt 13:22 and parallels

When love of these weighs down the soul, it becomes like a hedgehog armed with its spines, trusting *in its own virtue and* taking pride *in the vastness of its riches.** *Ps 48:7; Jerome, In Isa 6.31

But barren swamps, foul and muddy, in which animals joyfully crawl in the filth,† are like lust and impurity, †Jerome, In Isa 6.31

which are filthy and vile qualities. Unclean spirits rejoice in these vices, and their chief *sleeps* pleasantly *in the shade* amid the verdure *of the shoots and the reeds,** which grow *Isa 35:7

primarily in swamps and *damp places.** This kind of soul *Gregory, Mo 33. III.9; Aelred, S 55.8; Job 40:16

is swept not to be cleaned, but to be crushed.† †Isa 14:23; Matt 12:44 and parallels

20. Next it says, *The Lord of Hosts swore an oath, say- ing, "Surely, just as I have thought, so will it be; just as I have considered in my mind, so will it come to pass."§* Ev- §Isa 14:24-25

erything that the holy prophet describes about the burden of Babylon, he confirms on the authority of the Lord's oath. Thus, no one can doubt that what the Lord himself foretold under oath will come to pass. Now the greatest mark of truth and certainty is the claim that the Lord swears something. The Lord, after all, must be believed even when he does not swear.

21. *Surely, just as I have thought, so will it be; just as I have considered in my mind, so will it come to pass.** He *Isa 14:24-25

speaks to humans humanly; if he were to speak di- vinely, humans would not understand. The phrase *I* *think* is not always used to express doubt. A master who is angry with his servant quite frequently says to him, "I think that I am your master." Likewise, we should not attribute uncertainty, worry, or mental wavering to God's nature just because he says that he thinks or considers something. Rather, we should believe that he explains his eternal and unchanging providence in words that we can understand. For this reason, *judgment or consideration* is ascribed to him: just as people get the best result when they do not act hastily, but slowly and with deliberation, so also God, not rashly or by accident but by his own eternal counsel,* *reaches powerfully from end to end, delightfully ordering all things.** Just as he has ordered, thought, wished, and considered it to be, *so will it come to pass.**

*Ps 32:11

*Wis 8:1

*Isa 14:24

22. What will come to pass? He says, *I will crush the Assyrian in my land, and trample him amid my mountains.** Understand *the Assyrian* as that entire crowd of proud spirits who are crushed in the land of the Lord and trampled amid his mountains. Ascribe this, if you will, to the first coming of the Lord, when the devil was crushed in the land of the Lord. So *land* should be interpreted as the infants and fleshly people who are in the church. Because they are less able to eat solid food, the apostle gives them milk to drink,* saying, *I judged myself to know nothing among you except the Lord Jesus and him crucified.** In such a land, the Lord crushed the Assyrian. Laying bare his cunning by the light of faith shining forth, the Lord crushed his head with divine power.** The devil's head is the unbelief in their hearts.

*Isa 14:25

*Heb 5:12-13;
1 Cor 3:1-2

*1 Cor 2:2

*Gen 3:15

23. Further, understand *mountains* as the apostles and the perfect, to whom *the Lord gave the power to trample snakes and scorpions and all the enemy's power.** The devil's terribly heavy yoke was removed from them when *the yoke rotted from the oil.** After binding the strong man,† the one anointed *with the oil of gladness before* his *companions led captivity captive.*§ By his power he removed the burden that weighed upon their

*Luke 10:19;
Jerome, In Isa 6.32

*Isa 10:27; Aelred,
S 43.11–16 for
§§23–25

†Matt 12:29

§Pss 44:8; 67:19;
Eph 4:8

shoulders: *And his yoke will be removed from them, and
his burden will be taken from their shoulders.**   *Isa 14:25

24. There is the yoke or burden of iniquity, which
humanity placed on its own neck with the devil's en-
couragement. There is also the yoke or burden of bad
habit, to which people subject themselves by living
badly. There is also the yoke or burden of misfortune,
by which divine justice brought low sinful humanity.
And of course there is the heavy yoke or burden of
sin,* which, until the Lord's passion, weighed upon   *Sir 40:1; Ps 37:5
mortals to such an extent that no one's virtue or justice
could cast it off. Rather, it submerged everyone into
hell;* not only the condemned went there but even   *Luke 10:15;
the chosen, though *a great abyss was fixed between*   Isa 14:15
them.* The chosen, though not in glory, were granted   *Luke 16:26
rest; the condemned were unhappily assigned to
places of punishment. After the devil was trampled
and crushed through Christ's passion, this yoke and
burden was removed, so that the just and perfect
could then fly unhindered all the way up to heaven.

25. And yet, dear brothers, the Assyrian's yoke or
burden still weighs us down. We perceive, undoubtedly, *another law in* our members *fighting against the
law* of our *minds, leading* us captive *to the law of sin that
is in* our *members.** This yoke is heavy, brothers, this   *Rom 7:23
burden is heavy and unbearable.* *Who will free us from* *Sir 40:1; Ps 37:5
the body of this death?* What shall I say about the bur-   *Rom 7:24
den of habit? Whoever rashly takes it on their shoul-
ders will not be able to remove it again without
profound anguish and heavy labor.*   *Oner 15.9

26. But *heavy*, too, *is the yoke on the children of Adam
from their birth from their mothers' womb until their return
to the womb of the mother of us all.** Poverty burdens us,   *Sir 40:1
sickness burdens us, drowsiness weighs us down,
sloth casts us down. Sadness pulls us down, anger
disturbs us, hunger and thirst afflict us, mistrust per-
plexes us. I will not mention persecutions, bereave-
ments, banishment, and countless diseases of various
sorts; terrors, too, and fears, and unavoidable troubles;

injuries, false accusations, violence, temptations, murmuring, slander, hatred, curses, blasphemies, rebellion, false judgments, and shipwrecks. The world is full of all of these. As blessed Job said, *A human being, born of a woman, living only a short time, is filled with many miseries.** Clearly, all of these—with death itself, which is the last and heaviest of all—are included in the one yoke or burden of misfortune.

*Job 14:1

27. This is the burden of Babylon, which burdens not only Babylon but also the citizens of Jerusalem sojourning there.* Happy, happy is the one who, though weighed down by such things, is not overwhelmed. A day will surely come when the Assyrian will be utterly crushed in the land and trampled among the mountains. Not in just any land or among just any mountains, but as the Lord says, *Just as I have thought, so will it come to pass; I will crush the Assyrian in my land, and in my mountains I will trample him down.**

*Heb 11:13; 12:22; 13:14; 1 Pet 2:11

*Isa 14:25

28. Indeed, brothers, Satan was crushed by the Lord's passion;* he was trampled down by apostolic preaching. He was crushed in the land of the weak and trampled among the mountains of the perfect. This happened when first by the Lord himself, then by the apostolic preaching, all the nations rejected Satan with his terribly cruel laws, when he was cast out everywhere from people's bodies and hearts by the faith of those believing through the sign of the holy cross.* Did he not seem crushed and trampled when he could not even control pigs on his own?*

*Rom 16:20

*John 12:31

*Mark 5:12-13; Luke 8:32

29. But in fact, brothers, he was not altogether crushed and trampled. His ability to tempt still remained, and he will be given the power to commit violence and persecution through the Antichrist. But he will be completely crushed and trampled when the *very last enemy, death, is destroyed;** when no trace of the diabolical power remains in the land of the Lord, that is, in our flesh made glorious by an everlasting resurrection. He will be completely crushed and trampled when no temptation will be able to approach the

*1 Cor 15:26; Jerome, In Isa 6.32

mountains of the Lord, that is, our spirits raised up in the heights of divine contemplation. He will be completely crushed and utterly trampled, I say, when he is thrust down into the abyss to be tormented by eternal fires after every possibility of tempting, persecuting, or terrorizing has been taken from him.* ^{* see Luke 8:31; Matt 25:41}

30. This terribly heavy yoke of misfortune, this massive burden that we bear in this life *at different times and in varying ways,** will be removed from our necks or *shoulders* when, after the power of the resurrection absorbs every corruption and weakness,* we shall burst forth in this jubilant and mocking cry:† *Where, death, is your victory? Where, death, is your sting?*§ This is surely the end of this burden: that the city of confusion, Babylon,‡ will sink into hell with its leader the devil, where eternal punishments will burden it.* The city of peace, Jerusalem†—which, though burdened by the burden of Babylon, prudently exercised care, or bravely endured the burden, or powerfully escaped it—will be borne to heaven to be crowned with Christ its leader. Indeed, Jerusalem was careful lest it be overwhelmed by its vices, it endured when persecutions pressed in, and it escaped when, leaving the body, it was taken up by rest.*

Notes in margin:
*Heb 1:1
*1 Cor 15:43; 2 Cor 5:4; Phil 3:10
†Ps 41:5; Isa 48:20
§1 Cor 15:55
‡Jerome, Nom 3 and passim
*Luke 10:15; Matt 11:23; Isa 14:15
†Jerome, Nom 50 and passim
*2 Cor 5:13; 12:2

31. Lest someone suppose that the prophet composed his prophecy about one particular region or city, the Lord himself left no doubt, adding, *This plan that I have devised is upon all the earth, and this hand is stretched forth over all the nations.** What could be clearer? He demonstrates that what is said in this burden applies to the whole world and all the nations.* Because what is said is split between the chosen and the condemned, I think *plan* applies to the former and *hand stretched forth* to the latter.

*Isa 14:26
*Jerome, In Isa 6.33

32. It is a deep and lofty plan that the chosen, always living together with the condemned, are weighed down by the same burden of miseries, and astonishingly helped so as not to be overwhelmed. Though they often labor under the same sins and faults, their conversion of life and a reformed way of living separate them from

the condemned. *Though vices, grief, torments, or tempta-*
tions burden them, all things work together for their *good.**

*Rom 8:28

33. But how the hand of the Lord is stretched forth over the condemned! It neither receives their good deeds nor mitigates their bad ones. How the hand of the Lord is stretched forth, insofar as everything works together for their harm:* they are both burdened by pains and ruined by pleasures! They are proud of their virtues and so receive no reward for them. They are not humbled by their sins and so do not win forgiveness. If they abandon evil, they return to it again; if they begin some good work, they do not persevere in it.* In the end, the wicked are eternally condemned, while the chosen are crowned with the joys of eternal life. You should remember everything described in this burden and the way I explained it.

*Rom 8:28

*Oner 5.16

34. After the Lord's words of confirmation, the prophet, speaking for himself, adds, *The Lord of Hosts decreed it; who can weaken it?** I think this refers to the chosen ones. No one can weaken the divine plan for their salvation. For *If God is for us, who is against us?** Hear, too, the fixed and eternal decree, which no one dare resist, which no one can or ought to alter: *The firm foundation of God stands bearing this sign: The Lord has recognized those who are his.**

*Isa 14:27

*Rom 8:31

*2 Tim 2:19

35. It then follows, *And his hand is stretched forth; who will turn it away?** I think this must refer to the condemned, as we said above. Just as his mercy is sure and stable for the salvation of the chosen, so too his justice is surely stable and unchangeable for the damnation of the condemned.

*Isa 14:27

36. But with the end of this burden, let us also put an end to this sermon.* Let us beseech our Lord and God that we may be careful of the burden of the vices, that we may courageously sustain the burden of temptations and miseries, and that we may deserve to avoid that burden of eternal punishment, through our Lord Jesus Christ, who lives and reigns for ever and ever. Amen.

*Oner 4.18; 21.28; 26.34

Homily 20

1. Having finished explaining the burden of Babylon, we will now take up the explanation of the burden of the Philistines, relying more on your prayers than our abilities. In short, the prophet described the world in general with the name of Babylon. He understood the world to be divided between the chosen and the condemned, and that each would be either weighed down or crushed. He described it thus in a mystic word, with God bearing witness, who said, *This is the plan that I have devised over all the earth, and this is the hand stretched forth over all the nations.** Now passing over from genus to species, he describes the burdens of each nation one by one. What he had prophesied concerning the whole in few words, he here elaborates more explicitly in its components.*

2. First he records the plan of divine judgment against the Philistines, whose name can be translated as *falling down from drink.** I think this refers to the Jews, who, drunk on the letter of the law as though on old wine,* fell from grace.† For *not knowing God's righteousness and wanting to establish their own, they were not subjected to God's justice.** For those who thought that they were justified by the law fell away from grace.* This is that old wine that ran out at the wedding,† because our Lord Jesus Christ, *coming forth* from the Virgin's womb *as a bridegroom from his chamber,*§ put an end to the mysteries of the law like old wine‡

* Isa 14:26

* Aelred, Spec car 2.18.56; 3.7.20; Aelred, S 67.8

* Jerome, In Isa 6.35

* Luke 5:39
† Gal 5:4

* Rom 10:3

* Gal 5:4;
Rom 3:28
† John 2:3;
Luke 5:39
§ Ps 18:6
‡ Aelred, S 50.25

191

and supplied *the new wine** of the Gospel to all those
called *to the wedding of the great king*'s son.[†]

3. Therefore, clinging to the letter of the law and
ignorant of the lawgiver, as though drunk, the Jews
shouted, *We have the law, and according to the law he
should die.** O ruin, O fall! *We do not have any king except
for Caesar!** A great fall, a great ruin, to fall from Christ
and cling to Caesar! And fittingly enough, at the outset
of discussing the destruction of many nations, the text
begins with the Jews, who first received the faith of
Christ and were the first to fall from his faith.

4. It therefore begins thus: *This burden took place in the
year that King Ahaz died.** Ahaz, that wicked and proud-
est of kings, despiser of the divine law and worshiper
of idols,** represents the devil. His life can be understood
as the devil's kingdom, which took hold of humanity
on account of the fault of the first transgression. When,
therefore, did Ahaz die? Of course, when what the Lord
said through the prophet was fulfilled: *I will be your
death, O death!** Then *he exposed* on the cross *principalities
and powers, openly defeating them in himself.**

5. So, brothers, as long as the devil held power in
these nations, the Jewish people rejoiced in its prosperity, having the temple, the altar, the ephod, the thera-
phim, priests, and sacrifices.** But *in the year*, that is, at
the time, *that King Ahaz died,** when the devil's kingdom
was destroyed, a heavy weight of afflictions began to
encumber the Jewish people. Indeed, they added burden upon burden, sin upon sin,** and those who had
first crucified the Lord later attacked his disciples. From
there misfortune followed upon misfortune until, having been erased *from the land of the living,** they would
be wiped out even from the land of the dying[†] that had
been left to them as an inheritance.[§] Therefore, this burden began to take place spiritually when that intellectual Ahaz lost his empire among people. This *happened*,
that is, it was revealed to the prophet, *in the year that the
king* of Israel *Ahaz* paid the debt of death.**

*Luke 5:37-39 and parallels

†Matt 5:35; 22:2, 9; Ps 71:1

*John 19:7
*John 19:15

*Isa 14:28

*2 Kgs 16:2-4

*Hos 13:14
*Col 2:15; Aelred, S 78.5

*Hos 3:4
*Isa 14:28

*Isa 30:1

*Isa 53:8; Jer 11:19; Ps 26:13 †Oner 11:12 §Lev 20:24; Deut 3:18

*Isa 14:28

6. *Do not rejoice, Philistia, all of you, that the rod of your attacker has been broken.** Remember, brothers, the reading about that *council* that the people convoked against the Lord,* in which the high priest Caiaphas decreed that it was necessary for *one person to die* lest the *entire nation* perish.* For *if*, they say, *we let him go free in this way, everyone will believe in him, and the Romans will come and take away our place and nation.** They shook with fear where there was no fear.** The holy patriarch Joseph had seen in a dream that his brothers would bow down to him.* He was sold into Egypt so that this would not happen, but through that very act, it happened anyway.* They state that Christ must be killed so that the people will not believe in him, and *the Romans* will not take *both* their *place* and *nation* from them.* Although he was killed for that reason, the entire world believed in him, and the Romans came nevertheless and took away their place and nation. Yet they appeared to have freed themselves from this fear when, after Jesus was stretched out dead on the cross, they rejoiced to have abolished his name and power.

7. Recall what sacred history tells us about the Philistines and Samson.* There the Philistines clearly represent the Jews and Samson the Lord and Savior, who was *sent to the sheep* that were lost from *the house of Israel.** He longed for the embrace of the prostitute Delilah, that is, the Gentile church.* The holy gospels relate to us how many snares this Samson suffered from the Philistines, with how many ropes they attacked him, and with how many threats they assailed him. The scribes and Pharisees watch his mouth, they ask questions, they demand opinions on various matters, they oppose him with much from the law and the prophets, so that they have cause to accuse him, to judge him, to hand him over to a death sentence.*

8. They come with questions like ropes, but he broke them and walked away free whenever they attacked

*Isa 14:29

*John 11:47

*John 18:14; 11:49-50

*John 11:48

*Ps 13:5

*Gen 37:9-10

*Gen 37:28; 42:6; 43:26, 28

*John 11:18

*Judg 16

*Matt 15:24

*Judg 16:4; Aelred, S 63.12

*Luke 6:7 and parallels; 11:53-54; 22:20 and parallels; John 8:6

*Judg 16:9, 12
*Matt 22:17
*Ps 56:7
*Matt 22:21 and
parallels
*John 8:5
†Judg 16:9, 12

*John 8:7-9

him.* *Is it lawful,* they asked, *to pay Caesar tribute or not?** *They had prepared a snare for* his *feet,* but *they fell in* it.* *Render,* he said, *what is Caesar's to Caesar and what is God's to God.** So too of the adulterous woman, *Moses commanded us to stone such people; what do you say?** He broke the ropes in such a way that,† after the adulterous woman was freed, they would be struck by their own judgment and stoned by their own conscience's accusations.*

9. Finally, after being undone in sleep by the love of a prostitute and shorn of his hair, that Samson is also robbed of his strength. Handed over to the power of
*Judg 16:19-21
the Philistines, he was exposed to mockery and pain.* So too, loving the prostitute who lay *under every green*
*Jer 2:20; 3:6;
Ezek 6:13
*tree and on every shady hill,** who was stained by as many adulteries as the idols she worshiped, my Samson cut off his hair, hid his strength, and took up his
*Aelred, SS 62.16;
63.12
†2 Kgs 2:23; Luke
23:33, 35 and
parallels
§Aelred, SS 36.19;
62.17; 63.22
‡Ps 21:9
#Matt 27:39-44
bonds.* After the disciples escaped, as though bald *he climbed the place of Calvary,*† and, handed over to the will of the Jews, is mocked while hanging on the cross.§

10. The prophet saw in the spirit those disturbed with a mad joy, shaking their head before the cross,‡ mocking the miracles, and urging him to come down.# He spoke against this misplaced joy, saying, *Do not rejoice, Philistia, all of you, that the rod of your attacker has*
*Isa 14:29
*Isa 11:4
*been broken.** They thought their attacker was Jesus, who struck *the land with the rod of his mouth.** With saving words Jesus corrected those thinking of the
*Phil 3:19; Col 3:2
earth and tasting the earth.* At times he rebuked the scribes and Pharisees, at times he pointed out hypoc-
*Matt 23:13, etc.
risy, at times he condemned greed.* *Woe to you,* he says, *scribes and Pharisees, you who are like whitened*
*Matt 23:27
*tombs!** And again, *Woe to you, scribes and Pharisees, you who tithe mint, dill, and every oil, and every herb, and*
*Matt 23:23;
Luke 11:42
*dismiss the weightier parts of the law!**

11. Or consider the parable in which the tillers to whom the vineyard was entrusted killed first the ser-

vants and finally the heir. The Lord asked his listeners
what the vineyard's owner would do to such farmers.* *Matt 21:33-40
They answered, *He will destroy those wicked tillers and
will entrust his vineyard to other farmers!** How they *Matt 21:41
were struck when the Savior fully agreed with their
opinion, saying, *Therefore, the kingdom of God will be
taken from you and given to a people that produces its fruit.** *Matt 21:43

12. How they were struck, moreover, when they
asked his opinion of Caesar's census. He said, *Render
what is Caesar's to Caesar and what is God's to God.** But *Matt 22:21 and
the rod of his *mouth* also mightily struck those who parallels
demanded judgment on the adulterous woman so that
he would either oppose Moses or disregard the laws
of mercy.* To them he said, *Let the one among you with-* *Isa 11:4
out sin cast a stone first. One by one they departed,* leav- *John 8:7, 9
ing the wretched woman alone with only mercy.* *Augustine, In
ev Ioann 33.5

13. Therefore, as though freed from his blows, they
scoff at him as he hangs on the cross, joyfully *moving
their heads** *and saying, If he is the Son of God, let him come* *Matt 27:39 and
down from the cross.† O Philistia, O besotted, drunken, parallels
mad Philistia: you are falling, you are crashing, you †Matt 27:40, 42
are lying prostrate on the ground.* *The rod*, or the *Jerome, Nom 6
power, *of your attacker* seems *broken* to you.* You mock *Isa 14:29
captive Samson, whose head has been shaved, whose
eyes have been gouged out.* *Do not rejoice, Philistia,* *Judg 16:19-21
all of you.* Samson will die, his power will seem bro- *Isa 14:29
ken, but his death is your desolation,* the crushing of *Aelred, SS 61.12;
your children, the fading of your glory, the temple's 62.19
destruction, the suppression of your priesthood, the
scattering of all your people. Therefore, *do not rejoice,
Philistia, all of you, that the rod of your attacker has been
broken.** *Isa 14:29

14. When it says *all of you*, it expresses the great joy
with which they exulted in Christ's death. *Do not rejoice*, do not be glad, do not exult or scoff, for divine
justice will not allow such wickedness to pass un-
avenged.* For because *they did not receive the love of* *Job 24:12
truth in order to be saved, God will send a worker of error

2 Thess 2:10-11 upon them, so that they believe in a lie. Hence, the Lord says in the gospel, *I came in my Father's name, and you did not accept me. Another will come in his own name; you*

*John 5:43 *will accept him.* This is the worker of error whom the Jews will receive at the end of the world by God's just

Wis 16:18 Judgment, so that those who condemned Christ

Gregory, Mo 25. might have the Antichrist. That is why it follows, *For*
XVI.34;
29.XXXII.75 *a basilisk will come forth from the snake's root, and its seed*
†Isa 14:29 *will consume the bird.*†

15. When the holy patriarch Jacob blessed his sons, and Dan approached to be blessed with the others, Jacob said of him, *May Dan become a snake on the road,*

*Gen 49:17 *a horned serpent on the path.* Some think he was called a snake because from his seed, instrument of that

Isa 27:1; twisted serpent, the Antichrist would be born.† There-
Job 26:13
†Gregory, Mo 31. fore, just as *a rod* came forth *from the root of Jesse, and a*
XXIV.43
§Isa 11:1 *flower* grew up *from his root*,§ and that rod and flower

*Isa 14:29; was Christ, so too *a basilisk will come forth from the root*
Gen 49:17 of Dan, who was called a *snake*,* and that basilisk will be the Antichrist. The basilisk is called the king of the serpents, killing people with the breath of its mouth

Jerome, In and gaze. This serpent is compared to the Antichrist,
Isa 6:34 who will be full of the basilisk's might and ill-will. He is the king of the serpents, that is, the chief of the de- mons. Inspired by his wickedness and illuminated by his knowledge, many will fall from the faith of the

2 Thess 2:13; 1 truth. For his gaze strikes those whom his cunning
Tim 4:1; 2
Tim 2:18 deceives; his breath kills those whom his ill-will compels.

*Isa 14:29 **16.** *And its seed*, it says, *will absorb the bird.* *Seed* is in the singular rather than the plural. Just as the *good*

*Matt 13:38; *seed is the word of God,* so too is the *wicked seed* the
Luke 8:11
†Isa 14:20 LXX word of the Antichrist.† So his word, his preaching, and his teaching will absorb the Jews like a seed. Yet it will not absorb them all, but only those who, puffed up with pride, neither can go up to heaven nor want to come down to earth through humility. Rather, like

Oner 28.15; birds hanging in the void between heaven and earth,
2 Sam 18:9-10

they deserve the fellowship of those who, cast down from heaven, have found their place in this dark air.* *Oner 17.5; Augustine, Gen ad litt 11.26; Rev 12:9

17. *The snake's root* can also mean the devil's ill-will, which God's just judgment allowed him to carry out against the Jews.† The devil roused the nations to the Jews' destruction, and he hardened their hearts lest they should be mindful of their salvation.* *For from the snake's root,* that is, from the devil's suggestion, a *basilisk* came forth:* the Romans' pride, hatred, and disdain. The Romans' emperor at that time, the wicked Nero, is fittingly compared to a poisonous basilisk, whose *seed* or will, which he conceived from the snake's breath, sent Vespasian[1] to Judea. Vespasian and his son Titus[2] absorbed all the power, pride, and glory of the Jews.

†Wis 16:18; 2 Thess 1:5

*Ps 94:8; John 12:40, etc.

*Isa 14:29

18. *And the firstborn of the poor will be fed.** The prophetic word reproaches that unhappy people for the hatred that they carried out not only against Christ but indeed also against his disciples. The Jewish persecution of Christ's disciples did not cease for as long as the Jewish reign lasted. Some of the disciples were killed, some stoned, some chased from their dwellings, some crushed with scourging.* The prophet saw in the spirit that, after all this, many evils would befall the Jews. But Christ's disciples, after their persecution, or rather during the persecution itself, would be cheerful in the confidence of a good conscience. Therefore the prophet said, *And the firstborn of the poor will be fed.**

*Isa 14:30

*Matt 23:34, 37, etc.

*Isa 14:30

19. The poor are those of whom the Lord speaks in the gospel: *Blessed are the poor in spirit, for the kingdom of heaven is theirs.** These are the poor who, renouncing the world and all its riches, saying good-bye even to father and mother, brothers and sisters, fields and possessions,* nakedly follow the naked Christ.† The holy firstborn of all these were the apostles and disciples

*Matt 5:3

*Matt 19:29; Luke 14:33 †Oner 26.5; Jerome, Ep 125.20.5

---

[1] Roman emperor, AD 69–79.
[2] Roman emperor, AD 79–81.

of Christ, who, first hearing this teaching from his mouth, said with a sure conscience, *Behold, we have abandoned everything and followed you; what, then, will* * Matt 19:27   *we receive?**

20. Therefore these *firstborn of the poor* saw the Jews * Amos 8:11   laboring, famished for the word of God,* living in terror after the Romans attacked their capital. They themselves fed on the banquets of the divine word and on the faith of the many who were turning to God * Acts 2:47; 5:14   daily.* Resting in the tranquility of a good conscience * Sir 24:24   and the certitude of a holy hope,* with great confidence they cried out, *Who will separate us from the char-* * Rom 8:35   *ity of Christ? Tribulation, want, hunger, or sword?**

21. Therefore he said, *And the firstborn of the poor will* * Isa 14:30   *be fed, and the poor will rest in confidence.** Truly, Peter rested *in confidence* in Christ when the priests ordered * Acts 4:18; 5:28   the apostles *not to speak in Jesus' name.** He answered * Acts 5:29   them, *We must obey God rather than human beings.** How great, too, was the confidence in which Paul rested when, standing in the presence of the judge, he argued so forcefully concerning Christ and his precepts that * Job 26:14   Festus could not bear the thunder of his words,* saying, * Acts 26:24   *Paul, too much education has driven you mad.**

22. Of course this rest means mental stillness, in which they were not angered by their persecutors, nor moved by hatred against those hating them. Rather, they had learned to pray even for their enemies, to do * Matt 5:44 and   good to those who did evil to them,* and to work for parallels; RB 4.72   the lives of those desiring their death. So it is that * Acts 7:59-60   Stephen interceded for those stoning him,* Peter did not take back the word of salvation from those beating * Acts 5:40,   him,* and Paul was greatly saddened and bore a con- 42; 13:26   stant pain in his heart† for those who stoned him once † Rom 9:2 § 2 Cor 11:24-25   and beat him five times.§ Many of them planned to ‡ Acts 23:12-14   have him killed.‡

23. But while these people acted in confidence and rested in the gentleness of charity, what happened to the Philistines, who mocked our Samson? Listen to

what follows: *And I will make your root perish from famine, and your remnants I will kill.** *Isa 14:30

24. We can understand that people's *root* to be that
city on which other cities and every surrounding town
rely. The smaller towns are like branches depending
on their root, expecting from it the greenness of their
standing and prosperity. And after a plague ravaged
many in the city itself during the siege, famine overcame the others.* The famine left the city defenseless, *Ezek 5:12;
2 Kgs 25:3
exposing it to easy capture. The city then gave victory
to the Roman army. Therefore, its *root* perished from
hunger when, after the temple was burned down, the
city likewise fell, and all that grandeur perished either
from hunger or the sword.* Yet a small remnant sur- *Jer 14:16;
Ezek 5:12
vived in that place, which, receiving no correction
from that disaster, were killed or scattered by Aelius
Hadrian.[3]* Thus not even one Jew can be found in that *Jerome, In Ez
2.5.1-4; 7.24.1-14
land that had been given to them to be possessed
forever.* *Isa 60:21

25. Pontiffs and priests can also be called the people's root. Just as life-giving sap comes forth from the
root and spreads throughout the entire trunk and
branches, so the priests' teaching of the law prepared
healing cures for a remnant of the people. But because
the priests rejected Christ's word and judged themselves unworthy of God's kingdom,* they perished *Acts 13:46;
Luke 9:62
from famine. Their remnants, that is, the remaining
crowd, abandoned the life that is Christ* and were *John 11:25
punished with eternal death.

26. What has been said here regarding the foretelling of future events must now be repeated with a
moral sense. Thus the faith that the truth of prophecy
established may be adorned by conduct, commended
by life, and crowned by death. We should not understand this burden of the Philistines only as that by

---

[3] Roman emperor, AD 117–138.

which the Philistines are weighed down or crushed. We should also understand it as the burden with which they weigh down or crush others. Let us beware, therefore, dear brothers, of being crushed by the Philistines, because we cannot avoid being weighed down by them.

27. Let us, like Samson, be Nazirites,* that is, consecrated to the Lord. Let us be made holy after the hair of our head has grown.* May our hair, in which our greatest strength resides,* not be given over to the prostitute. Thus, bonds will not be able to constrain us, nor swords frighten us, nor prisons enclose us, nor crowds overcome us.* And if by chance the Philistines should exult, if at some point we seem to be captured, just about to be caught in their ropes, let them hear from the prophet, *Do not rejoice, Philistia, all of you, that the rod of your attacker has been broken.**

28. But because we need to pursue this topic more broadly and clearly, let us renew our powers with silence and our understanding with prayer. Let us come together tomorrow to explore these mysteries to the praise of our Lord Jesus Christ, *to whom is the honor and the glory, forever and ever. Amen.**

*Judg 13:5

*Num 6:5
*Judg 16:17

*Oner 21.24

*Isa 14:29

*Rom 16:27;
Heb 13:21

Homily 21

1. We will now take up for discussion with you, dearly beloved, the burden of the Philistines, which follows the burden of Babylon. The prophet narrated it in few words, yet the deeply meaningful subject he provided gives rise to many words.* So, brothers, descending from the allegorical mountains to the moral plains, let us return to the beginning of the burden itself. Let us say that we should take the Philistines to mean the proud *who trust in their own power and boast in the extent* of their spiritual gifts.* It is they who, going forth with Lot from Sodom and climbing the mountain of the virtues, become drunk from those two sisters, pride and vainglory.* Thus imperceptibly drawn to do shameful things, they fall into even *the worst of abominations.*† Rightly they are called Philistines, that is, *falling down from drink.*§

2. Take a look at what happens, dear brothers, when the virtues naturally take the place of uprooted vices. The more progress one makes, the more pride, now closer to the virtues than to the vices, grows bitterly strong. This beast takes many guises. One can hardly be on one's guard against it. There is no way to get rid of it in this life. Indeed, its own death feeds its life: it would rise up even stronger the more certainly it was regarded as extinct. You understand what I am saying. Whoever longs for honors is clearly proud. Whoever eliminates pride by despising honor often becomes more fatally vain by taking pride in pride's elimina-

*Oner 8.1

*Ps 48:7

*Origen, In Gen, Hom 5.6; Gen 19:30-35
†Ezek 8:9
§Jerome, Nom 6

tion. Whenever you do good, you look for a hiding place for fear of pride. But because you are careful of it, you soon suffer it more acutely. Therefore, brothers, judge how violent it is and how much danger is in it, because the mind, poisoned by this deadly venom, will not be cured except by an antidote of another venom equally deadly, although less dangerous.

3. Who does not know that lust brings eternal death to the soul just as much as pride does? Yet pride is more dangerous. Lust is granted entry so that pride can be driven out. For rarely do the proud escape the whirlpool of lust. Lust is either justly inflicted on them for their error or mercifully applied to heal that worst of wounds. For *God handed over to disgraceful passions in filth** those who *became vain in their thoughts, calling themselves wise when they were foolish.** David too, after the foreigners were brought under him, lifted his mind above its native humility. But crashing down, he collapsed in his love for Bathsheba, as though falling from heaven into the mud.* The more he knew his own weakness, the happier he was to be raised up.

4. *This burden took place in the year that King Ahaz died.** That beast does not dare raise its head as long as the vices, whose director is Ahaz, live in you, and the violent struggle with flesh and blood is within you.* The vices constantly inflict wounds upon you, even if you fight very well. The beast does not dare enter into deadly conflict against a fearful and trembling person who is armed for battle and fears death daily.* But if after Ahaz dies the stings of lust grow quiet—if generosity, tranquility, spiritual joy, and sobriety check the waves of avarice, the attack of anger, the horror of sadness, and the chasm of gluttony—then *the twisted serpent* will soon raise its venomous head.* After its injection of venom makes the soul swell up, this snake empties it of virtues. It then takes the soul down, causing rot under the swelling of the very vices that the soul had boasted of having escaped.

*Rom 1:26, 24
*Rom 1:21-22

*2 Sam 11:1-5

*Isa 14:28

*Eph 6:12

*1 Cor 15:21

*Job 26:13

5. Thus the prophetic word addresses those who, placed at the summit of the virtues, begin to boast not in the Lord, but in themselves:* *Do not rejoice,* it says, *Philistia, all of you, that the rod of your attacker has been broken.** *Do not rejoice, Philistia,* it says, you who have been given to drink from the cup of pride, you who became drunk on the wine of rejoicing,* you who now begin to fall from the higher to the lower: *Do not rejoice that the rod of your attacker has been broken.** This Ahaz is our attacker, him to whom God often hands the rod to strike us, to whip us, afflicting us through temptations and battering us through suggestions. This rod is broken when the power of tempting is taken away. Still, *do not rejoice, Philistia,** as if you had already escaped: do not boast, as if you had already destroyed that venomous snake by your own power. Be careful of the snake's root as well. If it is stuck deep within you, it will reproduce wicked fruit in you.

6. You know, brothers, that *pride is the beginning of all sin.** It is like the root of *the body of sin,*† which the apostle calls the worst of trees. This root produces many branches and fills all of them with its fatal sap. So beware of being Philistia, beware of the snake's root. Because *a basilisk will come forth from the snake's root;** from pride, contempt for God. The basilisk is the king of the serpents,* and contempt for God is the most powerful of all the vices. This is because vices are judged more worthy of damnation when they are born of contempt rather than of ignorance or weakness. Contempt is born of pride, because unless the human mind first becomes puffed up, it does not burst in wrongdoing against its Creator.

7. *And its seed will consume the bird.** The seed of contempt is a desperation that prevents confession, mocks repentance, and refuses to make amends. *The ungodly, when they come into the depth of sin, condemn.** They are blasphemous toward God and hostile toward their neighbor, and they rage destructively against

*1 Cor 1:31

*Isa 14:29

*Jerome, Nom 6

*Isa 14:29

*Isa 14:29

*Sir 10:15
†Rom 6:6

*Isa 14:29
*Jerome, In Isa 6.34

*Isa 14:29

*Prov 18:3

themselves. Because they despair of grace, they apply thick kindling to the despair itself, heaping vice upon vice.*

*Aelred, SS 40.8, 54.39; Gregory, Mo 26.XXXVII.69

8. Hope is represented by the bird, a winged animal that seeks higher things with swift flight. By hope, we prefer the heavenly to the earthly, the eternal to the temporal, and the divine to the human. By hope, too, we have already been saved, and reign together with Christ in heaven.* Desperation consumes this bird when the feathers with which it flew to heaven are plucked. This desperation then turns the soul to the basest things, so that, disregarding what is to come, it embraces the earthly. It desires nothing beyond the earthly, because it does not hope that anything beyond the earthly exists.

*Rom 8:24; Eph 2:6; 2 Tim 2:12

9. But *Do not rejoice, Philistia, all of you,** can also appropriately be addressed to those who do not willingly accept the divine *scourge.** They are lavish in prosperity, and they complain in adversity. Good treatment lifts them up, and persecution confounds them. Hear, brothers, what the apostle says: *What child does the father not correct?** Indeed, *he scourges every child whom he accepts.** And so he too can be called an attacker who *strikes* and heals, who *kills and gives life,* who *brings down to Hell and leads back again.** He certainly sends forth *the rod of* his *strength from Zion to punish* our *iniquities with the rod and* our *sins with blows.** This is a great sign, brothers, a great sign of divine compassion when he does not spare us in the present, when he does not show pity,* when he fences in our paths with *thorns* and encloses us with a *wall* so that seeking death we do not find it,† when he sprinkles many forms of bitterness on all the sweet things for which we yearn so that we do not cling to them.

*Isa 14:29

*Jdt 8:27

*Heb 12:7
*Heb 12:6

*1 Sam 2:6; Job 5:18; Deut 32:39

*Pss 88:33; 109:2; Isa 26:21

*Jerome, In Isa 6:34; Oner 1.15, 19.17
†Hos 2:6; Rev 9:6

10. What of you, Philistia, *falling down from drink? The Lord filled* you *with bitterness and made you drunk.**

*Ant 5 HM (Hesbert 3.4615); Lam 3:15

He made you drink *from the cup of his anger,** and his *Isa 51:17; Rev
arrows are stuck in you, *whose anger drinks up your* 14:10
*spirit.** Of course if you are angry, if you murmur, if *Job 6:4; Ps 37:3
you are displeased, if you reject the physician's hand,
if you hate the father's rod, then you are a Philistine
falling down from drink. You are rushing from a place
where you might have hoped to stand upright to your
own destruction.

11. Woe to you, if he turns his *zeal* away *from you*
and grows angry *with you no more.** It is like what he *Ezek 16:42
says to certain people through the prophet: *I will not
punish your daughters when they fornicate nor your wives
when they commit adultery.** Unhappy are those for *Hos 4:14; Oner
whom the psalms lament, *My people did not listen to* 1.15
*my law, and Israel did not pay me heed.** They did not *Pss 80:12; 77:1
listen to the teacher, they did not bear the corrector.
On the one side are *rebels and unbelievers,** on the other *Num 20:10
are murmurers, and both sides are ungrateful.** How *RB 4.39; Jude 16;
will they therefore be punished, how will they be af- 2 Tim 3:2
flicted if not with these torments? Listen to what follows: *So I left them to the desires of their heart.** *Ps 80:13; Oner,

12. Understand, my beloved brothers. The Lord cor- Adv 23 = Aelred,
rects many people for their sins. They are afflicted by S 47.23; Oner 6.5;
poverty, ground down by persecutions, weakened in Aelred, Spec car
their members, and tortured by various kinds of dis- 1.26.75
eases. If they do not accept correction but are excessive
in the good times and blasphemous in the bad,** he *2 Tim 3:2
holds back the rod and returns *the sword to its sheath.** *John 18:11
He hands *them* over *to the desires of their heart,** that *Rom 1:24; Ps
they may go according to their own counsels. Then 80:13
*they rejoice when they do evil and exult in the worst of
things.** The prophet speaks to people such as these, *Prov 2:14
saying, *Do not rejoice, Philistia, all of you, that the rod of
your attacker has been broken.** *Isa 14:29

13. Do not rejoice that he who educated you has
stopped beating you.** It was his rod that shut out the *Deut 8:5
head of the snake, removed the basilisk's venom, and

*Isa 14:20 LXX dried up its *wicked seed.** *Do not rejoice, therefore, that*
*Isa 14:29 *the rod of your attacker has been broken.** For the twisted
Job 26:13 snake will then easily implant its root in you. The
snake's root is the will's corruption, from which, as
from a wicked root, wicked branches come forth. *For
*Isa 14:29 *a basilisk will come forth from the snake's root;** that is to
say, unclean pleasure will come forth from a corrupted
will. The seed of unclean pleasure is our wicked
works, which overwhelm and absorb all that was lofty
Rom 11:20 in our soul before, and all that, like a winged bird,†
†Ps 148:10 sought higher things by means of desire and affection.
But what will the poor, that is to say, the humble, do
to the Philistines, that is to say, to the proud brought
low by such a burden?

14. It continues: *And the firstborn of the poor will be
*Isa 14:30 *fed, and the poor will rest in confidence.** These are the
poor to whom the Lord says, *Blessed are the poor, for
*Matt 5:3; Luke *yours is the kingdom of heaven.** This poverty is judged
6:20 according to disposition, not according to wealth,
since an eminent person abounding in riches and
*Ps 69:6 kingdoms says, *I am truly needy and poor.**

There are certain virtues with which we begin, others by which we advance, and still others by which
we are completed. The first of all the virtues is faith,
which hope strengthens and charity rewards. *Faith* is
*Gal 5:6 that virtue that *works through* love,* since no one works
well without hope of reward. These are the firstborn
of the poor, that is, of the humble, who boast not in
1 Cor 1:31 themselves, but in the Lord. These firstborn need to
*Matt 15:32 be fed *so that they do not faint on the way.** They are fed
by reason, authority, and experience. Reason com-
mends, authority confirms, and experience proves
what we believe or hope.

15. For when we say, *Faith does not have merit for those
*Gregory, Eu 26.1 *to whom human reason offers proof,** we are not referring
to the kind of reason that seeks to investigate what
should be believed or hoped, but rather to the kind
that tries to seize what is to be believed by fixed

proofs, and to see what is to be hoped for with the naked eye. But *a hope that is seen is not hope*,* and a faith that crosses over into knowledge is not faith. Yet reason works together with our faith when reflection on natural things proves what should be believed.

* Rom 8:24

16. For example, by reflecting on the natural mutability of creation, reason proves that we should believe that whatever changes did not exist at one time. Its existence, therefore, has a beginning. It did not take its beginning from itself, because it could not have created itself when it did not exist. Reason thus persuades us to believe that something exists that has no beginning and therefore always existed. It is this that gave being to all other things. All other things, of course, would not exist unless they were many. The many would not be able to come together in one harmony unless the one wisdom of the One led the many back, unless all things were brought under the one power of the One. This is why reason teaches us to believe that every creature is brought under the will of the Creator, made subject either willingly, unwillingly, or naturally. But every creature earns its reward willingly or its punishment unwillingly; anything without a will neither fears punishment nor expects a reward. All these things are believed and hoped here, but they will be better perceived in the future in charity itself.

17. Authority also feeds us when we provide our faith and hope in Christ with witnesses. The more clearly we see the fulfillment of what such witnesses foretold long ago, the more firmly we believe. This is a kind of experience in the present age that nourishes our faith. By this kind of experience, our own eyes prove that what we read in the prophets is true.

18. There is another kind of experience in this life that proves faith, strengthens hope, and nourishes charity. This is the experience of that *anointing* of the Spirit that *teaches* us *all things*.* It pours into us a kind

* 1 John 2:27

of firstfruit of future beatitude while it illuminates
and kindles our heart.* The heart thus sees and loves,
tastes and understands, when *the Spirit himself gives
testimony to our spirit that we are children of God.*

19. If these virtues are thus fed, if they are nourished, then we will easily advance in the other virtues
that they introduce. Fear adheres to faith, patience to
hope, and chastity to charity. From there, fear gives
birth to prudence, patience to fortitude, chastity to
temperance, and charity to righteousness. Through
these we finally ascend to wisdom, as from streams
to the source. Faith passes over to sight, hope to possession, charity to fullness. Then what follows will
certainly occur: *And the poor will rest in confidence.*

20. For when the humble, those who do not boast
in their own merits, those whom the prophet calls *poor*,
arrive at the peak of the virtues, *they will rest in confidence. Pride's foot does not press upon these poor,* and
so they can neither be moved by the hand of the sinner
nor struck by the impending whirlwind.* *There*, that
is, in pride, *those who worked iniquity fell. They have been
cast out; they could not stand.* These are the Philistines
falling down from drink, in whom the snake grafted its
root.* That root brought forth the basilisk, whose seed
absorbs the bird.* The prophet adds still more to this:
*And I will make your root perish from famine, and your
remnants I will kill.*

21. Both the proud who exalt themselves in their
virtues and the humble who boast in the Lord rely on
the catholic faith as the root of all virtues.* If this root
is rotten by the venom of any error, if it is as though
already dead, a kind of dryness withers that entire
tree of the virtues. But just as the Spirit's anointing
feeds and nourishes the faith in the holy and humble
heart,* as we said before,† so too the faith of the proud
and puffed up is easily cast down because they are
starving for spiritual grace, and they fall into various
errors and blasphemies. Those who called *themselves*

*Rom 8:23

*Rom 8:16;
Aelred, S 34.25

*Isa 14:30

*Ps 35:12

*Isa 30:30

*Ps 35:13
*Jerome, Nom 6
*Job 26:13
*Isa 14:29

*Isa 14:30

*1 Cor 1:31

*Matt 11:29; 1
John 2:27
†Oner 21.19

wise were made foolish and changed the truth of God into a lie.* *Rom 1:22, 23, 25

22. Therefore, it says, *And I will make your root perish from famine.** Because you do not deserve the grace by which it is nourished, the root will dry up and die, *and your remnants I will kill.** After the root has perished, why would the branches not die as well? After the first has passed away, will not whatever is last also be destroyed? Faith is the root; the other virtues are the remnants. Thus, where faith is corrupted, all the virtues likewise disappear, because *Everything that is not from faith is sin.** What, then? Is there no cure, no hope left for the Philistines? There is indeed, if they do what follows: *Wail, door; cry out, city.** But because we have not yet explained this allegorically, let us also postpone for now the moral explanation.

*Isa 14:30

*Isa 14:30

*Rom 14:23

*Isa 14:31

23. Because the burden of the Philistines can be understood not only as the burden by which they are weighed down but also as that with which they weigh down others, let us say that the Philistines are unclean spirits who,* drunk on pride, fell from that heavenly abode.* They tire us with their suggestions, weigh us down with temptations, and burden us with pain. Our struggle is against those who sometimes wound and strike us,* whom we in turn also both strike and wound. Therefore, brothers, *put on the armor of God, so that you can stand against the snares of the devil and remain perfect in all things.**

*Acts 8:7

*Isa 14:12; John 14:2

*Eph 6:12

*Eph 6:11, 13

24. Protect your great strength, which, like for Samson, *seven locks of hair* preserve for you.* The Philistines draw near, they bind with ropes those who are asleep. But they accomplish nothing if the seven locks have not been cut off first.* The prophet says this about these ropes: *They have encircled me with the ropes of sin.*† But because he did what follows—*And I did not forget your law**—he can confidently proclaim in another psalm, *You have broken my bonds.** There are three ropes with which the Philistines assail us: *concupiscence of*

*Judg 16:17, 19; Aelred, S 35.13

*Oner 20.27; Aelred, S 35.6, 17

†Ps 118:61

*Ps 118:61

*Ps 115:16; Aelred, S 35.5

*1 John 2:16;
Aelred, S 63.10,
13

the flesh, concupiscence of the eyes, and pride of life. Look,
O Samson, or you will fall asleep. Look, or you will
grow negligent with idleness. Look, or you will be
seduced by the prostitute's enticements, namely,

*Judg 16:19

vainglory.*

*RB 48.1

25. *Idleness is the enemy of the soul,* for all idle people
are attentive to their desires. Let them hear this, those
who look for opportunities to wander around, those
to whom the common manual labor is a burden, and
those who devote themselves to leisure and idle tales

*RB 48.18

while the brothers are engaged in necessary tasks.*
We often see such people bound by the ropes of the
Philistines. They are sometimes agitated by the goads

*2 Cor 12:7

of the flesh,* sometimes unhappily entangled in foolish affairs, and sometimes driven to wander by violent
passions, open to the criticism of many. The Philistines
drag them by the rope of carnal concupiscence to lust,
by the rope of concupiscence of the eyes to vanity, and
by the rope of pride to superstition.

*Aelred, S 35.10

26. Hair comes from the head, and thoughts from
the heart.* Seven thoughts maintain your strength. Of
these, two concern the past, two the future, and three
the present. To the past belongs the memory of creation and redemption; to the future, dread of damnation and contemplation of eternal reward; to the
present, reflection on our weakness and on divine
goodness and, with these, the memory of the consola-

*Aelred, S
35.14–16

tion that we often experience.* Of course, if in a deadly
sleep you senselessly betray these thoughts to a prostitute—that is, if you hand them over to vainglory to
be cut off—then you, powerless and weak, will be
handed over in turn to the Philistines, that is, to evil

*Judg 16:19-21;
Acts 19:12; Matt
20:19

spirits, to be mocked.*

27. One could say to those exulting, *Do not rejoice,
Philistia, all of you, that the rod* of Samson *has been bro-*

*Isa 14:29
†Judg 16:22

*ken.** His hair can grow again,† with which he will be
able to turn aside both the snake's root and the basi-

*Isa 14:29

lisk's birth.* This he will be able to do if, like a poor

person in a place of pasture, he is able to avoid famine for the word of God* and if he rests confidently in the hope of divine mercy.† It will come to pass that, by the grace of God, when the material of sin is removed, the snake's root will perish as though from famine, having nothing on which to live. And so too for the other vices that had sprouted from that worst of roots; after the root dies, they will wilt.*

*Jerome, In Isa 6.34; Ps 22:2; Amos 8:11
†Ps 4:9-10

*Isa 14:30

28. But let us now at last conclude this sermon, beseeching the mercy of God that we may deserve to feed interiorly on that word that has no end,* which is Christ, *to whom is the honor and the glory, forever and ever. Amen.*

*Oner 26.34; 4.18; 19.36; Bar 3:25

*Rom 16:27

Homily 22

1. We said that the Philistines, which means *falling down from drink,** were a type of what was to come, representing the Jews.† The Romans brought down and crushed the Jews because they killed our Lord and Savior. *They were cast out* and scattered, *because God despised them.** For this reason, the prophet said, *And I will make your root perish from famine, and your remnants I will kill.** Still describing their disaster, he added, *Wail, O gate; cry out, O city; all of Philistia has been brought low.**

2. History is not silent about what happened after the Romans besieged the city of Jerusalem and used weapons and war machines to wear down those within. There was often a cry at the gate and in the city. This was especially so when the towers, butted as though by a ram, fell to the ground and the army burst in and struck down whomever they came across. This is when it became clear that Philistia had been brought low. The temple had been burned down and the chiefs and priests were either killed or led captive for the victory procession. The sword killed a great crowd of the common people, another large faction had died from famine,* the victors led away not a small number and subjected them to base slavery, and more than a few were delivered to wild beasts or assigned to arenas *to fall by the blows they inflicted on one another.**

*Jerome, In Isa 6.35
†Col 2:17; Heb 10:1; Oner 20.2

*Pss 52:6; 72:2

*Isa 14:30

*Isa 14:31

*Jer 14:16

*2 Chr 20:23

3. We can also understand *gate* to signify the teachers through whom others received entrance to *the rites and sacrifices.** For the preachers of the New Testament are called the church's gates: *The Lord loves the gates of Zion above all Jacob's tents.** Understand *city*, on the other hand, to be the synagogue, which was indeed at first a *city of God** but is now called *the synagogue of Satan.*† Therefore, a cry and a wail are prophesied for both the leaders and subjects of that people, expressing pain and labor,* their heart's anguish and their voice's lamentation.*

4. It therefore says, *Wail, O gate; cry out, O city.** It goes on to show why they should wail or cry, saying, *All of Philistia has been brought low.** This is that desolation of a city and its people that holy Ezekiel describes based on what the Lord said to him: *And you, son of man, take up your sharp sword, and run it over your head and beard. And you will take up your scale, and will weigh and divide the hair. You will burn a third part with fire, you will cut a third part with your sword, and you will scatter a third part to every wind, and you will unsheathe your sword after them.** All of this needs no explanation, only reflection.*

5. There is another destruction of that people, a destruction all the more serious insofar as the soul is more precious than the flesh. Think, then, of that fruitful, fertile olive tree, whose root is Abraham and the other patriarchs. From this root, the useless—or rather harmful—branches were cut off. Having grown completely dry of that richness of faith and love that, proceeding from the best of roots, had communicated itself to all the branches, they were pruned for the eternal fire.* This was a hard fall from faith to treachery, from truth to lies, from heaven to hell!† On account of this fall, the gate wails and the city cries out.§

6. Understand, if you will, that here the gate is the apostle Paul, through whom *all the nations* came to

*Wis 14:15

*Ps 86:2

*Ps 86:3; Tob 13:11
†Rev 2:9

*Ps 89:10
*Ps 60:3; Jer 9:19

*Isa 14:31

*Isa 14:31; Jerome, In Isa 6.35

*Ezek 5:1-2
*Jerome, In Ezek 2.5.1-4

*Rom 11:16-17, 22; Matt 3:10 and parallels
†Rom 1:25
§Isa 14:31

*Col 1:6; 2 Tim 4:17
†Rom 9:2-3

*Ps 86:3

*Isa 14:31; Jerome, In Isa 6.35

*Isa 1:3
*Isa 6:10
*Rom 10:3; 1:21

*Jerome, In Isa 6.35; Isa 14:13, 31; Jer 1:14; 8:2
†Rom 11:25-26

*Isa 14:31

*Isa 14:32

*1 Tim 2:7; Acts 11:19-21

*Isa 14:32

*Rom 11:25

know *the grace of God.** For he was *very sad, and in constant pain for* his *brothers according to the flesh.*† I think the other apostles were also in mourning, even if Paul was more ardent. Not only they, but also the entire *city of God,** that is, the church, laments the fall of the Jews and desires their conversion. The prophet was not silent about why this people would suffer these things: *For smoke will come from the north, and no one will escape from its army on the march.**

7. Smoke, which darkens or blinds the eyes, represents the ignorance that hid the Savior's coming from them and took away their recognition of him. As the Lord said through the same prophet, *The ox has recognized its owner and the donkey its master's lodging, but Israel did not recognize me.** And much later, *Blind this people's heart.** These are the ones who, *not knowing God's righteousness,* fell into foolishness.* But where did this *smoke* come from? *From the north,* where Satan's throne is, from where *evil* advances *over the face of the land.** This is the *blindness* that *has occurred in Israel until the fullness of the nations enters in, and thus all Israel is saved.*† But this smoke comes with an army on the march, because many abominations follow ignorance: hatred, curses, and blasphemies. That wretched people becomes worse and worse with such abuses, so that there is no one among those condemned who *escapes* that smoke's *army on the march.**

8. It follows, *And what answer will the nations' messengers receive?** The nations' messengers are the preachers, apostles, and apostolic men who, driven out of Judea, went over to the Gentile people.* The Holy Spirit responds to these messengers who were mourning Israel's fall and wondering at the cause of such blindness, saying, *The Lord has founded Zion.** This is how the Holy Spirit answered Paul, and how Paul, in turn, answered many others: *Because blindness has in part occurred in Israel until the fullness of the nations enters in.** This is the very church from the nations,

namely, Zion, which *the Lord has founded,** and *its foundations are in the holy mountains.** Therefore, blindness occurred in Israel and *the natural branches* were cut off from the *natural* olive tree.* This is so that there would be room to graft other branches, even though they were less natural according to the flesh.* Zion, that is, the church, was founded from these very branches. But because *many are called, but few are chosen,** only *the poor of his people*, that is, *Zion, will hope in it.*†

9. *I announced*, it says, *and I spoke, they have grown beyond number.** And so the condemned enter the church with the elect, and the apostolic nets gather both good and bad fish. It will remain thus until *on the shore,* that is, at the end of the world, the angels go forth and separate *the wicked ones from amid the just.** And so the rich *trust in their wealth, the wise in their wisdom, and the strong in their strength.** But the poor, that is, those who have learned from the Lord to be meek and humble of heart,* show their path to the Lord and hope in him,† saying with the prophet, *Because you, O Lord, are my hope.*§ But the proud, too, in whom *the ancient serpent* has fixed the root of ungodliness,‡ have nowhere to run except to the humility of repentance. After the root of faith has dried up, the other virtues also perish.* Just as *confession perishes from the dead as though they did not exist,*† so too, the person who confesses and repents is returned to the favor of life.

10. *Wail*, therefore, *O gate; cry out, O city; all of Philistia has been brought low.** All of Philistia is brought low when reason falls into error, the memory of God falls into forgetfulness, and the will falls into wantonness. *All* is brought low when the heart occupies itself with shamefulness, speech with duplicity, and works with base affairs and iniquity. Therefore, *wail* in contrition of heart, *cry out* in confession. For the heart itself is called a *gate*, from which *evil thoughts go forth, murder, theft, blasphemy, and false witness.** But perhaps you

*Isa 14:32
*Ps 86:1

*Rom 11:21, 24-25

*Rom 9:3

*Matt 20:16 and parallels
†Isa 14:32

*Ps 39:6

*Matt 13:47-49; John 21:4

*Jer 9:23; Prov 11:28; Ps 48:7

*Matt 11:29; Jerome, In Isa 6.35
†Ps 36:5
§Ps 90:9
‡Rev 12:9; Isa 14:29

*Isa 14:30; Oner 21.22
†Sir 17:26

*Isa 14:31

*Matt 15:19

*Jerome, In Isa
6.35

prefer to understand the gate as a person's mouth.* In that case, it seems appropriate that the mouth, which had encouraged and drawn others to the vices, should wail fearfully in repentance to frighten others.

*Isa 14:31
†Jerome, In Isa
6.35

11. *Cry out,* it says, *O city.** The prophet calls the soul a *city.*† Depending on its state, the soul receives various names. Sometimes it is fit to be called Jericho, sometimes Jerusalem, and sometimes Babylon. Its walls are its virtues or vices, its houses are its natural gifts, its people are its thoughts and feelings. Now this city cries out in different ways: at times by praising God, at times by accusing itself, quite frequently by lamenting, and often by asking for something. Now, one can say that the city cries out when the soul draws together its entire being within itself and to itself and thus breaks forth in a *voice of praise, confession,* pain,

*Pss 65:8; 41:5;
114:1
†Ps 102:1

or *prayer.** *Bless the Lord, my soul, and may all that I have within bless his holy name,* says the prophet.† Not just any part, but the entire city will ring forth the blessing of the Lord.

*Isa 14:31

12. *Wail,* therefore, *O gate; cry out, O city,** so that there is contrition in the heart and confession in the mouth. Thus what blame had brought low, repentance may raise up, and what was written may be done: *Sodom will be restored to its former state.**

*Ezek 16:55; Isa
23:16 Var
†Isa 14:31
§Jer 1:13

13. It follows, *Smoke will come from the north.*† *What do you see,* the Lord asked Jeremiah, *What do you see?*§ And Jeremiah answered, *A pot on the fire, and it is fac-*

*Jer 1:13

*ing north.** You know who takes pleasure in the north-

*Isa 14:13

ern region,* that is, in the cold hearts of mortals that are hostile to God's warmth. He who sits in them

*Jer 1:13; Job
41:11

often lights a fire under the pot of temptation,* from which *smoke* comes forth, blinding the eyes of many

*Jerome, In Isa
6.35; Gregory, Mo
33.XXXVII.66
†Isa 14:31

and keeping them from the light of truth.* For he says that *Philistia is brought low;*† for this reason, one can also be sure of pardon if worthy repentance leads the way.

14. For Paul was brought low in faithlessness but raised up in faith; he was a persecutor in faithlessness* but *an instructor in faith.*† He said, *I have received mercy, because I unknowingly acted in unbelief.*§ His very ignorance was like smoke, coming forth, of course, from the north, encompassing his mind in the darkness of error. Therefore he easily obtains forgiveness, because *out of zeal* he persecuted *the church of God,** blinded by the smoke of ignorance rather than spurred on by ill-will.

15. Neither should you despair of forgiveness. Even if the smoke of ignorance perhaps did not influence you, yet the smoke of another's suggestion and the smoke of carnal concupiscence certainly did. Therefore, he who knows *our make* is all the quicker to show us mercy, because we bear in ourselves what is easily darkened by the smoke from that pot on the fire.* Therefore, Philistia, or any given proud soul, is certainly brought low. For the smoke of ignorance or concupiscence coming from the north—that is, from the devil's temptation—either encircles such a soul if it is careless or allures it if it is weak.*

16. But you, wail, you, cry out, so that what this prophet wrote may be done: *Take up the harp, go around the city, O prostitute who has been forgotten; sing well and often so that you are remembered.** You too, then, sing a song of pain with the harp of mortification, so that you may be remembered in the presence of the Redeemer's mercy. For he knows that *no one* can *escape* this wicked smoke's *army on the march.** For whose flesh and mind does that northern enemy not kindle at times like a *boiling pot,** rousing the smoke of concupiscence with fiery darts?†

17. *What answer,* then, *will the nations' messengers receive?** Understand, if you will, the nations' messengers to be the angels of the opposing power. They place the hard path of virtue and the flesh's fragility and corruption before the eyes of those worn out by

* Acts 9:4 and
parallels
† 1 Tim 2:7
§ 1 Tim 1:13; 2:7

* Phil 3:6

* Ps 102:14; Job 41:11; Jer 1:13

* Jas 1:14

* Isa 23:16

* Isa 14:31

* Job 41:11; Jer 1:13
† Eph 6:16

* Isa 14:32

various temptations, so that, downcast, they turn and run away from the path of salvation in a kind of hope-lessness.* I am speaking to those who have experience of this. In the beginnings of our conversion it seemed impossible to endure the severe temptations of flesh and spirit. At times the spirit of fornication burns us, at times anger catches fire, at times gluttony stirs up our desires. These seem especially impossible to en-dure since the slippery state of youth and the manifold cunning of temptation threaten an easy fall due to weakness. And so, what answer will be given when the spirits suggest such things? What is our hope, what is our refuge? *That the Lord has founded Zion.**

18. Brothers, *The firm foundation of God stands bearing this sign: The Lord has recognized those who are his.*[†] O Zion, O holy soul, placed, as it were, on a watchtower, you are waiting for your Lord's coming.* Do not fear, do not be disturbed, because if the *winds* should whip *and the rivers overflow,*[†] you may grow tired but you will not be knocked down. *For you were founded on firm rock.*[§] For *the Lord has founded Zion,*[‡] he who will not permit us *to be tempted beyond what* we are capable of, *but will provide a way out with the temptation, so that we might withstand it.*[#] This is the consolation of the wretched in this life, this is fortitude amid tempta-tions, this is security amid tribulation, this is constancy amid adversity. Certainly *The Lord has founded Zion,*[≈] which is the soul lofty in the contemplation of God. He has established it on the foundation of true humil-ity, which is all the more solidly and securely laid the more frequently temptations try it. Neither can care-lessness deceive it, nor can it be enticed once it has been tested nor overcome once it has been trained.* And so *the Lord has founded Zion, and in it the poor of his people will hope.**

19. O dear brothers, if some fault seizes you or if excessive temptation strikes you, you should note if your heart was exalted before the fall.* If you mourn

*Matt 7:14; RB Prol 48

*Isa 14:32; Ps 90:2, 9; Aelred, Inst incl 18
†2 Tim 2:19

*Isa 21:8; Judg 6:18; Luke 12:36; 1 Tim 6:14; Aelred, S 32.3–4; Jerome, Nom 39
†Matt 7:25
§Matt 7:25; Eccl 1:7; Ant et Resp Haec est domus In comm Dedic Eccl (Hesbert 3.2998; 4.6801)
‡Isa 14:32
#1 Cor 10:13
≈Isa 14:32

*Jas 1:12

*Isa 14:32

*Prov 16:18; 18:12

the cause of the sin, you will more easily obtain forgiveness for having committed it. For you will be made poor *in spirit, humble* in mind,* because it is not those who trust in their riches who hope in the Lord, but those who boast in Christian poverty.* *Matt 5:3; 11:29

20. However, *watchtower,* which is what *Zion* means, can also express spiritual knowledge.† The soul stands in this watchtower and protects the fruit of the virtues from thieves and wild beasts. But neither can the proud trust nor the puffed up hope in this knowledge that the Lord establishes in holy souls. It is only *the poor of his people,** that is, the humble, who can hope in this knowledge. These are the ones who, increasing knowledge, also increase sorrow,* so that they may one day boast in that beatitude that the Lord commends in the gospel: *Blessed are those who mourn, for they will be consoled.** In Christ Jesus our Lord, to whom with God the Father in the unity of the Holy Spirit be *honor, glory, and power,* for endless ages.* Amen.

*Ps 48:7; Jer 9:23; 1 Cor 1:31 and parallels
†Jerome, Nom 39

*Isa 14:32

*Eccl 1:18

*Matt 5:5; Aelred, S 42.12–13

*1 Pet 4:11; 1 Tim 6:16

Homily 23

1. After explaining the burden of the Philistines, the prophetic word arms itself against Moab. I realize that I should first explain its name to you. Holy Lot, after leaving Sodom, after *his wife, looking back,* had been changed *into a pillar of salt,** climbed up a mountain alone with his two daughters. After dwelling in an unclean city, he became the new inhabitant of a cave.* There each daughter stole intercourse from their drunken father and incestuously conceived sons. The firstborn daughter gave birth to Moab and the other to Ammon.* *Moab means from the father* or *paternal water.** Lot of course unknowingly fathered Moab with his daughter. It was not from a feeling of love, which joins those lawfully coming together in a kind of sweetness of spirit. Rather, it was from that fluid that comes forth like water from someone asleep or drunk, without a feeling of love.*

2. What can I say, dear brothers? Would you think me blasphemous if I said that holy Lot represented our Lord and Savior in all of this? Remember, if you will, that Judah in his relations with Tamar, who he thought was a prostitute,* and David in his forbidden embrace of Bathsheba represented forms of our Lord Jesus according to the holy fathers.† Do not be surprised that here too *Joshua§ the great priest* is depicted *in filthy clothes,* as in Zechariah.‡

*Gen 19:26; Wis 10:7; Luke 17:31-32

*Gen 19:30

*Gen 19:32, 36-38
*Jerome, In Isa 6.36

*Gen 19:33, 35; Jerome, In Isa 6.36

*Gen 38:12-26
†2 Sam 11:2-5; Augustine, C Faust Manich 22.86.87
§*Jesus*
‡Zech 3:1-3; Gregory, Mo 20.XXII.48

3. Christ, as you know, is the Power of God and the Wisdom of God.* From the Wisdom of God is produced, like two daughters, a double knowledge: practical and theoretical knowledge.* And so when the Wisdom of God led these two daughters into the cave,† namely, the pagans' dark hearts, they conceived a certain "knowledge of divine and human things" from the good father.* But this was not from the Father's willing seed,† which is charity, but from their own curiosity and vanity. They conceived as though from incest, and not according to the rightful order.§ For Paul bears witness that even the wise of this world have learned much about human and even divine realities from God's revelation, saying, *What was known of God was brought to light in them, for God revealed it to them.** But they did not cling to the Wisdom of God in the rightful order. So they were puffed up rather than humbled;* they called *themselves wise* and *became foolish.**

4. And so Moab, which means *from the father* or *paternal water,* represents the wise of this world or the *world's wisdom* itself.* Although such wisdom came from God, the philosophers did not use it for the taste of divine charity, but for the pomp of worldly vanity. These are the ones who, after grace had been revealed, fought against Christ's cross *in wisdom of speech.** After the destruction or conversion of the Jews, the apostles drew up a magnificent battle-array against these philosophers. This is why, after the burden that set right or suppressed the Jews' madness, the prophet prophesies of the burden of the wise of this world or of worldly wisdom itself,* that is, its sinking, saying, *Because Ar was destroyed at night, Moab kept silence.**

5. *Night* means opposition and trouble. It is written that the Savior himself, inhabiting this valley of darkness, suffered from this *night* by his own free will.* Remember, if you will, that he was betrayed and

*1 Cor 1:24

*Hugh of St. Victor, Didasc 2.2
†Gen 19:30

*Augustine, C acad 1.6.16; Cicero, Off 1.43:153; 2.2:5; Cicero, Tusc 4.26.57
†Jas 1:18; 1 Pet 1:23; 1 John 3:9
§Augustine, Civ Dei 19.3.5
*Rom 1:19

*1 Cor 4:19; 8:1
*Rom 1:22

*1 Cor 1:20

*1 Cor 1:17

*1 Cor 1:20; 3:19
*Isa 15:1

*Isa 53:7, 12; John 10:17-18

*Matt 26:47 and parallels; Luke 22:63-65 and parallels
†Matt 27:57-60 and parallels; Acts 13:29
§Isa 15:1
‡Jerome, In Isa 6.37
#1 Pet 5:8

mocked at night.* We know that he was taken down from the cross when night was already falling.† In this *night Ar was destroyed.*§ *Ar* means *opponent*,‡ that is the opponent about whom blessed Peter wrote, *Be sober and keep watch, because your opponent the devil is roaming around like a lion looking for someone to devour.*#

6. This opponent's city can rightly be called hell. It is certain that this city, opposed to the city of God, was destroyed with its prince through Christ's death. Thus the Lord, addressing hell itself, said, *I will be your death,*

*Hos 13:14

*O death; I will be your sting, hell.** For *he went down to hell,* and *having undone the suffering* of many *ascended*

*Symb apost; Acts 2:24; Eph 4:8

on high and *led captivity captive.** This is why the church, addressing him with sublime voice, proclaims with great rejoicing,

> Piercing the gates of hell,
> Redeeming your captives,
> The victor with noble triumph

*Hymn, *Iesu nostra redemptio* st. 3, ad vesp Ascens

> Is sitting at the right hand of the Father.*

This is that opposing city, namely, the hall of that armed strong man who, conquered when someone stronger overtook him, lost his booty and cast down

*Luke 11:21-22

his weapons.*

7. Therefore, everyone wise in this world—everyone who understood that Christ's passion had destroyed the devil's power as though *at night*—fell silent in great amazement. They did not know what to counter or how to resist. But one could also understand this very crowd of people as the city of Ar. Opposing God,

*Ezek 20:32

they worshiped *wood and stones.** In a certain fashion, this crowd was destroyed at night. Stunned by the suffering and patience of the saints, the majority destroyed this opposing city by their very absence from it. Then certainly, Moab, that is, *the wisdom of the world,*

*1 Cor 3:19; Isa 15:1

kept silence,* its voice too weak either to develop its own teaching or to dismiss Christ's. For the philosophers' very teaching can be called *Ar.* Such teaching is opposed to God's wisdom, by which it was proven to be destroyed, as it is written, *I will destroy the wisdom of the wise and condemn the prudence of the prudent.**

8. It goes on to say, *Because at night the wall was destroyed, Moab kept silence.†* The opposing city's *wall*, that is, hell's *wall*, was idolatry. We see that the power of the Lord's passion has destroyed idolatry throughout the entire world. Or the godless crowd's *wall* was worldly power, which divine power overthrew through the mystery of the holy cross. Furthermore, the opposing doctrine's *wall* was disputation and cunning argumentation.* Christian simplicity overturned this opposing doctrine *at night*, that is, under persecutions, and faith's sincerity laid waste all its arguments. *Moab*, that is, this world's understanding, *kept silence** when *the Lord* thundering over *many waters** barri- caded *the mouth of those speaking wickedness** and emp- tied out *all knowledge lifting itself up against the knowledge of God.** Therefore what follows happened: *The house* *went up and Dibon to the heights in mourning.†*

9. *Houses* refer not only to walls with a roof and foundation but also to the family that lives there. It is called a good or a bad house according to the family's good or bad habits. Understand the house of Moab, then, to be the heart of the wise of this world.* Not a small family of perceptions, thoughts, and affections lives in this house. Further, *Dibon*, which means *their flow*,* represents the variety and wantonness of these perceptions, thoughts, or even opinions.

10. In the city of Dibon there was a high place consecrated to an idol,* to which those offering sacrifices were accustomed to go up with shouts and joy. There was also a high place in the teaching of the philosophers. This high place was pride. Here they worshiped idols instead of God, exchanging *the glory of the incorruptible God for the image of a corruptible person, beasts and snakes.** Although they had known God

*per scientiam;
Rom 1:21

theoretically,* they fell headlong into idolatry because of their pride.

11. But they perceived that their empty doctrine had fallen silent *through the foolishness of the apostolic preach-*

*1 Cor 1:21

*ing.** Therefore they shifted their whole heart and all their thoughts, like a house or family, and all the astuteness of their perceptions, like *Dibon,* to higher

*Ezek 3:14

things in pride and *in indignation of spirit.** They mourned that their teaching was about to be overturned and sought a way to subtly oppose sound teaching. Therefore, *The house went up and Dibon to the*

*Isa 15:2

*heights in mourning.**

12. We can also understand it in this way: after Christ's teaching had shone forth, the house of Moab, that is, the philosophers' family—their disciples—and the city of Dibon, that is, the crowd of teachers who

*Jerome, In Isa
6.38; 1 Cor 10:14

had joyfully worshiped idols,* mournfully went up to these same idols and demanded the answers and help of demons against the Gospel. While many of the wise of this world renounced their errors and turned

*1 Cor 1:20; 3:19

to Christ,* many others stood firm in their inborn illwill. This burden uses this verse to refer to both, teaching that the former are burdened by repentance, but the latter by narrowness of heart. For many philosophers, both students and teachers, abandon the valley of error to climb to the heights of the virtues like the house and the city in the verse. They then mournfully and tearfully confess their sins and humbly repent of their former errors and blasphemies.

13. And the prophet added, *Over Nebo and over*

*Isa 15:2

*Medeba Moab will wail.** *Nebo* means *sitting; Medeba,*

*Jerome, In Isa
6.39

*from woodland.** *Sitting* is appropriate for teachers, according to the following: *Scribes and Pharisees sat on*

*Matt 23:2

*the seat of Moses.** The woodland, a place with infertile,

*Jerome, In Isa
6.39

fruitless trees,* where beasts rather than people dwell, expresses the Gentiles' untilled hearts. Such hearts, clinging to teachers of error, defended their precepts with the authority of the crowd. This verse describes,

then, Moab's wail over the teachers and common folk
who withdrew from their fellowship and turned
toward the catholic faith. They could not watch this
without great pain, which is what *wail* means.

14. This is why it follows, *All their heads are bald.**   *Isa 15:2
Understand Moab's heads to be the most illustrious
teachers of the various sects: Socrates, Plato, Diogenes,
Epicurius, Porphyry, and other similar figures. These
are indeed Moab's heads, namely, the princes of
worldly wisdom. Who among them has not had his
hair shaved off through Christ's grace? Their students,
accustomed to clinging to their teachers as hair to its
head,* left their sects and united themselves to the   *Oner 18.15; 20.9;
grace of our Savior. We ourselves certainly now see   Aelred, SS 36.19;
that the philosophers are bald; the wisdom of fisher-   62.17; 63.22
men is preferred to their teaching.* There is no one   *Aelred, SS 15.4;
who would profess or follow their sects now. For al-   71.3
though many may read them, everyone hates their
blasphemies.

15. Therefore the prophet fittingly adds, *Every beard
is shaved.** A person is regarded as a boy for as long as   *Isa 15:2
he is beardless, but the designation *man* is given to the
bearded. Impulsiveness is feared in a boy, but wisdom
is expected from a man. It was as though the philosophers were bearded when their wisdom and teaching
ruled the people. But after Christ's Gospel had re-
sounded everywhere and had refuted their errors,
everyone regarded them as foolish and senseless. It
was then as though their beards had been shaven; they
appeared unattractive and of no account, as though
reduced to childish foolishness.*   *Jerome, In Isa
                                                                6.39
16. But where it says, *Over Nebo and over Medeba
Moab will wail,** you can interpret it as the wail of those   *Isa 15:2
who turned from the wisdom of the world to the fool-
ishness of the cross.* They mourned the madness and   *1 Cor 1:21, 23
ruin of the others who persevered in their pride. For
when they perceived that their heads were bald* and   *Isa 15:2
every beard shaved by Christ's razor, the many who

had believed had compassion on the error of the few who remained. This minority was able neither to bend down with their *broken necks* nor to feel shame, although shaven or bald.* For it is natural that those turned toward the Lord should mourn such people above all others and have compassion on them with a kind of special affection, since the converts too were once held in the same vices or entangled in the same errors with them.

17. But let us look at the following: *At their fork in the road they were girded with sackcloth, and on their roofs and in their squares they all wail, and come down weeping.** Three elements are put forth here: the fork in the road, the roofs, and the squares. The fork in the road represents the deviations of the philosophers, the roofs represent pride, and the squares represent a dissolute life. The deception of sophistry brought about their deviations; human opinion, their pride; and the corruption of flesh and mind, their dissolute life. Many of these people, turning to the Lord, were punished for all their sins. For the prophet tells us that they are *girded with sackcloth* in a sign of repentance for the deceit and fallacies that are expressed in the *fork in the road.* He depicts them as wailing in contrition and confession for the pride with which they had been accustomed to announce with prattling cheeks* opinions on things divine and human, as though standing on a rooftop. And he announces that, humbled and washed by their tears, they will return from that broad way by which they went forth to their death, to the constricted and *narrow* gate *that leads to life.**

18. He says, therefore, *at the fork in the road*—undoubtedly, Moab's fork in the road—*they were girded with sackcloth.** They remembered the deviations and fallacies with which they had deceived human simplicity. Girded with sackcloth, that is, afflicted by the harshness of repentance, they were careful to appease him against whom they had sinned with worthy sat-

*1 Sam 4:18

*Isa 15:3

*Augustine, Conf 4.16.28

*Matt 7:13-14; Jerome, In Isa 6.39; RB 5.11

*Isa 15:3

isfaction: *and on their roofs and in their squares they all wail, and come down weeping.**

19. The Lord said in the gospel, *What you hear with your ears, preach on the rooftops.** *On the rooftop* indicates a certain altitude and openness. This is because those who preach something on a rooftop seem lofty and are clearly heard. Interpret the squares, which represent breadth, as the broad way of perdition,* in which they themselves entered and thus offered an example to others. But those who had climbed to the rooftop through self-exaltation came down humbled through compunction, and those who had preached their errors publicly as in the squares wailed pitifully in everyone's ears.

*Matt 10:27

*Matt 7:13

20. It follows, *Heshbon will shout, and Elealeh; their voice was heard as far as Jahaz.** We can translate *Heshbon* as *thoughts, Elealeh* as *ascent,* and *Jahaz* as *deed* or *command.** The philosophers were disturbed upon seeing many thousands of people daily flocking to faith in Christ and the sacraments. It is not easy to say how confused their thoughts were then: at times they were amazed, at times offended; at times they resisted, raised up in their pride. All this is expressed through the shout of Heshbon and Elealeh, namely, of thought and elation. Nor did this cry and murmuring cease until they proceeded from voice to work, either openly persecuting or obeying the faith and divine commandments.* Therefore, *their voice was heard as far as Jahaz.*†

*Isa 15:4

*Jerome, In Isa
6.39

*Jerome, In Isa
6.39
†Isa 15:4

21. I should explain this morally, brothers. But *fear and trembling has come upon me, and the darkness has covered me.** Moreover, *zeal for* God's *house eats at me,*† indignation drives me, pain compels me. Tears burst forth, but anger restrains them, jealousy swallows them. *My zeal made me waste away,** and my speech now longs to rage. But the pain of my mother the Roman Church indicates mourning to me instead. The church seems to shout in a wretched voice with *both*

*Ps 54:6
†Ps 68:10

*Ps 118:139

*2 Macc 15:21   *hands stretched out to heaven,** saying, *My mother's sons*
*Song 1:5   *fought against me.**

22. For although there is only *one dove* of Christ,
*Song 2:10; 6:8   Christ's *beautiful* one, Christ's *perfect* one,* which has
*Eph 4:5-6   *one God, one faith, and one baptism,** yet, on account of
the many peoples and nations, we say that there are
many churches, agreeing with one, subject to one, and
obedient to one. This is the holy Roman Church,
whose *children*, as you have heard, *have fought against*
*Song 1:5   her.** For some are *estranged from the womb, have wan-*
*Ps 57:4   *dered from the uterus, have spoken falsehoods.** Moreover,
*Ps 72:8   *they have spoken wickedness from on high.**

23. *The kings of the earth stood upright* at Pavia,[1] *and*
the chiefs gathered together as one against the Lord and
*Ps 2:2   *against his anointed,* Alexander.* There *many dogs circled*
*Ps 21:17   *around* him, *a council of the wicked besieged* him.* There
the wicked witnesses, Giovanni and Guido,[2] *rose up*
*Ps 26:12   *against* him, but *wickedness deceived itself.** Unhappy
and wretched are those who, coming down *from Jeru-*
*Luke 10:30   *salem to Jericho*, fell upon a robber.* It is he, the most
wicked Ottaviano,[3] who, *lurking in ambush* like a rob-
Ps 9:29 (10:8)   ber for a long while, regarded the papacy as prey,
Christ as a traveler, and the church as his spoils. Un-
happy is the one who ascended *the bed of* his *father* and
*Gen 49:4   stained *his quilt.**

24. This is that most proud Haman who prepared
*Esth 5:14; 7:9   the *cross* for *Mordecai,** who made a king *propose the*
*Esth 3:12-15;   *death sentence* against Israel.* Oh, when will the king
16:9   keep watch, when *will he rise from his sleep?*† When will
†Job 14:12   he finally stay awake during this dark night covered

---

[1] The Council of Pavia (February 1160), which was called by
Emperor Frederick I, supported Antipope Victor IV against the
legitimate pope, Alexander III.

[2] Giovanni Morrone and Guido di Crema, supporters of the
antipope.

[3] Ottaviano de Monticelli, elected Antipope Victor IV (1159–
1164).

in the gloom of death?* When will he hear in his chronicles how much good our Mordecai did for him?* When will he notice that this wicked person tried to *crush* the *queen* herself in his *presence?**

25. This queen is the wife not of Artaxerxes but of Christ, of whom the prophet says, *The queen stood at your right.** It is she who today in her sick members and *in those knowing little of the law* cries out and says,* *Show me, you whom my soul loves, where you are pasturing, where you lie down at noon.** Rightly threatening and rebuking, he answers, *If you do not know yourself, depart.**

26. How many people, brothers, these days *knowing neither the Scriptures nor God's power,* have departed from the Church,* and, separating themselves from Christ's vicar, follow the Antichrist's forerunner? Brothers, *let no one mislead you with empty words.** Let no one say to you, *Look, Christ is here, or look, he is there,** since Christ is always in the faith of Peter, which the holy Roman Church specifically obtained from Peter and keeps in the rock that is Christ.* Let us look at where this church began, from whom it began, and to where it proceeded.

27. *This Gospel,* said the Lord, *must be preached to the entire world, beginning with Jerusalem.** So its beginnings were in Jerusalem. The church was small, as though still nursing, when *the days of Pentecost were fulfilled,* and they were all together *in the same place.** The Holy Spirit, visiting the church in tongues of flame, both enlightened it with wisdom and inflamed it with love. Then the voices of all nations became universal in the mouth of the church. The coming together of all tongues foretold what would happen afterward in the conversion of all the nations.* The first head of this church was Peter, to whom it was said, *On this rock I will build my church.** And again, *Feed my sheep.*† And *To you I will give the keys of the kingdom of heaven.*§ And *Whatever you bind on earth,*‡ etc.

*Job 10:21

*Esth 6:1-2
*Esth 7:8

*Ps 44:10
*Rom 7:1; 2 Cor 11:23

*Song 1:6

*Song 1:7

*Matt 22:29

*Eph 5:6
*Mark 13:21; Luke 17:21

*1 Cor 10:4

*Mark 16:15; Luke 24:47

*Acts 2:1

*Acts 2:3-4

*Matt 16:18
†John 21:17
§Matt 16:19
‡Matt 16:19

28. This is what the holy apostle calls the church of the *firstborn*.* The fullness of its power passed over from East to West in its first ruler. On the Holy Spirit's authority, this power now resides in the Roman Church. No one of sound mind doubts that it is the clergy first ordained by blessed Peter that should be called the Roman Church, not the walls and stones. Therefore, just as Clement succeeded Peter, Anacletus succeeded Clement, and Evaristus succeeded Anacletus; so too, of course, for the clergy ordained and instituted by Peter. One ordained the next, who then obtained the rank and dignity.

29. Thus *children were* always *born to us in place of their parents*.* When the church received the earthly empire given by Constantine, human law also established these children as *princes over all the earth*.* Then on account of a special excellence of this particular Church, bishops, priests, and deacons were called cardinals, obtaining the honor of this designation from those of whom it is written, *For the earth's beams* are the Lord's, and he placed the world upon them*.* For just as the supreme pontiff obtains the chief place from the legal—and if I may put it thus—hereditary succession from Peter, so too did the power of the other apostles pass over to the cardinals.

30. This is the Roman Church. Whoever is not in communion with it is a heretic. It is for this church to see to all things, to judge concerning all things, to provide for all things. It is to the Roman Church in Peter that these words are addressed: *And you, once converted, strengthen your brothers*.* Whatever the Roman Church dictates, I uphold, I approve whatever it approves, and I condemn whatever it condemns. It is for the Roman Church to choose for us *the shepherd and bishop of our souls*.*

31. For the role that begetting had in the establishment of the fleshly high priesthood in the Old Testament is the same role that regular election, which is a

*Heb 12:23

*Ps 44:17

*Ps 44:17

*cardines
*1 Sam 2:8

*Luke 22:32

*1 Pet 2:25

kind of spiritual begetting, plays in the New. For it is
as though those electing were begetting, and the one
elected were begotten. And so, brothers, just as it was
Aaron's to bring forth sons,* so it was Christ's to *1 Tim 5:14
choose* apostles. Just as one of Aaron's children, El- *eligere
eazar, was chosen over the others,* so too one apostle, *Num 20:25-26
Peter, was chosen over the others. And Peter, when he
had begotten many spiritual children, chose Clement
over the others. Clement too abounded with children.
After his death, his curia elected Anacletus alone to
succeed him in a kind of spiritual begetting. Just as
there were always lawful successors to Peter whom
the church itself chose, so too those whom Peter's successors chose to be their assistants at various times
were true successors of the other apostles. And so we
have had no doubt concerning lawful succession from
blessed Sylvester and his cardinals up to Adrian[4] and
his cardinals in our time.

32. Consider this. After Adrian, the lawful successor
of Peter, had died, the lawful succession of the other
apostles continued with the cardinals.* Call to mind *Alexander III,
now those in their midst, Rolando and Ottaviano.[5] Let Ep Aet (PL 200:70
us call them thus for the time being, as though they A–72 B)
were in the womb of their mother the Holy Roman
Church, which was already in the labor of childbirth.* *Gen 25:24
I ask you, my brothers, is this not similar to Rebecca's
labor? Look at how wretched Esau, *red and hairy,** *Gen 25:25
twists the very maternal belly and seizes with furious
hands that simple Jacob,* whom all the harmony of *Gen 25:27
the womb embraces with every affection! For you
have heard how that demon-filled wretch removed
the mantle from the neck of that most holy man. And
when the other did not willingly yield to him, he came
forth from the womb to his mother's great pain. He

---

[4] Adrian IV (1154–1159).
[5] Rolando Bandinelli, the future Pope Alexander III, and Ottaviano de Monticelli, the future Antipope Victor IV.

inspired dread when the hair of his cupidity and ambition appeared. Two followed him, who themselves, also *estranged from the womb, have wandered from the belly;** two from all those choosing Alexander, clinging to Alexander, and following Alexander.

33. Now imagine Giovanni and Guido on one side with Ottaviano,* and imagine the rest of the Curia on the other side with Alexander. I ask you, whose voice is this: *They went forth from us, but they were not from us?** Of course, the Roman Curia is either in those three, or in all the others, or it has *vanished from the earth,** and in vain did the Savior pour out that prayer in which he says, *I prayed for you, that your faith would not fail*—which is mad to suppose. For who would be so foolish as to exclude so many cardinals—bishops, priests, and deacons—and to believe the power of the Roman Curia to rest with these two? I am now speaking, brothers, as though they were still in the Church of blessed Peter, when they separated themselves from the others as soon as the election took place.

34. Clearly the Roman Church did not pass away. Clearly no reason, no human understanding permits that all the rest should be condemned and that the Church should survive in those three. It follows, then, that the Church preserved the power of apostolic dignity in that great number that chose Alexander. For far be it from us to say that five cardinal bishops and fifteen or even more cardinal priests or deacons departed from those three, rather than the latter from the former. The former's reputation was greater, their lives were holier, their perception more profound, their number greater, and their authority loftier. Therefore, since it is well known that the church that chose Alexander is Roman, from which church it is clear that the others departed, whoever subsequently clung to

*Ps 57:4

*Oner 23.23

*1 John 2:19

*Mic 7:2

*Luke 22:32

them—the wicked Imar[6] or anyone else—is a heretic and schismatic. Such people have joined themselves to heretics rather than Christians, to schismatics rather than catholics, to *Satan's* synagogue rather than Christ's church.*   *Rev 2:9

35. Let our enemies say whatever they like, let them lie as much as they like, let them pretend whatever they like. Wherever the eyes perceive the church to be Roman, wherever reason proves it to be, wherever authority confirms it to be, there is my heart, there is my mind, there is my desire. Thanks to God's help, *neither death nor life nor any creature will separate* me*   *Rom 8:35, 38-39 from the church's faith, which Christ prayed would never fail,* from its unity, which, since Christ pre-   *Luke 22:32 serves it, the schismatics' perversity will not divide, and from submission to it, whose chief will open heaven for me.

36. What we have said ought to be enough for your safety, brothers, against the wicked lips and cunning tongues with which this land boils.* After our powers   *Ps 119:2 have recovered a bit through silence, let us return to the pleasures of God's word, *to whom is the honor and the glory forever and ever. Amen.**   *Rom 16:27; Heb 13:21

[6] Imar of Cluny consecrated Antipope Victor at the abbey of Farfa on October 4, 1159.

Homily 24

1. As you remember, beloved, yesterday we explained as best we could what the prophecy said about the beginnings of the burden of Moab. But we postponed for today the moral explanation, which fear prevented me from pursuing.* First, therefore, let us inquire according to the rules of moral interpretation who Moab is, so that we will be equipped to investigate more clearly how Moab burdens or is burdened.

2. Moab means *from the father*,* signifying something communicated from a father to his son. It can also signify those who live according to what they naturally received from their father. We know that Holy Scripture uses the word *father* in many ways. It can refer to nature, creation, adoption, imitation, age, or dignity.

3. It refers to nature when a man is called the *father* of the person whom he physically begot, as when Abraham is called the father of Isaac; Isaac, the father of Jacob; and Jacob, the father of the twelve patriarchs. Another example is when someone is called the father of an entire race that he begot. This is why the Lord said to the Jews, "Do not boast that you have *Abraham* as your *father*."*

4. It refers to creation when God is called the father of every creature, *from whom all fatherhood, in heaven and on earth, takes its name*.* It refers to adoption when all the chosen are called *children of God*,* the apostle

*Oner 23.21

*Jerome, In Isa 6.36

*Matt 3:9 and parallels

*Eph 3:15
*1 John 3:1

234

having said, *You have received the Spirit of the adoption of children in whom we cry out, Abba, Father.** For all who boast in this adoption cry constantly to God, saying, *Our Father, who art in heaven.** *Rom 8:15

*Matt 6:9

5. It referred to imitation when Christ himself called the faithless Jews the devil's children, saying, *You are from your father, the devil.** He makes this judgment on the basis of their imitation of the devil. For he said, *And you want to do the works of your father.** Hence we whom the Lord raised up *from stones* are also called *children of Abraham* by imitating Abraham's faith.* *John 8:44

*John 8:44, 41

*Matt 3:9 and parallels; Gal 3:7

6. It refers to age when Paul speaks to Timothy: *Do not rebuke your elder, but beseech him as a father.** It refers to dignity when Naaman becomes displeased with Elisha, because the prophet purported to heal his leprosy not by looking at it, or praying, or touching it, but by a command. Naaman's servants said to him as he angrily departed, *Father, even if the prophet had ordered that you do some great thing, you certainly should have done it. How much more since he said to you, Wash and you will be made clean?** *1 Tim 5:1

*2 Kgs 5:13

7. And so we owe what we are to the Father of all, who created us. We owe it to be good to the Father who adopted us as his children. We owe our mortality, our corruptibility, and our susceptibility to suffer from various passions to the father who begot us in the flesh. And so it is from the carnal father, that is, from corruptible nature, that we have within us the pricks of lust, the movements of concupiscence, the rush to anger, the sloth of sadness, a boundless fear, and the swelling of pride. This is the nation opposed to the one that the good Father, who adopted us rather than begot us, kindly infused in us, which is *charity, joy, peace, patience,* humility, *chastity,* etc.* The former nation is mystically called Moab; the latter, Israel. *Gal 5:22-23

8. Our battle against this Moab is constant. *Moab* can also fittingly be translated as *paternal water,** because it is the flow of this fatherly seed that instills *Jerome, In Isa 6.36

such corruptions in us. May the Lord Jesus be with us and burden this Moab. Although it cannot be completely destroyed in us, may it nevertheless be weighed down in such a way that it cannot reign in us. Let us hear, then, about the burden of this Moab. *Because Ar was destroyed at night, Moab kept silence. Because at night the wall was destroyed, Moab kept silence.** *Isa 15:1

9. Night, as you know, means *tribulation.* Ar, a Moabite city, means *adversary.** That nation of natural passions in our soul builds a city when original sin breaks forth in actual sin, with us supplying our *limbs* as *arms of iniquity for sin.** We turn what we previously suffered as sin's punishment into the will to and the carrying out of sin. The more we surrender to sins, the more wicked citizens we receive in this city. Now this city, founded on the vices, is clearly against that opposing city founded on the virtues. Moreover, the wall of the Moabite city is stubbornness, which shuts out the humility of repentance and stops up the voice of confession. *Jerome, In Isa 6.37 *Rom 6:13

10. O dear brothers, when everything goes favorably for us, when joyful times smile on us, when abundance gives birth to excess in all things, then this Moab bitterly rises up and violently sways us. It burns the flesh, distracts the mind, and suggests harmful, delightful things. A kind of cry of the vices arises in the mind. The vices cry *one to the other,** saying, *Tear it down, tear it all the way down to its foundation.** *Isa 6:3; Ezek 1:9 *Ps 136:7

11. Hence the most kind Savior acts as the best doctors do and cuts away the ailments' cause first. After what is joyful has been somewhat removed, and hard, sad things take its place, pleasures likewise disappear. But when we are thus forced to return to ourselves,** we find nothing bright there, nothing tranquil, nothing pleasing, nothing delightful. Rather, everything is dark, full of shadows and horror, full of night and darkness. *Luke 15:17

12. Ar is destroyed in this night,* when amusements
lose their allure and satisfactions vanish, when neither
social interaction is pleasurable nor forbidden drinking bouts are appealing. The wall, that is, stubbornness of mind, is also destroyed, and all its ramparts,
which are the *pretexts to sin*, are torn down.* Why
would Moab not keep silence? For after the vices' fuel
has been cut off during such a night, the vices' impulses likewise take their rest.

13. They stray, dear brothers! They stray, those who
delude themselves of their chastity while they constantly or frequently linger in the company of women
or guests, in gluttony and drunkenness, in idleness
and frivolity. I know by experience, beloved, and I believe you do too, that even after frequent fasting, constant vigils, and continuous labors have beaten Moab
as though with hammer blows, it still raises its crushed
head.* After a long period of silence, it drives on the
careless with renewed shouts and weighs down those
caught off guard. Hence it is that many tremble before
this Moab to such an extent that they would prefer to
crush their very bodies beyond measure in times of
crisis than to be liable to slavery under this desire.*

14. Therefore, brothers, whenever gluttony makes
this plain food disgusting to you, whenever drowsiness or bodily warmth makes you dread vigils, whenever mental lukewarmness compels you to neglect the
holy practice of daily work, call to mind, I beg you,
the pricks of lust, the shame of uncleanness, the restless and agitated movement of limbs, and, on the other
hand, the sweetness of chastity, the purity of feelings,
and the tranquility of the limbs. Soon everything that
had previously seemed difficult will be found quite
easy. Moab will thus grow silent, and natural corruption will cease to fight against the beginnings of good
will after the night of distress or pain has come upon
us. Then *the house [and] Dibon* will go up *to the heights
in mourning.**

*Isa 15:1

*Ps 140:4

*2 Cor 6:5;
Gen 3:15

* *tumor*

*Isa 15:2

15. Understand the soul's *house* to be the conscience, in which the soul stores all the mind's treasures, where it finds a place to rest.* Such a conscience welcomes with joyful breast the soul fleeing from the disturbances of the age and the commotion of the world, and the conscience's tranquility soothes all the pain coming from outside itself. Which of these things does a healthy and untroubled conscience not do? The city of vices has been *destroyed* and the *wall* of the passions has tumbled to the ground in such a conscience.*

16. Dibon, which means *their fluid,* expresses tenderness of feeling. This tenderness, seeping out into what is forbidden, spread its *legs for everyone who passed by.** When it is purified from the mire of the Moabite corruption, it climbs from the depths to the heights of the conscience itself, from vices to virtues, from the beginnings of good intentions to the carrying out of good works.

17. It *went up,* moreover, *in mourning.** For leaving the fool's laugh behind in the lower places, it finds the grief and mourning of the wise in the higher regions. It constantly mourns that the Moabite errors have deluded it for so long, it mourns that it consented for so long to its forbidden suggestions. It mourns that it lacked for so long the sweetness that it now begins to taste. It mourns that it spent so much time in empty and harmful affairs. Happy is the soul for whom Moab has thus fallen silent, as well as Nebo and Medeba, of whom the prophet added, *Over Nebo and over Medeba, Moab will howl.** Nebo means *sitting;* Medeba, *from woodland.*

18. *Sitting* represents the carelessness that is the mother of negligence and producer of neglect. For of those who profess this penitential life after many offenses, it pains me to say that some then hand themselves over to idleness and sloth and look down on the necessary exercises of the Order. They behave *as though they were a nation that had acted righteously and had not*

*Isa 66:1

*Isa 15:1

*Ezek 16:25 LXX; Aelred, Spir amic 1.39; Aelred, S 35.17-18

*Isa 15:2

*Isa 15:2

abandoned its God's law.* There are others whom daily *Isa 58:2
passions disgrace. Although the enemies' missiles often
attack them, they sit and laugh, free from care, as
though the enemy already lay dead or the entire interior
battle had fallen silent. Fruitless, wandering, and unstable people are said to be *from woodland,* that is,
Medeba.* The prophet speaks of those spiritual beasts *Jerome, In Isa
that dwell in such people, saying, *Do not hand over to* 6.39; RB 1.11
*the beasts the souls that confess you.** Moab does not, of *Ps 73:19
course, fall silent for people like this, but suggests vices,
heaps up unclean feelings, and urges wicked deeds
with frequent wailing. For Moab's wailing expresses
the violent temptation of the natural passions.

19. It follows, *All their heads are bald and every beard
is shaved.** It seems to me that the three natural human *Isa 15:2
impulses are fittingly called Moab's heads. These are
the irascible, the concupiscent, and the rational impulses. From their corruption, I believe, the stings of
all the natural passions arise. The hair of the head is
an adornment, while the beard is manly and is a sign
of virtue.

20. And so the impulse of anger is adorned, as it
were, when one is moved against one's own vices, as
where it is written, *Be angry, and do not sin.** It is also *Ps 4:5
adorned when one takes it up with discretion in zeal
for God against those who despise his law,* as where *1 Macc 2:54
it is written, *My zeal makes me waste away, because my
enemies have forgotten your words.** It is truly adorned, *Ps 118:139
since the Lord rewards this zeal often and in many
places. For Phinees *struck down* the fornicators *with a
dagger* in this very anger of which we are speaking,
and he received the eternal priesthood in recom-
pense.* And for the zeal with which he burned against *Num 25:7-8, 13;
the house of Ahab, Jehu, son of Nimshi, passed down Judg 16:7
the kingdom of Israel with God's help to his posterity
*to the fourth generation.** *2 Kgs 10:30

21. So too, a kind of ornament veils the shame of
the concupiscent impulse when one uses it only for

the procreation of children or when one takes food or drink only insofar as is necessary for physical sustenance. Hence it is that a certain saint did not hesitate to equate Abraham's marriage with the blessed John's virginity.* He took into account, of course, the obedience with which Abraham submitted to the divine will in this work of marriage, and also the integrity of his intention of procreating children. By this intention, a kind of noble veil, as it were, covered the concupiscent impulse, without which the conjugal duty is not fulfilled.*

*Augustine, Bon
coniug 21.26

*1 Cor 7:3

22. But the rational impulse, too, is adorned in this way if we do not use reason against reason. For theft, robbery, adultery, and other vices are committed against the laws of reason, yet these crimes are only carried out with the use of reason. For a thief could not foresee a fitting place to lie in wait or a fitting time to carry out his deeds without the force of reason. Thus the adulterer, acquiring cunning from the power of reason, looks for nightfall, a way of access, and the husband's absence. And so whoever misuses reason to carry out the vices disfigures the rational impulse itself, but whoever always uses it for the virtues and for beneficial knowledge adorns it with a most beautiful ornament.

23. It is well said of Moab, where all things have been corrupted, *All their heads are bald.** The wise use their impulses well. But in those whom natural stings rule, these impulses from whose corruption all the vices come forth look base and misshapen, stripped of every virtue and bald.*

*Isa 15:2

*1 Cor 11:5-6

24. What follows is also well put: *Every beard is shaved.** The beard, as we said, is a sign of manly virtue. Now, the highest virtue and manliest work is to resist these natural stings, and to turn the impulses themselves, which one cannot live without, back to the practice of the virtues. Those who yield to their passions and hand themselves over, stripped of every

*Isa 15:2

virtue, to serve their vices, are revealed as beardless and reduced, as it were, to the form of a woman.* Pay attention to this, beloved brothers. It is much easier to turn away from the vices before a fall than to free oneself from them after one has already yielded. For if someone is restrained by the bonds of habit, he is found in all things weak, beardless, and womanly.*

25. It follows, *At their fork in the road they were girded with sackcloth, and on their roofs and in their squares they all wail, and come down weeping.** Some of the Moabites are *at the fork in the road,* some are *in the squares,* and some are *on the roofs.* Whoever is at a fork in the road can turn in either direction to escape everyone's notice. The square is open to everyone's eyes; nothing can be hidden there. It is customary in the lands of Jerusalem, where the houses' roofs are not very high but stretch out broadly, that anyone who wishes to announce something or preach to the people climbs onto the roof.*

26. Therefore, those who sin secretly are at Moab's fork in the road, those who disgrace themselves publicly with wicked deeds are in the squares, and those who not only sin but also excuse their sins and preach them are on the roofs. Simple contrition of heart and body is enough for those who sin secretly. This contrition is fittingly expressed by sackcloth. But those who commit a shameful act openly need to wail. Just as they did not hide the greatness of their offenses, so too they must not hide their true conversion. Further, those who, bursting with pride, preach *their sin like Sodom** must *come down weeping.*† They climbed the mountain of pride by sinning; so too, they must come down humbled to the valley of lamentation.*

27. Further, because a fork in the road is where three roads come together, it can represent a threefold concupiscence: *concupiscence of the flesh, concupiscence of the eyes, and worldly ambition.** The three forms of sin— in thought, word, and deed—can also be called a fork

*Jerome, In Isa 6.39

*Jerome, In Isa 6.39

*Isa 15:3

*Matt 10:27

*Isa 3:9
†Isa 15:3
*Ps 83:7 Var

*1 John 2:16 Var

in the road. The three powers of the soul, through which every sin occurs, namely, memory, will, and reason, can also fittingly be called a fork in the road. Therefore, those who give in to this triple concupiscence—those who do wrong in thought, word, and deed—have the wretched lot of living at Moab's fork in the road. Their memory is disfigured by thought, their will is corrupted by pleasure, and their reason is weakened by consenting to sin.

28. Sackcloth is a sign of mourning. This is the mourning of which the Lord spoke in the gospel, saying, *Woe to you who are laughing now, because you will cry and lament.** Those, therefore, who *rejoice when they do evil and exult in the worst of things* at Moab's fork in the road will be girded with sackcloth,* that is, they will pine away, mourning wretchedly.

*Luke 6:25; John 16:20

*Prov 2:14

29. Interpret the roofs, if you will, to be the power and preeminence of the world, but the squares, where games and shows are put on, represent freely sinning. And so holy Isaiah prophesies going down and weeping for those who boast in this world's grandeur and who fall headlong into vices, having no bridle of discipline to restrain them.* They should thus know that they will go down to hell with a wail on account of the power with which they raise themselves above others as though *on roofs* and sin without restraint as though *in the squares.* They will be cast *into the outer darkness,* where *there will be weeping and grinding of teeth.**

*Isa 15:3

*Matt 8:12 and parallels

30. The prophetic discourse goes on to teach how they will arrive at this unhappiness, saying, *Heshbon shouted, and Elealeh; their voice was heard as far as Jahaz.** We posited a double meaning for what was written previously: the first meaning treated the repentance of the converted, the second the eternal punishment of the godless. Let us keep to the same order in this verse. Heshbon means *thoughts;* Elealeh, *ascent.**

*Isa 15:4

*Jerome, In Isa 6.39

31. If, therefore, you seek to learn how the repentant get from the fork in the road to simplicity of life, from the roofs of pride to humility, from the squares of self-will to the narrow way of holy necessity—clothed in the sackcloth of repentance and pain, giving forth a wail of confession and climbing down to tears of contrition—if, I say, you seek to learn by which road they travel so far, God's word tells you: *Heshbon shouted, and Elealeh.** *Isa 15:4

32. These are the thoughts that accuse and defend us by turns. They do not stop shouting in the hearts of those who labor to undertake a new life, as though making an ascent (which is what *Elealeh* means). These thoughts continue until the will to which they shout hears their voice, and, once heard, their voice arrives all the way to Jahaz. Jahaz means *command* or *deed.** *Jerome, In Isa 6.39

33. There are many people, brothers, in whom these thoughts shout quite often, and there is a kind of preliminary ascent of the interior person to abandon sins' fork in the road and to turn to the simplicity of the virtues. But *their voice* is not heard *as far as Jahaz.** Even if they conceive a desire* for the good, they do not bring it to fulfillment.* *Isa 15:4 *affectum *ad effectum

34. How often, dear brothers—when, forgetful of our intention, we fall into empty and idle activity, and become entangled in this world's forks in the road*— do our very thoughts cry out against us? How often does our desire to ascend, that is, to make progress, cry out? But as long as we repeat the same actions and our actions do not follow what we will, *their voice* is not heard *as far as Jahaz.** But may our thoughts cry out continually, may they cry out rudely, may they not be silent, may they not grow weary. May they continue until we are conquered by weariness or compelled by fear, and we at last fulfill the commandment. Then what has long been present in our thoughts will appear in our deeds. *2 Tim 2:4 *Isa 15:4

35. But just as good thoughts rouse the good to make progress, so too do evil thoughts always provoke the wicked to revolt. Therefore, both Heshbon and Elealeh, that is, twisted thoughts and the swelling of pride, cry out in these wicked people. Nor do they cease to weary the wretched soul within them with various temptations until their will is persuaded to act, which is what it means to shout *as far as Jahaz.**

*Isa 15:4

36. We must therefore examine our thoughts, brothers. If they suggest twisted things, we should immediately pass by them with deaf ears.* If they are useful and honorable, we should pursue what they suggest *as far as Jahaz.** But we should be mindful of the burden in both cases. Whether we voluntarily punish ourselves for what we have done, resist twisted thoughts, or assent to the good ones, we cannot escape without suffering a burden that either weighs us down or crushes us. But neither can we avoid the bad nor carry out the good by our own power. Let us then ask God to bestow on us both the power to resist and the ability to work, through his beloved Son our Lord, who, with him in the Holy Spirit, lives and reigns forever and ever. Amen.

*Isa 33:15

*Isa 15:4

Homily 25

1. We are still dealing with the burden of Moab, brothers. In this burden, the names of the cities and places express certain mystical realities. Now, we said that Moab prophetically represented worldly wisdom, or the wise people of the world who oppose the Gospel's teaching.* The prophecy says of such people, *Heshbon shouted, and Elealeh; their voice was heard as far as Jahaz.* We ended our explanation of the prophetic meaning of this verse the day before yesterday.* We will now take up with you, beloved, the verse that follows, which we need to explain today.

2. It follows, *For this the lightly armed soldiers of Moab will wail, its soul will wail to itself.* There was a *great shout* in the thoughts of the wise when,* on the one hand, the truth revealed through the Gospel reproved them, and, on the other, those puffed up in their pride resisted divine wisdom. The contest came to an end when some, wanting *to please people, were put to confusion, because God despised them,* while others humbled themselves *under God's mighty hand.* The slower these latter had been to believe and the more careful to examine, the less encumbered they became in the faith and teaching. These are the *lightly armed soldiers of Moab,* either because they freed themselves from the nets of false wisdom or because they entered unencumbered on the road of the Gospel. They wailed for what they had done before, not only by raising their voices "but also with an inner feeling of the heart."*

*Oner 23.4

*Isa 15:4
*Oner 23.20

*Isa 15:4
*Exod 11:6; 12:30

*Ps 52:6; Gal 1:10
*1 Pet 5:6

*RB 7.51

For when it says, *For this the lightly armed soldiers of Moab will wail*, it refers to outer confession; but when it continues, *Its soul will wail to itself*, it refers to inner contrition.*

*Isa 15:4

3. Now, it happens that those who forsake Moabite wisdom and follow the *foolishness of the cross* are all the more competent in divine wisdom for having been sharp in human affairs.* This is why the prophet, speaking on the Lord's behalf, added, *My heart will cry out to Moab.** The secret understanding of Holy Scripture is called God's *heart*, because in it, his will and the hidden mysteries of his decrees are revealed.* Therefore God's *heart* cries out *to Moab* when spiritual knowledge abundantly illuminates the mind of someone passing over from the world's philosophy to God. But if you prefer to understand this as the prophet speaking, it does not change the meaning, since the secrets of the prophecy itself could appropriately be called the prophet's heart.

*1 Cor 1:18, 23

*Isa 15:5

*Augustine, In
Ps 21.2.15

4. *Its bars as far as Zoar, a three-year-old calf.** Interpret Moab's *bars* as dialectical argument. Such argument, which had opposed the church, has begun to serve it in the wise who have converted. For when the subtle arguments of the philosophers serve the church, Moab's *bars* have reached *as far as Zoar*. For the church, in its state at that time, is rightfully called *Zoar*, that is, *small*.* The Song of Songs says of it, *Our sister is small and has no breasts; what will we do with our sister* who is so little?* For it was plainly little when it did not reach past the borders of Palestine but lurked behind them, small and contemptible. It was small in number, I say, but not in merit.* For this reason, just as fruitful Peninnah insulted sterile Hannah,† so too did the synagogue insult the church, *until the sterile woman gave birth to many, and she who had many children grew ill.**

*Isa 15:5

*Jerome, In
Isa 6.39

*Song 8:8

*Bede, In
Cant 5.8.8
†1 Sam 1:4-6

*1 Sam 2:5

5. Zoar, that is, the church, is beautifully called *a three-year-old calf*. Its first year is before the law, its second year under the law, and its third year under

grace.* Or its first year can be understood as under
the patriarchs, its second under the prophets, and its
third under the apostles. Of course, this type of animal
abounds in milk and great tenderness for its offspring.
For unless it is deceived by some trick, it neither accepts another calf at its breast nor gives milk unless
its own calf is present. This can be appropriately
adapted to mother church. It abounds in the milk of
charity and sweet teaching but judges as foreigners
unworthy of the most sacred mysteries those whom
it does not regenerate through the bath of saving
water. We can also say that the church is three years
old, because, by means of solid faith, hope, and love,
it proceeds to that perfect age,* *to the measure of the age
of the fullness of Christ.**

6. Therefore, when the *bars* of Moab reach *as far as
Zoar,* that is, when the wise of this world bring together all the support of their knowledge and all their
arguments to the church,* then what the prophet immediately adds will take place: *For by Luhith's ascent,
they will go up weeping, and they will raise a shout of
contrition on the way of Horonaim.**

7. *Luhith* means *cheeks.** For we often perceive people's inner state by their cheeks. Fear turns them
white; shame, red; pain makes them twitch; joy makes
them lively; and love fills them with sweetness. There
are two factors by which we judge the state of the
human mind: by actions and by words. For *from an
abundance of heart the mouth speaks,** and one acts according to what one loves. Therefore, when a wise
person enters the church and, remorseful for past
deeds, goes up to the height of the virtues by both
words and works, Moab goes up *by Luhith's ascent*
weeping.

8. *And they will raise a shout of contrition,* it says, *on
the way of Horonaim.** *Horonaim* means *chink of grief.*†
This is that *narrow way that leads to life,*§ namely, that
needle's eye through which the humped camel cannot

*Rom 6:14;
Aelred, Spec car
1.32.91

*Luke 2:52
*Eph 4:13

*1 Cor 1:20

*Isa 15:5

*Jerome, In Isa
6.39

*Matt 12:34

*Isa 15:5
†Jerome, In Isa
6.39
§Matt 7:14

*Matt 19:24

pass.* It is well called *a chink of grief,* because those who give themselves to this narrow chink will think that there is nothing sweeter than grieving. For such people grieve for forbidden acts committed, for the misfortune perceived in the present moment, for the evils that they fear will follow, and for the good things desired in the future. Therefore, *on the way of Horonaim,*

*Isa 15:5

the wise of the world raise *a cry of* contrition,* knowing that *a crushed spirit is a sacrifice to God, a contrite and*

*Ps 50:19; Jerome,
In Isa 6.39
†Isa 15:6
§Jerome, In Isa
6.39
*Jer 13:23

*humbled heart God does not reject.**

9. *For the waters of Nimrim will be desolate.*† Nimrim means *leopards* or *transgressors.*§ Understand *leopards* to represent variety, and transgression to represent ungodliness.* Therefore, interpret the waters of Nimrim to be worldly philosophy. In this sort of philosophy, there is such a great variety of sects and opinions that what one person constructs, another tears down; what this one approves, that one condemns; and what one person takes for the best, another regards as the worst. Now, one ungodliness rules in all of those changing *the truth of God into a lie*

*Rom 1:25, 18
*Acts 9:35

and serving *the creature rather than the Creator.** But among those *who have turned to the Lord,** the waters of Nimrim are desolate, because, trained in the Gospel's teaching, what before had seemed gain now

*Phil 3:7

seems loss on account of Christ.*

10. *Because the grass has dried up, the shoot has failed,*

*Isa 15:6

*and everything green has perished.** It is grass on which the unthinking flock grazes. If the grass should dry up, the flock does not even bother to touch it. *Grass* thus expresses the knowledge with which the philosophers used to address and instruct the unlearned masses. But *the grass dried up and the flower fell, because*

*Isa 40:7;
1 Pet 1:24

*the Lord blew on it.** For since the Spirit of the Lord has blown everywhere and breathed heavenly teaching into the hearts of mortals, all that knowledge has dried up to such an extent that it does not please even peasant simplicity anymore. When the grass dries up, the shoot also fails. When wicked preaching came to an end, the shoot that used to spring from it also failed for want of listeners. Everything green also perished, because the shining glory that common opinion had bestowed on it *quickly withered.** *Gen 32:25

11. But if you prefer, understand the grass as the knowledge of clear things, the shoot as the discernment of subtle and profound things, and the greenness as outer eloquence. All of this dried up, failed, and perished for those who held fast to the Gospel, so that the true could take the place of the false, and what was useful could enter in when what was harmful had been shut out.

12. It follows, *According to the greatness of their work is their visitation also.** *Visitation* can refer to either a *Isa 15:7 punishment or a help.** *I will visit them with evils,* it *profectus says, *and I will use all my arrows on them.** And else- *Deut 32:23; Isa where, *I will not punish your daughters when they forni-* 13:11 *cate nor your wives when they commit adultery.** But also, *Hos 4:14 *God visited us with* his *salvation,** and *the dawn from on* *Ps 105:4 *high* visiting *us* illuminated those *who* sat *in darkness and the shadow of death.** Understand here whichever *Luke 1:78-79; you like better. If it is a punishment, understand them Ps 106:10 to be visited *according to the greatness* of *their* wicked *work* in such a way that they receive fitting retribution either by inner contrition or outer affliction.** But if it *Jerome, In is a help, notice that the greater and loftier they were Isa 6.39 in their own eyes, so much the more did the Spirit's visit humble them. Or certainly they were visited in such a way that, *according to the measure by which they measured* by renouncing worldly glory *for Christ's name,* the abundance of Christ's grace was measured to them.** *Luke 6:38;

13. Therefore, visited in this way, they will be led *to Acts 15:26 the torrent of the willows.** It is thought that if this tree's *Isa 15:7 seed is swallowed, it takes away the ability to repro- duce.** For this reason, it suitably represents the virtue *Jerome, In Isa of chastity, or those who, having decided against 6.39; Jerome, In Zach 3.16

having children, take joy in dwelling in spiritual torrents on account of purity's sweetness. Therefore, Moab, that is, any wise person turned toward the Lord, walks *from virtue to virtue,** from self-awareness to repentance, from repentance to humility, and from humility to chastity.

*Ps 83:8

14. We can also interpret the willows as those sterile and fruitless people who, dwelling in the pleasures of this world as though in torrents, are rendered incapable of bearing any spiritual fruit.* After the orators and philosophers converted, either the Holy Spirit or the church's teachers with whom these converts were affiliated led them to guide and instruct such sterile people. Thus they taught the faith that they had attacked and built up the doctrine that they had previously hated. We can also take the torrents *of the willows* to be the troubles and passions that they too sustained with the dissolute, imitating the one who drinks *from the torrent on the way* and *therefore* lifted up *his head.**

*Jerome, In Isa 6.39; Cassian, Conl 4.2; Aelred, S 50.28

*Ps 109:7; Aelred, S 11.22

15. The prophet then shows how all of this would take place, saying, *Because a shout went around the border of Moab.** This is the shout of the apostolic preaching: *Repent, for the kingdom of heaven will draw near.** Their preaching could not have escaped the notice of any of the wise *of this world* after *their sound went forth to all the land and their words to the ends of the earth.** Therefore *a shout went around the border of Moab.*†

*Isa 15:8
*Matt 4:17

*Ps 18:5; Rom 10:18; 1 Cor 1:20
†Isa 15:8

16. But perhaps you prefer to understand this as the cry of Moab itself. Thus, its *cry went around the border of Moab* when Moab shouted among all people.* Everyone struggled against one another in a wide-ranging argument: the converts against those who turned away from God, the godless against the righteous, and the stubborn against the repentant.

*Isa 15:8

17. It then follows, *As far as Eglaim is its wail, and as far as Elim's well its shout.** *Eglaim* means *mound of sand.** Moab's wail, therefore, arrived as far as the mounds of sand in those who mourned with foolish

*Isa 15:8
*Jerome, In Isa 6.39

loyalty for those who had repented and turned away from their error. In these mounds of sand, nothing is firm, nothing stable, inasmuch as they are easily scattered by every wind. And in the converts, its shout arrived *as far as Elim's well. Elim* means *rams,** because, while the stubbornness of some deserved to be scattered, the repentance of others merited consolation from the ram's well, that is, from the apostles' teaching.* It thus says, *As far as Eglaim is its wail, and as far as Elim's well its shout,*† teaching that the same kind of people are pricked, but some respond with a sterile wail and others with a saving shout.

18. For Sacred Scripture has this custom—while speaking of the same people—of now announcing the best of things about them, now the worst. This is what the apostle does when writing to the Romans about the Jews, saying, *According to the Gospel, they are enemies because of you; according to the election, they are beloved because of their fathers.** He calls the same people both enemies and beloved, because in the same people we find both enemies who persecute Christ and beloved people who cling faithfully to Christ. You will often find this rule of speaking in Isaiah. Unless you pay attention to it, you will find everything to be confused and contradictory.

19. You should thus understand that the one name or people *Moab* represents the wise of this world, of whom some are condemned and others are chosen. In this way, the text subtly deals with each group. Since it does not use a different name but treats both groups as though they were one, it seems to offer contradictory judgments.

Moab, howling and shouting against sound teaching, accomplished nothing in the condemned. Rather, like mounds of sand driven by the wind of vanity, the condemned either came together or were scattered. It is thus fittingly said of Moab, *As far as Eglaim is its wail.** But because Moab deserved to attain the knowl-

*Jerome, In Isa 6.39

*Augustine, In Ps 28.2
†Isa 15:8

*Rom 11:28

*Isa 15:8

edge of saving doctrine in the chosen by their repenting, preaching, or praying, the following is also rightly
said of it: *And as far as Elim's well its shout.**

*Isa 15:8

20. It follows, *Because the waters of Dibon were full of
blood.** We read that *Dibon* means *flowing,*† referring to
those who, *calling themselves wise, became foolish,*§ and
flowed away in empty and base affairs. Their waters,
that is, their teaching, are full of blood. This is the
blood from which the prophet asked to be freed, saying, *Free me from blood, God,** and of which Isaiah himself said, *Their hands are full of blood.**

*Isa 15:9
†Jerome, In Isa
6.38-39
§Rom 1:22

*Ps 50:16
*Isa 1:15

21. O brothers, the sword of ungodliness has struck
down as many people as the philosophers have
brought together in their sect. For *fast are their feet to
shed blood,* because *they behaved deceitfully with their
tongues, vipers' poison behind their lips.** We should thus
read the verse in this way: Let no one be amazed that
most philosophers preferred *Elim's well* to the mounds
of sand, the apostolic teaching to worldly wisdom,
*because the waters of Dibon were full of blood.** For perverse doctrine does not give life to the souls of those
whom it deceives, but rather puts them to death.** Nor
does it cleanse them from filth, but pollutes them with
the blood of sin.

*Ps 13:3

*Isa 15:9

*1 Sam 2:6

22. And the prophet added, *For I will place more on
Dibon for those who flee the lion, leaving Moab, and for the
rest of the land.** Now clearly separating *the valuable
from the worthless,** it says, *For those who flee the lion,
leaving Moab*—that is, for their benefit, for their consolation, for their progress—*I will place more on Dibon.**
For I will add wounds to their wounds, pains to their
pains, anxieties to their anxieties, and fears to their
fears.** For here they will rot in their own fluid,† which
is what *Dibon* means, and in the end they will go down
to hell to suffer eternal punishments.** And this will
benefit those *who flee, leaving Moab;* in fleeing *the lion*
they will escape the one *roaming around looking for
someone to devour.** Those who, continuing among the

*Isa 15:9
*Jer 15:19

*Isa 15:9

*Lev 26:21
†Joel 1:17

*Job 21:13

*1 Pet 5:8

dissolute Moabites, receive *more* punishment for the flow of temporal things will not only benefit those *who flee the lion, leaving Moab.* They will also benefit *the rest of the land,* namely, *those who flee* that *lion,* the devil, abandoning earthly vices and eager for the virtues.*   *Isa 15:9

23. The verse *I will place more on Dibon** can also be read in another way. It is as though you asked in what way he was speaking of Dibon. He explains it by saying, *To those who flee Moab.** For Dibon can also mean *adequate mourning.** It thus represents those who, weeping and mourning in the manner that we described above, ran away from Moab, abandoning the fellowship of the faithless and clinging to the Christian people. The Lord assigned them persecutions in addition to the hardships they endured in repentance, *because it was given* to them *not only* to believe *in* Christ *but also* to suffer *for Christ.**   *Phil 1:29

  *Isa 15:9

  *Isa 15:9

  *Jerome, In Isa 6.39

24. The prophet explains this *more* that the Lord would place on them by adding *the lion.*[1] This expresses the persecution that that *roaring lion* roused up against the faithful,* not only against converts from worldly wisdom but also, as we said above, against *the rest of the land.* And if we are to interpret *the rest of the land,* let us read it as follows: Just as *Moab* represents the Gentiles, so too does *the rest of the land* represent the Jews. For the apostle said of the Jews, *The rest were saved according to the election of grace.** For the lion's persecution tormented both Gentiles and Jews who took up faith in Christ.   *1 Pet 5:8

  *Rom 11:5

25. O brothers, we have briefly and uninterruptedly clarified as best we could a section of the prophecy that is highly obscure on account of the abundance of proper names. We did this so that it might be more easily understood and more difficult to forget. You may thus listen with greater pleasure to the moral

---

[1] Isa 15:9 could also be translated as follows: "I will place . . . a lion on those fleeing from Moab and the rest of the land."

explanation that ought to follow. I want to put this off until tomorrow, however, lest I seem to burden you who are either satiated with food or tired from work. But armed with your prayers, we will bring to light tomorrow whatever the Spirit himself *who reveals mysteries* suggests for your upbuilding,* to the praise and glory of our Lord Jesus Christ,† who lives and reigns with God the Father and the same Holy Spirit, forever and ever. Amen.

*Dan 2:29; 1 Cor 2:10; 14:3; Eph 3:5; 4:29
†Oner 27.24

Homily 26

1. Be present, dear brothers; listen attentively and pray with understanding,* so that we can explain morally for your upbuilding the things that we touched on yesterday according to their prophetic explanation.* For these matters are exceedingly deep, and a veil of proper names covers them. They therefore demand more than a little concentration from both the listener and the speaker.

2. You remember well enough, beloved, what Moab, which means *from the father,* represents according to the moral law.* It represents those vices that are passed from father to son through carnal generation, such as the pricks of lust, the stings of anger, and other similar impulses.* Or else it represents the people who yield to such vices, having chosen to live according to them. But it also represents those who, abandoning the vices, engage in spiritual combat against them. As long as such temptations weary them, we have reason to call them *Moab*. Of such people, some are overcome because they are more encumbered—among whom what was said is fulfilled, *Heshbon will shout, and Elealeh,* etc.*—while others, because they fight lightly armed, shout to the Lord when they are in trouble, and he rescues *them from their difficulties.** It is written of them, *For this the lightly armed soldiers of Moab will wail, its soul will wail to itself.** It seems that we should first say who these *lightly armed soldiers of Moab* are.

*1 Cor 14:15

*1 Cor 14:3;
Eph 4:29

*Jerome, In
Isa 6.36

*Oner 24.2, 7

*Isa 15:4

*Ps 106:6

*Isa 15:4

3. Here our patriarch Abraham's memorable work took place. With 318 lightly armed soldiers born in his house, he invaded, put to flight, and brought low the enemy. Additionally, he powerfully snatched all the booty that they had taken from the Sodomites.* With nearly this number, holy Gideon scattered the Midian army, which was terrified by the light of their lamps and the sound of their trumpets.* I could also use lightly armed *soldiers* to refer to them; many were prudently and boldly excluded from their company because some hindrance made them unfit for war. For, instructed by the divine oracle, that wise leader ordered that all should depart from the war whom fear had made tremble and love* had made inattentive, whom cupidity had weakened or desire had engulfed.* After these had been sent away, others were led to be tried at the water. Soon, some were flat on their stomachs, eagerly drinking water; others, stooped slightly, considered their need and refrained from superfluity.*

4. You see, then, that not only vices but also superfluous things are a hindrance to those progressing and a burden to those fighting. Many, attracted by natural provocations, have fallen into filthy things. They decide both to repent for past deeds and to refrain from future ones when it comes to the riches, delights, and worldly affairs in which they have sinned. They thus grab on to a kind of conversion of life, but they give it very little time. For they are not lightly armed soldiers. For Heshbon, or wicked thoughts, and Elealeh, or a proud mind, shout within them,* until *their voice is heard as far as Jahaz,* and wicked deeds follow from wicked thoughts.

5. Therefore, wishing to make his soldiers *lightly armed* for this spiritual war, our leader says, *Those who do not renounce all their possessions cannot be my disciples.* And again, *Those who do not hate their father and mother and wife and children, and even their own soul,*

*Gen 14:14-16

*Judg 7:19-22

*amor

*Deut 20:5-8; Judg 7:3

*Judg 7:4-6

*Jerome, In Isa 6.39

*Luke 14:33

*cannot be my disciples.** And so *the lightly armed soldiers*   *Luke 14:26
of Moab are those who disentangle themselves from
all this world's affairs and riches, from all their long-
ings and even from their own will.*   *RB Prol 3
safely resist the Moabite vices into which they had
fallen and nakedly follow the naked Christ.*   *Oner 20.19;
                                                              Jerome,
6. When these lightly armed soldiers feel themselves   Ep 125.20.5
attacked by natural provocations, demonic sugges-
tions, or their own thoughts, they send forth to God
a loud wail of the heart and a wretched lamentation
of voice with tears and sighs, saying with the prophet,
*I am terribly afflicted and lowly; I roared out my complaint
from my heart.** This is exactly what Isaiah said: *For this*   *Ps 37:9
*the lightly armed soldiers of Moab will wail.**   *Isa 15:4

7. What follows—*Its soul will wail to itself*—   *Isa 15:4
expresses a hidden contrition of heart, a contrition that
rejects human eyes but longs for the divine face. The
prophecy thus blames those *who,* praying *on the street
corners so that others may see them,* do not have *a reward
with the Father who is in heaven.** The soul of those who   *Matt 6:5
fill bystanders' ears with shouts and sobs does not
wail to itself either. Seeking neither a fitting time nor
an opportune place, such people provide nothing useful for themselves, but plenty of hindrances to
others.*   *RB 52.3-5

8. It follows, *My heart will cry out to Moab.** Thanks   *Isa 15:5
be to you, good Jesus! Truly, your *compassion is over all*
your *works!** If inwardly where God sees,† a person's   *Ps 144:9
heart turns to God and is crushed, then God's heart   †Matt 6:6
will soon turn to that person. God's *heart* expresses
his goodness and compassion. *My heart will cry out to
Moab.** Moab wails in repentance; Christ cries out in   *Isa 15:5
mercy. Moab wails in fear; Christ cries out by showing
pity. Moab wails in confession; Christ cries out with
forgiveness. Moab, *seeing the strong wind* coming, fears
and wails; Christ, stretching out his hand and crying
out, rebukes the hesitating, trembling one, saying, *You
of little faith, why did you doubt?** The cry thus answers   *Matt 14:30-31

the wail, desire answers desire, mercy answers the wretched one; the doctor, the sick one; compassion, the one laboring and in pain.

9. Truly, Lord, *according to the great number of sorrows in my heart, your consolations have made my soul glad.** You cry out, Lord, you cry out from within my soul when you raise up what is desperate in hope, when you soothe what is fearful and trembling with an amazing goodness and sweetness,* when you pour the dew of saving consolation into the soul now stooped over from its body's burning, when you settle the mind laboring against anger, hatred, revenge, and so on by a kind of interior peace. And so, however often my soul wails to itself in and for this state, so often does the heart of my God cry out, showing me compassion. And so, Jesus, when you were about to raise up Lazarus, you cried out *in a loud voice*, expressing with a great cry the great desire of your goodness.* O Lord, how long will the heavy temptation of these passions rage against me? How long will Moab, whom I thought I had escaped at the beginning of my conversion, continuously renew its wars against me?

10. Listen to what follows: *Its bars as far as Zoar, a three-year-old calf.** *Zoar* means *small*,† representing the humility that makes the rich poor, the haughty simple, the great small, and the proud humble. This humility is fittingly called a *calf*, which is a kind of animal that abounds in milk, because *God resists the proud, but gives grace to the humble.** *And on whom*, it says, *will my Spirit rest if not on the humble, the quiet, those trembling at my words?** Further, it is called a three-year-old calf. At this age, the animal is fit both for the yoke and for breeding. The three-year-old calf, therefore, represents the fullness of humility.

11. The *bars* represent the strength and resilience that the habit of sinning lends to the vices. For we first discover our sins' resilience when, turned toward God, we resolve to resist these ingrained habits.*

*Ps 93:19

*Mark 5:33-34

*John 11:43

*Isa 15:5
†Jerome, In Isa 6.39

*1 Pet 5:5 and parallels

*Isa 66:2 LXX; 11:2

*Aelred, Spec car 1.28.79; Aelred, SS 43.13; 56.18

These habits undoubtedly weary us until deep humility puts an end to that cruel beast, pride. Therefore, Moab's *bars* reach *as far as Zoar, a three-year-old calf.*[*Isa 15:5]

12. The *three-year-old calf* can also express the three steps in which perfect humility makes itself known, which consists in a threefold contempt. The first step, then, is that one should condemn oneself, putting oneself under a superior according to God's will.*[*RB 7.34] Then one should despise nothing, regard nothing as lower than oneself, and thus be subjected to every creature for God. Finally, one should willingly, or at least patiently, allow oneself to be despised by all and long for God alone. Perfect humility consists in these three steps. All things will be peaceful and calm for whoever has advanced to this humility in God's compassion. Thus there will be nothing in the flesh that fights against the spirit, nor anything in the spirit that opposes God's will for such a person.*[*Gal 5:17]

13. Be sure of this, then, dear brothers. When fleshly concupiscence drives us to vice,*[*1 John 2:16] it results in one of the following: hidden pride is rebuked, open pride is put to confusion, or, lest the awareness of any virtue should cause pride to raise its wicked head, the tickling of previous vices makes such pride ebb again. For this reason, whoever desires to be freed from the rule of fleshly passions should devote much eagerness and work to acquiring or preserving humility. All the perfection of chastity and peace consists in humility's perfection. For Moab's *bars,* that is, the resilience of the fleshly passions, reach *as far as Zoar, a three-year-old calf.*[*Isa 15:5] This is because, when humility is perfect, all the strength and heat of such passions cool off.

14. Further, that we may know by which route we should climb to this perfection, let us hear what the prophet says next: *For by Luhith's ascent they will go up weeping, and they will raise a shout of contrition on the way of Horonaim.*[*Isa 15:5] *Luhith* means *cheeks; Horonaim, chink of grief.*[*Jerome, In Isa 6.39] *Do the widow's tears not run down her cheeks,* says Scripture, *and the Lord God will not take delight in them?** For tears run down the cheeks, but the power and secret motive for which they are shed *climb to heaven.** Therefore, people reflecting on their *early years with a bitter soul* often break down in tears,* and washing their *beds each night* and soaking their *blankets with tears,†* *they* say with the prophet, *Tears flowed from my eyes because they did not keep your law.§* Thus, *by Luhith,* that is, with tears on their cheeks, they go up *weeping* until, arriving at the *chink of grief,* that is, Horonaim, they raise *a shout of contrition.**

15. O brothers, we must not pass lightly over the phrase *on the way of Horonaim.** For *it is the way that leads to* Horonaim,* that is, to *the chink of grief.* What sort of chink is this? Who has seen it? Who has heard of it?* Who has learned of it?† Who has experienced it? Saving grief has a door, a window, and a chink. The door is the entrance to a house, the window allows one to see, and the chink lets nothing substantial pass through. Accessible to the light and air alone, the chink allows the eye to explore freely without letting it examine anything closely. Therefore, take the door to be faith, the window to be hope, and the chink to be manifestation.* Through faith, we lay open the secrets of God; through hope, we catch their scent; through manifestation, we touch them. Faith teaches all things, hope promises the things to come, and manifestation shows the things promised.

16. O dear brothers, where does your faith not arrive? Where does the soul not arrive through that faith? For through faith, not even the Divine Trinity's one and indivisible substance, wisdom, majesty, power, and goodness escape me. Through it, I have a firm grasp on the angels' blessedness, the demons' wickedness and unhappiness, the world's creation, and human nature with its rise, progress, and fall. The true and saving doctrine of Christ's incarnation and, following from it, humanity's restoration, also come

---

Marginal notes:

*Sir 35:18-19

*Sir 35:19
*Isa 38:15; Heb 10:32; Aelred, Orat past 2; Aelred, S 51.8
†Ps 6:7
§Ps 118:136

*Isa 15:5

*Isa 15:5
*Matt 7:14

*Isa 66:8
†Rom 11:34 and parallels

*species

through faith. I have likewise learned through faith what punishments await the wicked and what rewards await the just. We comprehend all these things through faith; with hope we catch scent of a few of these things that are to come as though from afar.

17. What of manifestation? Can it not be my door? Can it not be at least my window? If only that light would at least shine for me through a small chink, I could then at least explore that heavenly secret with one eye, drawing for myself at least a small droplet of divine sweetness and a pleasant memory of the delight explored!* Who or what could open this chink for me, through which I could at least fleetingly and partially, as though with one eye, contemplate what we believe and hope?* Who, I ask, if not Jesus? What, if not grief? Then let my soul go up, I beg you, *by Luhith's ascent,* that is, compunction's ascent, and in the way of divine fear let it raise up its voice in contrition. Let it pass through the chink of grief and arrive at the prick of contemplation's light. *Aelred, Spec car 1.18.51; 2.11.27; 3.37.102; Ps 30:20

*Oner 2.23; 1 Cor 13:9, 12

18. Grief is therefore threefold. First, there is the grief through which one passes on the way to faith; second, the grief through which one is raised up to hope; and third, the grief through which one is enlightened at the manifestation. The first pertains to fear, the second to consolation, and the third to desire and love. For since *faith without works* is *dead,** and dead faith is no faith at all, then one returns to faith again when, pricked by saving grief, one moves from a wicked life to a change of conduct. First one grieves to become worthy to obtain forgiveness of sins. Then one grieves to be consoled by the hope of the divine promise. One thus raises up a voice of contrition *on this way,* so that a chink opens up for the one grieving. The manifestation then appears through this chink as in a mirror.* O sweet and desirable grief, through which the dead are raised, the sick are healed, the blind enlightened, and the doors of heaven opened!* *Jas 2:20, 26

*1 Cor 13:12

*Ps 77:23

19. The feigned grief of the hypocrites is not like this.* Of their grief, the prophet says, *For the waters of Nimrim will be desolate.* Nimrim* means *leopards.*† The leopard is a spotted, mottled animal, which corresponds to hypocrites' lives and morals. Outwardly, such people are pure white, but they are dark within.* They outwardly project modesty, but lust stinks within them. They outwardly boast of humility, but they feed on vanity within. Their clothing indicates simplicity, but cupidity occupies their minds. Truth is in their words, but impurity in their lives. *Tears* flow *from* their *eyes,** but these *waters will be desolate.*† He *who will shine a light on the hidden places of darkness and lay bare hearts' counsels** will come and show that these barren and fruitless tears are devoid of any grace or reward, only squeezed out to be seen by others.

20. *Because the grass has dried up, the shoot has failed, and everything green has perished.** The beginning of a good way of life is like grass, the fruit of good works is like a shoot, and purity of intention is like greenness. But the grass will dry up in hypocrites when vanity corrupts the beginning of a good way of life. The shoot fails when they do not persevere in praiseworthy works. Everything green perishes when they abandon purity of intention, taking delight in cupidity.

21. It follows, *According to the greatness of the work is their visitation also.** If you think this verse refers to the hypocrites, then it pronounces a hard sentence against them. The greatness of their punishment will be measured to them according to the greatness of their evil deeds. But perhaps you think that this refers instead to those of whom it was said before, *For by Luhith's ascent, they will go up weeping,* etc.* Thus, after the parenthetical remark about the hypocrites' damnation, the prophecy returns to its previous referent, saying, *According to the greatness of the work is their visitation also.** This visitation should be taken in the positive sense; by it, his holy presence gives joy to the hearts

---

Marginalia (left column):

* Ps 1:4

* Isa 15:6
† Jerome, In Isa 6.39

* Matt 23:27

* Ps 118:136
† Isa 15:6

* 1 Cor 4:5

* Isa 15:6

* Isa 15:7

* Isa 15:5

* Isa 15:7

of the saints.* He bestows with just measure on everyone his share, just as each deserves.* Therefore, *According to the greatness of the work is their visitation also.*[†]

22. *To the torrents of the willows they will lead them.*[§] In other words, they will lead the Moabites who cross over from the vices to the virtues. These Moabites eagerly seek a place where they might exercise these virtues. These will be led, therefore, *to the torrents of the willows. The torrents of the willows* are the various orders of those who have renounced the world. They are called *torrents* on account of either the flood of their tears or the violence of their temptations.

23. Such was the torrent from which Elijah drank when *the ravens left him bread and meat in the morning, and bread and meat in the evening.** That torrent was called *Cherith,* which means *bald.** Because hair grows out[†] of the head, the bald are those who renounce whatever is superfluous and who are content to use only what is necessary.[§] These are *the lightly armed soldiers of Moab,*[‡] among whom was Elisha, whom the boys insulted, saying, *Go up, bald man; go up, bald man!*[#] These soldiers drink *on the path from the torrent,** until *the river's gush* brings joy *to God's city*[◊] and *the Most High* dedicates his *house.*[∞]

24. For a torrent does not flow continuously. Rather, when a strong south wind melts the ice,* or when rain falls more abundantly, water fills the valleys. Such is this present visitation, by which God floods us with saving water. The Holy Spirit at times blows, melting our hardness with sweet compunction; at other times, he soaks the humble with spiritual knowledge like heavenly water.*

25. Willows grow in torrents of this sort. These willows are the people who refuse to have carnal children. They *have cut themselves off for the kingdom of heaven,** having *a name in* God's *house better than sons and daughters.*[†] This is the highly pleasing virtue of chastity and cleanness, to which holy souls are worthy

*Ps 18:9
*Ps 61:13 and parallels; Aelred, SS 45.15; 56.1
†Isa 15:7
§Isa 15:7

*1 Kgs 17:6
*Rabanus Maurus, In 3 Reg 16 (PL 109:206C)
†*superfluere*
§1 Tim 6:8; Aelred, S 69.7–8
‡Isa 15:4
#2 Kgs 2:23; Aelred, S 36.18–19
≈Ps 109:7
◊Ps 45:5
∞2 Chr 7:5
*Acts 28:13; Job 37:10; Ps 147:18

*Aelred, S 69.10

*Matt 19:12; Gal 5:12
†Isa 56:5

to arrive. The Spirit of God leads such souls, and the holy angels accompany them to this virtue *by Luhith's ascent* and the way *of Horonaim*,* after the soul has suffered the troubles of the body, countless lustful temptations, frequent burning in the flesh, and the filthy demon's dangerous suggestions.*

26. *Because a cry went around the border of Moab.** This is the same cry of which it said above, *My heart will cry out to Moab.** This cry goes around *the border of Moab,* because the voice of God speaking in us shatters the boundaries of the vices and instills a horror of these same vices in us. How often, brothers, have I heard this cry of his with the ear of my heart. The uproar of the vices clamors on every side, and he opposes each of them. To those telling of delights,* he shuts up their cry with his own, holding forth the *border,* that is, the end, of this delight, making known its baseness, and setting forth the sweetness of spiritual delights to the captive mind! But let us now hear what the destination of each cry is.

27. *As far as Eglaim is its wail, and as far as Elim's well its shout.** By your leave, let us take each phrase separately. We may thus understand *Moab's wail* to be the wail of the vices, of which the prophet said earlier, *Over Nebo and over Medeba Moab will wail.** The *cry* refers to what was said before, *My heart will cry out to Moab.** The *wail* arrives at the *mounds of sand,* which is what *Eglaim* means, whereas the *cry* arrives at *Elim,* which means *rams' well.** For thoughts are unsettled and unstable like sand,† and this *wail* drives them together like a howling wind to make mounds of vices.§ Further, the rams' well is the depth of Scripture, which is served through rams, that is, through the prophets and apostles. Its secrets are opened to us when the Lord cries out in our hearts.

28. And so, brothers, the more outer persecution or inner disturbance saddens us, the more does divine consolation from the sacred writings cheer us.* *For*

*Isa 15:5;
Tob 5:21, 27

*Matt 4:1
*Isa 15:8

*Isa 15:5

*Ps 118:85, as cited by Augustine

*Isa 15:8

*Isa 15:2

*Isa 15:5

*Jerome, In Isa 6.39
†RB 1.11
§Oner 28.15

*Ps 93:19

whatever has been written was written for our instruction, so that we might have hope through the patience and consolation of the Scriptures.* I say to you, brothers, nothing adverse can happen, nothing so sad or bitter can take place, which does not quickly vanish or is not more easily endured as soon as the sacred page is opened to us. This is the field to which Isaac went to meditate when the day was already drawing to a close;* Rebecca met him there and relieved his pain with her sweetness.* *Rom 15:4

*Gen 24:63

*Gen 24:67;
Aelred, S 55.3

29. How often does day give way to evening for me, good Jesus! How often does unbearable pain take the place of what little consolation I have, just as the dark of night succeeds daylight. All things turn to boredom, and everything that I see is a burden. If someone speaks, I barely hear; if someone knocks, I barely perceive it. My heart grows as hard as a rock, my tongue clings to my palate, and my eyes dry up.* What then? I go out, of course, *to the field to meditate,** I reflect on the sacred book,* and I fix my meditations in wax. Then suddenly, Rebecca comes to meet me. In other words, your grace, good Jesus, scatters the darkness with your light, drives away boredom, and breaks up the hardness. Soon tears follow sighs, and heavenly joy accompanies tears. Unhappy are those who do not enter this field and rejoice in this way when some sadness disturbs them!* *Hos 13:15

*Gen 24:63

*Luke 4:17

*Aelred, S 55.14–
15, 18–19

30. You know, brothers, that when some sadness befalls the lovers of this world, they seek consolation in vain or harmful pursuits. The prophet thus rightly adds about such people, *Because the waters of Dibon were full of blood.** *The waters of Dibon,* which means *their flow,** represent the tears of those who laugh over the flow of temporal things if they have them, or weep if they lose them. Therefore, *the waters of Dibon were full of blood.** Just as those who laugh over temporal things laugh to their own detriment, so also those who weep over temporal things weep to their own *Isa 15:9

*Jerome, In Isa
6.38, 39

*Isa 15:9

detriment. For tears of this sort offer no purgation but rather pollute such people more completely with the blood of sin.

*Isa 15:9   **31.** It therefore follows, *I will place more on Dibon.**

Jer 45:3   For the Lord will add sorrows to their sorrows, so that they pass from tears to tears, enter the *land by two*

*Sir 2:14; Jer 17:18 *ways,* and are crushed *by a double contrition.** How wretched is the lot of those born *of woman,* who live but *a brief time*! Here they are filled *with many miseries,* and after this life they are handed over to eternal pun-

Job 14:1   ishments! Happy, on the other hand, are those whom the Word of God's visitation and light console in this world's labors, and who enjoy eternal delights when

John 14:23; 13:1 they pass from this world! For this reason, he will
*Isa 15:9   also place *more* for those *who flee the lion, leaving Moab.** These are the ones who, fleeing the vices, escape the leader of the vices as well. But he will also *place more*

*Isa 15:9   *for the rest of the land.**

32. Three kinds of people are noted here: one kind has given itself entirely to the vices and the world; another, renouncing the world, takes up Christ's

Matt 11:29   yoke; the third abstains from crimes in this world, yet devotes itself to earthly deeds. The first kind is represented by Dibon; the second, by those who flee from Moab; the third, by the rest of the land. The Lord will place more on all of them.

33. For he will repay the condemned for their sins with temporal sorrows in this life and with everlasting torture of both soul and body after this life. The gospel narrative relates how the Lord will multiply his gifts to those renouncing this world: *Everyone who gives up father and mother,* etc., *for me, will receive a hundredfold*

*Matt 19:29;   *now and eternal life in the future.** Those who shun *lead,*
Mark 10:29-30   *iron, and tin* and build *on the foundation* of the catholic faith with *wood, hay, and straw* will receive *from the*

*Isa 40:2; Ezek *Lord's hand double for all their sins.** For such people are
22:18; 1 Cor 3:12 crushed by many misfortunes. They will finally be

rescued from the fire, but they will suffer loss. They will be saved, *yet only as though through fire.**

34. The name of Moab is fitting for all three kinds of people. The Moabite vices will swallow up the first kind; the second kind will either completely destroy or nobly restrain the Moabite vices; these same vices sometimes disgrace and always weary the third kind. But the burden of Moab can be seen everywhere. This burden is weighed down in some people, others it weighs down, and others it crushes. But let us end this sermon here, pleading for our God's mercy,* so that he may render us, restored from the Moabite vices, acceptable to his will, through Christ our Lord. Amen.*

*1 Cor 3:15; Aelred, S 33.17; Augustine, Enchir 18.68–69

*Oner 21.28; 4.18; 19.36; 27.24

* see Orat fer IV hebd III Quadrag; Orat fer V hebd III Quadrag in Corpus Orat 8.5314, in CCSL 160G; Corpus Orat 1.750, in CCSL 160

Homily 27

1. *God will come from the south, and the Holy One from* *Hab 3:3 Var *a shady, dense mountain.** Behold, dear brothers, as our Lord Jesus bursts forth from this dense forest of allegorical words. He was hidden in its shady thickness up to the point where the prophet says, *Send forth the lamb, O Lord, the ruler of the land, from the rock of the* *Isa 16:1 *desert to the mountain of the daughter of Zion.** Truly, *my beloved stands behind our wall, looking through the win-* *Song 2:9 *dows, peering through the lattice.**

2. Is there anyone who has heard the Lord Jesus *John 5:39 saying in the gospel, *Examine the Scriptures*, etc.,* who does not know that we must seek him in the Scriptures? But the darkness of these very Scriptures, the riddles of words, and the narrative's allusions are like a kind of wall between us and him. In fact, those spiritual craftsmen who raised this wall for us installed windows and lattices in it, through which the beloved often lets his lovers see him. Thus no one may doubt that he whom the clear parts of Scripture plainly show is also to be found everywhere in the obscure parts.

3. Therefore, it says, *Send forth the lamb, O Lord, the* *Isa 16:1 *ruler of the land.** We said in the beginning that the prophets recorded future events sometimes by narrating, sometimes by commanding, and sometimes *Oner 3.6 even by praying.* The prophet perceived in the spirit that even the wise of the world would be brought under the power of the cross, and that *those believing* *1 Cor 1:21 would be saved *through the foolishness of the preaching.**

Yet he also perceived that the *wisdom of the wise* would be lost, *the prudence of the prudent* would be condemned,* and the other things foretold in this burden. The prophet burns with desire, he complains about the delay,* he wishes that Christ were present even now to fulfill the promises and to show forth what was foretold. And turned toward the Father, he demands the coming of the Son with burning feeling,* saying, *Send forth the lamb, O Lord, the ruler of the land, from the rock of the desert to the mountain of the daughter of Zion.** *1 Cor 1:19 *Hab 2:3 *Aelred, SS 1.24; 60.4 *Isa 16:1

4. This is the lamb who speaks through Jeremiah, saying, *And I was like a blameless lamb who is carried to be a victim and did not open its mouth.** This same Isaiah said of him, *As a sheep he will be led to the slaughter and as a lamb before the shearer he will be silent.*† John the Baptist recognized him when the Holy Spirit revealed him and said, *Behold, the lamb of God.** The prophet prophesied with desirous longing that the Father would send this lamb, that he would come into the world and subject all things to himself: *Send forth the lamb, O Lord, the ruler of the land.** David sang of him, saying, *He will rule from sea to sea and from the river to the boundaries of the earth.** *Jer 11:19; Isa 53:7; Ant et Resp 5 HM (Hesb 3.2422; 4.6660) †Isa 53:7 *John 1:29 *Isa 16:1 *Ps 71:8

5. *From the rock of the desert to the mountain of the daughter of Zion.** I take *rock of the desert* to refer to the cave that, carved in the rock by nature or art in a deserted place, received Lot fleeing from Sodom.* The prophecy says that the lamb would wonderfully come forth from this *rock of the desert*. For it was in that cave that Moab was begotten,* from whose seed Ruth was born, whose son was Obed, whose son was Jesse, whose son was David, from whose stock Christ was born.* Moreover, Christ is sent forth *from the rock of the desert to the mountain of the daughter of Zion,*† because, born of the Virgin in Bethlehem,§ he visited Jerusalem with his presence. Jerusalem is where Mount Zion is literally located. It is the mountain—that is, the *Isa 16:1 *Gen 19:30; Wis 11:2 *Gen 19:37 *Matt 1:5-6; Rev 22:16; Jerome, In Isa 5.60; 6.40 †Isa 16:1 §Matt 2:1

excellence and glory—of the daughter of Zion, that is, of the synagogue. This excellence and glory should be understood as the nobility of the temple.

6. The synagogue is allegorically called the rock of the desert. When it was led out of Egypt and made an inhabitant of the desert for forty years, it drank *from the spiritual rock that followed them.** The synagogue is fittingly called *the rock of the desert,* because it preserved the steadfastness of the faith in the perfect for such a long exile after many had died in infidelity.* The apostles came from this synagogue and brought the lamb *who took away the sins of the world* to the Gentiles with their preaching.* In this way, the lamb could reign over the entire world. The church would thus be born from the synagogue as though it were Zion's daughter, whose mountain is the height of faith, the grandeur of hope, and the more excellent way of charity.* For this reason the Lord said in the gospel, *It was necessary for the Christ to suffer and to rise again from the dead on the third day, and for repentance and the forgiveness of sins to be preached in his name to all nations, beginning from Jerusalem.**

7. Or surely the lamb was sent forth as ruler *of the land from the rock of the desert to the mountain of the daughter of Zion** when Christ passed over from the shadow of the law to *the truth of the Gospel.** It was then that he crossed over *from the rock of the desert* from which the children of Israel *drank,** which was the mystery of our redemption, *to the truth* of his most holy body and blood. It was then, after the veil of the letter was taken away, that he unlocked the secret of the spiritual understanding of the New Testament to his preachers.*

8. *And it will come to pass.** What? When the lamb, the ruler *of the land,* is sent forth *from the rock of the desert to the mountain of the daughter of Zion,** as a bird fleeing and the chicks flying from the nest, so will the daughters of Moab be in the passage of Arnon.** Understand the

*1 Cor 10:4

*1 Cor 10:5

*John 1:29

*1 Cor 12:31;
Jerome, In Isa
5.60

*Luke 24:46-47

*Isa 16:1

*Heb 10:1;
Gal 2:14

*1 Cor 10:4

*2 Cor 3:13-16

*Isa 16:2

*Isa 16:1

*Isa 16:2

daughters of Moab to be carnal and weak souls deceived by Moabite errors. Perceiving that the prophets'
oracles would be fulfilled and Christ would reign
everywhere, Moab's daughters turned *from the darkness to the light.** When the *devil's snares* in which they
had been bound were broken and the darkness of ignorance was cast off,* they crossed over to the light of
true knowledge.*

9. *As,* it says, *a bird fleeing* from a hawk avoids the
raptor's snares now by seeking the heights, now by
hiding in the depths, now by cutting through the air
on avian wing; *and as chicks* fly away terrified if a snake
unexpectedly invades the nest, and, having rejected
the nest's softness, are carried here and there by a
headlong flight, *so will the daughters of Moab be in the
passage of Arnon.** *Arnon* means *their illumination.*† The
birds of prey, which is what we call the demons according to our Lord and Savior's interpretation,§
pursue many who have recently converted to Christ's
faith and are already *in the passage* of heavenly wisdom
as Arnon. The demons intend to make them abandon
the truth and seize them in the claws of their ill-will.
It is gratifying to see these new converts oppose the
demon's stratagems and persevere by God's grace in
the faith they received. For there *also* had *to be heresies
so that those who are approved* might *also come to light,**
and a more thorough investigation might make known
the truth of the faith.

10. The enemy mocked Christian simplicity through
heretics or philosophers and reproached with sly insults our Lord and Savior's human weakness, the
stumbling block of the cross,* and the injustice of his
hungering, thirsting, and death. The faithful then
avoided these snares of scandal, quickly flying to the
heights of the divinity itself in mental contemplation.
But the heretics pursued them even there, using the
perfection of divine majesty to argue against the lowly
things of the flesh. They claimed that such lowly

*Acts 26:18;
1 Pet 2:9

*2 Tim 2:26

*Jerome, In
Isa 6.40

*Isa 16:2
†Jerome, In
Isa 6.40
§Luke 8:5, 12,
and parallels

*1 Cor 11:19

*Gal 5:11

things either had no place in God or were a product of the imagination. The saints knew that the evangelists and apostles had in truth preached the Savior's hunger, thirst, fatigue, and sadness. Descending from the heights to the depths, they confessed that just as his true divinity was on high, so too was his true humanity here below, and thus they made sport of the hunters' nets.

11. But if the shrewd enemy sought to cast the saints from the stronghold of the virtues by pointing to the Gospel's steep path with many hidden suggestions, immediately those saints wisely made light of the birdlime of worldly pleasures. Rather, avoiding the material of vices and carried on the wings of the virtues, their journey between heaven and earth split the mean of discretion as though it were air.

At times that languid snake would try to pour the hidden venom of heretical teaching into those who, dwelling in silence and rest as though in a nest, refused to take part in public arguments. But they avoided the bites of the Moabite snakes by immediately abandoning their nest of leisure and submitting what had been suggested to them to the consideration of many others.* Therefore, it says, *As a bird fleeing and the chicks flying from the nest, so will the daughters of Moab be in the passage of Arnon.**

12. It was truly necessary that many people gather together. The judgment of all the saints could thus condemn every perverse doctrine that was contrary to the faith and could establish a fixed rule of faith. The unlearned could then easily avoid heretics and false philosophers and distinguish the truth of the catholic faith from their error. For this reason, it is highly fitting that the prophet speaks to the church itself, which hesitated regarding these affairs and others like them, prophesying, *Take counsel, gather an assembly, cast your shadow like night at midday.** The sacred writings are not silent about these gatherings, which

*Jerome, In Isa 6.40

*Isa 16:2

*Isa 16:3

first the apostles and later the holy fathers quite often invoked.

13. We read about this in the Acts of the Apostles. After the Christian religion had grown and both Jews and Gentiles eagerly came together to the faith of Christ, certain people came to Antioch, where there was quite a large crowd of disciples.* Those who had *John 6:5 newly arrived said that the Gentiles must be circumcised and walk according to the law, and that they could not be saved without observing it.* For this rea- *Acts 15:1, 5 son, the apostles took *counsel* in Jerusalem and gathered an *assembly.* The liberty of faith, which had been hidden from many like a shadow and the night, was thus placed in the clear light as though *at midday.* It shone forth to all from the judgment of truth that the apostles announced.* What had been hidden was then *Acts 15:6-29 accessible to all, that circumcision is nothing and foreskin is nothing, but what matters is faith and the keeping of God's commandments.* *1 Cor 7:19; Gal 5:6

14. We should thus read the verse as follows: the church perceived that the shrewdness of heretics or philosophers had entangled Moab's daughters in error. Moab's daughters are those weak souls who had converted from Moabite vices. *So that* everyone might know *the Gospel's truth,** the church took counsel with the wise *Gal 2:5 and the learned. After the assembly had convened, the church offered a fixed and enlightened judgment concerning the matters in doubt. It thus cast its shadow— namely, the hidden mysteries of the faith that before had seemed as dark as night—at midday, that is, in the open. The prophet foretells by commanding or advising that all these things should come to pass, saying, *Take counsel, gather an assembly, cast your shadow like night at midday.** *Isa 16:3

15. We read about the evangelist John acting in this way. Ebion and Cherintus[1] and other plagues had

---

[1] Leaders of an early Christian sect.

corrupted the sincerity of the faith with twisted dogma while John was in exile. When he was called back, he took counsel and gathered an assembly, and what he had recorded in the gospel by God's revelation was brought to light. He thus drove away the darkness of error with the light of truth and transformed the night into midday.*

*Jerome, In
Matt, Pref

16. Then, during Constantine's rule, wicked Arius pined for the souls of both the birds and the chicks, namely, those who were spiritual and those who were carnal. He infected many with the venom of his ill-will and tempted them to divide and scatter the one and the same essence and equal power of the Father and the Son. A council was called and an assembly gathered. By the convening and authority of many saints, the undivided unity of the very Trinity, which had hitherto seemed to the simple like night and a dark shadow, was openly manifested to be believed by all. And the holy church has always kept this custom, so that as often as something doubtful or obscure would come up concerning the purity of faith, it might come to a fixed judgment, reached by the weight of counsel and by the authority of the assembly.

17. The prophet announces why all this should be done when he adds, *Hide those who are fleeing and do not betray the wanderers.** Understand *the fleeing and the wanderers* to be the birds and chicks of which the prophet had earlier said, *And it will come to pass that, as a bird fleeing and the chicks flying from the nest, so will the daughters of Moab be in the passage of Arnon.** Therefore, counsel must be taken and an assembly gathered to hide those fleeing—that is, so that the authority of many may defend Moab's daughters from the snares of the heretic, whom they flee like birds from a hawk— and so that *the wanderers*, that is, those who flit about here and there like chicks, are not carried about *by every wind of doctrine* and exposed to various errors.* After the truth has been brought to light, a fixed rule

*Isa 16:3

*Isa 16:2

*Eph 4:14;
Aelred, Spec
car 2.14.35

of faith will protect those fleeing, and the wanderers will be strengthened in this faith.*

18. It follows, *My refugees will dwell with you, Moab.*† Understand *Moab* here to be the wise, of whom we said above that the more attentive they had been in worldly wisdom, the more prudent they became in divine realities.* This is that Moab whose *bars* reach *as far as Zoar, a three-year-old calf.** Such was the blessed martyr Cyprian; such were Ambrose, Augustine, and Jerome, who brought everything that they had drawn from worldly wisdom for the church's support and progress.* People such as these were more effective in conquering the heretics. Their teaching protected the weak from the attack of false apostles.* Under their care as under motherly wings, the weak were more safely hidden, so that the demons could not lead them astray and carry them off.

19. Christ addresses this Moab, that is, this sort of wise person, saying, *My refugees will dwell with you, Moab; be their hiding place before the face of the destroyers.** Christ calls his *refugees* those whom, formerly led astray and carried off by the devil, he recovered by right with his victory over the enemy. The devil, grieving for those taken from him, raised up heretics, stirred up philosophers, and attacked with false dogma. By thus deceiving the simple, he hoped to console himself by their ruin for the wound he suffered at losing them. But until wickedness passes away and truth comes to light,* the imperfect depend on the faith of the perfect, and *before the face of* such *destroyers,* the wise provided the simple with the saving hiding place of their teaching and care.

20. It therefore says, *My refugees will dwell with you, Moab; be their hiding place before the face of the destroyers.** And so that this should not seem difficult to someone considering the devil's power and shrewdness, the prophecy immediately adds, *For the dust has come to an end; the wretched one has been consumed.** The devil's

*Jerome, In Isa 6.40
†Isa 16:4

*Oner 25.3
*Isa 15:5

*Oner 25.4

*2 Cor 11:13

*Isa 16:4

*Ps 56:2

*Isa 16:4

*Isa 16:4

teaching is compared to dust, because it came to an end of sorts when the world took up the saving teaching after the Gospel shone forth.*

*Jerome, In Isa 6.40

The prophet appropriately calls the devil *the wretched one*. Condemnation has been prepared for him in eternal fire in the future.* Now vain concern spurs his wicked breast forward. He always labors but never advances; he always desires the souls of the chosen but can never subdue them. Everyone considers him to be all the more wretched to the extent that earthly, mortal beings easily overcome a heavenly, immortal spirit. Truly wretched is he who is pressed down by the angels, mocked by humans, condemned by the perfect, and conquered by the weak.

*Matt 25:41

21. It therefore says, *The dust has come to an end; the wretched one has been consumed.** This is because, as soon as the devil's doctrine was blown away from human hearts like dust from the face of the earth,* that wretched one was confused and consumed everywhere on earth. All his effort came to nothing as far as the chosen are concerned. For this reason, the prophecy adds, *He who trampled the land has failed.** Let us give thanks, dear brothers, to that lamb who, sent forth *from the rock of the desert to the mountain of the daughter of Zion,** rescued the land that the devil had trampled from the beginning of the world in his tyranny. The lamb brought low and trampled him who had trampled his land under his feet, giving to that land *the power to trample snakes and scorpions and all the enemy's power.** For this reason the apostle addressed the believers, saying, *God will quickly crush Satan under your feet.**

*Isa 16:4

*Ps 1:4

*Isa 16:4

*Isa 16:1

*Luke 10:19

*Rom 16:20

22. For the holy fellowship of the chosen is called *land*. This land, of course, is fertile and abundant, bearing fruit that sometimes yields thirtyfold, sometimes sixtyfold, and sometimes even *a hundredfold.** Until the Savior's coming, the ancient enemy crushed this fruit with the feet of his ill-will on account of the guilt

*Matt 13:23

from the first transgression. He exercised the right of wicked rule even in the chosen, until, exceeding the decree on which he depended,* he put his ungodly hands on him who was not bound to him by any obligation of sin, sentencing to death him in whom no cause for death could be found.* The transgressor of the decree usurped what was not his. Thus justice pronounced the sentence so that this highly greedy and unjust overseer should rightly also lose what was his. For this reason, *he who trampled the land has failed.**

23. For the Lord, *wiping out the decree that was against us and nailing it to his cross, led forth principalities and powers, openly triumphing over them in himself.** Thus, after defeating the enemy, *he led captivity captive, receiving gifts among people.** *Because of that,* it says, *God exalted him and gave him the name above every other name,* etc.* From that time, what the prophet added began to be fulfilled: *And a throne will be prepared in mercy, and he will sit on it in truth in David's tabernacle, judging and seeking judgment and swiftly rendering what is just.** *I will sing to you of mercy and judgment, Lord.**

24. *Let us approach,* brothers, *let us approach with confidence the throne* of mercy that he prepared within David's tabernacle, that is, in the church.* *Because now is the time of showing mercy;** the time of judging will follow.† But although what we have said today begins to explain the moral sense, these matters need to be treated more fully. Let us bring this sermon to an end now,* and tomorrow, *God willing,*† we will repeat the same section, bringing to light whatever he himself suggests, to the praise and glory of our Lord Jesus Christ,* who lives and reigns, forever and ever. Amen.

*Col 2:14

*Luke 23:22;
Acts 13:28

*Isa 16:4

*Col 2:14-15

*Eph 4:8; Ps 67:19

*Phil 2:9

*Isa 16:5
*Ps 100:1

*Heb 4:16; 10:22
*Ps 101:14;
2 Cor 6:2
†Jerome, In Isa
5.63; Oner 13.8

*Oner 26.34
†Jas 4:15

*Oner 25.25

Homily 28

1. A clear prophecy concerning the Lord should be neither wrapped up in allegorical layers nor diminished by moral allusions. For nothing nourishes faith or builds up morals more than to read that the holy prophets foretold what we now perceive to be so clearly fulfilled. For what is clearer than to hear the blessed Baptist point out the lamb, of whom we read in the prophet that he would come? The prophet said, *Send forth the lamb, O Lord, the ruler of the land,** whereas the Baptist cried out, *Behold, the lamb of God, who takes away the sins of the world.** The same Baptist says elsewhere of him, *He who has the bride is the bridegroom.**

2. Who is this bride? It is she whom the Father addresses in the psalm: *Listen, daughter, and see, and bend your ear, and forget your people and your father's house.** It is she, then, who now having *God as father,** previously had the devil as a father, she who used to say *to stone: You are my father; and to wood: You begot me.** This is the church gathered from the Gentiles, which, at first begotten by Moab, that is, from the *father the devil,** crossed over *to the adoption of the children of God.*† All Christian souls are his daughters; they are *daughters of Moab* according to nature,§ but daughters of God from grace.

3. Since we said that morally Moab represents the natural corruption that we contract from the father,* we can fittingly say that Moab's daughters are those souls that carnal vices entangle or their suggestions

*Isa 16:1

*John 1:29
*John 3:29

*Ps 44:11
*John 8:41, 44

*Jer 2:27

*John 8:44;
Jerome, In
Isa 6.36
†Rom 8:23;
Eph 1:5
§Isa 16:2

*Oner 24.2, 7; 26.2

and desires wear out. It thus says of Moab's daughters, *As a bird fleeing and the chicks flying from the nest, so will the daughters of Moab be in the passage of Arnon.* *Arnon* means *their illumination.** *Isa 16:2

*Jerome, In Isa 6.40

4. So Moab's daughters must climb from the lower to the higher to be joined in saving marriage to that lamb *who*, sent forth *from the rock of the desert,** takes away *the sins of the world.** After abandoning the darkness of error and ignorance, they must be bathed in saving light and say with the prophet, *The light of your face is imprinted upon us, Lord.** Ascending thus, they are compared to a bird fleeing and chicks flying *from the nest*, because *in vain is the net thrown before the birds' eyes.** This is the flight that the prophet Jeremiah urges upon us, saying, *Take flight from the midst of Babylon.** *Isa 16:1

*John 1:29

*Ps 4:7

*Prov 1:17

*Jer 51:6; Aelred, S 82.3–4

5. But there are different kinds of birds. Just as their natures are diverse, so too do souls resemble them depending on the various states of their habits, life, or nature. For this reason, a certain holy soul, impatient of the darkness it was suffering—this soul had just said, *Fear and trembling came upon me and the darkness covered me**—thought about flying away, saying, *Who will give me wings like a dove's, and I will fly and take rest?** This very person is sometimes compared to a pelican, sometimes to a raven, sometimes to a sparrow, and sometimes to an eagle.** *Ps 54:6

*Ps 54:7

*Pss 101:7-8; 102:5

6. Pay attention, beloved. It often happens that, living amid a crowd, surrounded on all sides by the vices of sinners, the soul both longs for the virtues* and desires to put such longing into action.† It strives to ascend, but habit weighs it down. A *newness of spirit* raises it up,§ but the nearness of sin drags it back. It delights in the peace of the virtues, but the example of evil people entices it to do again what it hates, as though compelled against its will.* Hence it experiences pain if it should fall, fear if it should stand firm, trembling lest it perish in this state, and desire to take flight.* *virtutum affectum concipere

†effectum desidere

§Rom 7:6

*Aelred, S 72.10

*Ps 54:6

7. Darkness occupies the conscience, sadness the heart, and anguish the thoughts. Thus, speaking *in the bitterness of his soul,** the psalmist says, *Who will give me wings like a dove's, and I will fly and take rest?** And he adds, *Behold, fleeing, I have gone far away.** This daughter of *Moab* received what she was looking for. Flying away like a bird, fleeing the crowd, and turning away from the occasions for sin,** she chose hidden places in the desert.** There, mortifying her *members that are on earth,** she became *like a pelican of the desert.**

*Job 10:1
*Ps 54:7
*Ps 54:8

*Isa 16:2
*Ps 54:8
*Col 3:5
*Ps 101:7

8. They say that the pelican has a pale color. It kills its chicks with its beak as soon as they hatch. It then revives them with an extraordinary groan and the shedding of its own blood.** Happy is the soul that, taking up the wings of a dove, has flown to hidden places in the desert to mortify there its *members that are on earth.** Happy is the soul that kills its earlier deeds like its chicks, and then brings them to life again by pain and sweat, as though *with the spilling of blood and unspeakable groans,** and with saving compunction.

*Augustine, In Ps 101.1.8; Isidore, Etym 12.7.26

*Ps 54:7-8; Col 3:5

*Luke 22:44; Heb 9:22; Rom 8:26

9. Then, borrowing heavenly food for itself at the home of the Scriptures, the soul is made a spiritual *raven.** As a raven, it rejoices both at night and during the day, in adverse circumstances as well as prosperous ones, in the joyful and the sad, in temptations and consolations. Flying, it advances *from virtue to virtue** until, transformed into a kind of mystical sparrow* and keeping watch from the darkness of this unhappiness until that *inaccessible light,** it crosses over *to the place of the wonderful tabernacle up to the house of God, with a voice of rejoicing and confession, a sound of one feasting.**

*Ps 101:7; Isidore, Etym 12.7.41

*Ps 83:8
*Pss 101:8; 83:4

*1 Tim 6:16

*Ps 41:5

10. Therefore, the soul entangled in Moabite vices, progressing *from darkness to light* as through the passage of Arnon,** is compared to a bird fleeing and chicks flying *from the nest.*† We should understand *fleeing* here as the conversion of those renouncing the

*1 Pet 2:9; Isa 42:16
†Isa 16:2

world, and *flight* as the contemplation of the perfect ones. For chicks live in the nest and are fed by both their mother and father until their feathers have grown. But after their wings' feathers have grown and become strong, they prefer the free wind to the nest. Seeking sustenance by their own effort, they sometimes climb the heights of heaven in flight, and sometimes they sink down with tucked wings. Now, there is a nest of concupiscence, a nest of idleness and inactivity, and a nest of discipline.

11. There are also birds that try to fly but are unable. They seem to want to support themselves with their wings, but they soon sink down to the lowest places under the flesh's weight.* Such were the quails, which, rising by as much as two feet from the ground, immediately fell like stones upon the earth, satisfying the Israelites' gluttony with the fullness they desired.* These quails are the vices of the flesh and bodily desires, which lift the soul up in a kind of empty joy but thrust the conscience down once wantonness has been fulfilled. These quails are fed in the nest of concupiscence but by no means reach heavenly flight.

*Oner 13:13

*Num 11:31-32;
Ps 77:27-29

12. There are also other birds whom the sweetness of the nest delights so much that even their parents' pecks can scarcely drive them out. Such are those lazy and sluggish souls that are dissipated by a kind of unhappy calm to such an extent that they are equipped for absolutely no works of virtue, not even when rebuked.

13. The dove is not like this, nor the pelican, nor the raven, nor the sparrow.* Neither is the soul that goes to the nest of discipline like this. Such a soul can grow feathers there under a spiritual father and be fed by mother grace with saving food. Thus raised up on the wings of innocence and simplicity, it climbs from the darkness of the vices to the brilliance of the virtues, from the crowd to solitude, through solitude to knowledge, through knowledge to wisdom.*

*Ps 1:4

*Aelred, Spec car
1.5.16

14. Furthermore, our thoughts can be compared to birds, which are carried about, fluttering here and there with an astonishing quickness.* Now they seek what is lofty, now what is lowly, now what is filthy, and now what is clean. For there are birds that busy themselves with corpses and rotting flesh, preferring mud to heaven. Such are the thoughts of those who pursue filth and love wantonness, preferring the desires of the stinking flesh to the delights of the soul. Busied with uncleanness the entire day, they flit from disgrace to disgrace. They restore themselves with the most wicked and polluting feasts of the vices, running through assorted images of wantonness and shame. Wretchedly nourished in the nest of concupiscence, they unhappily receive not the wings with which they could be lifted on high, but those with which they will sink downward.

15. There are other birds that are so inconstant and unsteady that they are nearly always in motion.* They sometimes flit through the wind and sometimes float, but they live nowhere except in the emptiness.* All empty thoughts that are fantasies, desiring this world's honors and glory, and that feed on imagination and pride in this way as though they were wind can be compared to these birds.*

16. Unhappy are those who prepare a nest for these birds in their breasts, so that they cannot stay to Christ's path even if they seem to wish to.* The Lord has condemned them, saying, *Foxes have holes and the birds of heaven have nests, but the Son of Man has nowhere to rest his head.** Blessed above all such people are those who nourish their thoughts in the nest of wisdom. Like an eagle that, borne on the wings of contemplation, flies in the highest heaven, they may thus open their eyes to gaze fixedly on the splendor of the very sun near at hand.*

17. *The daughters of Moab* are the thoughts of the heart that, after natural corruption had allured them

*1 Sam 23:13; Aelred, Spec car 2.14.33

*RB 1.11

*Oner 20.16

*Oner 26.27; Aelred, Spec car 3.40.113

*1 Pet 2:21

*Matt 8:20

*Gregory, Mo 9.XXXII.48; 31.XLVII.94

to the vices,* committed adultery *with many lovers.*† *Jas 1:14
When they then strive to cross over from carnal to †Jer 3:1; Matt 5:28
spiritual love as though *from darkness to light,** they are *1 Pet 2:9; Acts 26:18
compared to a bird fleeing and chicks flying *from the
nest.** This is because they must first flee both the vices *Isa 16:2
and occasions for vice. Thus, growing feathers first in
the nest of discipline and later in the nest of wisdom,
they may climb from the lower to the higher, from the
human to the divine, and from the earthly to the
heavenly.

18. But now, the divine word speaks to the many
people who not only converted from Moabite vanity
and pleasure to the discipline of the Rule but were
also perfected in divine contemplation. The prophet
saw that they would advance the salvation and growth
of many others and so said to them, *Take counsel, gather
an assembly, cast your shadow like night at midday.** It is *Isa 16:3
as if he said, *O Moab,* you who now have become Is-
rael, until now you have rid yourself of former errors
and vices in the nest of discipline and have hidden
yourself in the nest of wisdom among the virtues and
delights of the Scriptures as though *in the hiding place
of* my *face.** Now rise up, go forth, fly, run about, so *Pss 30:21; 88:16
that you who until now have listened may then say,
*Come!** But because you still have less practice in these *Rev 22:17
exterior affairs,* *take counsel,* that is, learn the virtue *Heb 5:14
of discretion, and thus *gather an assembly,* namely,
bring many together to salvation for the benefit of
many. You who took pleasure in the angelic discourse
with Elijah *under the shadow of the juniper,** where all *1 Kgs 19:5
your works were concealed as though it were night,
bring forth *like light your justice and your judgment like
midday,** so that your *light may shine in the presence of* *Ps 36:6
others, that they may see your *good works and glorify* your
*Father who is in heaven.** *Matt 5:16

19. O my brothers, pay careful attention to which
steps one must climb to arrive at pastoral care. You
may thus more easily avoid the common plague of

humanity, namely, the desire to rule. It may be, as they say, that you would rather remain safely below than attempt what is above. First of all, do not *emulate evil-*
*Ps 36:1 *doers,** those who are *fornicators, adulterers, effeminate,*
*1 Cor 6:9-10 *homosexuals,** who shamelessly and irreverently climb
*Gen 49:4 their *father's bed* and stain *his quilt,** changing Christ's marriage chamber into a brothel and trampling his
*Heb 10:29 blood.** They ruin its worth not only in what is vain and harmful but—it is frightful to say—also in payment for dishonor, forgetting all shame. Do not emulate such people, even if they are prosperous in their
*Ps 36:7 ways,** *because they will quickly dry up like hay and will*
*Ps 36:2 *soon fall away like green vegetables.** For the Lord orders the *useless servant* to be thrown out *into the outer dark-*
*Matt 25:30 *ness.** What, then, will he do with the unworthy, the shameless, the unwholesome, with those disgracefully forcing themselves onto Christ's throne? But leaving
*RB 1.13 these things aside,** observe the path that the prophetic word describes to you.

20. First of all, fleeing the world and turning away from every vice, you should make yourself "a stranger
*RB 4.20 to the world's deeds."** Then you should subject your-
*RB 7.34 self "to a superior in all obedience."** You should purge and punish yourself *in hunger and thirst, in vigils* and *labors,* in poverty *and nakedness* for any wrongs
*2 Cor 6:5; 11:27 you remember having committed.** In this way, when habit has taken the place of habit, when the best has taken the place of the worst, you may obtain the wings of the virtues in the nest of discipline. For one can never rule well who has not first learned to be a subject. Therefore, purged of the vices and adorned with the virtues in this way, you may pass on to the investigation of the Scriptures. As you were formed for life, so too may you be illuminated for knowledge. When you learn from the Scriptures to refer everything that lives and perceives to the love of God and neighbor, you will climb the mountain of contemplation borne on two wings, namely, knowledge and love. You will

then learn to form the structure of this earthly tabernacle according to the heavenly one, and you will hear with Moses, *Look, make everything according to the pattern that was shown to you on the mountain.** *Exod 25:40; Heb 8:5

21. The first step, therefore, is conversion; the second, purgation; the third, virtue; the fourth, knowledge; the fifth, contemplation; and the sixth, love. These are perhaps those six steps of Solomon's throne, as Sacred Scripture says, *King Solomon made a throne for himself,* etc.* And so that we may give *occasion for the wise* to become *wiser,** the priestly chair can fittingly be called Solomon's throne. If someone advances to the priestly chair without these steps, he climbs not so much to sit on it as to fall from it. Now I leave it to your meditations to investigate whether the *twelve small lions* could refer to the twelve children of that great lion *from the tribe of Judah**—of which children it says, *The children of the bridegroom cannot fast for as long as the bridegroom is with them**—whether the gold could refer to wisdom;[†] its roundness, to eternity; its back, to the end; its *two arms,* to the double work of love.[§]

*1 Kgs 10:18-20
*Prov 9:9; 1:5

*1 Kgs 10:20; Rev 5:5

*Matt 9:15; Mark 2:19; Aelred, S 75.51
†1 Kgs 10:20; Aelred, S 75.7
§1 Kgs 10:19; Aelred, S 75.9–11

22. It follows, *Hide those who are fleeing and do not betray the wanderers. My refugees will dwell with you, Moab; be their hiding place before the face of the destroyers.** It is Moab thus converted, thus changed, thus purged of its vices, thus adorned with virtues, thus advanced to lofty heights, whom the divine Word addresses, ordering it to do what the prophet had foreseen that it would do with grace's help. For just as Moab had to hide when it fled, so now Moab is worthy of hiding others who take flight. And just as Moab while still a wanderer was not betrayed by those who received it, so too it is rightly told not to reveal to their persecutors the wanderers whom it now receives. Therefore, those fleeing fornication according to the apostle's command* must be hidden. One must be careful lest those who are still wanderers, inconstant at heart* and prone

*Isa 16:3-4

*1 Cor 6:18
*RB 1.11

to the vices, be readily betrayed to wicked teachers or
provokers of the vices.

23. O my brothers, of those who have recently arrived from the world,* some are simple and uneducated,* some are learned and subtle, some are bound
by the wicked habit of vice, some, though sinners, are
strangers to every fault, some are accustomed to pleasure, some have been worn down by a hard way of
life, some are idle, some hardworking, some are of
such a nature that they are scarcely moved to wantonness, some are such that they are tempted by the
slightest occasion, some are hot-tempered, some naturally gentle. Therefore we must consider and carefully
weigh the quality and nature of each person taking
flight from the world.* We should thus foresee what
might prove a greater hindrance to one person and
what to another and, further, which spirit might tempt
one person and which attachment might disturb another. In this way, although a person may be attacked
by vices, demons, or that person's own nature; by corruption, inclination, or habit; or by the company kept,
suggestion, or another's example, a fitting *hiding place*
may be offered to each.*

24. Some must be hidden from every exterior affair,
others from their previous intimacy and shared life.
Some are profitably hidden from anger and displeasure under the shade of silence. Others are beneficially
protected from natural urges under scant nourishment
and poverty. Others are sheltered from a wandering
heart and instability of spirit under the shadow of
work and vigils.* Others are defended from the snares
of unclean spirits by psalms and prayers, by meditation and reading.*

25. It therefore says, *Hide those who are fleeing and do
not betray the wanderers. My refugees will dwell with you,
Moab; be their hiding place before the face of the destroyers.*
Destroyers include the spirit of fornication, the demon
of pride, the inciter of gluttony, the raging of avarice,
the assault of anger, the enervation of sadness, the

Margin notes:
* RB 58.1
* Acts 4:13
* Gregory, Reg past 3.3; Mo 6. XXXVII.57
* Isa 16:4
* Aelred, SS 9.37; 60.28
* Aelred, Spec car 3.33.79
* Isa 16:3-4

plague of envy, and the contempt of ambition. Moab thus offers a wholesome hiding place to those fleeing from destroyers of this sort. In this hiding place, a superior, formerly Moab but afterward Israel, trains each virtue to oppose the corresponding vices that attack that superior's subjects.

26. It follows, *For the dust has come to an end; the wretched one has been consumed*, etc.* Our previous sermon regarding the prince of the demons and the vices explained this verse.* Nothing else needs to be said regarding the moral explanation, except, perhaps, the following: we would like *the dust* to be understood as the sins that we contract from neglect, a wandering heart, or outside affairs.* *The wretched one* represents the sins on which we stumble through the law of this corruptible flesh,* a law that makes us wretched. The one who tramples the land represents crimes and shameful deeds, which trample and crush all humanity, represented by the barren land.* These acts render a person sterile and empty of every spiritual liquid and every fruit's sweetness, like the threshing floor after the threshing.*

27. Therefore this dust will come to an end through a humble way of life. Vigils, fasts, and labor will consume the nearly unendurable ardor of this natural flesh.* The crimes and shameful deeds committed will fail by worthy contrition of heart and confession of mouth and deed. When all this has taken place, Christ's *throne will be prepared in mercy* for those fleeing and hiding in this way.* This is the throne on which Christ sits *in David's tabernacle*,* that is, in the church, which still sojourns in the land, in which *mercy and truth have met; justice and peace have kissed*.* There too he judges and seeks Judgment, judging those who do not judge themselves and seeking our judgment from us, lest we be forced to feel his, because he will *swiftly* render *what is just*,* *giving to all according to their works*,* he who lives and reigns, forever and ever. Amen.

*Isa 16:4

*Oner 27.21–22

*Aelred, S 78.28

*Rom 7:23

*Aelred, S 53.10

*Jer 51:33

*2 Cor 6:5;
Aelred, Ss 69.12;
72.26

*Isa 16:5
*Isa 16:5

*Ps 84:11

*Isa 16:5

*Rev 22:12;
1 Kgs 8:32

Homily 29

1. Up to this point, holy Isaiah has composed his prophecy about those who renounced Moabite wisdom and vanity and chose Christ's *sweet yoke and light*

* Matt 11:30

burden over philosophical pride.* Now he directs his prophetic judgment against those who, blinded by their pride, persevere in the darkness of their errors. He therefore says, *We hear Moab's pride; it is extremely*

* Isa 16:6

*proud.** What is prouder than those philosophers who were not strong enough to climb to what we profess to be divine in Christ as though to heaven, but despised what is claimed of his humanity as something base and earthly? They hung in the wind *between*

* 2 Sam 18:9-10; 1
Cor 10:20
† Rom 1:22
§ 1 Cor 1:24

heaven and earth, companions of the demons.* What is prouder than those who, *calling themselves wise,*† despised the true *Wisdom of God?*§ They were exalted, puffed up, irreligious in their lives, and superstitious in their worship.

2. *Its pride, arrogance, and displeasure are greater than*

* Isa 16:6

*its strength.** The text proposes three qualities: pride, arrogance, and displeasure. Pride is found in the heart, arrogance in speech, and displeasure in deed. Pride begets arrogance, and arrogance, displeasure. Contempt for Christ came forth from pride, blasphemy against Christ from arrogance, argument against Christ from displeasure. What is prouder than Porphyry,[1] who preferred his own wisdom to the

---

[1] Neoplatonic philosopher of the third century.

prophetic and apostolic teaching? What is more arrogant than he who claimed that he would overthrow Christian doctrine with dialectical arguments? What expresses greater displeasure than he who railed against Christian simplicity in his writing, speech, and curses and defamed those whom he could not overthrow?* *Augustine, Civ Dei 19.23

3. Now the philosophers accomplished nothing, because they could do nothing. Those who were among them grew angry. They gnashed their teeth and wasted away;* they lamented and murmured to *Ps 111:10 one another. And this is what follows: *Therefore, Moab will wail at Moab, all will wail.** We have discussed this *Isa 16:7 *wail* thoroughly where we treated what was written: *For this the lightly armed soldiers of Moab will wail, its soul will wail to itself.* All of Moab wails* to all, the *Isa 15:4; wicked against the good, those turned away from God Oner 25.2 against those turned toward him, and the proud against the humble. Or everyone belonging to that wicked fellowship wails to one another, unable to resist the faith and unwilling to follow it. Furthermore, this *wail* could signify the pain that they will undoubtedly endure in the eternal fire.* *Matt 25:41

4. For this reason, the prophet addresses the holy preachers, saying, *To those who rejoice on the walls of fired brick, speak of its wounds.** O my preachers, *speak *Isa 16:7 of the wounds* of Moab; *by chance they* will *see and understand and* be *converted and I* will *heal them.** But speak *Acts 28:27; mainly to those *who rejoice on the walls of fired brick.*† Isa 6:10 *The children of Adam,* who had come down at one time †Isa 16:7 *from the east, laid the foundation of a tower* in the field *of Shinar.* The tower, which reached up to heaven, would protect them from the danger of a flood, if one should by chance take place. But they had *bricks instead of stones, and pitch instead of cement.** Pharaoh also com- *Gen 11:2-5; pelled the children of Israel, whom he weighed down Jerome, In Isa 6.41 with hard slavery, to build cities with brick walls.* But *Exod 1:11, 14; Solomon built the temple from precious stones that Isa 14:3

were cut, polished, smoothed, and joined together in such a way that when they were inserted in the walls one could hear neither a hammer ringing nor an axe falling.*

5. Now, turn your eyes, beloved, to those living stones that our *Solomon's masons,** namely, the doctors and shepherds of the church, work in the courtyard of the heavenly Jerusalem.* They beat these stones with corrections, cut them with lashes, grind them with doctrine, shape them to themselves with faith and morals, and make them square with the virtues. In this way, after crossing over from the depths to the heights, they may be inserted in those sacred walls of which holy David sang, *Holy is your temple, wonderful in its symmetry.** These builders take delight in stones of this sort, and they rejoice greatly in the progress of those who they see are to be inserted in heaven.

6. The teachers of error withdraw *from* the true *east* and raise up a *tower* of pride in Shinar's field.* Shinar means *their stench,** as though it were that broad way *that leads to death,** in which lust gives forth its stench. The teachers of error look for *bricks* that are made from soft mud and are hardened by fire.* These bricks have the likeness of stones, but they know nothing of their virtue.* Such are the muddy hearts of the carnal, which the habit of sinning and stubbornness of mind harden, allowing them to fend off the sharp arrows with which Christ's soldiers are armed to conquer the Moabite cities.

7. It was from these bricks that Pharaoh built cities, and he forced the children of Israel, whom he had reduced to slavery, to labor in clay and straw.* From these bricks, too, the wise of this world and the advocates of wicked teaching raised a wall against Christ's church,* creating for themselves disciples who would both stubbornly defend error and subtly ward off objections. Therefore, those who raise up this wall *of fired brick* rejoice on it. It is best that the holy preachers tell

*1 Kgs 6:7; 7:9;
Jerome, In Isa 6.41

*1 Kgs 5:17-18;
1 Pet 2:5

*Ps 121:2;
Heb 12:22

*Ps 54:5-6

*Gen 11:2, 4
*Jerome, Nom 10
*Matt 7:13;
Prov 12:28
*Gen 11:3

*2 Tim 3:5

*Exod 1:11, 14;
Wis 19:13; Jdt 5:10

*1 Cor 1:20

them of this wall's downfall *and wounds*, so that fear may correct those whom too much safety imperils.

8. Therefore, the prophet said, *To those who rejoice on the walls of fired brick, speak of its wounds, because Heshbon's suburbs will be abandoned and Sibmah's vineyard.** *Heshbon* means *thoughts.** So it seems to me that Heshbon represents the sect of philosophers, which was founded with great eagerness and anxious thoughts. Coming together in this sect by common agreement, many constructed a city, as it were, that was fortified with dialectical arguments like towers and walls against those understanding differently. Each sect then created its own school like the cities' suburbs. Many disciples devoted themselves to these suburbs and extended out like vineyards.

*Isa 16:7-8

*Jerome, In Isa 6.41

9. But *from Sodom's vineyard is their vineyard, and from Gomorrah's suburbs. Their grapes are grapes of gall and their clusters are very bitter. Dragons' gall is their wine,** which, pressed from their errors as from the worst of grapes, made many mortal hearts drunk and deprived them of all sense. *Sibmah's vineyard* is fittingly spoken of.* *Sibmah* means *raising on high,*† expressing that puffed-up knowledge of which the apostle says, *Knowledge puffs up.*§ For they raised up this knowledge *against the knowledge of God,** but God *chose the weak things of the world to confound the strong, and God chose the foolish things of the world to confound the wise.**

*Deut 32:32-33; Jerome, In Isa 6.42

*Isa 16:8
†Jerome, In Isa 6.41
§1 Cor 8:1
*2 Cor 10:5

*1 Cor 1:27

10. *The lords of the nations* are those who cut down the shoots of the wicked vineyards, as it follows, *The lords of the nations cut off its shoots.** These are the lords of the nations whom the prophet saw and, astonished at their rule, said, *To me your friends are greatly honored, God, their rule has been greatly strengthened.** These lords made deserts of the philosophers' school, they destroyed the sects, and they cut down their disciples with the sword of God's word as though they were shoots of that vineyard.* What is more remarkable, *they arrived as far as Jazer,** which means *their*

*Isa 16:8

*Ps 138:17; Resp In comm Apost (Hesbert 4.7216–17)

*Eph 6:17
*Isa 16:8

*Jerome, In
Isa 6.42

*strength.** For because *the world did not know God through wisdom, it pleased God to save those believing through the foolishness of the preaching. Because while the Jews look for signs and the Greeks demand wisdom, we preach Christ crucified, a stumbling block to the Jews and* *1 Cor 1:21-23   *foolishness to the gentiles.**

*Pref Mass   **11.** *Let us,* therefore, *give thanks to the Lord our God,** brothers, who by *the word of the cross,* which *is foolish-* *1 Cor 1:18   *ness to those who are perishing,** *made the wisdom of this* *1 Cor 1:20   *world foolish.** He overthrew every wicked doctrine and power of argumentation, which was the world's greatest strength, by the simplicity of the Christian faith. Where is that famous academy of which the Socratics and Platonists boasted as though it were the very source of divine wisdom? Where are those peripatetic sects, where are the Epicurean teachings, where are the judgments of the Stoics, once accepted by so many? They are all despised, abandoned, blown away, and the entire world flocks to the simple teaching of *1 Cor 1:23;   fishermen and the foolishness of the cross.*
Aelred, SS 15.4;
71.3   **12.** It follows, *They wandered in the desert.*† I think this
†Isa 16:8   phrase refers to the vineyard's shoots, namely, to the disciples of error. Seeing that worldly wisdom had everywhere been abandoned, they reviewed the philosophers' various sects in their thoughts and minds as though they were wandering through a remote area. They did not know which sects they should abandon, which they should retain, and which they should defend.

                 13. But *the lords of the nations,* as is later shown,
*Isa 16:8   *crossed the sea.** This is because, crossing over not only
*Acts 18:6; Luke to the wise of this world, but also *to all the nations,**
24:47 and   which are represented by the word *sea,* they subjected
parallels; Rev
17:15; Ezek 26:3 them to Christ's yoke and the Gospel's teaching.† For
†Matt 11:29   *they* went down *to the sea in ships,* and *doing work on the great waters,* that is, performing miracles among
*Ps 106:23-24;   the Gentile peoples, *they saw God's works*—namely,
Augustine, In   what a *change in the right hand of the Most High* would
Ps 106.12

take place in the conversion of the nations*—*and his wondrous acts in the deep,* in these dark human hearts.† For Christ's grace inwardly supplies an increase for those outwardly planting and watering.§

14. O dear brothers, many saints perceived that such a great subtlety of character and liveliness of perception in human and divine matters would be lost. By what great tenderness were they moved, by what compassion did they melt, by what mercy were they touched, and how many tears did they spill for them! Who could doubt that the Holy Spirit worked this feeling in the saints. This is what the Holy Spirit describes in detail through holy Isaiah, saying, *For this I will weep with the tears of Jazer.** *We do not know,* says Paul, *what to pray for as we should, but the Spirit himself intercedes for us with unspeakable groaning.** Therefore, it is said that the Holy Spirit weeps for *Jazer,* that is, for the power and strength of worldly knowledge, and for *Sibmah's vineyard,* namely, for the crowd of wanderers. For he makes the saints groan and weep* from desire for their salvation, or from pain at their loss, although the prophet could have also said this for himself or on behalf of the saints.

15. For this reason it follows, *I will make you drunk with my tear, Heshbon and Elealeh.** He said *tear,* that is, *tears,* using the singular instead of the plural, as in the psalm, *He spoke, and the locust and grasshopper came.** Therefore, those who converted from error and vices by the saints' mourning and prayers become drunk on their wailing, weeping, and tears. By a kind of wholesome delirium of mind, forgetting the things *that are behind* and stretching themselves forth *to what is before* them,* they cease to be what they were and begin to be what they were not. This spiritual drunkenness takes place in the thoughts, by which the mind climbs from the lower to the higher and from the vices to the virtues by a kind of intoxication of spirit. For *Heshbon* means thoughts, and *Elealeh* means *ascent.**

*Ps 76:11

†Ps 106:23-24; Augustine, In Ps 106.12; Jerome, In Isa 6.42

§1 Cor 3:6

*Isa 16:9

*Rom 8:26, 34

*Ant Salve Regina

*Isa 16:9

*Ps 104:34

*Phil 3:13

*Jerome, In Isa 6.39, 42

16. For we climb up and down in our thoughts. We climb down from memory to imagination, from imagination to pleasure, from pleasure to consent, and from consent to action. At which point, when the mind has subjected itself to a bad habit, it is clouded and shaken as though drunk, and all its integrity is lost.* But if the Spirit has first made our thoughts holy, and the soul has conceived the fear of God by the Spirit's holy inspiration, as though from a kind of spiritual infusion of seed, then it goes up from there to devotion,* from devotion to knowledge, from knowledge to strength, from there to judgment,* and thus to understanding.† At last, reaching wisdom, it grows drunk *from the abundance of* God's *house and* is intoxicated *from the river of* his *delight.**

17. What follows shows from where this drunkenness arises: *Because the voice of the treaders has broken out over your vintage and over your harvest.** *Vintage* and *harvest* have the same meaning. You have the Lord saying to his disciples in the gospel, *The harvest is indeed great, but the laborers are few. Therefore, ask the lord of the harvest to send laborers to his harvest.** *The voice* of these laborers broke out *over* the *vintage and over* the *harvest* of Moab when the apostolic and evangelical preaching gathered many disciples from the followers of worldly wisdom.* These disciples are the spiritual grapes that *the lords of the nations,** namely, the holy apostles, gathered from the vineyard to be crushed in the winepress of the passion. Or else they are the crops gathered from the field to be threshed on the threshing floor of persecution and stripped from the chaff of their bodies.

18. They are called *treaders,* of course, on account of that special power to trample of which the Lord spoke in the gospel, saying, *Behold, I have given you the power to trample snakes and scorpions.** For this reason, the prophet says to a certain holy and perfect person, *You will walk on the asp and the basilisk, and you will trample*

*Ps 106:27

*pietas

*consilium
†*intellectus;*
Isa 11:2-3

*Ps 35:9

*Isa 16:9

*Luke 10:2

*Isa 16:9
*Isa 16:8

*Luke 10:19

the lion and the dragon.* One can also say that they are
called *treaders* because they make those whom they
convert to the faith humble and patient. This is so to
such an extent that their converts calmly endure this
world's lovers' trampling them, casting them down,
tormenting them, and mocking them. By the prayers
and tears of these converts, God's Spirit often visits
and pricks the teachers of error, those who *rejoice on
the walls of fired brick,** who then grow drunk on a kind
of saving ecstasy of the soul. Or breaking down in
tears on account of the loss of so many companions,
they are thrown into a kind of frenzy by their unbearable sadness and by their great pain.

19. It follows, *And joy and exultation will be taken from
Carmel.** Carmel is a mountain and is translated as
circumcision.* Now, there is a physical circumcision, a
sensory circumcision, and a spiritual circumcision.
The physical circumcision belongs to the Jews, the
sensory circumcision to philosophers or heretics, and
the spiritual circumcision to Christians. One member
of the body was made clean for the Jews; the philosophers boast of being clean in all their senses; Christians are cleansed *from every defilement of flesh and
spirit.**

20. The circumcision of the philosophers, whose
wondrous abstinence and public continence serve
worldly vanity, is compared to a mountain on account
of their proud minds. For they did everything to be
seen by others.* Now they enjoyed their continence
in two ways: pleasing themselves inwardly,* they
boasted in themselves and not in God,* and striving
for the praise of others outwardly, they delighted in
their esteem. But after the preaching of Christ's disciples, *joy and exultation* were taken from *Carmel,** because all their superstition began to be despised. For
that reason their outer joy, having nothing to support
it, vanished, and their inner exultation, deprived of
its desired fruit, faded.

*Ps 90:13

*Isa 16:7

*Isa 16:10
*Jerome, In
Isa 6.42

*2 Cor 7:1

*Matt 23:5
*2 Pet 2:10
*1 Cor 1:31 and
parallels

*Isa 16:10

21. *And they will neither exult nor shout in the vineyards.** The same meaning is repeated, except that it says that their exultation or shout mainly rang out *in the vineyards.* For in the crowd of their disciples, they argued brilliantly about contempt for the world, the shame of pleasure, and punishment of the body. Their pride swelled while they argued, and with an inner shout of joy and outer arrogance, they took delight in their listeners who looked on and praised what they said. All of this was taken away when the Gospel's trumpets blared.* It therefore says of Moab, *And they will neither exult nor shout in the vineyards.*†

22. And it added, *Those who were accustomed to treading will not tread the wine in the press.** For those who were from Moab had toiled in the winepress of their own wisdom so that the wine of faithlessness might be pressed out from their listeners, of whom it was written, *Their wine is dragon's gall and incurable asps' venom.** But they no longer work in that vineyard, which the householder took from the wicked teachers and entrusted to the best farmers *so that they would render him fruit in due season.**

23. *I have taken away the voice of the treaders.** The metaphor continues. When the abundance of produce or grapes is favorable, the gatherers, treaders, or harvesters often gesture and sing with great gladness. They express their inner joy through their voices, by clapping, leaping, and moving their limbs.* But when the vineyard is cut down, snatched by enemies, hailed upon or burned by lightning, or when the field is laid waste, rarely do any harvesters or gatherers show themselves. Finding scarcely anything to gather, they sadly and silently go on their way with bowed heads and gloomy faces.*

24. So it is then that the teachers of error with their disciples gathered around them would boast of their great number as of a barren vineyard. Cheeks rattling and gesticulating with great vanity, they demanded

*Isa 16:10

*Leo the Great, Tract 27.1
†Isa 16:10

*Isa 16:10

*Deut 32:33; Jerome, In Isa 6.42

*Matt 21:33, 41
*Isa 16:10

*Augustine, In Ps 99.4

*1 Kgs 21:27; Job 30:28

faith in what they said as though they were squeezing the wine of treachery from unripe grapes. But after the apostles and their successors preached the Gospel of God, the teachers of error both mourned in pain and fell silent for shame, since they never or rarely had a listener.

25. *Let us give thanks,* brothers, *to the Lord our God,** who *made the wisdom of this world foolish* and emptied out the prudence and subtlety of philosophers with the simplicity of fishermen,* *so that all who boast should boast in the Lord,*† *to whom is the honor and glory,* forever and ever. Amen.§

*Pref Mass

*1 Cor 1:20; Matt 10:16; 11:25 and parallels; Acts 4:13

†1 Cor 1:31

§Rom 16:27

Homily 30

1. O brothers, today we will repeat with a moral explanation what we discussed yesterday allegorically. The prophecy spoke of those who, turned from the vices to Christ, advance *to a perfect man.** Saying how much comfort such people give to others who turn away from a similar vanity, the prophet says, *My refugees will dwell with you, Moab; be their hiding place before the face of the destroyers.** And behold, with a fine reproach, he then mocks the presumption of the many who show pride for the grace bestowed upon them. *Not knowing the justice of God,** they boast in themselves rather than *in the Lord,** arrogantly putting their virtues on display. The prophet says of them, *We hear Moab's pride; it is extremely proud.**

2. May we not be found, brothers, like those who daily break forth in Elihu's words.* Whatever they seem to have acquired in virtue, they waste by bandying it about! They promise great things, everything they propose is bold, they walk *in great and wonderful things above* themselves,* declaring with a proud mouth that no labor is too much for them, nothing in the Scriptures too obscure, and no deed too difficult. The prophet added of such people, Moab's *pride, arrogance, and displeasure are greater than its strength.** Very well said. The deeds of the arrogant do not match their words. Neither does a kind of *strength* in good works result from their presumption of spirit, by which they inwardly swell,* nor from their *pompous tongue,* by

*Eph 4:13

*Isa 16:4

*Rom 10:3
*1 Cor 1:31 and parallels

*Isa 16:6

*Job 32:10

*Ps 130:1

*Isa 16:6

*Eccl 6:9

298

which they praise themselves outwardly,* nor from
their pride, in which they claim to have transcended
everyone, scorning others as inferior to themselves. *Ps 11:4

3. *Therefore, Moab will wail at Moab.** Behold, you
have Moab, and then Moab. Moab to whom it is said,
*My refugees will dwell with you, Moab,** and Moab of
whom it is said, *We hear Moab's pride.** The first is
humble, the other is proud. The first presumes something of itself; the other offers everything it is to God.
The first scatters its works on the wind of vanity; the
second conceals its good works in the storehouse of
its conscience. The first does everything to be seen by
others;* the second, to be pleasing to the gaze of God
alone. The first Moab, then, wails to the second, when,
engulfed in all sorts of filth because of the vice of
pride, it confesses its error to the latter with sadness.
The second wails to the first when, mourning the first
Moab's downfall, it provokes it to repentance by its
groans and warnings. Thus, *all Moab* wails,* the good
and the bad, the humble and the proud, those turned
toward God and those turned away from him.

*Isa 16:7
*Isa 16:4
*Isa 16:6
*Matt 23:5
*Isa 16:7

4. Therefore, brothers, we should not immediately
praise the way of life of those whose intention is unknown, because *if the eye is wicked, the entire body will
be dark.** For this reason, the holy prophet restrains the
joy of those who indiscreetly extol certain arrogant
people, believing everything to be true that such
people claim for themselves. The prophet orders those
who discern these things more sensibly to alert the
others to how much evil these arrogant ones will suffer, saying, *To those who rejoice on the walls of fired brick,
speak of its wounds.** *Matt 6:23

*Isa 16:7

5. The wall *of fired brick* refers to the inner state of
those who are proud and arrogant.* This interior condition does not rest firmly on a stable foundation of
*square stones,** that is, of true virtues, but on a foundation made from the mud of base intention and from
false and hypocritical virtues. Hardened in the fire of

*Rom 7:22;
Eph 3:16
*Isa 9:10

cupidity, such people *indeed* display an *appearance of*
*2 Tim 3:5   *goodness** but do not know *its power*. Gold is mud, sil-
Wis 7:9   ver is mud, the fulfillment of any desire is mud, one
Hab 2:6   person's opinion of another is mud. Just so, every
thought concerned with such things is muddy; every
intention that stretches forth to these things is muddy.

6. Yet those who are arrogant form thoughts in their
hearts from all of this. They heap up images of honors,
pleasures, and riches. When they give their will and
intention over to these images, they do *all their works*
*Matt 23:5   to be seen *by others.** They cook and harden the appearance of the virtues in the fire of their desires, and
they strive to get what they want by this appearance.
In this way, hard and rough tasks seem quite easy to
RB 58.8   them because of their wicked goal. People such as
this become more willing for vigils than others, more
ready for manual labor, and more zealous in fasting,
with a more austere countenance and more sober
speech. They look down on the weak, they disparage
the simple, and they speak such great and firm things
that those who practice these disciplines less fre-
Heb 5:14   quently regard them as holier. These admirers are the
*Isa 16:7   ones *who rejoice on the walls of fired brick,** to whom the
wounds of Moab must be announced. But now, let us
hear of these *wounds*.

7. *Because Heshbon's suburbs will be abandoned and*
*Isa 16:8   *Sibmah's vineyard.** *Heshbon* means *thoughts,* while
*Jerome, In   *Sibmah* means *raising on high.** These are the thoughts
Isa 6.41   that compose that muddy wall, in which the images
of countless affections are heaped up. The intention
formed from these thoughts or feelings is like a city;
the virtues and works that arise from this intention are
like suburbs. These virtues and works will lose even
the appearance of goodness in which they seemed en-
veloped after the proud person abandons God's help
2 Tim 3:5   and protection. For often when the proud, disappointed in their hope, can fulfill their cupidity, they are
unable to restrain themselves further and burst forth

in open wickedness. They suffer that with which the Lord threatened such a soul through another prophet: *Behold, I will strip you, and your shame will be known.** Therefore, *Heshbon's suburbs will be abandoned* and *Sibmah's vineyard,* too, will be abandoned.*

8. We read of many vineyards in Sacred Scripture, and also of many kinds of wine. For there is the wine of love, on which holy Noah got drunk, hiding what was strong and laying bare what was weak as a type of our Lord and Savior. He is mocked while he sleeps, but when he awakes he will avenge the wrong done to him.* There is the wine of rejoicing on which Lot got drunk; surreptitious incest stained him because of this wine after he had escaped the Sodomite destruction.† There is further the wine of *saving wisdom,*§ on which Joseph's brothers got drunk at midday.‡ Squeezed from the vineyard of Scripture, this wine *makes glad the* entire *city of God.*#

9. You also have the wine of bitterness, of which Jeremiah said, *My enemy made me drunk with bitterness.** Furthermore, Scripture is not silent about the wine of lust, of which Moses said, *From Sodom's vineyard is their wine,* etc.* Additionally, the psalmist mentions the wine of compunction, saying, *You showed your people hard things, you gave us the wine of compunction to drink.** Finally, there is the wine of the evangelical and apostolic teaching, *the new wine,** which, coming down from the heavenly storeroom into the apostles' hearts, begets virgins throughout the entire world* and makes the hearts of the faithful drunk with the desire for perfection.

10. The proud and arrogant approach the vineyard of the Scriptures and take from it the plants of various opinions, placing them in the fields of their hearts. Tilling there with many meditations, they create for themselves a vineyard of a kind of puffed-up knowledge.* They press a wine of doctrine for themselves from this knowledge, and from this wine they seek to

*Jer 13:26;
Ezek 16:37

*Isa 16:8

*Gen 9:21-25;
Bede, In Gen
2.9.20–21;
Augustine, C
Faust Manich
12.23
†Gen 19:32-35
§Sir 15:3
‡Gen 43:25, 34
#Ps 45:5

*Lam 3:15; Ant
Replevit 5 HM
(Hesbert 3.4616)

*Deut 32:32

*Ps 59:5

*Luke 5:38 and
parallels

*Zech 9:17

*1 Cor 8:1

*Job 32:10;
Prov 29:11

*Jerome, In
Isa 6.42
†Rom 11:20
§Job 9:18

*Job 32:19

*Wis 6:13

*Isa 16:8

*Dan 10:20
*Acts 19:12

*Isa 16:8

*Isa 16:8
*Jerome, In
Isa 6.42
†Acts 19:15

make public their own spirit and show their wisdom.* Not wrongly, then, is this vineyard called *Sibmah's vineyard*, that is, *raising on high*.* For if such people taste something elevated,† their spirit does not rest until it becomes known.§ They seem to proclaim in their manner of speaking, their pride, and the winks of their eyes, *My belly is like a recent wine without air, which splits the new wineskins.** But this vineyard is abandoned when the proud, having none of the fruit that they expected from their knowledge, grow bored with their works and set aside their studies. Thus, all their doctrine wilts.*

11. It follows, *The lords of the nations cut off its shoots.** We read that the princes of the nations are the opposing powers, as were the prince of the Persian kingdom and the prince of the Greek kingdom in Daniel.* The wicked spirits* are said to be lords or princes of those nations, perhaps because of the vices with which they especially took pleasure in staining them by their suggestions. Perhaps it was thus too for other nations. Perhaps their spirits boasted that they were the lords and princes of such nations before they received faith in our Lord and Savior, for example, the Goths, the Gauls, or the Germanic peoples. Such princes or lords of the nations *cut off* the *shoots* of *Sibmah's* vineyard,* namely, the branches from which clusters come forth. This happened when wicked spirits used the sickle of suggestions and unclean thoughts to cut out the meditations with which the arrogant would press the wine of doctrine from the vineyard of the knowledge of Scripture.

12. But because good feelings or wicked thoughts and what follows from them sometimes disturb even faith itself, in which the strength of all the virtues resides, it rightly follows, *They arrived as far as Jazer.** For *Jazer* means *their strength.** For when a wicked spirit takes a soul captive,† it first cuts out all the virtues, and thus, sowing vices, it strives to topple even faith itself.

13. It continues, *They wandered in the desert.** Where   *Isa 16:8
there used to be a city and suburbs, where there used
to be a vineyard, where Jazer used to be, there was
then a desert, a place empty of all virtues, a place
without a drop of charity.* Someone walking   *Oner 25.14
through a desert without vineyards, fields, houses,
or walls to stand in the way can wander here and
there with unfettered steps.* Such is the case for wan-   *Judg 15:5;
dering spirits in the soul in which the spiritual   1 Sam 23:13
vineyard has been cut down, the virtues cut off, and
faith itself put to confusion. The spirits walk safely
without resistance as though in a desert. They cast
the soul down, drunk and staggering, into all sorts of
errors. Therefore, it is rightly said of the princes or
lords of the nations who cut down the shoots of the
vineyards and arrived *as far as Jazer, They wandered in
the desert.**   *Isa 16:8

14. And it follows, *Its slips were abandoned.** Continu-   *Isa 16:8
ing the metaphor of the vineyard, the prophecy asserts
that not only was it reduced to a desert* but also that   *Jer 50:13;
its slips, which can be moved and transplanted else-   Ezek 35:14
where, were left behind. We said that proud people
create for themselves a kind of knowledge in the vineyard of the mind from various scriptural verses. If the
temptation of wicked spirits cuts away such knowledge, even *its slips*—the judgments and meditations
with which the vineyard itself could have been prepared again—perish, abandoned by God's grace.

15. *They crossed over the sea.** The sea represents the   *Isa 16:8
bitterness of repentance. Now it happens that, after
displaying the appearance of holiness,* those who fall   *2 Tim 3:5
into the abyss of disgrace at first grow sad, weep, become alarmed, judge and condemn themselves, rise
up against themselves, swear and decide *to keep the
judgments of God's justice,** and vow and bear witness   *Ps 118:106
never to repeat such deeds. But *drawn by concupiscence,**   *Jas 1:14
thwarted by error, or crushed by the power of diabolic
temptation, they then repeat the wicked act. They thus

make their desire for pleasure stronger, their longing for the good is reduced, and, by adding their fuel, the fire of ill-will grows. Finally, conquered by habit, they fall into the abyss of hopelessness and are thus carried headlong to death, so that no prick of fear, confusion of shame, or bitterness of mind can call them back from the disgrace of their scandals.* Therefore, con-cerning the thoughts and desires of people of this sort, it is rightly said, *They crossed over the sea.**

16. And the prophet adds, *For this I will weep with the tears of Jazer for the vineyard of Sibmah.** It is Christ's voice that speaks through Isaiah. It is he who, *seeing the city* of Jerusalem, *wept over it, saying, If you too had only known! Because the days will come to you and they will squeeze you from all sides and cast you down to the ground,* etc.* The prophet agrees with the evangelist. For Jesus saw the city abounding in honors, overflow-ing with riches, reveling in pleasures, puffed up by pride, and undone by joy. Foreseeing its coming di-saster, he weeps over those laughing, mourns over those rejoicing, and groans over those who do not know what will happen to them. The prophet, too, sees the soul that raises itself up in its own virtues. Both he and the other holy souls to whom God's Spirit often reveals these things compassionately weep when they see what a terrible fall of morals such a soul will suffer. After he counted up the wounds of the vices that would be inflicted on them,* he said, *For this I will weep with the tears of Jazer for the vineyard of Sibmah.**

17. The prophet weeps over two things: *Jazer* and *the vineyard of Sibmah.* He already said that *Sibmah's vineyard* would become a desert, and that the lords of the nations had cut off *its shoots* and arrived *as far as Jazer.** We have already said enough about this above. This is what causes the prophet's groaning, of which it says, *For this I will weep with tears for Jazer, for the*

*Aelred, SS 43.15–16; 72.10, 16

*Isa 16:8

*Isa 16:9

*Luke 19:41-44

*Isa 16:7-8

*Isa 16:9

*Isa 16:8

vineyard of Sibmah.[1]* He wept for Jazer, that is, for the great strength with which the soul withstood the world, itself, and the demon. Although it stood higher than other souls in human judgment, it perished by the one vice of pride. The prophet also wept for Sibmah's vineyard, that is, for the doctrine that could have helped many if it could have been preserved in the shade of humility. But it withered, cut off by the hoe of arrogance and reduced to a desert.*

18. It follows, *I will make you drunk with my tear, Heshbon and Elealeh.** Severe pain multiplies tears, not leaving unmourned anything that could be lamented. *I will make you drunk,* he says, *with my tear, Heshbon and Elealeh.** The person who suffers, weeps, and mourns makes others drunk. For if those who have fallen into forbidden acts because of the sickness of pride should see certain saints who, hating their wicked deeds and moved with pity, tenderly* lament their ruin, these sinners too may repent for their past deeds and return to themselves. Drunk on the wine of compunction,* they may embrace bitterness instead of pleasure, labor instead of rest, and tears instead of laughter.

19. Thus, drunk on charity, conscious of the storehouses of kindness and mercy that lay hidden in Christ's breast, he* chases those who have fallen from disciples to thieves, from Christians to robbers to wicked murderers after encountering the hidden mysteries of the church. He chases them all the way to the hidden places of the desert. He then restores these sinners, drunk on repentance, to the members of Christ from whom they had been cast out. Therefore the prophet addresses Heshbon and Elealeh, that is, the thought and pride of any wicked person.* Just as

*Isa 16:9

*Jer 50:13;
Ezek 35:14

*Isa 16:9

*Isa 16:9

pietatis affectu

*Ps 59:5

*Isaiah or
another speaker
of Isa 16:9

*Jerome, In
Isa 6.42

---

[1] The Vulgate text of Isa 16:9 can be translated "I will weep with the tears of Jazer" or "I will weep with tears for Jazer," depending on the context.

he had grown drunk on charity for their loss, so too should they grow drunk on compunction.

20. Then, having described the cause of his sadness, he added, *Because the voice of the treaders has broken out over your vintage and over your harvest.** The fruit of the year's labor is reaped during the harvest and grape-gathering seasons. Wicked spirits are called *treaders,** which, shouting, overtake and attack the soul that, deluded by vanity, does all things in pride and hypocrisy. Just when such a soul believes that it will receive the fruit of its work, these wicked spirits wrench it away to satiate their cruelty. This was the wine that the holy angels were supposed to bring to the heavenly kingdom because of its apparent virtues.

*Isa 16:9

*Acts 19:12

21. *And joy and exultation will be taken from Carmel.** Carmel represents circumcision,* and circumcision, continence. Now those who feed on the esteem of others normally are eager to preserve their chastity above all else. But pain and sadness will take the place of exultation and joy at the harvest and grape-gathering seasons, when they see that it was all without merit because of their twisted intention.

*Isa 16:10

*Jerome, In Isa 6.42

22. It therefore follows, *And they will neither exult nor shout in the vineyards.** Who? Moab, of course, who used to exult inwardly and shout outwardly in the vineyards of knowledge, with which we dealt sufficiently above.

*Isa 16:10

23. And the prophet adds, *Those who were accustomed to treading will not tread the wine in the press. I have taken away the voice of the treaders.** Here the treaders, who would press wine from this vineyard's grapes, represent those who were accustomed to taking something from the knowledge of the arrogant for themselves. They used to boast in this knowledge with their teachers and had, as it were, a sweet song to sing.* And so, after such teachers pass away, the prophet threatens that all their joys will be condemned to eternal silence.*

*Isa 16:10

*Jer 48:33; Jerome, In Isa 5.71

*Jerome, In Isa 6.42

24. We have touched on these matters briefly, brothers, so that everything that we explained yesterday allegorically or prophetically in one sermon, we might also make clear morally in one sermon. Let us now restore our faculties in silence. Let us discuss the little that remains to be explored of the burden of Moab tomorrow, to the praise and glory of our Lord Jesus Christ, who lives and reigns with the Father and the Holy Spirit, forever and ever. Amen.

Homily 31

1. We have covered the burden of Moab, brothers, up to the harp, to which holy Isaiah, or *Christ speaking in him*,* believed his belly should be compared: *On this account*, he said, *my belly will sound forth to Moab like a harp.** The beginning of this sermon should be seen as a continuation of the one from the day before yesterday concerning the prophecy of future events. We said that every joy was taken away from the wise of the world,* who are expressed prophetically through Moab, on account of the conversion of many after Christ's gospel shone forth.* And now, *On this account*, he says, *my belly will sound forth to Moab like a harp.** This is the voice of the prophet, or of Christ speaking in the prophet. *On account of this*, he said—on account of what I said concerning Moab, its conversion, sinking down, or damnation—*On account of this*, he said, *my belly will sound forth to Moab like a harp.**

2. We can call the holy church Christ's belly. For the belly contains the interior organs. There the heart provides a living impulse for the entire body, there the liver feeds the body's heat and distributes life-giving blood to all the limbs, there reside the other interior organs, each with its appointed function for the body's nourishment. So it is in the church, where the Lord has appointed *some apostles, some prophets, some pastors and teachers in the work of ministry, in building up the body of Christ.**

*2 Cor 13:3

*Isa 16:11

*see 1 Cor 1:20; Isa 16:10

*Oner 29.20-24

*Isa 16:11

*Isa 16:11

*Eph 4:11-12

308

3. There are also many strings on the harp, each with its own sound. Yet all are arranged by certain proportions and calculations in such a way that all agree in one harmony, and one beautiful tone arises from them all. So too in Christ's church there are various ranks and various orders, each with diverse gifts of virtues.* Yet all are founded in one charity.† Through charity, they compose one beautiful tone by bringing together many virtues.

4. We can also understand God's belly to be Sacred Scripture, which contains his secrets as a belly contains organs. There various opinions and precepts, agreeing in the one root of faith, send forth a kind of sweet melody to both the hearts and the ears of the faithful.

5. Therefore it says, *On this account, my belly will sound forth to Moab like a harp.** On account of everything spoken against Moab, that is, against the wise of the world,* the holy church sent out the most beautiful and harmonious sound of preaching in various ways: now teaching, now admonishing, now rebuking, now coaxing, now conquering with robust reasons all the arguments of the dialectical art, namely, the support of the philosophical discipline, like a wall of fired brick.

6. When it says, *And my inner organs to a wall of fired brick,** the same meaning is repeated. Yet because we explained above that Moab could be spoken of in two ways,* according to the conversion of some and the turning away of others, this verse seems to explain which Moab is being talked about: the one that hardened itself like a wall against the preachers' voices. Therefore it says, *My inner organs will sound forth to a wall of fired brick.**

7. Further, every holy person has a spiritual belly. Thus Jeremiah said, *My abdomen, my abdomen aches, my heart's perceptions are troubled.** Just as the belly's contents are locked up in a prison from everyone's

*Rom 12:6; 1 Cor 7:7
†Eph 3:17

*Isa 16:11

*1 Cor 1:20

*Isa 16:11

*Oner 25.2, 19

*Isa 16:11

*Jer 4:19

eyes and concealed from everyone's knowledge, so *no one knows what is worked in a person except for* that person's conscience *that is within.** Happy the soul in which all things have been arranged and ordered like the strings of a harp, in which the virtues agree with one another and the inner corresponds to the outer.

*1 Cor 2:11; Augustine, Conf 10.3.3; Aelred, Spec car 1.34.113; Aelred, S 52.3

8. Virtues are like spiritual strings, which, stretched between two pieces of wood, the upper and the lower, represent the mystery of the cross. The first string of all is temperance, through which people, putting to death their *members that are on earth,** crucify them all with Christ.* This string is fixed to the bottom of the cross. Originating from fear, it sends forth a deep sound of compunction and confession. The second string, justice, is at the top of the cross. Rendering to all what pertains to them, it breaks forth in a high pitch of charity.* The string of prudence, as though on the transverse board of the cross, takes its place between the other two. There it moderates the fineness of the one string and the deep tone of the other with its sweet sound of discretion. The fourth string, fortitude, embraces the length of the cross, lending a sustaining power to the others and sending forth a pleasing sound of patience. Indeed, the strings of many other virtues come from the side to accompany these, and they bring together a variety of many voices and fixed ratios of spiritual numbers into one harmony.

*Col 3:5

*Gal 2:19; Aelred, S 8.18

*Cicero, De fini bon et mal 5.23.65

9. As we have already often said,* according to the rules of moral interpretation, Moab, which means *from the father,** signifies the natural corruption inserted in our members, or those people who live according to corruption.* So the belly of the prophet sounds forth *to Moab* like a harp when a perfect person persuades someone who is unsteady that there is harmony in the virtues and dissonance in the vices, setting moderation against wantonness, patience against anger, shame against lust, and love against cupidity.

*Oner 26.2

*Jerome, In Isa 6.36

*Rom 7:23

10. But also each one of us should play the harp when we see in ourselves Moab raising its abominable head and shaking all our limbs by the law of natural corruption.* Let us blunt Moab's thorns by imitating or meditating on the Lord's passion. By the power of the cross, let us knock down the brick wall of faults that has grown hard by habit. Surely this melody is well suited to the task: *My belly will sound forth to Moab like a harp, and my inner organs to a wall of fired brick.** This is David's harp, whose most holy sound puts the demons to flight, calms anger, and extinguishes lust.* Happy, O happy are those who dedicate everything they have within them like the inner organs of the belly to the cross, so that thundering against the desires of the flesh* they may say with the prophet, *Bless the Lord, my soul, and may all that I have within bless his holy name.**

11. It follows, *And it will happen when it comes to light that Moab has labored in its high places.** It certainly came to light how vainly *Moab labored* after churchmen defeated the wise of this world* and converted others. Everything appeared vacant and empty* after what is written was fulfilled: *Where is the wise person? Where is the scribe? Where is the conqueror of this age? God has made the wisdom of this world foolish, has he not?** This is why the apostle also announced beforehand, *I will destroy the wisdom of the wise, and I will condemn the prudence of the prudent.**

12. And well enough it says, *in its high places.*† For the philosophers always boast of both *speaking of lofty things* and doing perfect deeds.* This vanity, indeed, meant not a little labor for them as they struggled against the evangelical and apostolic teaching with all their might. But what end was there to this labor? *And it will happen,* it says, *when it comes to light that Moab has labored in its high places.** In other words, the wise of the world saw that they had worn themselves out in vain against the church,* and the brilliance of their

*Rom 7:23

*Isa 16:11

*1 Sam 16:23

*1 John 2:16

*Ps 102:1; Jerome, In Isa 6.43

*Isa 16:12

*1 Cor 1:20

*Gen 1:2

*1 Cor 1:20

*1 Cor 1:19; Isa 29:14
†Isa 16:12

*1 Sam 2:3

*Isa 16:12

*1 Cor 1:20

tenets had fallen to the ground before the simplicity of faith. They then turned to prayers and tears, awaiting the aid of the demons *whom they had regarded as* *gods,** whose *holy places* they had revered.

*Wis 12:27

13. Therefore it says, *He will enter his holy places to* *pray, and it will do no good.** So when every argument had failed and all knowledge that raised *itself against* *the knowledge of God* had been destroyed,* they tried *to resist the Holy Spirit* and overthrow the divine purpose by beseeching, tricks, and accursed demonic rites.* But this wickedly careful foresight of theirs did no good, because the *sound* of the apostles had already *gone out to all the land, and their words to the ends of the* *earth.**

*Isa 16:12

*2 Cor 10:5

*Acts 6:10; 7:51

*Ps 18:5

14. Everyone's end, death,* reveals how vainly those who have dedicated themselves to the Moabite corruption labor *to work iniquity,** even though they devote a lot of time to satisfying their desires. But *the* *foolish virgins* too carried lamps without oil *in their high* *places,* namely, *in pride and fullness of heart.** After all their lamps had gone out, receiving no consolation from the oil sellers,* they returned to *the holy places.*† There they offered prayers, saying, *Lord, Lord, open the* *door for us!*§ But that terrible answer shows how little they accomplished with this prayer: *Amen, I say to you,* *I do not know you.**

*Rom 6:21

*Jer 9:5

*Isa 9:9

*Matt 25:1-10
†Augustine, Div quæst 59.3; Aelred, S 93.9.15– 10, 16
§Matt 25:11

*Matt 25:12

15. At this point the prophet puts an end to the burden, saying, *This word which the Lord spoke to Moab from* *that time.** The divine discourse calls everything that had been proclaimed about or to Moab a *word.** But the end corresponds to the beginning. In fact, it began like this: *The burden of Moab.** *From that time* therefore, that is, from the time in which he began to speak of Moab, *he said* all these things.* The prophet shows that what he said was true and firm.* He is not delusional, speaking about what he does not know after the fashion of raving Montanus. Rather, he prophesied what he understood, full of the Spirit of God.* After ap-

*Isa 16:13
*Jerome, In Isa 6.43

*Isa 15:1

*Isa 16:13
*Heb 2:2

*Acts 4:8; 13:9;
Jerome, In Isa 1.1- 2; Jerome, In Naum prol

propriately making that comment, he mystically declared at what time the things he had prophesied of
the burden of Moab would be fulfilled, saying, *And
now the Lord spoke, saying, in three years time, as though
hired years, the glory of Moab will be taken away from over
all the many people.* *   *Isa 16:14

16. The prophecy describes three periods of the
church: the times of calling, of trial, and of consolation.
The church was called by the preaching of the apostles,
tried by the persecution of the martyrs, and consoled
by the conversion of rulers. In these three periods as
though *in three years time the glory of Moab* was taken
away *from over all the many people.* * For the philoso-   *Isa 16:14
phers still appeared to be glorious at the time when
the church was called, when catholic men attacked
their perverse teaching only with great difficulty.
When many temptations tried the patience of the
saints, the philosophers' glory appeared all the greater
insofar as Christ's faith was regarded as more lowly.
But when the kings of the world, having received the
saving faith, raised Christ's church up, the philosophers' *glory* was taken away *from over all the many
people,* * from those, that is, who had been deceived by   *Isa 16:14
their error.

17. But it says that these years are *as though hired
years.* * *Just as a hired worker awaits the end* of the year†   *Isa 16:14
and regards every season as long in the desire for pay-   †Job 7:2
ment, so the wise of this world during these three
periods,* as though *for three years,* waited daily for the   *1 Cor 1:20
catholic teaching to be destroyed. For this reason,
duped by the oracles of the unclean spirits, they assumed that the faith of Christ would endure for a certain number of years, beyond which they falsely
declared that it could not continue.

18. It follows, *And there will remain in it a small cluster,
as it were, and not a great quantity.* * When the harvest   *Isa 16:14; 17:6
is finished, few clusters are still to be found in the
vineyard. So it is that scarcely anyone is found who

still professes worldly wisdom in present times, after the church's sickle has cut many away from such wisdom.

19. But returning to us, dear brothers, let us consider the Moab that is sown in us, namely, that corruption of the flesh that we contracted from our fathers. Let us consider this corruption's author and inciter, the devil. There is a great people of thoughts, affections, and delights in each of us. Moab boasts of its dominion over these peoples for as long as the mind acquiesces to its suggestions. But *in three years time, as though hired years, the glory of Moab will be taken away from over all* *the many people.** For like the three years, there are three stages of progress: conversion, purgation, and contemplation. The first takes place in pain, the second in fear, and the third in love.

*Isa 16:14

20. The beginning of our conversion is therefore like the beginning of the first year. The will is changed, then wicked habits are overcome, and thus what is evil is abandoned and what is good is sought. And this is the first year. Moab still boasts more than a little during this time, since often by his suggestion the will cools off, habit grows strong, evil creeps up and resists our intentions, and the good that the mind seeks does not find fruition.*

*Rom 7:18-19

21. Moab's glory is lessened, of course, when a person perfectly turned toward the Lord enters into *hand-to-hand combat* with the vices.* Beginning the second year, such a person stays as busy as possible making sure that the Moabite corruption decreases like an old habit and that the new, untested life increases.* Moab still has some glory in this year, because although it might not defeat its opponent, yet of necessity it at times wounds even the best adversary.*

*1 Sam 17:10; Heb 10:32

*Augustine, Conf 8.11.25

*Heb 12:4

22. By the third year, the soul has been purged by spiritual exercises. It advances on to the contemplation of heavenly things and meditation on the Scriptures. Then the soul begins to find virtue sweet and vice contemptible. By a kind of infusion of love it tastes *how sweet the Lord is.** *The glory of Moab will be taken away from over all the many people*[†] when the experience of a new sweetness removes whatever unclean delight had remained in our thoughts and desires.

23. Yet like *a small cluster, as it were,** that law remains *in* our *members,** fighting against the law of our mind. Clusters are occasionally found in a vineyard even after it has been laid waste. Such is the case after the host of vices has been weakened. That unavoidable passion* necessarily remains, which often both infants suffer and the old are unable to avoid.*

24. Further, they are referred to as *hired years.*[†] Just as the hired worker longs for payment, so too do those who, having long borne the impossibility of self-control, desire to be converted. Such people burn with an extraordinary desire, waiting for the very possibility of chastity as though it were the fruit of their labor. They are also concerned for their purgation for as long as the vices attack them. Greatly desiring to be set free from their temptations, they await that rest like a generous payment. Finally feeling disgust even at this natural corruption itself, they long for the dew of chastity to bathe them thoroughly and for the gentleness of all the virtues to anoint their agitated breasts.

25. Hypocrites can also be described as *Moab.* While the Moabite corruption defiles them in secret, a kind of feigned honor elevates them publicly. Their years are *hired years,* because *they do everything to be seen by others.** They will hear the Lord say, *They have received their reward.** But when the three years have passed— the first of which is in this life, the second after death, and the third after the resurrection—then clearly all their *glory will be taken away.** After the oil runs out and no more is to be had from the sellers,* they will hear the bridegroom say, *Amen, I say to you, I do not know you.*[†]

*1 Pet 2:3;
Aelred, S 8.15
† Isa 16:14

*Isa 16:14; 17:6
*Rom 7:23

* *motus*
*Aelred,
SS 5.16; 43.14
† Isa 14:16

*Matt 23:5
*Matt 6:5; Jerome,
In Isa 6.44

*Isa 16:14
*Matt 25:8-10
† Matt 25:12;
Augustine, S
93.7.9–8.10;
9.15–10.16

26. Having explained in some fashion the three burdens of Babylon, Philistia, and Moab,* brothers, I now
lay down my pen. I wish to refer what I have said or
written to the consideration of the holy Gilbert, bishop
of London, whom I have chosen as judge and corrector
of my words and opinions. Depending on his will, I
will destroy this text, stop here, or continue further.*
Meanwhile, we will attempt something else that seems
either useful or pleasing for your instruction or for the
instruction of others.

*Isa 13:1-16; 14

*Oner, Ep 9

Scriptural Index

Scriptural references are cited by homily and paragraph number. For example, Genesis 1:2 is quoted in Homily 3, paragraphs 2 and 4, and in Homily 31, paragraph 11. Ep = Letter to Gilbert Foliot; Adv = Advent Sermon (Sermon for the Coming of the Lord).

Gen			
1:2	3.2, 4; 31.11	11:4	29.5
1:4	1.13	13:10	13.4
1:14	1.13	14:14-16	26.3
1:16	10.6–7, 11,	18:2	2.4
1:26	7.12; 15.11	19:5	13.4
1:27	15.11	19:24	13.4
2:2	8.8	19:26	23.1
2:9	17.10	19:30	23.1, 3; 27.5
2:24	Ep 3	19:30-35	21.1
3:3	17.10	19:32	23.1
3:5	19.4	19:32-35	30.8
3:6	17.10	19:33	23.1
3:14	19.4	19:35	23.1
3:15	19.22; 24.13	19:36-38	23.1
3:17	12.8	19:37	27.5
3:18	12.8	24:62	Adv 36
3:19	18.6, 8	24:63	26.28–29
4:7 LXX	12.5	24:67	26.28
4:13	3.6	25:18-22	3.11
5:1	7.12; 15.11; 16.14–15	25:24	23.32
9:21-25	30.8	25:25	23.32
10:2	11.19	25:27	23.32
11:2	29.5	25:29-33	13.14
11:2-5	29.4	26:34	13.14
11:3	29.5	26:35	13.14
		27:11	13.14

59:5	30.9, 18	84:8	3.6
60:3	7.6; 22.3	84:11	Ep 3; 28.27
61:12-13	1.13	85:5	13.34
61:13	8.5; 11.19; 26.21	85:15	13.34
62:12	23.8	86:1	7.4; 22.8
65:8	22.11	86:2	22.3
65:10	11.5	86:3	22.6
65:12	6.17; 15.20	88:3	Adv 5; 22.3
65:15	5.10	88:7	16.15
67:3	3.7	88:9	16.15
67:6	10.11	88:16	28.18
67:7	7.10	88:33	12.4, 9–10; 15.19;
67:14	18.14		19.17; 21.9
67:19	19.23; 27.23	88:33-34	1.15
67:20	14.19	88:34	19.17
68:10	23.21	89:4	13.22
68:16	18.9	89:10	Adv 41; 22.3
68:22	17.11	90:2	22.17
69:6	21.14	90:9	22.9, 17
70:13	Adv 25	90:13	29.18
71:1	20.2	93:19	26.9, 28
71:3	7.4	94:8	20.17
71:8	27.4	95:10	18.3
72:2	18.6; 22.1	98:8	12.9
72:5	1.15	100:1	Adv 1, 5–6, 44; 13.8;
72:8	23.22		27.23
72:28	17.8	101:7	28.7, 9
73:12	4.1	101:7-8	28.5
73:19	13.27; 24.18	101:8	28.9
76:11	29.13	101:14	13.8; 27.24
77:1	21.11	102:1	22.11; 31.10
77:26	26.18	102:5	28.5
77:25	8.17	102:14	22.15
77:27-29	28.11	102:19	17.15
77:49	Adv 11, 15; 8.2	103:23	13.8–9
79:6	8.16	103:29	12.11
80:12	21.11	103:30	12.11
80:13	Adv 23; 1.15; 6.5; 12.7;	104:34	29.15
	21.11-12	105:4	25.12
82:18	5.9	105:8	6.7
83:4	28.9	106:2	7.10
83:6	3.19	106:2-3	7.6
83:7 Var	24.26	106:6	26.2
83:8	25.13; 28.9	106:9	15.1

9:17	30.9
13:7	11.9

Tob

5:21	26.25
5:27	26.25
13:11	22.3

Jdt

5:10	15.12; 29.7
8:27	19.17; 21.9
16:3	15.15

Wis

1:7	5.15
1:11	15.14, 19
2:24	15.25
3:6	11.5
6:2	18.11
6:7	8.10
6:13	30.10
7:9	11.17; 30.5
7:27	1.3; 2.24
8:1	19.21
10:7	23.1
11:2	27.5
11:21	2.13; 12.16
12:27	31.12
14:15	22.3
14:27	3.9
16:18	10.3, 17; 11.19; 15.18; 20.14, 17
19:13	29.7

Sir

1:22	12.14
2:14	8.13; 26.31
5:11	8.11
7:40 Vulg	8.7
10:9	13.2
10:15	21.6
13:6	8.10
14:15	Adv 41
15:3	30.8

17:26	22.9
18:1	17.11
24:24	20.20
35:18-19	26.14
40:1	19.24–26
50:6	17.3

Bar

3:25	21.28
4:25	15.19

1 Macc

1:56	11.7
2:54	24.20
14:12-13	14.6

2 Macc

1:19	17.14
9:8	Adv 4
15:21	23.21

Matt

1:5-6	27.5
2:1	7.19; 27.5
3:2	4.4
3:10	22.5
3:12	10.4; 11.10
4:1	26.25
4:2	Adv 4
4:9	19.6
4:17	25.15
4:36-38	Adv 4
5:3	20.19; 21.14; 22.19
5:4	11.13; 13.36; 18.25
5:5	9.9; 22.20
5:14	2.11; 7.3; 10.6; 10.13
5:16	18.26; 28.18
5:28	28.17
5:35	20.2
5:44	20.22
6:1	4.8; 5.21; 18.26
6:5	26.7; 31.25
6:6	26.8
6:19	14.16

8:50	6.17		18:6	Adv 4
8:56	15.1		18:11	21.12
9:4	8.8–9, 11		18:14	20.6
9:31	19.8		19:7	20.3
9:39	1.14		19:15	20.3
10:12	11.9		20:23	Adv 37
10:17-18	23.5		21:4	22.9
10:36	4.11		21:11	14.3
11:18	20.6		21:17	23.27
11:25	20.25		21:19	18.12
11:43	26.9			
11:47	Adv 37; 4.9; 20.6		*Acts*	
11:48	20.6		1:4	14.18
11:49-50	20.6		2:1	23.27
11:51	Adv 37		2:3-4	23.27
12:31	Adv 10; 19.7, 12, 28		2:20	10.6, 10, 12, 15
12:40	20.17		2:24	23.6
12:43	6.17		2:47	20.20
13:1	26.31		4:8	31.15
13:2	8.2		4:13	16.14; 28.23; 29.25
13:5	4.12		4:18	20.21
13:23	18.14		4:32	Ep 4; 7.4; 9.10
13:25	18.14		5:12	4.6
13:35	4.10		5:14	4.17; 7.4; 13.25; 20.20
14:2	10.13; 17.1; 18.13;		5:28	20.21
	21.23		5:29	20.21
14:23	26.31		5:40	20.22
15:5	1.11		5:42	20.22
15:18	13.28		6:10	31.13
15:19	13.2		7:51	31.13
16:7	2.16		7:55-57	4.15
16:9	Adv 38		7:59-60	20.22
16:12-13	2.15–16		8:7	21.23
16:13	2.19		9:4	22.14
16:20	13.9; 24.28		9:6	Ep 8
16:21	9.6, 9		9:35	25.9
16:33	13.2, 9		10:10-13	2.11
17:1	6.3		10:13	12.3
17:5	6.3		10:34-35	2.11
17:6	13.2		11:5-7	2.11
17:9	13.2		11:7	12.3
17:17	6.3		11:19-21	22.8
17:18	4.11		12:23	5.5
17:19	6.3, 15		13:9	31.15

13:26	20.22	5:5	Adv 35, 37
13:28	27.22	5:12-14	19.3
13:29	23.5	5:14	19.2
13:46	4.15; 20.25	5:20	19.2
15:1	27.13	6:6	21.6
15:5	27.13	6:12	13.36
15:6-29	27.13	6:13	Adv 19; 24.9
15:26	25.12	6:14	19.3; 25.5
16:6	Adv 34	6:19	14.17
17:16	Adv 34	6:21	31.14
17:27-28	Adv 2	6:23	9.8
18:6	29.13	7:1	23.25
19:12	12.13; 21.26; 30.11, 20	7:6	3.19; 4.14; 28.6
19:15	15.18; 30.12	7:18-19	31.20
20:22	Adv 34	7:22	9.14; 30.5
20:28	11.16	7:23	Adv 19; 19.25; 28.26;
23:12-14	20.22		31.9–10, 23
26:13	Adv 16	7:24	19.25
26:18	7.9; 16.4; 27.8; 28.17	8:2	19.2
26:24	20.21	8:5	6.14; 12.13; 13.36
28:13	26.24	8:16	21.18
28:27	29.4	8:23	21.18; 28.2
		8:24	21.8, 15
Rom		8:26	Adv 20; 5.13; 28.8;
1:14	1.10		29.14
1:18	11.2; 25.9	8:28	5.16; 18.23; 19.32–33
1:19	23.3	8:29-30	3.3–4
1:19-21	Adv 29	8:30	1.19; 6.10; 19.3
1:21	22.7; 23.9	8:31	19.34
1:21-22	21.3	8:34	5.13; 29.14
1:22	23.3; 25.20; 29.1	8:35	6.8; 20.20; 23.35
1:22-23	21.21	8:38-39	23.35
1:23	23.9	9:2	20.22
1:23-24	Adv 29	9:2-3	Adv 35; 22.6
1:24	21.3, 12	9:3	18.15; 22.8
1:25	21.21; 22.5; 25.9	9:4-5	7.8
1:26	Adv 29; 21.3	9:5	16.17
1:28	Adv 29	9:17	6.7
1:30	Adv 23	9:18	8.2
2:2-3	16.2	9:22-23	3.22; 8.4
2:29	9.4	9:25	13.24
3:19	17.8	9:33	11.16
3:28	20.2	10:3	20.2; 22.7; 30.1
4:15	19.2	10:15	4.11

1:14-15	Adv 19		*1 John*	
1:17	5.12		2:15	4.4; 5.20
1:18	17.4; 23.3		2:16	13.36; 21.24; 26.13; 31.10
1:19	10.13			
1:26	12.10		2:16 Var	24.27
2:20	26.18		2:17	4.4
2:26	26.18		2:18	5.2; 9.23
4:6	4.10		2:19	23.33
4:11	10.14		2:27	21.18; 21.21
4:15	27.24		3:9	23.3
			3:13	13.28
			4:1	2.21
1 Pet			4:2	7.7
1:2	6.4		4:4	13.2
1:18-19	19.3		5:19	13.2
1:23	23.3			
1:24	25.10		*Jude*	
2:3	2.3; 13.34; 31.22		16	4.9; 8.11; 10.14; 21.11
2:5	29.5			
2:9	27.8; 28.10, 17		*Rev*	
2:11	19.27		1:7-8	Adv 1
2:14	10.3		2:7	14.12
2:21	28.16		2:9	22.3; 23.34
2:25	13.20; 23.30		2:16	11.15
3:19	17.5, 23; 19.4, 9		3:2	4.15
4:8	4.12		3:16	8.13
4:11	22.20		3:20	18.15
4:17	Adv 1; 10.2; 14.17		5:5	28.21
5:5	26.10		6:13	10.14
5:6	25.2		8:2-7	5.7
5:8	23.5; 25.22, 24		8:3-4	5.10
5:9	11.11		9:1	10.14
			9:6	21.9
			11:2	14.8
2 Pet			12:8	9.21
1:14	14.17		12:9	20.16; 22.9
2:3	15.2		12:12	14.13
2:4	17.5		12:14	10.16; 14.8
2:10	29.20		13:1-10	16.9
2:21 Var	6.6		13:7	13.3
3:3	16.2		14:7	5.5
3:10	9.20		14:10	21.10
3:12	9.20		14:13	8.8–9, 11; 18.11
3:14	14.19			

Topical Index

This index is intended to give a sense of topics emphasized or explored in these sermons but is necessarily incomplete. It includes neither *Christ* nor *God*. Topics are cited by sermon and paragraph number. Ep = Letter to Gilbert Foliot; Adv = Advent Sermon (Sermon for the Coming of the Lord).

Babylon, 13.8; 18.27; 19.27; 22.11
  as a dark mountain, 3.9; 4.13
  as love of the world, 13.27; 19.10
  as the soul, 1.20; 5.1
  as the world, 3.9; 4.13; 13.2; 19.10
  burdened by cross, 3.14; 4.14; 5.2
  city of confusion, 3.5, 8; 5.22; 7.7;
    13.3; 19.30
  destruction of, 3.5, 8; 8.1, 4; 13.7,
    10–11, 17; 14.5; 19.12, 15, 17–18,
    30
  end of Babylon's delights, 13.5
  the fallen, 9.18
  immoderate people, 9.18
  in hearts of many, 12.18
  king of, 3.12; 14.7; 15.3–4, 9
  land of ungodly, 11.12, 14
  meaning confusion, 5.1
  prince of, 18.1
  understood in two ways, 13.1
Balaam, Adv 37; 4.9; 10.8
Baptism, 6.10; 25.5
Beast of the south, Adv 11, 33–37
Belly, 9.2–4; 10.12; 31.2, 7, 10
  of Christ, 31.1, 2
  of church, 31.5
  of God, 31.4
  of the prophet, 31.1, 2, 9
  spiritual, 31.7
Birth
  harmful, 9.8
  physical, 9.6
  punitive, 9.6, 9
  spiritual, 9.6–7
  types of, 9.6
Blasphemy, 12.13; 21.12
Burden
  definition of, Adv 10; 1.12, 15–16

Caesar, 15.10; 20.3, 8, 12
Caiaphas, Adv 37; 17.15; 20.6

Captivity, 3.5
Charity, Ep 7–8; 4.10, 12; 5.12; 6.10;
  7.16; 10.2, 10, 17; 14.18; 15.2, 4;
  18.14–15; 20.23; 27.6; 31.3
  represented by sun, 12.9
Chastity, 5.3; 6.10, 12–13, 15, 18;
  7.15–16; 10.4, 13, 17; 15.4, 13;
  24.13–14; 25.13; 26.13, 25;
  31.24
  and marriage, 7.16
  types of, 6.13
Cherubim, 3.11
Chosen, the, 11.10; 19.3–4, 9, 24, 31,
  33–35; 20.1; 22.9; 25.18–19;
  27.20
  three groups, 1.19
Christmas, 16.1
Church, 7.6; 8.5; 9.1, 18; 10.1–2;
  11.6–7, 14–15; 22.6, 8–9; 25.6–7;
  27.6, 18, 24; 28.2; 31.2–3
  as heaven, 11.6
  as kingdom of God, 7.9
  at time of Antichrist, 10.16; 13.25;
    14.5–6; 16.7, 9–10; 18.3
  councils, 27.12–14, 16–17
  defended by kings, 10.11
  land of the saints, 11.12; 14.2;
    14.8
  leaders of, 11.16
  praying in, 5.5
  primitive, 11.5; 13.25; 25.4–5
  reign of, 7.3–4; 10.5; 11.14
  three stages of, 6.2; 31.16
Circumcision, 9.4; 27.13; 29.19–20;
  30.21
Compunction, 5.16; 8.16; 12.8;
  19.16; 23.19; 26.17, 24; 28.8;
  30.18
Concupiscence, Adv 9; 8.17; 9.17;
  10.17; 21.24–25; 22.15–16; 24.7,
  21, 27; 26.13; 28.10–11, 14